CW01432356

Selected Letters of John Keats

Selected Letters of John Keats

REVISED EDITION

EDITED BY

GRANT F. SCOTT

Based on the texts of Hyder Edward Rollins

HARVARD

UNIVERSITY

PRESS

Cambridge, Massachusetts

London, England

2002

Library of Congress Cataloging-in-Publication Data
Keats, John, 1795–1821.
[Correspondence. Selections]
Selected letters of John Keats / edited by Grant F. Scott.—Rev. ed.
p. cm.
Rev. ed. of: The letters of John Keats, 1814–1821. 1958.
"Based on the texts of Hyder Edward Rollins."
Includes bibliographical references and index.
ISBN 0-674-00749-2 (alk. paper)
1. Keats, John, 1795–1821—Correspondence.
2. Poets, English—19th century—Correspondence.
I. Scott, Grant F.   II. Title.

PR4836 .A4 2002
821'.7—dc21
[B]   2001051862

CONTENTS

1818

1819

1821

ILLUSTRATIONS

PREFACE

The selection of Keats's letters gathered here is based on Hyder E. Rollins, *The Letters of John Keats, 1814–1821* (2 vols., Harvard University Press, 1958), which is still considered the standard edition. Although nominally a revision, the present selection differs from Rollins in one other important regard: it is not a rigorously scholarly edition. This means that it does not include the detailed textual apparatus that has become a common feature of all diplomatic editions of personal letters for the last century. Rather, the letters have been edited for readability and with a more general audience in mind. My intent has been to make Keats's letters more accessible by reducing the scholarly annotations and by modernizing such features as punctuation and spelling. In doing so, I have hoped to recreate some of the spontaneity with which these letters were originally written as well as the excitement with which they were received. Keats's letters are some of the most lively and creative in the language, and they deserve to have a larger audience. There is no such edition of the letters currently in print, and this represents a serious gap.

The present volume differs from existing editions of Keats's letters not only in editorial procedures, which I shall discuss in more detail, but also in a number of other features. I have included a handful of letters *to* Keats and *among* his friends in an effort to lend further perspective to the portrait of Keats. This chorus of voices greatly enriches our sense of Keats's character and provides an illuminating contrast in epistolary styles. It also offers us a revealing glimpse of his "posthumous existence," the period of Keats's illness in Italy. Most editions close with the poet's last letter, written to Charles Brown at the end of November 1820. But Keats goes on living for another three months, and this period is faithfully recorded, often in painstaking detail, by Keats's deathbed companion, Joseph Severn. These letters are poignant, agonizing, and riveting in the extreme, and I believe their inclusion here will deepen the reader's understanding of the Keats story. For similar reasons I have also included letters from Dr. James Clark, Percy Bysshe Shelley, and Richard Woodhouse, all of which offer valuable additional testimony concerning Keats the man.

No new edition of the letters has appeared in over thirty years, and this alone is reason enough for the present volume. During this time two new Keats letters, along with the final page of an important journal letter, have come to light. These include the letter of 30 January 1818 to his brothers; the letter of 2 November 1819 to William Haslam; and the last leaf of the famous journal letter of 14 February–4 May 1819 to his brother and sister-in-law in America. I have printed these here in addition to Keats's verse epistle of September 1816 to Charles Cowden Clarke, which Rollins knew of but decided against printing (he published the slightly different version that Keats used in his *Poems* of 1817). I have also corrected a number of Rollins's minor errors having to do with names and dates and have provided translations for the two dozen or so foreign words and phrases that Keats sprinkled throughout the letters (all in French, Italian, and Latin). Finally, I have included ten illustrations that I hope will afford the reader a better sense of the original manuscripts as well as the people and prominent locations in Keats's life.

EDITORIAL PROCEDURES

If we did not already have scrupulously accurate transcripts of Keats's letters in Rollins's edition and a paperback selection edited by Robert Gittings, the appearance of the present book might seem unwarranted. As it is, both of these editions are widely available and will continue to serve the needs of scholars. Perhaps a stronger justification for the present book can be found in the implicit assumption made by all modern scholarly editions: that of exact fidelity to the original manuscript. In the foreword to *John Keats: Letters from a Walking Tour* (Grolier, 1995), Jack Stillinger makes a convincing case for a "principled modernization" of Keats's letters, arguing that in spite of their claims to accuracy, scholarly editions already constitute translations and interpretations of the originals. As he says, these editions "print the texts in conventional typography and with standard headings, justified margins, uniform spacing between letters, words, and lines, and a generous accompaniment of scholarly commentary" (xii). In this respect, they significantly recast the originals, especially their visual appearance, their "look" on the page. If we add to this uniformity the fact of their mass production in book format and the neat chronological ordering and arrangement of letters written to a variety of correspondents over a period of years, we can see just how artificial the standard edition actually is.

It is worth dwelling on this point at more length. The great advantage of conventional typography is its ability to reproduce ordinarily inaccessible texts and disseminate them in inexpensive forms to a wide audience. The drawback, of course, is that the resulting texts represent mechanical transla-

tions of handwriting, and thus regularize letters and words that in the originals possess their own unique physical body. In a conventionally printed
letter, then, readers cannot experience the idiosyncrasies of Keats's hand,
the loops and flourishes, the scorings out, the inkblots, the doodles or pictures in the margins. They must also do without the tactile elements of a
letter, sacrificing everything from its contours and creases to its smell. Perhaps a more serious shortcoming is the inability of modern typography to
capture what Keats called the "chequer work" of a "crossed" letter. To save
on postage, Keats frequently turned the sheet of paper on its side and added
another page of writing across the path of the first. This habit served a practical purpose, but it also resulted in palimpsests that are rich in graphic
meaning. In cases like this where the medium plays a significant role in the
message, the modern scholarly edition is helpless to render the unique features of Keats's "living hand."

By necessity, the present selection is also interpretive, though I have tried
to remain sensitive to the visual character of Keats's letters by including two
facsimile illustrations as well as noting where he exploited the graphic appearance of his text for puns. In more specific terms, I have modernized the
texts of Keats's letters by silently correcting small slips of the pen (e.g., sup-
plying missing letters and punctuation, correcting transposed letters), adding terminal punctuation to sentences that lack them, and converting many
of Keats's dashes to full stops. I have omitted Keats's deletions and cancellations, reduced most superscripts to the line, incorporated all interlineations
into the regular text, and expanded a number of abbreviations. I have also
dispensed with square and other types of brackets within the texts and kept
the annotations to a minimum, paring Rollins's notes considerably. For the
sake of clarity, I have created new paragraph divisions, usually where Keats
took up the same letter on a different day or started on a completely new
topic, and I have deleted all postmarks and addresses of correspondents
from the head and foot of each letter. Finally, the reader should note that
two kinds of notes appear in the texts, numbered, which are mine, and
asterisked, which belong to Keats or other correspondents.

I have made the occasional exception to these rules, specifically in matters of punctuation and spelling. In places where the punctuation appears

ambiguous, or where Keats appears to be deliberately taking advantage of syntactical ambiguity, I have retained the original grammar and syntax. This is also the case with a number of Keats's misspellings, which can be wonderfully spontaneous and creative. Apparent slips not only may contain puns and double entendres, but also may provide us with a sense of how a particular word sounded to Keats's ear. For these reasons, I have either retained or footnoted the more inventive and suggestive misspellings, words such as "rediculous," "Lawers," "philantrophy," and "atchievements."

Like his misspellings, Keats's habit of capitalization is eccentric, but may offer clues to his patterns of association and to his meaning. Thus, I have retained all but a dozen or so capitalized nouns, regardless of how insignificant they may appear. (I have converted to lowercase a handful of verbs and pronouns that appear to have been capitalized by accident.) The fact is that Keats will often use capital letters to emphasize significant phrases ("Nest of Debauchery," "Mouth of Fame," "Cliff of Poesy"), highlight alliterative groupings of words ("I must endeavor to lose my Maidenhead with respect to money Matters"), and even signal an internal rhyme ("A doze upon a Sofa does not hinder it, and a nap upon Clover engenders ethereal finger-pointings"). He almost always capitalizes nouns relating to family or social status ("Brother," "Sister," "Lady"), important abstract nouns ("Life," "Mind," "World," "Genius," "Beauty," "Imagination"), and words that refer to the fine arts, especially literature ("Volumes," "Verses," "Stanzas," "Lines," "Words," "Laurels"). He tends to use the uppercase for the names of animals, flowers, and the elements, and typically capitalizes words that begin with Q or C. This may have been simply a personal tic; he had difficulty writing the letter r, for instance, and could never manage the word "perhaps," which invariably came out "Perphaps." In any event, I have decided to retain capital letters because they do not in general affect readability and because readers may find them significant.

By the same token, I have left all words that would normally be capitalized ("Sunday," "Isle of Wight," "England") in lowercase letters, according to Keats's own manuscripts. Of course these may also be slips, but it is just as likely that they indicate Keats's sentiments on a particular subject and that they are deliberate subversions of grammatical convention. Thus, for example, Keats speaks disparagingly of Devonshire men, seldom dignifying them with a D and dismissing them as "dwindled englishmen." The same is true of the French, whom Keats frequently relegates to the lowercase, adding insult to injury by referring on one occasion to "french Meadows" and on another to a "french Ambassador," whose picture he discards in favor of "a head" of the properly uppercase "Shakespeare." Wordsworth comes off no better. In a famous letter to Richard Woodhouse, Keats invents his own category to contain the Lake poet's massive self-regard, the "wordsworthian or egotistical sublime," a phrase in which the belittling operates on more than one level. To alter expressions such as these, I believe, would be to misrepresent Keats's intentions.

ACKNOWLEDGMENTS

My first and largest debt is to Jack Stillinger, whose editorial wisdom, generosity, and good sense I have relied on throughout this project. This book was initially his idea, and I am grateful to him for entrusting me with its fruition. I also thank my colleagues at Muhlenberg College for their advice and encouragement. Barri Gold, Alec Marsh, and David Rosenwasser read a draft of my introduction and offered valuable criticism and commentary, and Patricia DeBellis, Lisa Perfetti, and Robert Wind helped with translations of various foreign words and phrases. Fellow Keatsian Carol Kyros Walker kindly sent me the map of Keats's walking tour that she used in her book, and Yale University Press granted permission for me to use it. I am grateful as well to Donald B. Hoffman, whose sponsorship of a yearlong research fellowship allowed me valuable release time to devote to this book.

A nod toward the scholar's home institution has become an obligatory part of any sensible acknowledgment, but I would like to pay more than customary thanks to Muhlenberg College, which, year after year, continues to support my scholarly endeavors with summer grants, travel money, and subventions. Without this institutional generosity, my task would have been considerably more difficult.

Least in size but certainly not last in regard is Oliver J. S. Scott, to whom I owe an odd sort of parental gratitude. If it were not for his booming wee voice and the uncanny precision of his predawn awakenings, I would never have been propelled into my office at this dim hour. I dedicate this book to him and to Markéta—*s láskou a vd'akou.*

For most modern readers it is hard to see Keats's poems for the sheen of their language. They appear too much like bright monuments in winter sun. No one, I suspect, could mistake a line like "And still she slept an azure-lidded sleep"—from "The Eve of St. Agnes"—for anything but poetry. Indeed, Keats has come to represent the poet of "silken phrases and silver sentences," exploiting language, rhyme, and allusion in ways that terrify students but thrill the ranks of professional scholars.

On first looking into Keats's letters, however, readers who bring with them some memory of the formal difficulty of his poems will be pleasantly surprised. Rather than the stately elegance of "Ode on a Grecian Urn" or the finely wrought agonies of "Ode to a Nightingale," the letters yield the spontaneous and frank observations of a young man: his insecurities, doubts, fears, enthusiasms, prejudices, ambitions, opinions, and ideas. If his greatest poems are characterized by their stillness and poise, his letters are masterpieces of motion. They read like mountain rivers: ragged, rough, full of raw energy, dangerous. They are alive with improvisational wit and verbal gusto, revealing an agile mind happily willing to dwell in contradiction or, as he says, "remain content with half knowledge" (21, 27 [?] December 1817). Keats never commits his speculations to the casket of a theory. A remarkable fact of the letters is that his most famous ideas—Negative Capability, the Chameleon Poet, the Vale of Soul-making, the Mansion of Many Apartments—appear only once. They are neither repeated to other correspondents nor formalized in published essays, but remain provisional, bound within the specific human context of a letter.

Perhaps what is most surprising and delightful about Keats's letters, especially next to the polished, anthology-ready gems of his poetry, is their unpredictability. In *The Use of Poetry and the Use of Criticism*, T. S. Eliot remarked that the letters "are what letters ought to be; the fine things come in unexpectedly, neither introduced nor shown out, but between trifle and trifle" (100). And he is right. What is so striking about the famous "Negative Capability" letter is not so much the term itself, though it has generated hundreds of pages of commentary, as the casual way in which it emerges out of the quotidian detail of Keats's life. He goes to see a play, mentions a publisher's trial for libel, talks about dining out with friends, and then—like a thunderclap—"I had not a dispute but a disquisition with Dilke on various subjects; several things dovetailed in my mind, and at once it struck me what quality went to form a Man of Achievement especially in Literature and which Shakespeare possessed so enormously—I mean *Negative Capability*, that is when man is capable of being in uncertainties, Mysteries, doubts, without any irritable reaching after fact and reason." Yet the sentence that immediately precedes this one is marvelously ordinary, providing not a clue of what is about to follow: "Brown and Dilke walked with me and back from the Christmas pantomime" (21, 27 [?] December 1817).

The proximity of the mundane and the profound leads to another salient feature of Keats's letters: their seamless integration of everyday life with the life of the mind. Today we have grown accustomed to think of intelligence as necessitating a special time and place. Thinking is segregated from other activities and has become the unique preserve of institutions such as the university, the foundation, and the "think tank," where it is carried out by a camera-friendly team of "experts" and "knowledge workers." In our time we have come to witness the complete professionalization of the intellect as well as the allotment of designated time to "mental work." The weekends are now reserved for the strenuous fun that constitutes authentic living. Such a belief makes Keats's letters all the more astonishing for their insistence that there need be no distinction between living and thinking; that thinking *is* living and in fact works best when it takes its measure directly from life. "Axioms in philosophy," he writes to his friend John Hamilton Reynolds, "are not axioms until they are proved on our pulses" (3 May 1818). This is one of the signs of Keats's health: that he can find no essential difference between the body and the mind, that such a split would be unnatural, and that the mind's activities are in every way as sensuous and exhilarating as the body's. In the same letter, Keats illustrates the danger of separating body and mind in a metaphor that suggests a scene out of Dante: "The difference of high Sensations with and without knowledge appears to me this: in the latter case we are falling continually ten thousand fathoms deep and being blown up again without wings and with all the horror of a bare-shouldered Creature. In the former case, our shoulders are fledged, and we go thro' the same air and space without fear." Only in tandem do "high Sensations" and "knowledge" equip the human creature with wings capable of navigating the abyss.

If the letters show no embarrassment in mingling serious ideas with bits of idle gossip, light-hearted banter, comments on women and the weather, they also seem perfectly at ease with the inclusion of poetry—Keats's own and that of others. For those who have encountered Keats's poems only in weighty anthologies, it is refreshing to come upon them in this warmer human environment. In this context they seem to breathe again, to take on new life and interest. Here the poems are not isolated aesthetic events or solemn attempts at initiation into the "Temple of Fame" so much as natural extensions of his ordinary existence. Some of Keats's most supple and original sonnets—for example, "On the Sea," "On Sitting Down to Read *King Lear* Once Again," "O thou whose face hath felt the winter's wind," "Four seasons fill the measure of the year"—grow organically out of specific contexts, reflecting both the patterns of his thought at the moment of writing and the interests of individual correspondents. His own commentary on works such as "The Eve of St. Agnes" and "La Belle Dame sans Merci" is also highly suggestive and serves to humanize poems that have become dauntingly canonical. The happy marriage of poetry and prose in the letters tells us that for Keats, poetry was not a job or a career but a necessity, like breathing. "I find that I cannot exist without poetry, without eternal poetry," he admits to Reynolds; "half the day will not do, the whole of it." Poetry becomes a physical appetite, almost an addiction: "I began with a little, but habit has made me a Leviathan." If he cannot get his fix, either by reading or writing it, he becomes "all in a Tremble" (17, 18 April 1817).

This attitude will no doubt surprise the modern reader who has been taught to see poetry like Keats's as a luxury, to be classed with opera or haute cuisine. Keats's poetry—serious poetry—is not a part of most people's workaday lives. It is a sign of his complexity that Keats too could share this belief in poetry as an elite club; indeed, he once signed one of his poems "Caviare" and was fond of playing the connoisseur, even the collector, of the beautiful. He notes, for instance, that "though a quarrel in the streets is a thing to be hated, the energies displayed in it are fine" (14 February– 4 May 1819), and on his walking tour with Charles Brown he relates to his brother Tom their first sight of a Scottish country dancing school: "There was as fine a row of boys and girls as you ever saw, some beautiful faces, and one exquisite mouth" (29 June, 1, 2 July 1818).

But more often Keats saw a vital connection between poetry and the "real world," the world of suffering and misfortune that beset those closest to him. "I am ambitious of doing the world some good," he confesses to his friend Richard Woodhouse, and he meant *through his poetry.* He begins his adult life in training to be an apothecary, what we would consider today a family doctor; he ends it determined to be a poet-physician, healing with the balm of his words. Poetry is what Keats prescribes, but not exclusively for spiritual health (as we might do today, insisting that it is "good for the soul"); rather, he sees it as genuinely medicinal and therapeutic. In a memorable passage Keats concludes the early poem "I stood tiptoe" with a vision of ethereal breezes reviving "the languid sick" as they lie feverish in their hospital beds. "Springing up," these invalids awake "clear eyed" to greet their friends, their tongues "loos'd in poesy." This powerfully vivid image tells us that for Keats, poetry was both a cure for disease—those breezes bear the burden of Apollo's song—and a vital sign of a person's health.

In his letters this association of poetry with health is made explicit on a number of occasions. The poems are conceived not only as diversions or amusements for his friends, but also as a means of speeding the time and soothing their cares. The poetic epistle to J. H. Reynolds of 25 March 1818, for example, is sent "in hopes of cheering [him] through a Minute or two" and "pleas[ing]" his friend, who is confined to his bed, "sick and ill." In another letter he calls his poems "Scribblings" and hopes that they "will be some amusement for you this Evening" (3 February 1818), and in yet another feels content if his words have been "sufficient to lift a little time from your Shoulders" (19 February 1818). He is continually jotting down nonsense rhymes for his brother Tom, who is battling tuberculosis, and his young sister, Fanny, who is "imprisoned" by their legal guardian, Richard Abbey. And it is clear that he sees these poems as a way of consoling his family, combating and ameliorating their respective hardships.

The epistolary context of his poems as well as their function as antidote suggests another important dimension of Keats's letters: their sociability. The stereotype of the isolated romantic poet—confined to some lonely hut in the wilds, generating poems in a visionary frenzy with "flashing eyes" and "floating hair"—could hardly be less appropriate for Keats. He is genial and gregarious, inseparable from the tight network of his friends. He goes to plays, public lectures, dinner parties, dances, exhibitions, picture galleries, concerts, "claret feasts," even boxing matches and bear-baitings. He is always dining with the Brawnes or the Dilkes, going to "routs" at the Reynoldses', visiting Haydon's studio or the British Museum with Severn, attending Hazlitt's lectures, or reciting his poetry for Bailey or Wordsworth. He cuts short his first sojourn at the Isle of Wight (where he had repaired to write *Endymion*) because he "was too much in Solitude, and consequently was obliged to be in continual burning of thought as an only resource" (10 May 1817), and a year later confides to Reynolds, "I could not live without the love of my friends" (9 April 1818).

Although literary critics have recently stressed the political aspect of Keats's life and thought, it is important to remember that Keats himself felt that "the first political duty a Man ought to have a Mind to is the happiness of his friends" (17–27 September 1819). That his friends felt the same way about him is poignantly illustrated in an unpublished letter of 4 December 1820 William Haslam sent to Joseph Severn, who was ministering to his dying companion in Italy: "Keats must get himself again, Severn, if but for us.

I for one cannot afford to lose him. If I know what it is to love, I truly love John Keats." This sort of devotion speaks well both of Haslam and of Keats's other close friends, who eventually win their own collective fame as the "Keats Circle."

Keats occasionally yearned for solitude, it is true. He announces to George and Georgiana that he will never marry, and in a beautifully evocative image says that "the roaring of the wind is my wife and the Stars through the window pane are my Children" (14–31 October 1818). But it is only in his last year that he begins to sequester himself, and this is more the result of financial distress and the burden of his illness than any permanent streak of misanthropy in his character. In health, Keats's sensibility was profoundly social. Even when he decides to embark on a well-deserved walking tour with Charles Brown in the summer of 1818, he feels some guilt at abandoning his friends; as he says to Mrs. Wylie, "It was a great regret to me that I should leave all my friends just at the moment when I might have helped to soften away the time for them" (6 August 1818).

It is more than a measure of compensation, however, that the tour itself takes on the character of a larger humanitarian mission. Keats vows to his brother Tom that he shall "learn poetry here and shall henceforth write more than ever, for the abstract endeavour of being able to add a mite to that mass of beauty which is harvested from these grand materials by the finest spirits and put into ethereal existence for the relish of one's fellows" (25–27 June 1818). For Keats the "abstract endeavour" of art is always tempered by "the relish of one's fellows"; the pursuit of beauty always fulfills a social obligation that benefits humanity. It is not for nothing that Keats calls both Milton and the Grecian Urn the "friend[s] of man." Nor is it accidental that his famous prediction—"I think I shall be among the English Poets after my death"—pivots on the word *among,* as if immortality were a congenial gathering of geniuses rather than a row of marble busts.

Keats's conception of fame is similarly inflected by this social imperative. He was always saddened by the quarrels of his friends and frequently tried to reconcile them, but nothing depressed him more than the bickering of artists. He writes to Benjamin Bailey that he is "quite disgusted with literary Men" because they envy one another's work and as a result are constantly "at Loggerheads" (8 October 1817). Keats sees fame not as the culmination of a competitive struggle, or as the image of a glorious trophy held aloft in individual triumph, but rather as an aesthetic heaven where great spirits may converse with one another. "So now in the Name of Shakespeare, Raphael, and all our Saints," he concludes a letter to Haydon, "I commend you to the care of heaven!" (10, 11 May 1817). No matter how much "Minds [will] leave each other in contrary directions, traverse each other in Numberless points," he muses in another letter, they will nevertheless "greet each other at the Journey's end" (19 February 1818). Such camaraderie advocates the "*gregarious* advance of intellect" (3 May 1818, my emphasis) while exposing—for Keats at least—the bankruptcy of the "egotistical sublime."

Even as he is dying of consumption, it testifies to the fundamentally social character of his mind that the genial Keats returns. The last sentence of his will, provided to his publisher John Taylor before he sailed for Italy, reads, "My Chest of Books divide among my friends" (14 August 1820). And he signs off his final letter to Charles Brown by admitting that he "always made an awkward bow" (30 November 1820), as if even in the end he was trying to close the gap between letter and life, write a gesture that would place him for one last moment in the physical presence of his friend. It is precisely the *awkwardness* of this final bow—especially coming from the Poet of Beauty—that lends it so much quiet grace.

It would be a mistake to conclude from these examples that because Keats was so generous and warm-hearted, he was also consistently amiable or overly compliant. In fact, he was possessed of a fiery temper and could get magnificently pissed off. Commentators have politely ignored this side of the man, perhaps because it does not square with the noble Keats of "exquisite manners" and "profound tolerance" that Lionel Trilling has portrayed, or perhaps because it is difficult to reconcile the person who claimed that he would "jump down Aetna for any great Public good" (9 April 1818) with the one who remarks bitterly that he likes "man" but hates "Men." But the Keats who confesses to "the violence of my temperament" (14 February–4 May 1819) is a very real presence in the letters, and we ignore him at the risk of painting an idealized or sanitized portrait.

In truth, Keats had a great capacity for anger, particularly when it came to acts of injustice against others. When he learns that his friend Benjamin Bailey's curacy has been delayed because of snobbery, for example, he can hardly contain his rage: "There is something so nauseous in self-willed yawning impudence in the shape of conscience, it sinks the Bishop of Lincoln into a smashed frog putrifying. That a rebel against common decency should escape the Pillory! That a mitre should cover a Man guilty of the most coxcombical, tyrannical and indolent impertinence!" (3 November 1817). This "Keats-like rhodomontade" (19, 20 September 1819), as one of his friends called it, goes on for another page. He demonstrates similar loathing for the figure of the parson, who "is an Hippocrite to the Believer and a Coward to the unbeliever" and "must be either a Knave or an Ideot" (14 February–4 May 1819), and he vehemently damns the Scottish Church elders for banishing "puns and laughing and kissing" in order to create "regular Phalanges of savers and gainers" (7 July 1818). In other letters he vents his spleen on the public, Devonshire men, the caretaker of Burns's cottage ("I hate the rascal . . . he is a mahogany-faced old Jackass who knew Burns"), and bluestocking women writers, whom he decries as "a set of Devils whom I detest so much that I almost hunger after an acherontic promotion to a Torturer purposefully for their accommodation" (21 September 1817).

Keats saves the brunt of his wrath, however, for Charles Wells, the perpetrator of a romantic hoax against his brother Tom. Though the man who impersonated Amena Bellafila in a series of trumped-up love letters no doubt meant the whole affair as a practical joke, Keats was furious at the deception and called it a "diabolical scheme." What most enraged him was that it was carried out "with every show of friendship," exploiting Tom's open and generous nature. It is this manipulation of the sacred bond of friendship that elicits an ire appearing nowhere else in Keats's letters: "I do not think death too bad for the villain," he writes to his brother and sister-in-law. "I consider it my duty to be prudently revengeful. I will hang over his head like a sword by a hair. I will be opium to his vanity, if I cannot injure his interests. He is a rat and he shall have ratsbane to his vanity. I will harm him all I possibly can. I have no doubt I shall be able to do so. Let us leave him to misery alone except when we can throw in a little more" (14 February–4 May 1819). This is Keats's "incendiary spirit" with a vengeance; it is the ready pugilist who as a five-year-old boy reputedly defended his mother's sickroom with a sword, "clench'd" his fist against his master Thomas Hammond, and knocked down an usher who had boxed his brother's ears at school.

If we acknowledge this more explosive side of his character, we need also come to terms with those troubling moments in Keats's letters that commentators have conspicuously overlooked. Because they have laid so much stress on the intellectual strain of his mind, influential critics such as A. C. Bradley, T. S. Eliot, and Lionel Trilling have ignored the darker Keats, the man who could be rash, cruel, unreasonable, jealous, intolerant, misogynistic, and even anti-Semitic. These qualities simply do not square with the man of "moral energy" and "firmness of character" who has been promoted in the last half century. In fact, a remarkable feature of Trilling's highly successful paperback edition of the selected letters is its complete omission of any passage that might contradict his portrait of Keats as the "Poet-Hero." Entire paragraphs simply disappear from the letters without editorial comment.

Such is the case as well with the sequence of notes and love letters that Keats sent to his fiancée, Fanny Brawne, which were not published until 1878 and then created a storm of controversy. Although they now form part of any legitimate edition of the letters, this sequence has been almost completely ignored by scholars. Even as perceptive a reader as W. H. Auden confesses that he is "sorry that they were not published anonymously." After quoting a few of the more distasteful passages, he then attempts to cordon them off like a crime scene: "Any discussion of Keats's letters, therefore, should confine itself to those written before February 3, 1820." These are the texts that embarrass academic critics not only because they cut too close to the bone but also because they thwart the attempt to enshrine Keats as secular humanist and gentleman, a man of "generosity" and "exquisite manners." As we have seen, Keats was certainly possessed of these qualities, but he could also be imperious and antisocial, self-pitying and suspicious. "I enclose a passage from one of your Letters which I want you to alter a little," he writes to Fanny Brawne. "I want (if you will have it so) the matter express'd less coldly to me" (August [?] 1820). In these brief notes and letters, Keats is prone to self-dramatization and hyperbole. He can be as melodramatic as a gothic novel—"Good bye! I kiss you—O the torments!" (May [?] 1820)—or as jealous as Othello: "How have you pass'd this month? Who have you smil'd with?" (5 July [?] 1820). Even as Fanny complains of his "illtreating [her] in word, thought and deed" (June [?] 1820), Keats bristles with accusations: "You do not feel as I do. You do not know what it is to love. One day you may, your time is not come . . . Do not write to me if you have done anything this month which it would have pained me to have seen. You may have altered. If you have not, if you still behave in dancing rooms and other societies as I have seen you, I do not want to live" (5 July [?] 1820).

It has been argued that Keats's illness distorted his normally sanguine temperament and that it is unfair to judge his character on this basis. But Keats's treatment of Fanny Brawne was no anomaly. The same man who could admire the "grand march of intellect" (3 May 1818) and endorse the progressive improvement of civilization could also denigrate and abuse women with disturbing candor. Women "appear to me as children," he writes to George and Georgiana in October 1818, "to whom I would rather give a Sugar Plum than my time," and two months later: "I never intend here after to spend any time with Ladies unless they are handsome, you lose time to no purpose" (2 January 1819). To Bailey he confesses that when he is among women he has "evil thoughts, malice, spleen" (18 July 1818), and to George that "the Dress Maker, the blue Stocking and the most charming sentimentalist differ but in a Slight degree, and are equally smokeable" (31 December 1818). He reserves his most venomous attack, however, for a letter of September 1819 to America. A scant page before an extended meditation on the humane progress of English history, where Keats argues that all civilized "countries become gradually more enlighten'd," he quotes a long passage from Burton's *Anatomy of Melancholy* describing a lover's mistress. It is one of the most extraordinary pieces of misogyny in romantic literature, a detailed catalog of female ailments that Keats patiently copies from Burton's book and then exuberantly endorses for his brother George: "There's a dose for you—fine!!" Perhaps even more remarkable is that the letter is addressed to both his brother *and* his sister-in-law Georgiana, whose response to this gruesome list we can scarcely imagine.

To arrive at a more honest estimation of Keats's character, then, it is important that we acknowledge these moments even (or especially) if they trouble our sense of his spiritual health or appear to compromise "the energy of his heroism." Such acknowledgment, I hasten to add, does not mean that we ought to drag Keats before a firing squad, or scold him for not being sensitive enough to issues of gender and ethnicity. This would demonstrate our own historical amnesia. But it does mean that we should recognize the fullness and complexity of Keats the man, resisting the spell of his considerable charms. To register the dark side of his character also helps us to recognize his capacity for role-playing and the ease with which he assumed a variety of social and psychological identities. In his letters he is finely attuned to his different audiences. By turns he is reflective and philosophical with Bailey and Reynolds, ambitious with Haydon, gossipy and colloquial with George and Georgiana, and paternal with his sister, Fanny. He plays the beleaguered poet with Taylor, the knowing rake with Dilke and Rice, the martyred lover with Fanny Brawne, and the solicitous older brother with Tom. To the Jeffery sisters he shows off, lacing his letters with puns, and to his close friend Charles Brown he reveals his deepest anxieties about writing, about money, and about death.

In sum, the Keats we experience in the letters bears striking similarities to the hypothetical "chameleon Poet" whom he refers to in a letter to Richard Woodhouse: "As to the poetical Character itself," he writes, "it is not itself, it has no self. It is everything and nothing. It has no character. It enjoys light and shade; it lives in gusto, be it foul or fair, high or low, rich or poor, mean or elevated. It has as much delight in conceiving an Iago as an Imogen" (27 October 1818). Such protean versatility allows Keats to explore a remarkable range of human character and emotion *without judgment;* that is, it allows him to entertain the very real existence of evil in the world (Iago's hatred, cynicism, and bigotry) alongside the existence of good (Imogen's loyalty and virtue) in isolation from any moral prerogative. It is this kind of disinterestedness—a word Keats liked and borrowed from William Hazlitt—that makes him vulnerable to moral critics, who see Keats sliding into the abyss of absolute aestheticism, art for art's sake. But such openness, really a kind of celebration of the question of the world, also makes him distinctly modern, especially in his efforts to forge an identity out of "uncertainties, Mysteries, doubts."

One of the great ironies of Negative Capability and of Keats's formulation and embodiment of the characterless character is that he leaves behind such a powerful trace of self after his death. Even as he enters what he calls his "posthumous existence" in Italy and stops reading and writing letters, Keats's voice is channeled through the words of his friends. Joseph Severn becomes both the chronicler of his last months and his scribe, writing a series of detailed letters back to England relating the progress of Keats's disease and recording portions of his conversation. These letters are then carefully copied and circulated among Keats's friends and family. Almost immediately after his death, Keats's publisher John Taylor begins collecting material for a biography, as does Charles Brown. So lasting is the impression that Keats leaves on Reynolds that he requests his tombstone bear the words "The Friend of Keats," the same phrase that is eventually included on Brown's stone as well. Although she eventually marries, Fanny Brawne wears mourning for three years after Keats's death and takes his engagement ring to her grave. Fanny Keats carefully collects and preserves all of her brother's letters, and Joseph Severn sustains the poet's memory the length of his long life, writing no fewer than five separate memoirs of his experiences along with countless letters of reminiscence; his many portraits and sketches of Keats now constitute Severn's most enduring legacy.

True to his own theories about the fragility of identity, Keats insists that no name appear on his tombstone but only the words "Here lies one whose name was writ in water." It is one of the saddest epitaphs ever written, expressing Keats's bitter disappointment and his sense of the futility of his career. In this respect, it is consistent with his other request to Severn, "that no mention be made of [me] in any manner publicly—in reviews, magazines or newspapers—that no engraving be taken from any picture of [me]" (Severn to Taylor, 24 December 1820). In both of these requests Keats attempts to erase himself from the world, to ensure that not a trace of his

character remain. A similar kind of evanescence appears at the end of a letter he wrote to J. H. Reynolds in March 1818, though it is predicated on air
rather than water. Keats apologizes for the brevity of his letter, for not crossing it with "a little innocent bit of metaphysic," but then invites Reynolds
to cross the letter himself in his own mind: "If you think for five minutes
after having read this, you will find it a long letter and see written in the Air
above you, Your most affectionate friend, John Keats." Here is a more accurate forecast of his eventual reception: the body of Keats's life and work inscribed in air, floating above us like a genial spirit, awaiting our imaginative
participation to give him presence.

FURTHER READING

Auden, W. H. "Keats in His Letters." Review of Trilling's *Selected Letters. Partisan Review* 18 (November–December 1951): 701–706.

Bradley, A. C. "The Letters of Keats." In *Oxford Lectures on Poetry.* London: Macmillan, 1950. 209–244.

Eliot, T. S. "Shelley and Keats." In *The Use of Poetry and the Use of Criticism.* London: Faber, 1933.

Gittings, Robert. "Introduction." In *Letters of John Keats.* London: Oxford University Press, 1970.

Homans, Margaret. "Keats Reading Women, Women Reading Keats." *Studies in Romanticism* 29 (1990): 341–370.

Kucich, Greg. "The Poetry of Mind in Keats's Letters." *Style* 21 (1987): 76–94.

Luke, David. "Keats's Letters: Fragments of an Aesthetic of Fragments." *Genre* 11 (1978): 209–226.

Trilling, Lionel. "The Poet as Hero: Keats in His Letters." In *The Opposing Self.* New York: Viking, 1955. Originally published as the introduction to *The Selected Letters of John Keats.* New York: Farrar, 1951.

Wolfson, Susan J. "Keats the Letter-Writer: Epistolary Poetics." *Romanticism Past and Present* 6 (1982): 43–61.

EVENTS IN THE LIFE OF JOHN KEATS

1795	31 October, born at the Swan and Hoop Livery Stables, 24 Moorfields Pavement Row, London.
	18 December, baptized at St. Botolph's, Bishopsgate.
1796	28 February, George Keats born.
1799	18 November, Tom Keats born.
1800	28 April, Edward Keats born. (Died 1802.)
1803	3 June, Fanny (Frances Mary) Keats born.
	Attends John Clarke's school at Enfield.
1804	16 April, Thomas Keats, father, dies in riding accident.
	27 June, Frances, his mother, marries William Rawlings.
1805	8 March, John Jennings, grandfather, dies. Alice Jennings, grandmother, takes children to live at Edmonton.
1806–1809	Mother leaves husband and lives apart from the children.
1810	March, mother dies. Guardians appointed for children.
1811	Leaves Enfield school and is apprenticed to Thomas Hammond, a surgeon at Edmonton.
1814	December, grandmother dies.
1815	October, enters Guy's Hospital as a student.
1816	3 March, entered at Guy's as dresser to the surgeons.
	5 May, first published poem in the *Examiner* ("O Solitude").
	25 July, passes examination at Apothecaries' Hall, becomes eligible to practice as apothecary, physician, surgeon.

October, writes "On First Looking into Chapman's Homer."
  Meets Hunt, Haydon, Reynolds.

1 December, his Chapman's Homer sonnet appears in Leigh
  Hunt's article on "Young Poets" in the *Examiner*. Abandons
  medicine for poetry.

1817   1 or 2 March, sees the Elgin Marbles with Haydon and writes
  the Elgin Marbles sonnets.

3 March, his *Poems* published by C. and J. Ollier.

April–August, writes Books I and II of *Endymion* at Isle of
  Wight, Margate, Canterbury, Hastings, and Hampstead.
  Meets Bailey, Brown, Dilke.

September, visits Bailey at Oxford, writes Book III of
  Endymion.

October, ill at Hampstead, taking mercury.

28 November, finishes Book IV and the first draft of
  Endymion.

December, meets Wordsworth at Haydon's "immortal dinner."
  Writes theater reviews.

1818   January–February, revises *Endymion;* attends Hazlitt's lectures.

March–April, nurses brother Tom at Teignmouth. Writes
  "Isabella, or the Pot of Basil." *Endymion* published.

28 May, George Keats marries Georgiana Wylie.

June, George and Georgiana sail for America. Keats begins
  walking tour with Brown.

July–August, walking tour of Scotland with Brown.

7, 8 August, returns to London.

August–December, nurses Tom at Hampstead; meets Fanny
  Brawne. His *Poems* and *Endymion* are attacked in *Blackwood's* and the *Quarterly*. Begins *Hyperion*.

1 December, Tom Keats dies. Keats moves to Wentworth Place
  to live with Brown.

1819   January, writes "The Eve of St. Agnes" at Chichester.

February, writes "Bright Star" and "To Fanny."

April, writes "La Belle Dame sans Merci," sonnets on Fame,

Sleep, "If by dull rhymes," and the "Ode to Psyche." Secretly engaged to Fanny Brawne.

May, writes "Ode on a Grecian Urn," "Ode to a Nightingale," "Ode on Melancholy," and "Ode on Indolence."

July, "Ode to a Nightingale" published in *Annals of the Fine Arts*.

August, writing *Lamia* and *Otho the Great*.

19 September, writes "To Autumn" at Winchester.

21 September, abandons *The Fall of Hyperion*.

October–December, returns to Hampstead. Officially engaged to Fanny Brawne.

1820   January, "Ode on a Grecian Urn" published in *Annals of the Fine Arts*. George returns to England to raise money.

1 February, George sails for America from Liverpool.

3 February, has a severe lung hemorrhage, confined.

13 February, offers to break his engagement to Fanny Brawne.

March, revising *Lamia* volume, has several attacks of heart palpitation.

May, moves from Hampstead to Kentish Town, near Leigh Hunt.

10 May, "La Belle Dame sans Merci" published in Hunt's *Indicator*.

22 June, has a second severe hemorrhage; moves in with the Hunts.

July, *Lamia, Isabella, The Eve of St. Agnes, and Other Poems* published.

5 July, ordered by doctor to Italy.

August, leaves Hunt's and is tended by Fanny Brawne at Wentworth Place.

17 September, departs for Italy with Joseph Severn aboard the *Maria Crowther*.

21 October, reaches Naples after a harrowing voyage. They are held in quarantine.

31 October, released from quarantine.

7 or 8 November, starts for Rome in hired carriage.

15 November, reaches Rome, enters lodgings at 26 Piazza di
   Spagna.

30 November, writes last known letter, to Charles Brown.

1821   23 February, dies at 11 P.M.

26 February, buried in the Protestant Cemetery.

17 March, news of his death reaches London.

KEATS'S CORRESPONDENTS

Benjamin Bailey (1791–1853). The early friend of Keats who matriculated at Oxford and became a country parson in Northamptonshire. Keats's friendship with him cooled when Bailey, after having ardently courted Mariane Reynolds, became engaged to Hamilton Gleig, daughter of the bishop of Brechin and primus of the Scots Episcopal Church. Their correspondence ended on 14 August 1819, the day on which Keats sent very stiff congratulations on the marriage. Bailey migrated to Ceylon, where he became senior colonial chaplain and later archdeacon.

Frances (Fanny) Brawne (1800–1865). Keats's fiancée, whom he met shortly after his return from Scotland in August 1818. Keats lived next door to the Brawnes from the middle of October 1819 until May 1820, and then, desperately ill, he convalesced in their home for a month in August–September. He saw Fanny for the last time on 13 September 1820. After this he never wrote to her again nor read her letters. More than twelve years after his death, in June 1833, she married Louis Lindo (later Lindon), who was twelve years her junior. They had three children and spent most of their time on the Continent.

Mrs. Samuel Brawne (1778?–1829). Fanny's mother, a widow since 1810 with three children, Fanny, Samuel, and Margaret. She rented Brown's half of Wentworth Place in the summer of 1818 and Dilke's half from about April 1819 to the end of 1829. Mrs. Brawne was severely burned at the door of her home, and died on 23 November 1829.

Charles Brown (1787–1842). A close friend of the poet whom Keats met in the summer of 1817. On his brother's death he inherited enough money to make possible what he called a life of literary pursuits. Keats roomed with Brown in Wentworth Place after the death of his brother Tom. In late 1819 Brown was illegally married to Abigail O'Donaghue, his house-keeper ("Our irish Servant," Keats calls her), by whom he had a son, Charles or "Carlino." In May 1820 he rented his house and set off alone for Scotland. He never saw Keats again after this, though the poet hoped in vain that Brown would accompany him to Italy. In 1841 he migrated to New Zealand, where he died the next year.

Dr. (later Sir) James Clark (1788–1870). Keats's attending physician in Rome. A Scotsman who was well read and fond of music, Clark knew Keats's poems and took a keen interest in his patient. He returned to London in 1826, and eventually became physician to Queen Victoria, who made him a baronet in 1837.

Charles Cowden Clarke (1787–1877). The son of the master of Enfield school, which the three Keats brothers attended. He greatly influenced the literary tastes and achievements of John, eight years his junior, inspired him to write verses, and introduced him to his first patron, Leigh Hunt. He left Keats's circle of friends fairly early, moving to Ramsgate in 1817 and seeing Keats for the last time in early 1819. Clarke later became a publisher and bookseller, and subsequently a popular lecturer on literary subjects and, with his wife, an editor of Shakespeare's works. He provided great assistance to Keats's first biographer, Richard Monckton Milnes, and published his own "Recollections" of Keats in the *Atlantic Monthly* (1861).

Charles Wentworth Dilke (1789–1864). A civil servant and author who worked in the Navy Pay Office, Somerset House, until 1836 and then retired on his pension. He published a useful six-volume edition of *Old English Plays* (1814–1816). He was joint owner, with Charles Brown, of Wentworth Place, later called Lawn Bank, and now the Keats House in Hampstead. Largely because of Mrs. Dilke's kindness and charm, Wentworth Place became a home for the Keats boys. The Dilkes' open disapproval of Keats's engagement to Fanny Brawne caused Keats to see little of them during his final months in England. After 1821 Dilke held together part of the old Keats circle, supervising the financial affairs of Fanny Keats and Fanny Brawne, and keeping in touch with George Keats in America. He championed George's honesty in money matters and defended him from Charles Brown's accusations of unscrupulousness.

William Haslam (1795 or 1798?–1851). A lawyer, Keats's schoolfellow, and one of the most engaging and devoted of the poet's friends. He lent money to Keats, forwarded letters to him, and in many other ways was "excessively kind." It is Haslam who at the last minute arranged for Severn to accompany Keats to Italy, having been prevented from going himself because of a new baby and business problems. He was instrumental in making the financial arrangements for the trip. Severn's letters to him from Italy constitute an invaluable record of Keats's last months.

Benjamin Robert Haydon (1786–1846). A historical painter, stalwart defender of the Elgin Marbles, and early friend of Keats, whom he met at Leigh Hunt's Hampstead cottage in October 1816. For a time Keats worshipped him and was greatly impressed by Haydon's huge painting *Christ's Triumphant Entry into Jerusalem,* wherein his face appears along with Wordsworth's, Lamb's, and Hazlitt's. Keats broke with him in June 1819, however, after learning of his quarrels with Hunt and Reynolds and after Haydon's refusal to pay back a loan. His ambitious historical pictures never caught on with art critics or with the public, and he commited suicide in 1846.

Leigh Hunt (1784–1859). An early mentor and friend of Keats. He lent books to Keats, praised and printed his verse in the *Examiner* and the *Indicator,* introduced him to Haydon, Shelley, and other celebrities, and in every way encouraged and fostered his protégé's talents. For a time Keats venerated him as a master. Then he perceived some of Hunt's limitations, and realized how damaging to his own reputation and style their friendship had been. Keats later reconsidered this opinion and came to appreciate Hunt's friendship and support. In 1828 Hunt published the first biographies of Keats in *Lord Byron and Some of His Contemporaries* and in John Gorton's *General Biographical Dictionary.*

The Jeffery Sisters—Marian, Sarah, and Fanny. Friends of the Keats brothers who lived in Teignmouth, Devon.

Frances (Fanny) Keats (1803–1889). Keats's sister. After the death of her grandmother, Mrs. Jennings, in 1814, she lived with her guardian, Richard Abbey, in one or the other of his houses in Walthamstow and London, except for four years (January 1815–December 1818) when she attended the Walthamstow school. Abbey made it as difficult as possible for her to see her brothers, and even offered objections to John's writing letters to her. Although John did write fairly often and visited her when he could, during his final year in Hampstead he saw little of her, and was forced to leave for Italy without saying good-bye. In 1826 she married Valentin Maria Llanos y Gutierrez, who is said to have spoken to Keats only three days before the latter's death. They moved to Spain in 1833 and never saw England again. During 1861–1864 they lived in Italy, where they saw much of Joseph Severn.

George Keats (1797–1841). Keats's middle brother. After completing Enfield school, George was lodged and set to work in Abbey's business house. In 1816, after a quarrel with Abbey's junior partner, George left Abbey's employment and moved in with his two brothers. He married Georgiana Wylie in May 1818 and in June they sailed to Philadelphia. Eventually they reached Kentucky, where George was swindled by the famous naturalist John James Audubon. They eventually settled in Louisville, where his financial affairs deteriorated. In search of funds, he returned to England in January 1820, managing to take back to America his own share of Tom's estate plus, his enemies charge, the larger part of John's. In a few years, however, George became a wealthy and influential citizen of Louisville, and he then paid all of John's debts.

Tom Keats (1799–1818). Keats's youngest brother. After returning from Scotland, Keats devoted practically every minute to looking after Tom, thereby injuring his own health beyond repair. Tom died of tuberculosis on 1 December 1818. His letters show him to have been, as Milnes phrases it, "of a most gentle and witty nature," and all of Keats's friends spoke of him with interest and affection.

John Hamilton Reynolds (1794–1852). One of Keats's dearest friends, Reynolds met Keats at Leigh Hunt's in October 1816, and in turn introduced him to Brown, Rice, Bailey, Taylor, Hessey, Dilke, and others. He talked about poetry with Keats, inspired him to write poems such as "Robin Hood" and "Isabella," and prevented him from publishing the first reckless preface to *Endymion*. He was initially a poet himself, though took up the study of law. From 1847 till his death in 1852, he was an assistant clerk of the County Court at Newport, Isle of Wight.

James Rice, Jr. (1792–1832). Through Reynolds, Keats met Rice sometime before April 1817, and a lasting friendship resulted. They spent a month together in the Isle of Wight during the summer of 1819, and, being both in poor health, got on each other's nerves. But their affection and admiration did not suffer, and soon Keats was referring to Rice as "the most sensible, and even wise Man I know." He was an attorney who persuaded Reynolds to enter the law and then took him into partnership. Together they became the solicitors of Fanny Keats de Llanos and handled business for her, Llanos, and George Keats in a fashion that displeased all three. Rice suffered from an incurable disease for many years and died at the age of forty.

Joseph Severn (1793–1879). Today the most famous of Keats's friends, Severn was a painter who accompanied Keats to Italy and nursed him in his final months. He was probably introduced to Keats by Haslam when Keats was a student at Guy's Hospital in late 1815. On occasion Severn conducted Keats around the British Museum or the art galleries, pointing out the beauties of the Elgin Marbles or the paintings of Titian. In 1819 he was awarded the Royal Academy's gold medal for his painting

The Cave of Despair. From 17 September 1820, when the *Maria Crowther* sailed to Gravesend, till 23 February 1821, when Keats died, Severn was a model cook, cleaner, entertainer, nurse, and companion. His subsequent life, long and eventful, was first a crusade on behalf of Keats's reputation, and then after 1848 a sort of reminiscence of his association with the poet. Twenty years after Keats's death he returned to England, where he led a financially precarious existence until 1861, when he was appointed British consul to Rome. During his life he painted and sketched many portraits of Keats. He died in his eighty-sixth year and was eventually buried next to the poet in the Protestant Cemetery in Rome.

John Taylor (1781–1864) and James Augustus Hessey (1785–1870). Taylor and Hessey, whose authors included Coleridge, Carlyle, De Quincey, and Hazlitt, took over Keats's 1817 *Poems* from Charles and James Ollier soon after its appearance, and published his next two volumes. In 1803 Taylor met Hessey, and in 1806 they established their own firm at 93 Fleet Street. Keats respected and liked both men, and they in turn were thoroughly convinced of his greatness. They made him welcome in their homes, introduced him to many interesting men, defended him against hostile reviewers, lent him books, and raised the necessary funds that made the Italian trip possible. Taylor was a scholarly man who wrote books on Junius, currency, banking, and scriptural subjects, as well as antiquarian articles. He planned to write the "Memoirs and Remains of John Keats," but never finished the manuscript. Hessey remained a bookseller until he became bankrupt in 1829. By 1834 he was in charge of a school at Hampstead.

Richard Woodhouse, Jr. (1788–1834). One of the most interesting and scholarly of Keats's friends, Woodhouse studied law and eventually became a legal and literary adviser to the publishers Taylor and Hessey. He was convinced of Keats's genius and devoted much time to collecting and copying every poem, letter, anecdote, and proof sheet he could lay his hands on. In Rollins's edition, twenty otherwise unknown letters are printed from his transcripts. He developed tuberculosis in 1829 and died five years later. Students of Keats today owe a heavy debt to Wood-

house for his diligence in collecting and transcribing Keats's letters and
poems.

Georgiana Augusta Wylie (1798–1879). Keats's sister-in-law, who married
George and immigrated with him to America in 1818. Keats "was very
fond of her" and found her "the most disinterested woman I ever knew."
To George and Georgiana, Keats's longest and brightest letters were addressed. They had eight children. After George died, Georgiana remar-
ried in 1843. Her second husband, John Jeffrey, a Scotsman living in
Lexington, Kentucky, was some sixteen years her junior. In 1845 Jeffrey
copied—or miscopied—a fair number of Keats's letters and autograph
poems for the use of Milnes in his biography.

Selected Letters of John Keats

1816–1817

To C. C. Clarke
SEPTEMBER 1816[1]

Margate—Sept. 1816—

To Mr C. C. Clarke—

Oft have you seen a Swan superbly frowning,
And, with proud breast, his own white shadow crowning:
He slants his Neck beneath the waters bright,
So silently, it seems a beam of light
Shot from the Galaxy; anon he sports—
With outspread wings, the Naiad Zephyr courts,
Or ruffles all the surface of the Lake,
In striving, from its crystal face, to take
Some diamond Waterdrops, and them to treasure
In milky Nest, and sip them off at leisure.
But, not a moment, can he there insure them;
Nor, to such downy rest, can he allure them:
For down they rush, as though they would be free,
And drop, like time into Eternity.
   Just like that Bird, am I, in loss of time,
Whene'er I venture on the Stream of Rhyme;
With shattered Boat, oar snapt, and canvass rent,
I slowly sail, scarce knowing my intent;
Still scooping up the water with my fingers;
In which, a trembling diamond never lingers.
   By this, Friend Charles! you may, full plainly, see

Why I have never pen'd a Line to thee:
Because my thoughts were never free, and clear,
And little fit to please a classic Ear:
Because my Wine was of too poor a savour
For one, whose Palate gladdens in the flavour
Of sparkling Helicon[2]—Small good it were,
To take him to a desert, rude, and bare,
Who had on Baiae's shore reclin'd at ease,
While Tasso's Page was floating in a Breeze
That gave soft Music from Armida's[3] Bowers,
Mingled with fragrance from her rarest flowers:
Small good, to one‹,› who had, by Mulla's Stream,[4]
Fondled the Maidens with the Breasts of Cream:
Who had beheld Belphoebe in a Brook,
And lovely Una in a leafy Nook,
And Archimage[5] leaning o'er his Book:
Who had, of all that's sweet tasted, and seen,
From silv'ry ripple, up to Beauty's Queen;
From the sequester'd haunts of gay Titania,
To the blue dwelling of Divine Urania.
One, who, of late, had ta'en sweet forest walks
With him who elegantly chats, and talks—
The wrong'd Libertas[6]—who hath told you Stories
Of laurel Chaplets, and Apollo's glories;
Of Troops chivalrous‹,› prancing through a City;
And tearful Ladies, made for Love and Pity:
With many else which I have never known.

    Thus have I thought; & days, on days have flown
Slowly, or rapidly—unwilling still,
For you to try my dull unlearned quill.
Nor should I now, but that I've known you long;
That you first taught me all the sweets of song:
The grand, the sweet, the Terse, the free, the Fine;
What swell'd with Pathos, and what right divine;

Spenserian vowels, that elope with ease,
And float along like Birds o'er summer Seas;
Miltonian Storms, and more, Miltonian tenderness;
Michael in Arms, and more, meek Eve's fair slenderness.
Who read for me the Sonnet, swelling loudly
Up to its Climax, and then dying proudly?
Who found for me the Grandeur of the Ode,
Growing, like Atlas, stronger from its load?
Who let me taste that more than cordial dram,
The sharp, the rapier pointed Epigram?
Show'd me that Epic was of all the King,
Round, vast, and spanning all, like Saturn's Ring?
You too, upheld the Veil from Clio's beauty,
And pointed out the Patriots stern duty;
The Might of Alfred, and the shaft of Tell,
The Hand of Brutus, that so grandly fell
Upon a Tyrant's Head.—Ah! had I never seen,
Or known your kindness, what might I have been?
What my Enjoyments in my youthful years,
Bereft of all that now my Life endears?
And can I e'er these Benefits forget?
And can I e'er repay the friendly debt?
No, doubly no—Yet, should these Rhymings please,
I shall roll on the Grass with two fold ease:
For I have long time been my fancy feeding
With Hopes, that you would one day think the reading
Of my rough Verses not an hour mispent:—
Should I e'er hear it what a rich content!
    Some Weeks have pass'd since last I saw the Spires
In lucent Thames reflected:—warm desires
To see the Sun o'er peep the eastern dimness,
And morning Shadows stretching into slimness
Across the lawny Fields, or pebbly water;
To mark the time, as they grow broad, and shorter;

To feel the Air, that plays about the Hills,
And sips its freshness from the little rills;
To see high, golden Corn wave in the light,
When Cynthia smiles upon a Summer's Night,
And <play> 'peers among the Cloudlet's jet, and white;
As though she were reclining on a bed
Of bean blossoms, in heaven freshly shed.
No sooner had I stepp'd into these Pleasures,
Than I began to think of Verse, and Measures:
The Air that floated by me, seem'd to say,
"Write! thou wilt never have a better day"
And so I did.—When many Lines I'd written,
Though, with their grace, I was not over smitten;
Yet, as my hand was in, I thought I'd better
Trust to my feelings, and write you a Letter.
Such an Attempt required an inspiration
Of a peculiar sort;—a consummation.
Which, had I felt, these scribblings might have been
Verses, from which the Soul would never wean.
But many days have pass'd, since last my heart
Was warm'd luxuriously, by divine Mozart;
By Arne[7] delighted, or by Handel madden'd,
Or by the Songs of Erin pierc'd, and sadden'd:
What time, you were before the Musick[8] sitting,
And the rich Notes, to each Sensation fitting.
Since I have walked with you through shady Lanes,
That freshly terminate in open Plains;
And revel'd, in a Chat, that ceased not,
When at night fall among your Books we got;
No, nor when Supper came, nor after that,
Nor when, reluctantly, I took my Hat;
No, nor till cordially you shook my Hand
Mid way between our homes:—your accents bland
Still sounded in my Ears, when I no more
Could hear your footsteps touch the grav'ly floor.

Sometimes I lost them, and then found again;
You chang'd the footpath for the grassy plain.
In these still moments, I have wished you joys
That well you know to honor—"Life's very toys
With him," said I, "will take a pleasant charm,
It cannot be, that ought will work him harm"
These thoughts now come o'er me with all their might:
Again I shake your hand:—Friend Charles—good Night!

1. Huntington Library, San Marino, California (HM 11903). This verse epistle appears for the first time in its entirety here. Rollins prints the version that Keats included in his *Poems* (1817), which reveals slight but significant changes from this original manuscript letter. Because it has never been published before, I depart from the editorial procedures discussed in the preface and transcribe the letter exactly as Keats wrote it, with his own punctuation and cancellations, which appear in angle brackets (< >).
2. The mountain residence of Apollo and the Muses and source of poetic inspiration.
3. In Tasso's *Jerusalem Delivered* an enchantress who made captives of Rinaldo and Tancred.
4. A stream near Spenser's home at Kilcolman. See *The Faerie Queene,* IV.xi.41, VII.vi.40.
5. For these characters, see *The Faerie Queene,* Books I and II.
6. Leigh Hunt is so called in Keats's "Specimen of an Induction to a Poem," line 61.
7. Thomas Augustine Arne (1710–1778), English composer.
8. Musical instrument, piano.

To C. C. Clarke
9 OCTOBER 1816

Wednesday Oct. 9th

My dear Sir,

The busy time has just gone by, and I can now devote any time you may mention to the pleasure of seeing Mr. Hunt. 'Twill be an Era in my existence. I am anxious too to see the Author of the Sonnet to the Sun, for it is no mean gratification to become acquainted with Men who in their admiration of Poetry do not jumble together Shakespeare and Darwin.[1] I have copied out a sheet or two of Verses which I composed some time ago, and find so much to blame in them that the best part will go into the fire. Those to G. Mathew[2] I will suffer to meet the eye of Mr. H. notwithstanding that the Muse is so frequently mentioned. I here sinned in the face of Heaven even while remembering what, I think, Horace says: "never presume to make a God appear but for an Action worthy of a God." From a few Words of yours when last I saw you, I have no doubt but that you have something in your Portfolio which I should by rights see. I will put you in Mind of it. Although the Borough is a beastly place in dirt, turnings and windings, yet No. 8 Dean Street is not difficult to find, and if you would run the Gauntlet over London Bridge, take the first turning to the left and then the first to the right, and moreover knock at my door, which is nearly opposite a Meeting,[3] you would do one a Charity which as St. Paul saith is the father of all the Virtues. At all events let me hear from you soon; I say at all events not excepting the Gout in your fingers.

Your's Sincerely
John Keats—

1. Erasmus Darwin (1731–1802), grandfather of Charles Darwin, naturalist, poet, author of *The Botanic Garden*.
2. George Felton Mathew (1795–?), early friend of Keats and subject of one of Keats's verse epistles.
3. A Baptist chapel.

To C. C. Clarke
31 OCTOBER 1816

My daintie Davie,[1]

I will be as punctual as the Bee to the Clover. Very glad am I at the thoughts of seeing so soon this glorious Haydon and all his Creation. I pray thee let me know when you go to Ollier's[2] and where he resides—this I forgot to ask you—and tell me also when you will help me waste a sullen day. God 'ield you.[3]

J—K—

1. "My dainty Davie" appears in Robert Burns's "To Davie Second Epistle," and "Dainty Davie" is the chorus to his "Now Rosy May."
2. Charles Ollier (1788–1859), publisher of Keats's first volume of poems.
3. *Hamlet,* IV.v.41, "God 'ild you!"

To B. R. Haydon
20 NOVEMBER 1816

Novr. 20th

My dear Sir—

Last Evening wrought me up, and I cannot forbear sending you the following—Your's unfeignedly, John Keats—

> Great Spirits[1] now on Earth are sojourning
>   He of the Cloud, the Cataract, the Lake
>   Who on Helvellyn's summit wide awake
> Catches his freshness from Archangel's wing
> He of the Rose, the Violet, the Spring
>   The social Smile, the Chain for freedom's sake:
>   And lo!—whose stedfastness would never take
> A Meaner Sound than Raphael's Whispering.
> And other Spirits are there standing apart
>   Upon the Forehead of the Age to come;
> These, These will give the World another heart
>   And other pulses—hear ye not the hum

Of mighty Workings in a distant Mart?
Listen awhile ye Nations, and be dumb!

Novr. 20—

Removed to 76 Cheapside

1. The "Great Spirits" are Wordsworth, Hunt, and Haydon.

To C. C. Clarke
17 DECEMBER 1816

Tuesday—

My dear Charles,

You may now look at Minerva's Aegis with impunity. Seeing that my awful Visage[1] did not turn you into a John Doree,[2] you have accordingly a legitimate title to a Copy. I will use my interest to procure it for you. I'll tell you what; I met Reynolds at Haydon's a few mornings since. He promised to be with me this evening and Yesterday I had the same promise from Severn, and I must put you in Mind that on last All hallowmas' day you gave your word that you would spend this Evening with me. So no putting off. I have done little to Endymion lately. I hope to finish it in one more attack. I believe you know I went to Richards's.[3] It was so whoreson a Night that I stopped there all the next day. His Remembrances to you. (Excpt. from the common place Book of my Mind—Mem.—Wednesday—Hampstead—call in Warner Street—a Sketch of Mr. Hunt). I will ever consider you my sincere and affectionate friend. You will not doubt that I am your's.

God bless you, John Keats—

1. A reference to a cast of Haydon's life mask of Keats.
2. A fish.
3. Thomas Richards worked in the Ordnance Department in the Tower from 1804 to 1831. His brother Charles printed Keats's 1817 *Poems*.

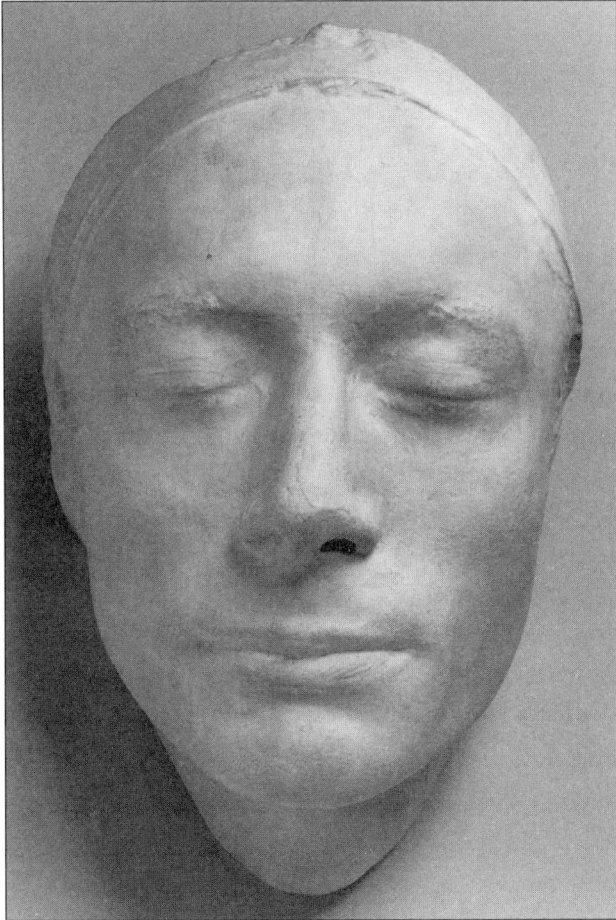

Haydon's life mask of Keats (1816).
National Portrait Gallery, London.

To J. H. Reynolds
17 MARCH 1817

My dear Reynolds,

My Brothers are anxious that I should go by myself into the country. They have always been extremely fond of me, and now that Haydon has pointed out how necessary it is that I should be alone to improve myself, they give up the temporary pleasure of living with me continually for a great good which I hope will follow. So I shall soon be out of Town.[1] You must soon bring all your present troubles to a close, and so must I, but we must, like the Fox, prepare for a fresh swarm of flies.[2] Banish money—Banish sofas—Banish Wine—Banish Music—But right Jack Health—honest Jack Health, true Jack Health—banish health and banish all the world.[3] I must [. . .] myself [. . .][4] if I come this Evening, I shall horribly commit myself elsewhere. So I will send my excuses to them and Mrs. Dilke by my Brothers.

Your sincere friend
John Keats

1. He left for Southampton on April 14.
2. A reference to "The Fox and the Hedgehog" in *Aesop's Fables*.
3. Keats adapts this passage from *1 Henry IV*, II.iv.520–527.
4. The letter is torn.

To George and Tom Keats
15 APRIL 1817

Tuesday Morn—

My dear Brothers,

   I am safe at Southampton after having ridden three stages outside and the rest in for it began to be very cold. I did not know the Names of any of the Towns I passed through. All I can tell you is that sometimes I saw dusty Hedges, sometimes Ponds, then nothing, then a little Wood with trees look you like Launce's Sister "as white as a Lilly and as small as a Wand."[1] Then came houses which died away into a few straggling Barns; then came hedge trees aforesaid again. As the Lamplight crept along, the following things were discovered: "long heath brown furze";[2] Hurdles here and there half a Mile; Park palings when the Windows of a House were always discovered by reflection; One Nymph of Fountain; *N. B. Stone;* lopped Trees; Cow ruminating; ditto Donkey; Man and Woman going gingerly along; William seeing his Sisters over the Heath; John waiting with a Lantern for his Mistress; Barber's Pole; Doctor's Shop. However, after having had my fill of these I popped my Head out just as it began to Dawn—*N. B. this tuesday Morn saw the Sun rise*—of which I shall say nothing at present. I felt rather lonely this Morning at breakfast so I went and unbox'd a Shakespeare; "Here's my Comfort."[3] I went immediately after Breakfast to the Southampton Water where I enquired for the Boat to the Isle of Wight as I intend seeing that place before I settle. It will go at 3, so shall I after having taken a Chop. I know nothing of this place but that it is long, tolerably broad, has bye streets, two or three Churches, a very respectable old Gate with two Lions to guard it. The Men and Women do not materially differ from those I have been in the Habit of seeing. I forgot to say that from dawn till half past six I went through a most delightful Country, some open Down but for the most part thickly wooded. What surprised me most was an immense quantity of blooming Furze on each side the road cutting a most rural dash. The Southampton water when I saw it just now was no better than a low Water Water, which did no more than answer my expectations. It will have mended its Manners by 3. From the Wharf are seen the shores on each side stretching to the isle of Wight. You, Haydon, Reynolds etc. have been pushing each other out of my Brain by turns. I have conned over every Head in Haydon's Picture.[4] You must warn them not to be afraid should my Ghost visit them on Wednesday. Tell Haydon to Kiss his Hand at Betty over the Way for me, yea and to spy at her for me. I hope one of you will be competent to take part in a Trio while I am away. You need only aggravate your voices a little and mind not to speak Cues and all.[5] When you have said Rum-ti-ti, you must not be rum any more or else another will take up the ti-ti alone and then he might be taken, God shield us, for little better than a Titmouse. By the by, talking of Titmouse, Remember me particularly to all my Friends. Give my Love to the Miss Reynoldses and to Fanny who I hope you will soon see. Write to me soon about them all, and you George particularly how you get on with Wilkinson's plan. What could I have done without my Plaid? I don't feel inclined to write any more at present for I feel rather muzzy. You must be content with this facsimile of the rough plan of Aunt Dinah's Counterpane.

Your most affectionate Brother
John Keats—

Reynolds shall hear from me soon—

1. *The Two Gentlemen of Verona,* II.iii.22f.
2. *The Tempest,* I.i.70f.
3. *The Tempest,* II.ii.47, 57.
4. *Christ's Entry into Jerusalem,* in which appeared the heads of Hazlitt, Wordsworth, and Keats.
5. *A Midsummer Night's Dream,* I.ii.83f. and III.i.102f.

$\mathcal{T}$o $\mathcal{J}$. $\mathcal{H}$. $\mathcal{R}$eynolds

17, 18 APRIL 1817

Carisbrooke, April 17th

My dear Reynolds,

Ever since I wrote to my Brothers from Southampton I have been in a taking, and at this moment I am about to become settled, for I have unpacked my books, put them into a snug corner, pinned up Haydon, Mary Queen of Scots and Milton with his daughters in a row. In the passage I found a head of Shakespeare which I had not before seen. It is most likely the same that George spoke so well of, for I like it extremely. Well, this head I have hung over my Books, just above the three in a row, having first discarded a french Ambassador. Now this alone is a good morning's work. Yesterday I went to Shanklin, which occasioned a great debate in my mind whether I should live there or at Carisbrooke. Shanklin is a most beautiful place; sloping wood and meadow ground reaches round the Chine, which is a cleft between the Cliffs of the depth of nearly 300 feet at least. This cleft is filled with trees and bushes in the narrow part, and as it widens becomes bare, if it were not for primroses on one side, which spread to the very verge of the Sea, and some fishermen's huts on the other, perched midway in the Balustrades of beautiful green Hedges along their steps down to the sands. But the sea, Jack, the sea—the little waterfall, then the white cliff, then St. Catherine's Hill, "the sheep in the meadows, the cows in the corn." Then, why are you at Carisbrooke, say you? Because, in the first place, I should be at twice the Expense, and three times the inconvenience. Next, that from here I can see your continent; from a little hill close by, the whole north Angle of the Isle of Wight with the water between us. In the 3rd place, I see Carisbrooke Castle from my window, and have found several delightful wood-alleys and copses and quick freshes. As for Primroses, the Island ought to be called Primrose Island, that is if the nation of Cowslips agree thereto, of which there are diverse Clans just beginning to lift up their heads and if an how the Rain holds whereby that is Birds eyes abate.[1] Another reason of my fixing is that I am more in reach of the places around me. I intend to walk over the island east, West, North, South. I have not seen many specimens of Ruins. I don't think, however, I shall ever see one to surpass Carisbrooke Castle. The trench is o'ergrown with the smoothest turf, and the walls with ivy. The Keep within side is one Bower of ivy. A Colony of Jackdaws have been there many years. I dare say I have seen many a descendant of some old cawer who peeped through the Bars at Charles the first, when he was there in Confinement. On the road from Cowes to Newport I saw some extensive Barracks, which disgusted me extremely with Government for placing such a Nest of Debauchery in so beautiful a place. I asked a man on the Coach about this, and he said that the people had been spoiled. In the room where I slept at Newport I found this on the Window: "O Isle spoilt by the Mil*a*tary." I must in honesty however confess that I did not feel very sorry at the idea of the Women being a little profligate. The Wind is in a sulky fit, and I feel that it would be no bad thing to be the favorite of some Fairy, who would give one the power of seeing how our Friends got on, at a Distance. I should like, of all Loves, a sketch of you and Tom and George in ink, which Haydon will do if you tell him how I want them. From want of regular rest, I have been rather *narvus* and the passage in Lear—"Do you not hear the Sea?"—has haunted me intensely.

On the Sea

It keeps eternal Whisperings around
  Desolate shores, and with its mighty swell
  Gluts twice ten thousand Caverns; till the spell
Of Hecate leaves them their old shadowy sound.
Often 'tis in such gentle temper found
  That scarcely will the very smallest shell
  Be moved for days from whence it sometime fell
When last the winds of Heaven were unbound.
O ye who have your eyeballs vext and tir'd,
  Feast them upon the wideness of the Sea.

O ye whose Ears are dinned with uproar rude
    Or fed too much with cloying melody,
Sit ye near some old Cavern's Mouth and brood
    Until ye start as if the Sea Nymphs quired.

                                        April 18th

Will you have the goodness to do this? Borrow a Botanical Dictionary, turn to the words Laurel and Prunus, show the explanations to your sisters and Mrs. Dilke, and without more ado let them send me the Cups, Basket and Books they trifled and put off and off while I was in Town. Ask them what they can say for themselves. Ask Mrs. Dilke wherefore she does so distress me. Let me know how Jane has her health. The Weather is unfavorable for her. Tell George and Tom to write. I'll tell you what, on the 23rd was Shakespeare born. Now if I should receive a Letter from you and another from my Brothers on that day 'twould be a parlous good thing. Whenever you write say a Word or two on some Passage in Shakespeare that may have come rather new to you, which must be continually happening, notwithstanding that we read the same Play forty times; for instance, the following, from the Tempest, never struck me so forcibly as at present:

                    "Urchins
   Shall, for that vast of Night that they may work,
   All exercise on thee."

How can I help bringing to your mind the Line,

    In the dark backward and abysm of time.

I find that I cannot exist without poetry, without eternal poetry; half the day will not do, the whole of it. I began with a little, but habit has made me a Leviathan. I had become all in a Tremble from not having written anything of late. The Sonnet over leaf did me some good. I slept the better last night for it. This Morning, however, I am nearly as bad again. Just now I opened Spencer, and the first Lines I saw were these:

   "The noble Heart that harbors vertuous thought,
   And is with Child of glorious great intent,

Can never rest, until it forth have brought
Th' eternal Brood of Glory excellent."[2]

Let me know particularly about Haydon. Ask him to write to me about Hunt, if it be only ten lines. I hope all is well. I shall forthwith begin my Endymion, which I hope I shall have got some way into by the time you come, when we will read our verses in a delightful place I have set my heart upon near the Castle. Give my Love to your Sisters severally, to George and Tom. Remember me to Rice, Mr. and Mrs. Dilke and all we know.

Your sincere Friend
John Keats

Direct J. Keats, Mrs. Cook's new Village
Carisbrooke

1. Robert Gittings states that bird's-eye, or germander speedwell, closes its petals in cloudy weather.
2. *The Faerie Queene*, I.v.i.

To Leigh Hunt

10 MAY 1817

Margate, May 10th

My dear Hunt,

The little Gentleman that sometimes lurks in a gossip's bowl ought to have come in very likeness of a *coasted* crab[1] and choked me outright for not having answered your Letter ere this; however, you must not suppose that I was in Town to receive it. No, it followed me to the isle of Wight and I got it just as I was going to pack up for Margate, for reasons which you anon shall hear. On arriving at this treeless affair I wrote to my Brother George to request C. C. C. to do the thing you wot of respecting Rimini,[2] and George tells me he has undertaken it with great Pleasure. So I hope there has been an understanding between you for many Proofs. C. C. C. is well acquainted with Bensley.[3] Now why did you not send the key of your Cupboard, which I know was full of Papers? We would have lock'd them all in a trunk together with those you told me to destroy, which indeed I did not do for fear of demolishing Receipts, there not being a more unpleasant thing in the world (saving a thousand and one others) than to pay a Bill twice. Mind you, old Wood's[4] a very Varmant, sharded in Covetousness. And now I am upon a horrid subject. What a horrid one you were upon last Sunday and well you handled it. The last Examiner was a Battering Ram against Christianity, Blasphemy, Tertullian, Erasmus, Sir Philip Sidney.[5] And then the dreadful Petzelians and their expiation by Blood. And do Christians shudder at the same thing in a Newspaper which they attribute to their God in its most aggravated form? What is to be the end of this? I must mention Hazlitt's Southey.[6] O, that he had left out the grey hairs! Or that they had been in any other Paper not concluding with such a Thunderclap. That sentence about making a Page of the feelings of a whole life appears to me like a Whale's back in the Sea of Prose. I ought to have said a word on Shakespeare's Christianity. There are two, which I have not looked over with you, touching the thing: the one for, the other against. That in favor is in Measure for Measure, Act 2, s. 2.

> Isabella: Alas, Alas!
>   Why, all the Souls that were, were forfeit once,
>   And he that might the vantage best have took,
>   Found out the Remedy.

That against is in Twelfth Night, Act 3, s 2. Mariana: "for there is no Christian, that means to be saved by believing rightly, can ever believe such impossible Passages of grossness!" Before I come to the Nymphs[7] I must get through all disagreeables. I went to the Isle of Wight, thought so much about Poetry so long together that I could not get to sleep at night, and moreover, I know not how it was, I could not get wholesome food. By this means in a week or so I became not over capable in my upper Stories, and set off pell-mell for Margate, at least 150 Miles, because forsooth I fancied that I should like my old Lodging here, and could contrive to do without Trees. Another thing I was too much in Solitude, and consequently was obliged to be in continual burning of thought as an only resource. However, Tom is with me at present and we are very comfortable. We intend though to get among some Trees. How have you got on among them? How are the Nymphs? I suppose they have led you a fine dance. Where are you now? In Judea, Cappadocia, or the Parts of Lybia about Cyrene, Strangers from "Heaven, Hues and Prototypes"? I wager you have given several new turns to the old saying, "now the Maid was fair and pleasant to look on," as well as made a little variation in "once upon a time." Perhaps too you have rather varied "thus endeth the first Lesson." I hope you have made a Horse shoe business of "unsuperfluous lift," "faint Bowers," and fibrous roots.[8] I vow that I have been down in the Mouth lately at this Work. These last two days, however, I have felt more confident. I have asked myself so often why I should be a Poet more than other Men, seeing how great a thing it is, how great things are to be gained by it. What a thing to be in the Mouth of Fame, that at last the Idea has grown so monstrously beyond my seeming Power of attainment that the other day I nearly consented with myself to drop into a Phaeton. Yet 'tis a disgrace to fail even in a huge attempt, and at this moment I drive the thought from me. I began my Poem[9] about a Fortnight since and have done some everyday except travelling ones. Perhaps I may have done a good deal for the time but it appears such a Pin's Point to me that I will not copy any out. When I consider that so many of these Pin points go to form a Bodkin point (God send I end not my Life with a bare Bodkin,[10] in its modern sense) and that it requires a thousand bodkins to make a Spear bright enough to throw any light to posterity, I see nothing but continual uphill Journeying. Now is there anything more unpleasant (it may come among the thousand and one) than to be so journeying and miss the Goal at last? But I intend to whistle all these cogitations into the Sea where I hope they will breed Storms violent enough to block up all exit from Russia. Does Shelley go on telling strange Stories of the Death of kings? Tell him there are strange Stories of the death of Poets. Some have died before they were conceived. "How do you make that out Master Vellum"?[11] Does Mrs. S—[12] cut Bread and Butter as neatly as ever? Tell her to

procure some fatal Scissars and cut the thread of Life of all to be disappointed Poets. Does Mrs. Hunt tear linen in half as straight as ever? Tell her
to tear from the book of Life all blank Leaves. Remember me to them all, to
Miss Kent and the little ones all.[13]

Your sincere friend
John Keats alias Junkets—[14]

You shall know where we move—

1. Pun on the "roasted crab" of *A Midsummer Night's Dream,* II.i.47f.
2. Hunt's poem *The Story of Rimini.*
3. The book printer for the second edition (1817) of *Rimini.* Charles Cowden Clarke corrected the proofs.
4. Gittings maintains that Wood was probably a bailiff, and that Hunt was heavily in debt.
5. Hunt's article in the issue of 4 May dealt with religious intolerance and ridiculed the charges of sedition and blasphemy made against the reformers.
6. In the same issue of the *Examiner,* Hunt printed news of a sect led by "Petzel, a priest of Branau," alleged to practice human sacrifice; the critic William Hazlitt (1778–1830) reviewed and attacked Robert Southey's *Letter to William Smith, Esq. M.P.* (1817).
7. "The Nymphs" is a long poem in Hunt's *Foliage* (1818).
8. All quotations from "The Nymphs."
9. *Endymion.*
10. Compare *Hamlet,* III.i.76.
11. Addison, *The Drummer, Or The Haunted House,* IV.i.
12. Mrs. Shelley.
13. Elizabeth Kent, sister of Mrs. Leigh Hunt, author of *Flora Domestica* (1823) and *Sylvan Sketches* (1825), both of which refer to and quote Keats. At this point, Thornton (1810), John (1812), and Mary Florimel Leigh (1814) made up Hunt's "little ones."
14. A contraction of "John Keats," but also an allusion to the sweet Spenserian confections of Keats's early verse. A "Junket" is a "dish consisting of curds sweetened and flavoured, served with a layer of scalded cream on the top" *(OED).*

To B. R. Haydon

Margate, Saturday Eve

My dear Haydon,

> Let Fame, which all hunt after in their Lives,
> Live register'd upon our brazen tombs,
> And so grace us in the disgrace of death:
> When spite of cormorant devouring time
> The endeavour of this present breath may buy
> That Honor which shall bate his Scythe's keen edge
> And make us heirs of all eternity.[1]

To think that I have no right to couple myself with you in this speech would be death to me, so I have e'en written it, and I pray God that our brazen Tombs be nigh neighbors. It cannot be long first the endeavor of this present breath will soon be over, and yet it is as well to breathe freely during our sojourn. It is as well if you have not been teased with that Money affair, that bill-pestilence. However I must think that difficulties nerve the Spirit of a Man; they make our Prime Objects a Refuge as well as a Passion. The Trumpet of Fame is as a tower of Strength; the ambitious bloweth it and is safe. I suppose by your telling me not to give way to forebodings George has mentioned to you what I have lately said in my Letters to him. Truth is I have been in such a state of Mind as to read over my Lines and hate them. I am "one that gathers Samphire dreadful trade."[2] The Cliff of Poesy Towers above me, yet when Tom, who meets with some of Pope's Homer in Plutarch's Lives, reads some of those to me they seem like Mice to mine. I read and write about eight hours a day. There is an old saying, "well begun is half done." 'Tis a bad one. I would use instead, "not begun at all 'till half done." So according to that, I have not begun my

Poem and consequently (a priori) can say nothing about it. Thank God! I do begin arduously where I leave off, notwithstanding occasional depressions, and I hope for the support of a High Power while I climb this little eminence and especially in my Years of more momentous Labor. I remember your saying that you had notions of a good Genius presiding over you. I have of late had the same thought, for things which I do half at Random are afterwards confirmed by my judgment in a dozen features of Propriety. Is it too daring to Fancy Shakespeare this Presider? When in the Isle of Wight I met with a Shakespeare in the Passage of the House at which I lodged, it comes nearer to my idea of him than any I have seen. I was but there a Week, yet the old Woman made me take it with me though I went off in a hurry. Do you not think this is ominous of good? I am glad you say every Man of great Views is at times tormented as I am.

Sunday Aft. This Morning I received a letter from George by which it appears that Money Troubles are to follow us up for some time to come, perhaps for always. These vexations are a great hindrance to one. They are not like Envy and detraction stimulants to further exertion as being immediately relative and reflected on at the same time with the prime object, but rather like a nettle leaf or two in your bed. So now I revoke my Promise of finishing my Poem by the Autumn, which I should have done had I gone on as I have done. But I cannot write while my spirit is fevered in a contrary direction and I am now sure of having plenty of it this Summer. At this moment I am in no enviable Situation. I feel that I am not in a Mood to write any today, and it appears that the loss of it is the beginning of all sorts of irregularities. I am extremely glad that a time must come when everything will leave not a wrack behind.[3] You tell me never to despair. I wish it was as easy for me to observe the saying. Truth is I have a horrid Morbidity of Temperament which has shown itself at intervals. It is, I have no doubt, the greatest Enemy and stumbling block I have to fear. I may even say that it is likely to be the cause of my disappointment. However, every ill has its share of good. This very bane would at any time enable me to look with an obstinate eye on the Devil Himself, aye, to be as proud of being the lowest of the human race as Alfred could be in being of the highest. I feel confident I should have been a rebel Angel had the opportunity been mine.

I am very sure that you do love me as your own Brother. I have seen it in your continual anxiety for me, and I assure you that your welfare and fame is and will be a chief pleasure to me all my Life. I know no one but you who can be fully sensible of the turmoil and anxiety, the sacrifice of all what is called comfort, the readiness to Measure time by what is done and to die in 6 hours could plans be brought to conclusions, the looking upon the Sun, the Moon, the Stars, the Earth and its contents as materials to form greater things, that is to say, ethereal things. But here I am talking like a Madman greater things than our Creator himself made!!

I wrote to Hunt yesterday, scarcely know what I said in it. I could not talk about Poetry in the way I should have liked, for I was not in humor with either his or mine. His self-delusions are very lamentable. They have enticed him into a Situation which I should be less eager after than that of a galley Slave. What you observe thereon is very true [and] must be in time. Perhaps it is a self-delusion to say so, but I think I could not be deceived in the Manner that Hunt is. May I die tomorrow if I am to be. There is no greater Sin after the 7 deadly than to flatter oneself into an idea of being a great Poet, or one of those beings who are privileged to wear out their Lives in the pursuit of Honor. How comfortable a feel it is that such a Crime must bring its heavy Penalty? That if one be a Self-deluder accounts will be balanced? I am glad you are hard at work. 'Twill now soon be done. I long to see Wordsworth's as well as to have mine in, but I would rather not show my face in Town till the end of the Year, if that will be time enough. If not, I shall be disappointed if you do not write for me even when you think best. I never quite despair and I read Shakespeare. Indeed, I shall, I think, never read any other Book much. Now this might lead me into a long Confab, but I desist. I am very near Agreeing with Hazlitt that Shakespeare is enough for us. By the by, what a tremendous Southean Article his last was. I wish he had left out "grey hairs." It was very gratifying to meet your remarks of the Manuscript.[4] I was reading Anthony and Cleopatra when I got the Paper and there are several Passages applicable to the events you commentate. You say that he arrived by degrees, and not by any single Struggle to the height of his ambition, and that his Life had been as common in particulars as other Men's. Shakespeare makes Enobarb say, "Where's Antony?" Eros: "He's walking in the garden—thus, *and spurns the rush that lies* before him, cries 'Fool, Lepidus!'" In the same scene, we find: "let determined things to destiny hold unbewailed their way." Dolabella says of Anthony's Messenger: "An argument that he is pluck'd when hither he sends so poor a pinion of his wing." Then again, Eno: "I see Men's Judgments are a parcel of their fortunes; and things outward do draw the inward quality after them, to suffer all alike." The following applies well to Bertram: "Yet he that can endure to follow with allegiance a fallen Lord, does conquer him that did his Master conquer, and earns a place i' the story."[5]

But how differently does Buonap bear his fate from Antony! 'Tis good too that the Duke of Wellington has a good Word or so in the Examiner. A Man ought to have the Fame he deserves, and I begin to think that detracting from him as well as from Wordsworth is the same thing. I wish he had a little more taste, and did not in that respect "deal in Lieutenantry."[6] You should have heard from me before this, but in the first place I did not like to do so before I had got a little way in the 1st Book and in the next, as G. told me you were going to write, I delayed till I had heard from you. Give my Respects the next time you write to the North[7] and also to John Hunt.[8] Remember me to Reynolds and tell him to write, Ay, and when you sent Westward tell your Sister that I mentioned her in this. So now in the Name of Shakespeare, Raphael and all our Saints, I commend you to the care of heaven!

Your everlasting friend,

John Keats—

1. *Love's Labor's Lost*, I.i.1–7.
2. *King Lear*, IV.vi.15.
3. *The Tempest*, IV.i.156.
4. Discussing "Bonaparte. 'Manuscrit venu de St. Helene'" in the *Examiner*, 4 May 1817, pp. 275f., Haydon concluded, "Never was a little book so interesting! . . . And if it be not by Napoleon, it is from an intellect of similar construction."
5. The quotations are from *Antony and Cleopatra*, III.v.16–18, III.vi.84f., III.xii.3f., III.xiii.31–34, 43–46.
6. *Antony and Cleopatra*, III.xi.38f.
7. To Wordsworth.
8. Leigh Hunt's brother (1775–1848), who called himself publisher and printer of the *Examiner*.

To Taylor and Hessey
16 MAY 1817

Margate, May 16—

My dear Sirs,

I am extremely indebted to you for your liberality in the Shape of manu-factured rag value £20 and shall immediately proceed to destroy some of the Minor Heads of that spring-headed Hydra the Dun,[1] to conquer which the knight need have no Sword, Shield, Cuirass, Cuisses Herbadgeon, spear, Casque, Greves, Pauldrons, Spurs, Chevron or any other scaly com-modity. But he need only take the Bank Note of Faith and Cash of Salva-tion, and set out against the Monster invoking the aid of no Archimago[2] or Urganda,[3] and finger me the Paper light as the Sybil's Leaves in Virgil whereat the Fiend skulks off with his tail between his Legs. Touch him with this enchanted Paper and he whips you his head away as fast as a Snail's Horn, but then the horrid Propensity he has to put it up again has discour-aged many very valiant Knights. He is such a never-ending still beginning sort of a Body, like my Landlady of the Bell. I should conjecture that the very Spright that the "green sour ringlets makes whereof the Ewe not bites"[4] had manufactured it of the dew fallen on said sour ringlets. I think I could make a nice little Allegorical Poem called "The Dun" where we would have the Castle of Carelessness, the Draw Bridge of Credit, Sir Novelty Fashion's[5] expedition against the City of Taylors, etc., etc.

I went day by day at my Poem for a Month at the end of which time the other day I found my Brain so overwrought that I had neither Rhyme nor reason in it so was obliged to give up for a few days. I hope soon to be able to resume my Work. I have endeavoured to do so once or twice but to no Purpose. Instead of Poetry I have a swimming in my head and feel all the effects of a Mental Debauch: lowness of Spirits, anxiety to go on without the Power to do so, which does not at all tend to my ultimate Progression.

However, tomorrow I will begin my next Month. This Evening I go to Canterbury, having got tired of Margate. I was not right in my head when I came. At Canterbury I hope the Remembrance of Chaucer will set me forward like a Billiard Ball. I am glad to hear of Mr. T's health and of the Welfare of the "In-town-stayers" and think Reynolds will like his trip. I have some idea of seeing the Continent some time in the summer.

In repeating how sensible I am of your kindness I remain

Your Obedient Servant and Friend
John Keats—

I shall be very happy to hear any little intelligence in the literary or
friendly way when you have time to scribble.

1. A creditor.
2. *The Faerie Queene,* Books I and II.
3. Urganda the Unknown, a leading character in the fifteenth-century romance *Amadis of Gaul.*
4. *The Tempest,* V.i.37f.
5. A character in Colley Cibber's *Love's Last Shift.*

To Taylor and Hessey
10 JUNE 1817

Tuesday Morn—

My dear Sirs,

I must endeavor to lose my Maidenhead with respect to money Matters as soon as possible, and I will too, so here goes. A Couple of Duns that I thought would be silent till the beginning at least of next month (when I am certain to be on my legs for certain sure) have opened upon me with a cry most "untunable."[1] Never did you hear such un "gallant chiding."[2]

Now you must know I am not desolate but have, thank God, 25 good notes in my fob. But then you know I laid them by to write with and would stand at bay a fortnight ere they should grab me. In a month's time I must pay, but it would relieve my mind if I owed you instead of these Pelican duns.

I am afraid you will say I have "wound about with circumstance"[3] when I should have asked plainly. However, as I said, I am a little maidenish or so, and I feel my virginity come strong upon me. The while I request the loan of £20 and £10, which if you would enclose to me I would acknowledge and save myself a hot forehead. I am sure you are confident in my responsibility and in the sense of squareness that is always in me.

Your obliged friend
John Keats—

1. *A Midsummer Night's Dream,* IV.i.28, "A cry more tuneable."
2. Ibid., IV.i.118f., "Never did I hear / Such gallant chiding."
3. *The Merchant of Venice,* I.i.154, "To wind about my love with circumstance."

To Jane and Mariane Reynolds

4 SEPTEMBER 1817

Oxf—

My dear friends,

You are, I am glad to hear, comfortable at Hampton where I hope you will receive the Biscuts we ate the other night at Little Britain. I hope you found them good. There you are among Sands, Stocks, Stones, Pebbles, Beaches, Cliffs, Rocks, Deeps, Shallows, Weeds, ships, Boats (at a distance), Carrots—turnips, Sun, Moon and Stars, and all those sort of things. Here am I among Colleges, Halls, Stalls, plenty of Trees, thank God, plenty of Water, thank heaven, plenty of Books, thank the Muses, plenty of Snuff, thank Sir Walter Raleigh, plenty of Sagars ditto, plenty of flat Country, thank Tellus's rolling pin. I'm on the Sofa, Buonaparte is on the Snuff Box, but you are by the seaside, argal[1] you bathe, you walk, you say how beautiful, find out resemblances between waves and Camels, rocks and dancing Masters, fire shovels and telescopes, Dolphins and Madonas, which word by the way I must acquaint you was derived from the Syriac and came down in a way which neither of you, I am sorry to say, are at all capable of comprehending. But as a time may come when by your occasional converse with me you may arrive at "something like prophetic strain,"[2] I will unbar the Gates of my Pride and let my Condescension stalk forth like a Ghost at the Circus. The Word Madona my dear Ladies, or the word Mad-o-na. So I say! I am not mad. Howsumever, when that aged Tamer Kewthon sold a Certain Camel Called Peter to the Overseer of the Babel Skyworks, he thus spake, adjusting his Cravat round the tip of his Chin: "My dear Ten Storyupinair, this here Beast, though I say it as shouldn't say't, not only has the Power of subsisting 40 days and 40 Nights without fire and Candle, but he can sing." Here I have in my Pocket a Certificate from Signor Nicolini of the King's Theatre,[3] a Certificate to this effect xxxxxxxx. I have had dinner since I left that effect upon you and feel too heavy in mentibus to display all the Profundity of the Polyglon, so you had better each of you take a glass of cherry branday and drink to the health of Archimedes who was of so benign a disposition that he never would leave Syracuse in his Life, so kept himself out of all knight errantry. This I know to be a fact for it is written in the 45 Book of Winkine's treatise on Garden rollers that he trod on a fishwoman's toe in Liverpool and never begged her pardon. Now the long and the short is this, that is by comparison, for a long day may be a short year, a long Pole may be a very stupid fellow as a Man.[4] But let us refresh ourself from this depth of thinking and turn to some innocent Jocularity. The Bow cannot always be bent nor the gun always loaded if you ever let it off. And the Life of Man is like a great Mountain, his breath is like a Shrewsbury Cake, he comes into the world like a Shoeblack and goes out of it like a Cobbler. He eats like a Chimney sweeper, drinks like a Gingerbread Baker and breaths like Achilles. So it being that we are such sublunary creatures, let us endeavour to correct all our bad Spelling, all our most delightful Abominations, and let us wish health to Marian and Jane whoever they be and wherever. Your's truly

John Keats—

1. Keats got this word, which was not in the dictionaries, from *Hamlet,* V.i.13, 21, 55.
2. Milton, "Il Penseroso," line 174.
3. Nicolino (or Nicolini) Grimaldi (1673–1726) sang at the King's, later the Haymarket, Theatre.
4. A possible reference to William Pole-Tylney-Long-Wellesley, fourth earl of Mornington (1788–1857), who is mentioned in the first poem, "Loyal Effusion," in James and Horace Smith's *Rejected Addresses:* "Long may Long Tilney Wellesley Long Pole live." After his death the *Morning Chronicle* candidly remarked that Mornington's life was "redeemed by no single virtue, adorned by no single grace."

To J. H. Reynolds

SEPTEMBER 1817[1]

"Wordsworth sometimes, though in a fine way, gives us sentences in the Style of School exercises. For Instance,

> The lake doth glitter
> Small birds twitter, etc.

Now I think this is an excellent method of giving a very clear description of an interesting place such as Oxford is:

> The Gothic looks solemn,
> The plain Doric column
> Supports an old Bishop and crosier;
> The mouldering arch,
> Shaded o'er by a larch,
> Lives next door to Wilson the hosier.

Vicè, that is, by turns,
O'er pale visages mourns
The black-tassel trencher, or common-hat.
The Chauntry boy sings,
The steeple bell rings,
And as for the Chancellor—dominat.
There are plenty of trees,
And plenty of case,
And plenty of fat deer for parsons;
And when it is venison,
Short is the benison,
Then each on a leg or thigh fastens.

// J.K.

1. The text of this letter comes from Richard Woodhouse, who copied this fragment into his book of Keats's poems (not letters).

To Fanny Keats
10 SEPTEMBER 1817

Oxford, Sept. 10th

My dear Fanny,

Let us now begin a regular question and answer, a little pro and con, letting it interfere as a pleasant method of my coming at your favorite little wants and enjoyments, that I may meet them in a way befitting a brother.

We have been so little together since you have been able to reflect on things that I know not whether you prefer the History of King Pepin to Bunyan's Pilgrim's Progress, or Cinderella and her glass slipper to Moor's Almanack.[1] However in a few letters I hope I shall be able to come at that and adapt my Scribblings to your Pleasure. You must tell me about all you read if it be only six pages in a week, and this transmitted to me every now and then will procure you full sheets of writing from me pretty frequently. This I feel as a necessity: for we ought to become intimately acquainted, in order that I may not only, as you grow up, love you as my only sister, but confide in you as my dearest friend. When I saw you last I told you of my intention of going to Oxford and 'tis now a Week since I disembark'd from his Whipship's Coach the Defiance in this place. I am living in Magdalen Hall on a visit to a young man[2] with whom I have not been long acquainted, but whom I like very much. We lead very industrious lives, he in general studies and I in proceeding at a pretty good rate with a Poem which I hope you will see early in the next year. Perhaps you might like to know what I am writing about. I will tell you.

Many Years ago there was a young handsome Shepherd who fed his flocks on a Mountain's side called Latmus. He was a very contemplative sort of a Person and lived solitary among the trees and plains little thinking that such a beautiful Creature as the Moon was growing mad in Love with him. However, so it was, and when he was asleep on the Grass she used to come down from heaven and admire him excessively for a long time, and at last could not refrain from carrying him away in her arms to the top of that high Mountain Latmus while he was a-dreaming. But I dare say you have read this and all the other beautiful Tales which have come down from the ancient times of that beautiful Greece. If you have not, let me know and I will tell you more at large of others quite as delightful.

This Oxford, I have no doubt, is the finest City in the world. It is full of old Gothic buildings, Spires, towers, Quadrangles, Cloisters, Groves, etc., and is surrounded with more Clear streams than ever I saw together. I take a walk by the side of one of them every evening and thank God we have not had a drop of rain these many days. I had a long and interesting letter from George, cross lines by a short one from Tom yesterday dated Paris. They both send their loves to you. Like most Englishmen they feel a mighty preference for everything English. The french Meadows, the trees, the People, the Towns, the Churches, the Books, the everything, although they may be in themselves good, yet when put in comparison with our green Island they all vanish like Swallows in October. They have seen Cathedrals, Manuscripts, Fountains, Pictures, Tragedy, Comedy, with other things you may by chance meet with in this Country such as Washerwomen, Lamplighters, Turnpikemen, Fish kettles, Dancing Masters, kettle drums, Sentry Boxes, Rocking Horses, etc. and now they have taken them over a set of boxing gloves. I have written to George and requested him, as you wish I should, to write to you. I have been writing very hard lately even till an utter incapacity came on, and I feel it now about my head: so you must not mind a little out of the way sayings, though bye the bye were my brain as clear as a bell I think I should have a little propensity thereto. I shall stop here till I have finished the 3rd Book of my Story, which I hope will be accomplish'd in at most three weeks from today, about which time you shall see me. How do you like Miss Taylor's essays in Rhyme? I just look'd into the Book and it appeared to me suitable to you, especially since I remember your liking for those pleasant little things the Original Poems.[3] The essays are the more mature production of the same hand. While I was speaking about france it occurred to me to speak a few Words on their Language. It is perhaps the poorest one ever spoken since the jabbering in the Tower of Babel and when you come to know that the real use and greatness of a Tongue is to be referred to its Literature, you will be astonished to find how very inferior it is to our native Speech. I wish the Italian would supersede french in every School throughout the Country, for that is full of real Poetry and Romance of a kind more fitted for the Pleasure of Ladies than perhaps our own. It seems that the only end to be gained in acquiring french is the immense accomplishment of speaking it. It is none at all, a most lamentable mistake indeed. Italian indeed would sound most musically from Lips which had begun to pronounce it as early as french is cramm'd down our Mouths, as if we were young Jackdaws at the mercy of an overfeeding Schoolboy.

Now Fanny you must write soon and write all you think about, never mind what, only let me have a good deal of your writing. You need not do it all at once, be two or three or four days about it, and let it be a diary of your little life. You will preserve all my Letters[4] and I will secure yours, and thus in the course of time we shall each of us have a good Bundle, which, hereafter, when things may have strangely altered and God knows what happened, we may read over together and look with pleasure on times past that now are to come. Give my Respects to the Ladies,[5] and so my dear Fanny I am ever

                                        Your most affectionate Brother
                                                    John

If you direct—Post Office Oxford—your Letter
    will be brought to me—

1. Francis Moore (1657–1715?) issued his first almanac in 1699. Several continuations of the almanac are still published.
2. Benjamin Bailey.
3. Jane Taylor's *Essays in Rhyme, or Morals and Manners* (1816) and Jane and Ann Taylor's *Original Poems for Infant Minds* (1804).
4. Fanny's biographer, Marie Adami, notes how as an old woman Fanny said that her letters from Keats had only once, and then but for a few days, been out of her possession.
5. Her schoolmistresses.

To J. H. Reynolds
21 SEPTEMBER 1817

                                                Oxford, Sunday Morn
My dear Reynolds,

So you are determined to be my mortal foe. Draw a Sword at me, and I will forgive; Put a Bullet in my Brain, and I will shake it out as a dewdrop from the Lion's Mane;[1] put me on a Gridiron, and I will fry with great complacency; but, oh horror! to come upon me in the shape of a Dun! Send me Bills! As I say to my Taylor, send me Bills and I'll never employ you more.[2] However, needs must when the devil drives and for fear of "before and behind Mr. Honeycomb,"[3] I'll proceed. I have not time to elucidate the forms and shapes of the grass and trees, for rot it! I forgot to bring my mathematical case with me, which unfortunately contained my triangular Prism so that the hues of the grass cannot be dissected for you.

For these last five or six days, we have had regularly a Boat on the Isis, and explored all the streams about, which are more in number than your eyelashes. We sometimes skim into a Bed of rushes and there become naturalized riverfolks. There is one particularly nice nest which we have christened "Reynolds's Cove," in which we have read Wordsworth and talked as may be. I think I see you and Hunt meeting in the Pit. What a very pleasant fellow he is, if he would give up the sovereignty of a Room pro bono. What Evenings we might pass with him, could we have him from Mrs. H., Failings I am always rather rejoiced to find in a Man than sorry for, for they bring us to a Level. He has them, but then his makes-up are very good. He agrees with the Northern Poet in this, "He is not one of those who much delight to season their fireside with personal talk."[4] I must confess however having a little itch that way and at this present I have a few neighbourly remarks to make. The world, and especially our England, has within the last thirty years been vexed and teased by a set of Devils, whom I detest so much that I almost hunger after an acherontic promotion to a Torturer, purposely for their accommodation. These Devils are a set of Women, who having taken a snack or Luncheon of Literary scraps, set themselves up for towers of Babel in Languages, Sapphos in Poetry, Euclids in Geometry, and everything in nothing. Among such the Name of Montague[5] has been preeminent. The thing has made a very uncomfortable impression on me. I had longed for some real feminine Modesty in these things, and was therefore gladdened in the extreme on opening the other day one of Bayley's Books, a Book of Poetry written by one beautiful Mrs. Philips, a friend of Jeremy Taylor's, and called "the matchless Orinda."[6] You must have heard of her, and most likely read her Poetry. I wish you have not, that I may have the pleasure of treating you with a few stanzas. I do it at a venture; you will

not regret reading them once more. The following to her friend Mrs. M. A.
at parting you will Judge of.

~1~

I have examined and do find
        of all that favour me
There's none I grieve to leave behind
        But only, only thee.
To part with thee I needs must die
Could parting sep'rate thee and I.

~2~

But neither chance nor Compliment
        Did *element* our Love;
'Twas sacred sympathy was lent
        Us from the Quire above.
That friendship fortune did create,
Still fears a wound from time or fate.

~3~

Our chang'd and mingled souls are grown
        To such acquaintance now,
That if each would resume her own
        Alas! we know not how.
We have each other so engrost
That each is in the union lost.

~4~

And thus we can no absence know
        Nor shall we be confin'd;
Our active souls will daily go
        To learn each other's mind.

Nay should we never meet to sense
Our souls would hold intelligence.

~5~

Inspired with a flame divine
    I scorn to court a stay;
For from that noble soul of thine
    I ne'er can be away.
But I shall weep when thou dost grieve
Nor can I die whilst thou dost live.

~6~

By my own temper I shall guess
    At thy felicity,
And only like my happiness
    Because it pleaseth thee.
Our hearts at any time will tell
If thou, or I be sick or well.

~7~

All honour sure I must pretend,
    All that is good or great;
She that would be Rosania's friend,
    Must be at least compleat,*
If I have any Bravery,
'Tis cause I have so much of thee.

~8~

Thy Leiger Soul in me shall lie,
    And all thy thoughts reveal;

---

*A compleat friend. This Line sounded very oddly to me at first.

Then back again with mine shall flie
    And thence to me shall steal.
Thus still to one another tend;
Such is the sacred name of friend.

~9~

Thus our twin souls in one shall grow,
    And teach the world new Love,
Redeem the age and sex, and show
    A Flame Fate dares not move:
And courting death to be our friend,
Our Lives together too shall end.

~10~

A Dew shall dwell upon our Tomb
    of such a Quality
That fighting Armies thither come
    Shall reconciled be
We'll ask no epitaph but say
Orinda and Rosannia.

In other of her Poems there is a most delicate fancy of the Fletcher Kind which we will con over together. So Haydon is in Town. I had a letter from him yesterday. We will contrive as the Winter comes on, but that is neither here nor there. Have you heard from Rice? Has Martin met with the Cumberland Beggar or been wondering at the old Leech gatherer?[7] Has he a turn for fossils, that is, is he capable of sinking up to his Middle in a Morass? I have longed to peep in and see him at supper after some tolerable fatigue. How is Hazlitt? We were reading his Table[8] last night. I know he thinks himself not estimated by ten People in the world. I wish he knew he is. I am getting on famous with my third Book, have written 800 lines thereof, and hope to finish it next week. Bailey likes what I have done very much. Believe me, my Dear Reynolds, one of my chief layings-up is the pleasure I shall have in showing it to you, I may now say, in a few days. I have heard twice from my Brothers; they are going on very well and send their Re-membrances to you. We expected to have had notices from little Hampton this Morning. We must wait till Tuesday. I am glad of their Days with the Dilke's. You are I know very much teased in that precious London and want all the rest possible; so I shall be content with as brief a scrall, a word or two, till there comes a pat hour.

Send us a few of your Stanzas to read in "Reynolds's cove." Give my Love and respects to your Mother and remember me kindly to all at home. Yours faithfully,

John Keats

I have left the doublings for Bailey who is going to say that he will write to you tomorrow.

1. *Troilus and Cressida,* III.iii.224f., "like a dew-drop from the lion's mane, / Be shook to air."
2. At his death, Keats owed his tailor £30 or £40.
3. See Goldsmith, *The Good Natur'd Man,* III.i.252–254.
4. Wordsworth's "Personal Talk" begins, "I am not One who much or oft delight / To season my" etc.
5. Elizabeth Montagu (1720–1800), a famous bluestocking.
6. Katherine Fowler (Mrs. James) Philips (1631–1664). "To Mrs. M.A. at Parting" is in her *Poems* (1710), pp. 94–96.
7. Wordsworth's "Old Cumberland Beggar" and "Resolution and Independence." John Martin (1791–1855) was a publisher and bookseller.
8. Hazlitt and Hunt collaborated in *The Round Table* (1817), a two-volume collection of essays.

To B. R. Haydon
28 SEPTEMBER 1817

Oxford, Sept. 28th

My dear Haydon,

I read your last to the young Man whose Name is Crips.[1] He seemed more than ever anxious to avail himself of your offer. I think I told you we asked him to ascertain his Means. He does not possess the Philosopher's stone, nor Fortunatus' purse, nor Gyges' ring,[2] but at Bailey's suggestion, whom I assure you is a very capital fellow, we have stummed up a kind of contrivance whereby he will be enabled to do himself the benefits you will lay in his Path. I have a great Idea that he will be a tolerable neat brush. 'Tis perhaps the finest thing that will befall him this many a year, for he is just of an age to get grounded in bad habits from which you will pluck him. He brought a Copy of Mary Queen of Scots. It appears to me that he has copied the bad style of the painting as well as coloured the eyeballs yellow like the original. He has also the fault that you pointed out to me in Hazlitt, on the constringing and diffusing of substance. However I really believe that he will take fire at the sight of your Picture and set about things. If he can get ready in time to return to Town with me which will be in a few days, I will bring him to you. You will be glad to hear that within these last three weeks I have written 1000 lines, which are the third Book of my Poem. My Ideas with respect to it, I assure you, are very low, and I would write the subject thoroughly again. But I am tired of it and think the time would be better spent in writing a new Romance which I have in my eye for next summer. Rome was not built in a Day and all the good I expect from my employment this summer is the fruit of Experience, which I hope to gather in my next Poem. Bailey's kindest wishes and my vow of being

Yours eternally
John Keats—

1. Charles Cripps was baptized in Iffley Church on November 27, 1796. He may have been a pupil of Haydon's, though there is no mention of him in Haydon's published journal.
2. Gyges, the Lydian monarch whose ring gave him invisibility.

To Benjamin Bailey
8 OCTOBER 1817

Hampstead, Oct. Wednesday

My dear Bailey,

After a tolerable journey I went from Coach to Coach to as far as Hampstead where I found my Brothers. The next Morning, finding myself tolerably well, I went to Lambs Conduit Street and delivered your Parcel. Jane and Marianne were greatly improved, Marianne especially, she has no unhealthy plumpness in the face, but she comes me healthy and angular to the Chin. I did not see John. I was extremely sorry to hear that poor Rice after having had capital Health during his tour was very ill. I dare say you have heard from him. From No. 19 I went to Hunt's and Haydon's who live now neighbors. Shelley was there. I know nothing about anything in this part of the world. Everybody seems at Loggerheads. There's Hunt infatuated; there's Haydon's Picture in statu quo. There's Hunt walks up and down his painting room criticising every head most unmercifully. There's Horace Smith[1] tired of Hunt. The web of our Life is "of mingled Yarn." Haydon having removed entirely from Marlborough street, Cripps must direct his Letter to Lisson Grove, North Paddington. Yesterday Morning while I was at Brown's in came Reynolds. He was pretty bobbish. We had a pleasant day, but he would walk home at night that cursed cold distance. Mrs. Bentley's[2] children are making a horrid row, whereby I regret I cannot be transported to your Room to write to you. I am quite disgusted with literary Men and will never know another except Wordsworth; no, not even Byron. Here is an instance of the friendships of such. Haydon and Hunt have known each other many years; now they live pour ainsi dire jealous Neighbours.[3] Haydon says to me, Keats don't show your Lines to Hunt on any account or he will have done half for you, so it appears Hunt wishes it to be thought. When he met Reynolds in the Theatre, John told him that I was getting on to the completion of 4000 Lines. Ah! says Hunt, had it not been for me they would have been 7000! If he will say this to Reynolds what would he to other People? Haydon received a Letter a little while back on this subject from some Lady which contains a caution to me through him on this subject. Now, is not all this a most paltry thing to think about? You may see the whole of the case by the following extract from a Letter I wrote to George in the spring[4]: "As to what you say about my being a Poet, I can return no answer but by saying that the high Idea I have of poetical fame makes me think I see it towering too high above me. At any rate I have no right to talk until Endymion is finished. It will be a test, a trial of my Powers of Imagination and chiefly of my invention, which is a rare thing indeed, by which I must make 4000 Lines of one bare circumstance and fill them with Poetry. And when I consider that this is a great task, and that when done it will take me but a dozen paces towards the Temple of Fame, it makes me say, God forbid that I should be without such a task! I have heard Hunt say and I may be asked, why endeavour after a long Poem? To which I should answer: do not the Lovers of Poetry like to have a little Region to wander in where they may pick and choose, and in which the images are so numerous that many are forgotten and found new in a second Reading, which may be food for a Week's stroll in the Summer? Do not they like this better than what they can read through before Mrs. Williams comes downstairs? A Morning's work at most. Besides, a long Poem is a test of Invention which I take to be the Polar Star of Poetry, as Fancy is the Sails, and Imagination the Rudder. Did our great Poets ever write short Pieces? I mean in the shape of Tales. This same invention seems indeed of late Years to have been forgotten as a Poetical excellence. But enough of this, I put on no Laurels till I shall have finished Endymion, and I hope Apollo is not angered at my having made a Mockery of him at Hunt's."[5]

You see Bailey how independent my writing has been. Hunt's dissuasion was of no avail. I refused to visit Shelley, that I might have my own unfettered scope, and after all I shall have the Reputation of Hunt's elevé. His corrections and amputations will by the knowing ones be trased in the Poem. This is to be sure the vexation of a day, nor would I say so many Words about it to any but those whom I know to have my wellfare and Reputation at Heart. Haydon promised to give directions for those Casts and you may expect to see them soon, with as many Letters. You will soon hear the dinning of Bells; never mind, you and Gleig[6] will defy the foul fiend. But do not sacrifice your health to Books; do take it kindly and not so voraciously. I am certain if you are your own Physician your stomach will resume its proper strength and then what great Benefits will follow. My Sister wrote a Letter to me which I think must be at ye post office—Ax Will to see. My Brothers' kindest remembrances to you. We are going to dine at Brown's where I have some hopes of meeting Reynolds. The little Mercury I have taken has corrected the Poison and improved my Health, though I feel from my employment that I shall never be again secure in Robustness. Would that you were as well as

your sincere friend and brother
John Keats

The Dilke's are expected today.

1. Horace Smith (1779–1849), poet, novelist, wit, and intimate friend of Hunt and Shelley.
2. Keats's landlady at Well Walk in Hampstead.
3. "Now they live as jealous neighbors, so to speak."
4. The letter is now unknown.
5. Where he allowed Hunt to crown him with laurel.
6. George Robert Gleig (1796–1888), student at Magdalen Hall, Oxford, and later Bailey's brother-in-law.

To Benjamin Bailey
28–30 OCTOBER 1817

My dear Bailey,

So you have got a Curacy! Good, but I suppose you will be obliged to stop among your Oxford favorites during term-time. Never mind. When do you preach your first sermon, tell me, for I shall propose to the two R's[1] to hear it, so don't look into any of the old corner oaken pews for fear of being put out by us. Poor Johnny Martin[2] can't be there. He is ill, I suspect, but that's neither here nor there. All I can say, I wish him as well through it as I am like to be. For this fortnight I have been confined at Hampstead. Saturday evening was my first day in town when I went to Rice's as we intend to do every Saturday till we know not when. Rice had some business at Highgate yesterday, so he came over to me and I detained him for the first time of I hope 24860 times. We hit upon an old Gent[3] we had known some few years ago and had a veray pleausante daye. In this World there is no quiet, nothing but teasing and snubbing and vexation. My Brother Tom look'd very unwell yesterday and I am for shipping him off to Lisbon. Perhaps I ship there with him. I have not seen Mrs. Reynolds since I left you, wherefore my conscience smites me. I think of seeing her tomorrow; have you any Message? I hope Gleig came soon after I left. I don't suppose I've written as many Lines as you have read Volumes, or at least Chapters, since I saw you. However, I am in a fair way now to come to a conclusion in at least three Weeks, when I assure you I shall be glad to dismount for a Month or two, although I'll keep as tight a reign as possible till then nor suffer myself to sleep. I will copy for you the opening of the 4th Book,[4] in which you will see from the Manner I had not an opportunity of mentioning any Poets, for fear of spoiling the effect of the passage by particularising them!

Muse of my Native Land. Loftiest Muse!
O First born of the Mountains, by the hues
Of Heaven on the spiritual air begot,
Long didst thou sit alone in northern grot
While yet our England was a wolfish den;
Before our forests heard the talk of Men;
Before the first of Druid's was a child.
Long didst thou sit amid our regions wild
Wrapt in a deep, prophetic Solitude.
There came a hebrew voice of solemn Mood
Yet wast thou patient: then sang forth the Nine
Apollo's Garland; yet didst thou divine
Such homebred Glory, that they cry'd in vain
"Come hither, Sister of the Island." Plain
Spake fair Ausonia, and once more she spake
A higher Summons—still didst thou betake
Thee to thy darling hopes. O thou has won
A full accomplishment. The thing is done
Which undone these our latter days had risen
On barren Souls. O Muse thou knowst what prison
Of flesh and bone curbs and confines and frets
Our Spirits' Wings: despondency besets
Our Pillows and the fresh tomorrow morn
Seems to give forth its light in very scorn
Of our dull uninspired snail-paced lives.
Long have I said "how happy he who shrives
To thee," but then I thought on Poets gone
And could not pray—nor can I now—so on
I move to the end in Humbleness of Heart.

Thus far had I written when I received your last, which made me at the
sight of the direction caper for despair. But for one thing I am glad that I
have been neglectful, and that is, therefrom I have received a proof of your

utmost kindness which at this present I feel very much, and I wish I had a
heart always open to such sensations. But there is no altering a Man's nature
and mine must be radically wrong for it will lie dormant a whole Month.
This leads me to suppose that there are no Men thoroughly wicked, so as
never to be self-spiritualized into a kind of sublime Misery. But alas! 'tis but
for an Hour. He is the only Man "who has kept watch on Man's Mortality,"⁵ who has philanthropy enough to overcome the disposition to an indolent enjoyment of intellect, who is brave enough to volunteer for uncomfortable hours.* You remember in Hazlitt's essay on commonplace people,
he says "they read the Edinburgh and Quarterly and think as they do."⁶
Now with respect to Wordsworth's Gipsies, I think he is right and yet I
think Hazlitt is right, and yet I think Wordsworth is rightest. Wordsworth
had not been idle, he had not been without his task, nor had they Gipseys;
they in the visible world had been as picturesque an object as he in the invisible. The Smoke of their fire, their attitudes, their Voices were all in harmony with the Evenings. It is a bold thing to say and I would not say it in
print, but it seems to me that if Wordsworth had thought a little deeper at
that Moment he would not have written the Poem at all. I should judge it
to have been written in one of the most comfortable Moods of his Life. It is
a kind of sketchy intellectual Landscape, not a search after Truth, nor is it
fair to attack him on such a subject, for it is with the Critic as with the
poet. Had Hazlitt thought a little deeper and been in a good temper, he
would never have spied an imaginary fault there.⁷ The Sunday before last I
asked Haydon to dine with me when I thought of settling all Matters with
him in regard to Crips and let you know about it. Now although I engaged
him a Fortnight before, he sent illness as an excuse. He never will come. I
have not been well enough to stand the chance of a Wet night, and so have
not seen him nor been able to expurgatorize those Masks⁸ for you. But I
will not speak; your speakers are never doers. Then Reynolds: every time I
see him and mention you he puts his hand to his head and looks like a son
of Niobe's, but he'll write soon. Rome, you know, was not built in a day. I

*You must forgive although I have only written 300 Lines. They would have been five but I
have been obliged to go to town. Yesterday I called at Lamb's St. Jane look'd very flush when
I first went in but was much better before I left.

shall be able, by a little perseverance, to read your Letters off hand.[9] I am afraid your health will suffer from over study before your examination. I think you might regulate the thing according to your own Pleasure, and I would, too. They were talking of your being up at Christmas. Will it be before you have passed? There is nothing, my dear Bailey, I should rejoice at more than to see you comfortable with a little Paeòna[10] Wife. An affectionate Wife, I have a sort of confidence, would do you a great happiness. May that be one of the many blessings I wish you. Let me be but the 1/10th of one to you and I shall think it great. My Brother George's kindest wishes to you. My dear Bailey, I am

your affectionate friend
John Keats

I should not like to be Pages in your way when in a tolerable hungry mood; you have no Mercy. Your teeth are the Rock tarpeian[11] down which you capsize Epic Poems like Mad. I would not for 40 shillings be Coleridge's Lays in your way. I hope you will soon get through this abominable writing in the schools and be able to keep the terms with more comfort in the hope of returning to a comfortable and quiet home out of the way of all Hopkinses and black beetles.[12] When you are settled I will come and take a peep at your Church—your house— try whether I shall have grown too lusty for my chair by the fireside and take a peep at my cardials Bower. A Question is the best beacon towards a little Speculation. You ask me after my health and spirits. This Question ratifies in my Mind what I have said above. Health and Spirits can only belong unalloyed to the selfish Man; the Man who thinks much of his fellows can never be in Spirits. When I am not suffering for vicious beastliness I am the greater part of the week in spirits.

1. Presumably Rice and Reynolds. Bailey's first curacy was at Carlisle.
2. Martin was a partner in the publishing and bookselling firm, Rodwell and Martin.
3. An old poet.

4. Of *Endymion.*
5. Wordsworth, "Ode: Intimations of Immortality," line 202.
6. "On Common-place Critics," in *The Round Table* (1817), II:204.
7. Keats is discussing Hazlitt's note to "On Manner," in *The Round Table,* I:120–22, in which Hazlitt criticizes Wordsworth's "Gipsies" (1807).
8. That is, to get copies of Keats's life mask from Haydon.
9. Bailey's handwriting was notoriously difficult to read.
10. Paeòna is Endymion's sister.
11. *Coriolanus,* III.i.213.
12. Slang term for the Oxford beadles.

To Benjamin Bailey
3 NOVEMBER 1817

Monday—Hampstead

My dear Bailey,

Before I received your Letter I had heard of your disappointment—an unlook'd for piece of villainy.[1] I am glad to hear there was an hindrance to your speaking your Mind to the Bishop, for all may go straight yet as to being ordained. But the disgust consequent cannot pass away in a hurry. It must be shocking to find in a sacred Profession such barefaced oppression and impertinence. The Stations and Grandeurs of the World have taken it into their heads that they cannot commit themselves towards an inferior in rank, but is not the impertinence from one above to one below more wretchedly mean than from the low to the high? There is something so nauseous in self-willed yawning impudence in the shape of conscience; it sinks the Bishop of Lincoln into a smashed frog putrifying. That a rebel against common decency should escape the Pillory! That a mitre should cover a Man guilty of the most coxcombical, tyrannical and indolent impertinence! I repeat this word, for the offence appears to me most especially *impertinent,* and a very serious return would be the Rod. Yet doth he sit in his Palace. Such is this World, and we live. You have surely been in a continual struggle against the suffocation of accidents. We must bear (and my Spleen is mad at the thought thereof) the Proud Man's Contumely.[2] O, for a recourse somewhat human independent of the great Consolations of Religion and undepraved Sensations—of the Beautiful, the poetical in all things. O, for a Remedy against such wrongs within the pale of the World! Should not those things be pure enjoyment, should they stand the chance of being contaminated by being called in as antagonists to Bishops? Would not earthly things do? By Heavens, my dear Bailey, I know you have a spice of what I mean. You can set me and have set it in all the rubs that may befall me, you have, I know, a sort of Pride which would kick the Devil on the Jaw Bone and make him drunk with the kick. There is nothing so balmy to a soul embittered as yours must be, as Pride. When we look at the Heavens we cannot be proud, but shall stocks and stones be impertinent and say it does not become us to kick them? At this Moment I take your hand; let us walk up yon Mountain of common sense. Now if our Pride be vainglorious such a support would fail, yet you feel firm footing. Now look beneath at that parcel of knaves and fools. Many a Mitre is moving among them. I cannot express how I despise the Man who would wrong or be impertinent to you. The thought that we are mortal makes us groan. I will speak of something else or my Spleen will get higher and higher, and I am not a bearer of the two-edged Sword. I hope you will receive an answer from Haydon soon; if not, Pride! Pride! Pride! I have received no more subscription,[3] but shall soon have a full health, Liberty and leisure to give a good part of my time to him. I will certainly be in time for him. We have promised him one year, let that have elapsed and then do as we think proper. If I did not know how impossible it is, I should say "do not at this time of disappointments disturb yourself about others." There has been a flaming attack upon Hunt in the Edinburgh Magazine[4]—I never read anything so virulent—accusing him of the greatest Crimes, depreciating his Wife, his Poetry, his Habits, his company, his Conversation. These Philippics are to come out in Numbers, call'd "the Cockney School of Poetry." There has been but one Number published, that on Hunt to which they have prefixed a Motto from one Cornelius Webb Poetaster,[5] who unfortunately was of our Party occasionally at Hampstead and took it into his head to write the following, something about we'll talk on Wordsworth Byron, a theme we

never tire on and so forth till he comes to Hunt and Keats. In the Motto
they have put Hunt and Keats in large Letters. I have no doubt that the second Number was intended for me, but have hopes of its non-appearance
from the following advertisement in last Sunday's Examiner: "To Z. The
writer of the Article signed Z in Blackwood's Edinburgh magazine for October 1817 is invited to send his address to the printer of the Examiner, in
order that Justice may be executed of the proper person." I don't mind the
thing much, but if he should go to such lengths with me as he has done
with Hunt, I must infallibly call him to an account—if he be a human being and appears in Squares and Theatres where we might possibly meet. I
don't relish his abuse.

Yesterday Rice and I were at Reynolds. John was to be articled tomorrow; I suppose by this time it is done. Jane was much better. At one time or
other I will do you a Pleasure and the Poets a little Justice, but it ought to
be in a Poem of greater moment than Endymion. I will do it some day. I
have seen two Letters of a little Story Reynolds is writing. I wish he would
keep at it. Here is the song I enclosed to Jane, if you can make it out in this
crosswise writing.

> O Sorrow
> Why dost borrow
> The natural hue of health from vermeil Lips?
> To give maiden blushes
> To the white Rose bushes
> Or is it thy dewy hand the daisy tips?
>
> O Sorrow
> Why dost borrow
> The Lustrous Passion from an orbed eye?
> To give the glow worm Light?
> Or on a moonless night
> To tinge on syren shores the salt sea spray?
>
> O Sorrow
> Why dost borrow
> The tender ditties from a mourning tongue?

> To give at Evening pale
> Unto the Nightingale
> That thou mayest listen the cold dews among?
>
> O Sorrow
> Why dost borrow
> Heart's lightness from the Merriment of May?
> A Lover would not tread
> A Cowslip on the head
> Though he should dance from eve till peep of day;
> Nor any drooping flower
> Held sacred to thy bower
> Wherever he may sport himself and play.
>
> To Sorrow
> I bade good morrow,
> And thought to leave her far away behind
> But cheerly, cheerly,
> She loves me dearly,
> She is to me so constant, and so kind.
> I would deceive her
> And so leave her
> But ah! she is too constant and too kind.

O, that I had Orpheus' lute and was able to charm away all your Griefs and Cares, but all my power is a Mite. Amid all your troubles I shall ever be

your sincere and affectionate friend
John Keats

My brothers' remembrances to you.
    Give my respects to Gleig and Whitehead.[6]

---

1. There was some difficulty over his curacy in the diocese of Lincoln. He was eventually ordained 19 July 1818 in the diocese of Carlisle.
2. *Hamlet,* III.i.71.
3. To pay for Cripps's studying under Haydon.

ie Cockney School of Poetry. No I," *Blackwood's Edinburgh Magazine*, Octo-
7 (II:38–41).
lius Francis Webb, or Webbe (ca. 1790–ca. 1848).
6. Reverend Joseph Charles Frederick Whitehead of Eccleston, Lancashire (1784–1825), who was a contemporary of Bailey's at Magdalen Hall.

To Benjamin Bailey

22 NOVEMBER 1817

My dear Bailey,

I will get over the first part of this (*un*said)[1] Letter as soon as possible for it relates to the affair of poor Crips. To a Man of your nature, such a Letter as Haydon's must have been extremely cutting. What occasions the greater part of the World's Quarrels? Simply this, two Minds meet and do not understand each other time enough to prevent any shock or surprise at the conduct of either party. As soon as I had known Haydon three days I had got enough of his character not to have been surprised at such a Letter as he has hurt you with. Nor when I knew it, was it a principle with me to drop his acquaintance, although with you it would have been an imperious feeling. I wish you knew all that I think about Genius and the Heart, and yet I think you are thoroughly acquainted with my innermost breast in that respect or you could not have known me even thus long and still hold me worthy to be your dear friend. In passing, however, I must say of one thing that has pressed upon me lately and encreased my Humility and capability of submission, and that is this truth: Men of Genius are great as certain ethereal Chemicals operating on the Mass of neutral intellect, but they have not any individuality, any determined Character. I would call the top and head of those who have a proper self Men of Power.

But I am running my head into a Subject which I am certain I could not do justice to under five years study and 3 vols. octavo, and moreover long to be talking about the Imagination. So, my dear Bailey, do not think of this unpleasant affair if possible, do not. I defy any harm to come of it—I defy.

Opening page of Keats's crossed letter to Benjamin Bailey,
22 November 1817 (Ms Keats 1.16).
By permission of the Houghton Library, Harvard University.

I shall write to Crips this Week and request him to tell me all his goings on from time to time by Letter wherever I may be. It will all go on well, so don't because you have suddenly discover'd a Coldness in Haydon suffer yourself to be teased. Do not, my dear fellow. O, I wish I was as certain of the end of all your troubles as that of your momentary start about the authenticity of the Imagination. I am certain of nothing but of the holiness of the Heart's affections and the truth of Imagination. What the imagination seizes as Beauty must be truth[2]—whether it existed before or not—for I have the same Idea of all our Passions as of Love; they are all in their sublime, creative of essential Beauty. In a Word, you may know my favorite Speculation by my first Book and the little song I sent in my last, which is a representation from the fancy of the probable mode of operating in these Matters. The Imagination may be compared to Adam's dream—he awoke and found it truth.[3] I am the more zealous in this affair, because I have never yet been able to perceive how anything can be known for truth by consequitive reasoning—and yet it must be. Can it be that even the greatest Philosopher ever arrived at his goal without putting aside numerous objections? However it may be, O for a Life of Sensations rather than of Thoughts! It is "a Vision in the form of Youth," a Shadow of reality to come, and this consideration has further convinced me for it has come as auxiliary to another favorite Speculation of mine, that we shall enjoy ourselves hereafter by having what we called happiness on Earth repeated in a finer tone and so repeated. And yet such a fate can only befall those who delight in sensation rather than hunger as you do after Truth. Adam's dream will do here and seems to be a conviction that Imagination and its empyreal reflection is the same as human Life and its spiritual repetition. But as I was saying. The simple imaginative Mind may have its rewards in the repetition of its own silent Working coming continually on the spirit with a fine suddenness. To compare great things with small: have you never by being surprised with an old Melody—in a delicious place—by a delicious voice, felt over again your very speculations and surmises at the time it first operated on your soul? Do you not remember forming to yourself the singer's face more beautiful than it was possible, and yet with the elevation of the Moment you did not think so? Even then you were mounted on the Wings of Imagination so high that the Prototype must be hereafter that delicious face you will see. What a time! I am continually running away from the subject; sure this cannot be exactly the case with a complex Mind, one that is imaginative and at the same time careful of its fruits, who would exist partly on sensation, partly on thought, to whom it is necessary that years should bring the philosophic Mind. Such an one I consider your's and therefore it is necessary to your eternal Happiness that you not only drink this old Wine of Heaven, which I shall call the redigestion of our most ethereal Musings on Earth, but also increase in knowledge and know all things. I am glad to hear you are in a fair Way for Easter. You will soon get through your unpleasant reading and then! But the world is full of troubles and I have not much reason to think myself pestered with many. I think Jane or Marianne has a better opinion of me than I deserve, for really and truly I do not think my Brother's illness connected with mine. You know more of the real Cause than they do, nor have I any chance of being rack'd as you have been. You perhaps at one time thought there was such a thing as Worldly Happiness to be arrived at, at certain periods of time marked out; you have of necessity from your disposition been thus led away. I scarcely remember counting upon any Happiness. I look not for it if it be not in the present hour. Nothing startles me beyond the Moment. The setting sun will always set me to rights, or if a Sparrow come before my Window, I take part in its existence and pick about the Gravel. The first thing that strikes me on hearing a Misfortune having befallen another is this: "Well, it cannot be helped. He will have the pleasure of trying the resources of his spirit." And I beg now, my dear Bailey, that hereafter should you observe anything cold in me not to put it to the account of heartlessness but abstraction, for I assure you I sometimes feel not the influence of a Passion or Affection during a whole week. And so long this sometimes continues I begin to suspect myself and the genuineness of my feelings at other times, thinking them a few barren Tragedy-tears. My Brother Tom is much improved. He is going to Devonshire whither I shall follow him. At present I am just arrived at Dorking to change the Scene, change the Air, and give me a spur to wind up my Poem, of which there are wanting 500 Lines. I should have been here a day sooner but the Reynoldses persuaded me to stop in Town to meet your friend Christie.[4] There were Rice and Martin. We talked about Ghosts. I will have some talk with Taylor and let you know when, please God, I come down at Christmas. I will find that Examiner if possible. My best regards to Gleig. My Brothers' to you and Mrs. Bentley.

Your affectionate friend
John Keats—

I want to say much more to you; a few hints will set me going.
    Direct Burford Bridge near dorking.

1. The word is a pun on the legal use of "said," as in "the said . . ."
2. See the final two lines of Keats's "Ode on a Grecian Urn."
3. See *Paradise Lost,* VIII.452–490.
4. Jonathan Henry Christie (d. 1876). On 16 February 1821 he mortally wounded John Scott, editor of the *London Magazine,* in a duel that resulted directly from the Cockney School reviews in *Blackwood's.* Scott died on 27 February.

To J. H. Reynolds

22 NOVEMBER 1817

Saturday

My Dear Reynolds,

There are two things which tease me here, one of them Cripps and the other that I cannot go with Tom into Devonshire. However, I hope to do my duty to myself in a week or so, and then I'll try what I can do for my neighbour. Now, is not this virtuous? On returning to Town, I'll damn all Idleness. Indeed, in superabundance of employment, I must not be content to run here and there on little two penny errands, but turn Rakehell, i.e.,

go a-*making* or Bailey will think me just as great a Promise-keeper as *he*
thinks you. For myself, I do not, and do not remember above one Complaint against you for matter o' that. Bailey writes so abominable a hand, to
give his Letter a fair reading requires a little time; so I had not seen when I
saw you last his invitation to Oxford at Christmas. I'll go with you. You
know how poorly Rice was. I do not think it was all corporeal. Bodily pain
was not used to keep him silent. I'll tell you what; he was hurt at what your
Sisters said about his joking with your Mother he was, soothly to sain. It
will all blow over. God knows, my Dear Reynolds, I should not talk any
sorrow to you; you must have enough vexations, so I won't any more. If I
ever start a rueful subject in a Letter to you, blow me! Why don't you? Now
I was a going to ask a very silly Question neither you nor anybody else
could answer under a folio, or at least a Pamphlet—you shall judge—Why
don't you, as I do, look unconcerned at what may be called more particularly Heart-vexations? They never surprise me. Lord! A man should have
the fine point of his soul taken off to become fit for this world.

I like this place very much. There is Hill and Dale and a little River. I
went up Box hill this Evening after the Moon—you a' seen the Moon—
came down, and wrote some lines. Whenever I am separated from you and
not engaged in a continued Poem, every Letter shall bring you a lyric. But I
am too anxious for you to enjoy the whole to send you a particle. One of
the three Books I have with me is Shakespeare's Poems. I ne'er found so
many beauties in the sonnets. They seem to be full of fine things said unin-
tentionally in the intensity of working out conceits. Is this to be borne?
Hark ye!

> When lofty trees I see barren of leaves
> Which erst from heat did canopy the herd,
> And Summer's green all girded up in sheaves,
> Borne on the bier with white and bristly beard.[1]

He has left nothing to say about nothing or anything, for look at Snails.
You know what he says about Snails; you know where he talks about "cock-

led snails."[2] Well, in one of these sonnets, he says—the chap slips into—no! I lie! This is in the Venus and Adonis. The Simile brought it to my Mind.

> Audi—As the snail, whose tender horns being hit,
>   Shrinks back into his shelly cave with pain,
>   And there all smothered up in shade doth sit,
>   Long after fearing to put forth again:
>   So at his bloody view her eyes are fled,
>   Into the deep dark Cabins of her head.

He overwhelms a genuine Lover of Poesy with all manner of abuse, talking about—

> "a poets rage
> And stretched metre of an antique song"—[3]

Which by the by will be a capital Motto for my Poem, won't it? He speaks too of "Time's antique pen" and "april's first born flowers," and "death's eternal cold."[4] By the Whim King! I'll give you a Stanza, because it is not material in connection and when I wrote it I wanted you to give your vote, pro or con.

> Christalline Brother of the Belt of Heaven,
>   Aquarius! to whom King Jove hath given
>   Two liquid pulse streams instead of feather'd wings—
>   Two fan-like fountains—thine illuminings
> For Dian play:
>   Dissolve the frozen purity of air;
>   Let thy white shoulders silvery and bare
>   Show cold through watery pinions. Make more bright
>   The Star-Queen's Crescent on her marriage night:
> Haste, Haste away!

Now I hope I shall not fall off in the winding up, as the Woman said to the——.[5] I mean up and down. I see there is an advertizement in the chronicle to Poets. He is so overloaded with poems on the late Princess.[6] I suppose you do not lack.[7] Send me a few. Lend me thy hand to laugh a little. Send me a little pullet sperm, a few finch eggs, and remember me to each of our Card-playing Club. When you die you will all be turned into Dice, and be put in pawn with the Devil, for Cards they crumple up like any King, I mean John in the stage play what pertains Prince Arthur. I rest

Your affectionate friend
John Keats

Give my love to both houses. Hinc atque illinc.[8]

1. Sonnet 12, lines 5–8.
2. *Love's Labor's Lost,* IV.iii.338.
3. Sonnet 17, lines 11f.
4. Sonnets 19, line 10; 21, line 7; 13, line 12.
5. This space blank in Woodhouse's transcription.
6. Princess Charlotte Augusta died on 6 November 1817.
7. That is, lack poems on the princess, for at this time Reynolds was in charge of the poetry department of the *Champion.*
8. Virgil, *Georgics,* III.257, "on each side."

To George and Tom Keats
21, 27 (?) DECEMBER 1817

Hampstead, Sunday
22 December 1818

My dear Brothers,

I must crave your pardon for not having written ere this, etc., etc. I saw Kean return to the public in Richard III, and finely he did it, and at the request of Reynolds I went to criticise his Luke in Riches;[1] the critique is in today's champion, which I send you with the Examiner in which you will find very proper lamentation on the obsoletion of christmas Gambols and pastimes, but it was mixed up with so much egotism of that drivelling nature that pleasure is entirely lost. Hone the publisher's trial you must find very amusing and as Englishmen very encouraging. His *Not Guilty* is a thing, which not to have been, would have dulled still more Liberty's Emblazoning. Lord Ellenborough has been paid in his own coin. Wooler and Hone have done us an essential service.[2] I have had two very pleasant evenings with Dilke, yesterday and today, and am at this moment just come from him and feel in the humour to go on with this, began in the morning, and from which he came to fetch me. I spent Friday evening with Wells[3] and went the next morning to see *Death on the Pale horse*. It is a wonderful picture, when West's age is considered, but there is nothing to be intense upon, no women one feels mad to kiss, no face swelling into reality. The excellence of every Art is its intensity, capable of making all disagreeables evaporate from their being in close relationship with Beauty and Truth. Examine King Lear and you will find this examplified throughout; but in this picture we have unpleasantness without any momentous depth of speculation excited, in which to bury its repulsiveness. The picture is larger than Christ rejected.[4] I dined with Haydon the sunday after you left, and had a very pleasant day. I dined too (for I have been out too much lately) with Horace Smith and met his two Brothers with Hill and Kingston and one Du Bois.[5] They only served to convince me how superior humour is to wit in respect to enjoyment. These men say things which make one start, without making one feel. They are all alike. Their manners are alike; they all know fashionables. They have a mannerism in their very eating and drinking, in their mere handling a Decanter. They talked of Kean and his low company. Would I were with that company instead of yours, said I to myself! I know such like acquaintance will never do for me and yet I am going to Reynolds on wednesday. Brown and Dilke walked with me and back from the Christmas pantomime. I had not a dispute but a disquisition with Dilke on various subjects; several things dovetailed in my mind, and at once it struck me, what quality went to form a Man of Achievement, especially in Literature and which Shakespeare possessed so enormously—I mean *Negative Capability*, that is when man is capable of being in uncertainties, Mysteries, doubts, without any irritable reaching after fact and reason. Coleridge, for instance, would let go by a fine isolated verisimilitude caught from the Penetralium of mystery, from being incapable of remaining content with half knowledge. This pursued through Volumes would perhaps take us no further than this, that with a great poet the sense of

Beauty overcomes every other consideration, or rather obliterates all consideration.

Shelley's poem is out and there are words about its being objected to, as much as Queen Mab was.[6] Poor Shelley, I think he has his Quota of good qualities, in sooth la!! Write soon to your most sincere friend and affectionate Brother

(Signed) *John*

1. Kean played Luke Traffic in Sir James Bland Burges's *Riches: Or, The Wife and Brother. A Comedy* (1817).
2. Thomas Jonathan Wooler (1786?–1853) and William Hone (1780–1842), radical journalists and booksellers, had been tried for libel and acquitted, one on 5 June, the other on 18–20 December. Lord Ellenborough (1750–1818), lord chief justice, presided at the second and third trials.
3. Charles Jeremiah Wells (1800–1879) was a schoolfellow of Tom Keats.
4. Benjamin West (1738–1820), an American painter, was president of the Royal Academy. Both pictures mentioned are now in the Academy of Fine Arts, Philadelphia.
5. Thomas Hill (1760–1840) was a well-known book collector and bon vivant; John Kingston, a comptroller of stamps; and Edward Dubois (1774–1850), a wit, man of letters, and editor.
6. *Laon and Cythna* (afterwards *The Revolt of Islam*) dealt with incest.

1818

To George and Tom Keats

5 JANUARY 1818

Featherstone Buildings, Monday

My dear Brothers,

I ought to have written before, and you should have had a long Letter last week, but I undertook the Champion for Reynolds who is at Exeter. I wrote two articles, one on the Drury Lane Pantomime, the other on the Covent Garden New Tragedy, which they have not put in. The one they have inserted is so badly punctuated that, you perceive, I am determined never to write more without some care in that particular. Wells tells me that you are licking your Chops, Tom, in expectation of my Book coming out. I am sorry to say I have not begun my corrections yet; tomorrow I set out. I called on Sawrey[1] this morning. He did not seem to be at all out at anything I said and the enquiries I made with regard to your spitting of Blood; and, moreover, desired me to ask you to send him a correct account of all your sensations and symptoms concerning the Palpitation and the spitting and the Cough, if you have any. Your last Letter gave me a great Pleasure, for I think the Invalid is in a better spirit there along the Edge,[2] and as for George, I must immediately, now I think of it, correct a little misconception of a part of my last Letter. The Miss Reynolds have never said one word against me about you, or by any means endeavoured to lessen you in my estimation. That is not what I referred to, but the manner and thoughts which I knew they internally had towards you. Time will show. Wells and Severn dined with me yesterday; we had a very pleasant day. I pitched upon another bottle of claret—Port. We enjoyed ourselves very much, were all very witty and full of Rhyme. We played a Concert[3] from 4 o'clock till 10, drank your Healths, the Hunts, and N. B. Severn, Peter Pindar's.[4] I said on that day the only good thing I was ever guilty of. We were talking about Stephens and the 1st Gallery. I said I wondered that careful Folks would go there, for although it was but a Shilling still you had to pay through the Nose. I saw the Peachey family[5] in a Box at Drury one Night. I have got such a curious,[6] or rather I had such, now I am in my own hand. I have had a great deal of pleasant time with Rice lately, and am getting initiated into a little Cant. They call drinking, "deep-dying scarlet," and when you breathe in you're "watering"; they bid you cry hem and play it off. They call good Wine a "pretty tipple," and call getting a Child "knocking out an apple." Stopping at a Tavern they call "hanging out." Where do you sup? is "where do you hang out?" This day I promised to dine with Wordsworth and the Weather is so bad that I am undecided, for he lives at Mortimer street. I had an invitation to meet him at Kingston's, but not liking that place I sent my excuse. What I think of doing today is to dine in Mortimer Street (Wordsworth) and sup here in Featherstone Buildings, as Mr. Wells has invited me. On Saturday I called on Wordsworth before he went to Kingston's and was surprised to find him with a stiff Collar. I saw his Spouse and I think his Daughter. I forget whether I had written my last before my Sunday Evening at Haydon's; no, I did not or I should have told you Tom of a young Man you met at Paris at Scott's of the name of Richer,[7] I think. He is going to Fezan in Africa there to proceed if possible like Mungo Park.[8] He was very polite to me and enquired very particularly after you. Then there was Wordsworth, Lamb, Monkhouse, Landseer, Kingston and your humble Sarvant.[9] Lamb got tipsey and blew up Kingston, proceeding so far as to take the Candle across the Room, hold it to his face, and show us wh-a-at-sort-fello he-waas. I astonished Kingston at supper with a pertinacity in favour of drinking, keeping my two glasses at work in a knowing way. I have seen Fanny twice lately. She enquired particularly after you and wants a Co-partnership Letter from you. She has been unwell but is improving. I think she will be quick. Mrs. Abbey was saying that the Keatses were ever indolent, that they would ever be so and that it was born in them. "Well," whispered fanny to me, "If it is born with us how can we help it?" She seems very anxious for a Letter. I asked her what I should get for her, she said a Medal of the Princess. I called on Haslam. We dined very snugly together. He sent me a Hare last Week, which I sent to Mrs. Dilke. Brown is not come back. I and Dilke are getting capital Friends. He is going to take the Champion. He has sent his farce to Covent Garden. I met Bob Harris in the Slips[10] at Covent Garden. We had a good deal of curious chat. He came out with his old humble Opinion. The Covent Garden Pantomime is a very nice one, but they have a middling Harlequin, a bad Pantaloon, a worse Clown, and a shocking Columbine who is one of the Miss Dennets. I suppose you will see my Critique on the new Tragedy in the next Week's Champion. It is a shocking bad one. I have not seen Hunt; he was out when I called. Mrs. Hunt looks as well as ever I saw her after her Confinement. There is an article in the sennight Examiner on Godwin's Mandeville, signed E. K. I think it Miss Kent's.[11] I will send it. There are fine Subscriptions going on for Hone. You ask me what degrees there are between Scott's Novels and those of Smollet. They appear to me to be quite distinct in every particular, more especially in their Aim. Scott endeavours to throw so interesting and ramantic a colouring into common and low Characters as to give them a touch of the Sublime. Smollet, on the contrary, pulls down and levels what with other Men would continue Romance. The Grand parts of Scott are within the reach of more Minds than the finest humours in Humphrey Clinker. I forget whether that fine thing of the Sargeant is Fielding's or Smollet's, but it gives me more pleasure than the whole Novel of the Antiquary. You must remember what I mean. Someone says to the Sargeant, "that's a non sequiter." "If you come to that," replies the Sargeant, "you're another."[12] I see by Wells' Letter, Mr. Abbey does not overstock you with Money. You must insist. I have not seen Loveless yet, but expect it on Wednesday. I am afraid it is gone. Severn tells me he has an order for some drawings for the Emperor of Russia. I was at a Dance at Redhall's and passed a pleasant time enough, drank deep and won 10.6 at cutting for Half Guineas. There was a younger Brother of the Squibs made himself very conspicuous after the Ladies had retired from the supper table by giving Mater Omnium.[13] Mr. Redhall said he did not understand anything but plain english, whereat Rice egged the young fool on to say the Wor[l]d plainly out. After which there was an enquiry about the

derivation of the Word C——t,[14] when while two parsons and Grammar-
ians were sitting together and settling the matter, William Squibs interrupt-
ing them said a very good thing: "Gentleman," says he, "I have always understood it to be a Root and not a Derivitive." On proceeding to the Pot in
the Cupboard it soon became full, on which the Court door was opened.
Frank Floodgate bawls out, Hoollo! Here's an opposition pot. Ay, says Rice,
in one you have a Yard for your pot, and in the other a pot for your Yard.[15]
Bailey was there and seemed to enjoy the Evening. Rice said he cared less
about the hour than anyone and the proof is his dancing. He cares not for
time, dancing as if he was deaf. Old Redall, not being used to give parties,
had no idea of the Quantity of wine that would be drank and he actually
put in readiness on the kitchen Stairs 8 dozen. Everyone enquires after you
and everyone desires their remembrances to you. You must get well, Tom,
and then I shall feel "Whole and general as the casing Air."[16] Give me as
many Letters as you like and write to Sawrey soon. I received a short Letter
from Bailey about Crips and one from Haydon ditto. Haydon thinks he
improves very much. Here a happy twelfth days to you and may we pass the
next together. Mrs. Wells desires remembrances particularly to Tom and
her respects to George, and I desire no better than to be ever your most affectionate

Brother John—

I had not opened the Champion before; I find both my articles in it.

1. Solomon Sawrey (1765–1825), surgeon, and the Keats's family doctor.
2. An escarpment and walk at Teignmouth.
3. Each person imitating vocally the instruments of an orchestra.
4. Peter Pindar, or John Wolcot (1738–1819), satirist and poet.
5. James Peachey was an attorney and a schoolfellow of Keats.
6. A bad pen, which he changed at this point.
7. Joseph Ritchie (1788?–1819), surgeon and explorer.
8. African explorer (1771–1806).
9. Thomas Monkhouse (1783–1825), a merchant and cousin of Mrs. Wordsworth.
   John Landseer (1769–1852), painter and engraver.
10. The slips are the sidings from which scenery was pushed onstage. Bob Harris may

have been related to Thomas Harris, who was the manager of Covent Garden for many years.
11. E. K. was not Bessy Kent, Mrs. Leigh Hunt's sister, but P. B. Shelley ("Elfin Knight").
12. Henry Fielding, *Tom Jones*, IX:vi.
13. "Mother of all." Perhaps a prayer or hymn, probably to the Virgin Mary, though Eve is also likely, given the discussion that follows.
14. Keats observed the taboo that had since about 1700 made it a legal offense to print the word in full.
15. From 1590 to 1780, "yard" was perhaps the most commonly used literary term for "penis," but was obsolete by 1850. (Partridge)
16. *Macbeth*, III.iv.23, "As broad and general as the casing air."

To B. R. Haydon

10 JANUARY 1818

Saturday Morn—

My dear Haydon,

I should have seen you ere this, but on account of my sister being in Town, so that when I have sometimes made ten paces towards you, Fanny has called me into the City; and the Xmas Holydays are your only time to see Sisters, that is if they are so situated as mine. I will be with you early next week. Tonight it should be, but we have a sort of a Club every Saturday evening—tomorrow—but I have on that day an insuperable engagement. Crips has been down to me, and appears sensible that a binding to you would be of the greatest advantage to him. If such a thing be done, it cannot be before £150 or £200 are secured in subscriptions to him. I will write to Bailey about it, give a Copy of the Subscribers' names to everyone I know who is likely to get a £5 for him. I will leave a Copy at Taylor and Hessey's, Rodwell and Martin and will ask Kingston and Co. to cash up. Your friendship for me is now getting into its teens, and I feel the past. Also, every day older I get the greater is my idea of your achievements in

Art, and I am convinced that there are three things to rejoice at in this Age: The Excursion, Your Pictures, and Hazlitt's depth of Taste.

Your's affectionately
John Keats

To George and Tom Keats
13, 19 JANUARY 1818

Tuesday, Hampstead 1818

My dear Brothers,

I am certain I think of having a letter tomorrow morning, for I expected one so much this morning. Having been in town two days, at the end of which my expectations began to get up a little, I found two on the table, one from Bailey and one from Haydon. I am quite perplexed in a world of doubts and fancies. There is nothing stable in the world; uproar's your only music. I do not mean to include Bailey in this and so I dismiss him from this, with all the opprobrium he deserves, that is in so many words. He is one of the noblest men alive at the present day. In a note to Haydon about a week ago (which I wrote with a full sense of what he had done, and how he had never manifested any little mean drawback in his value of me), I said if there were three things superior in the modern world, they were "the Excursion," "Haydon's pictures" and "Hazlitt's depth of Taste." So I do believe, not thus speaking with any poor vanity that works of genius were the first things in this world. No! for that sort of probity and disinterestedness which such men as Bailey possess, does hold and grasp the tiptop of any spiritual honours that can be paid to anything in this world. And, moreover, having this feeling at this present come over me in its full force, I sat down to write to you with a grateful heart, in that I had not a Brother, who did not feel and credit me for a deeper feeling and devotion for his uprightness than for any marks of genius however splendid. I was speaking about doubts and fancies; I Mean there has been a quarrel of a severe nature between Haydon and Reynolds, and another ("the Devil rides upon a fiddle-stick")[1] between Hunt and Haydon. The first grew from the sunday on which Haydon invited some friends to meet Wordsworth. Reynolds never went and never sent any Notice about it. This offended Haydon more than it ought to have done. He wrote a very sharp and high note to Reynolds and then another in palliation, but which Reynolds feels as an aggravation of the first. Considering all things, Haydon's frequent neglect of his Appointments, etc., his notes were bad enough to put Reynolds on the right side of the question, but then Reynolds has no powers of sufferance, no idea of having the thing against him, so he answered Haydon in one of the most cutting letters I ever read, exposing to himself all his own weaknesses and going on to an excess, which whether it is just or no, is what I would fain have unsaid. The fact is they are both in the right and both in the wrong.

The quarrel with Hunt I understand thus far. Mrs. H. was in the habit of borrowing silver of Haydon. The last time she did so, Haydon asked her to return it at a certain time. She did not. Haydon sent for it; Hunt went to expostulate on the indelicacy, etc. They got to words and parted forever. All I hope is at some time to bring them all together again. Lawk! Molly there's been such doings. Yesterday evening I made an appointment with Wells to go to a private theatre and it being in the neighbourhood of Drury Lane, and thinking we might be fatigued with sitting the whole evening in one dirty hole, I got the Drury Lane ticket and therewith we divided the evening with a Spice of Richard III.

Good Lord! I began this letter nearly a week ago, what have I been doing since? I have been—I mean not been sending last sunday's paper to you, I believe because it was not near me, for I cannot find it and my conscience presses heavy on me for not sending it. You would have had one last thursday but I was called away and have been about somewhere ever since. Where? What? Well, I rejoice almost that I have not heard from you, because no news is good news. I cannot for the world recollect why I was called away, all I know is that there has been a dance at Dilke's and another at the London Coffee House, to both of which I went. But I must tell you in another letter the circumstances thereof, for though a week should have passed since I wrote on the other side it quite appalls me. I can only write in scraps and patches. Brown is returned from Hampstead.[2] Haydon has returned an answer in the same style. They are all dreadfully irritated against each other. On sunday I saw Hunt and dined with Haydon, met Hazlitt and Bewick[3] there, and took Haslam with me. Forgot to speak about Crips, though I broke my engagement to Haslam's on purpose. Mem. Haslam came to meet me, found me at Breakfast, had the goodness to go with me my way. I have just finished the revision of my first book and shall take it to Taylor's tomorrow. Intend to persevere. Do not let me see many days pass without hearing from you.

Your most affectionate Brother
(signed) *John*—

1. *1 Henry IV,* II.iv.534f.
2. Keats meant either "to Hampstead" or "from Hampshire," for Brown had been at Bedhampton.
3. William Bewick (1795–1866), artist.

To B. R. Haydon

23 JANUARY 1818

Friday 23rd—

My dear Haydon,

I have a complete fellow-feeling with you in this business[1]—so much so that it would be as well to wait for a choice out of *Hyperion.* When that Poem is done there will be a wide range for you. In Endymion I think you may have many bits of the deep and sentimental cast. The nature of *Hyperion* will lead me to treat it in a more naked and grecian Manner, and the march of passion and endeavour will be undeviating. And one great

Haydon's drawings of Keats's head (1816).
National Portrait Gallery, London.

contrast between them will be that the Hero of the written tale being mortal is led on, like Buonaparte, by circumstance, whereas the Apollo in Hyperion being a fore-seeing God will shape his actions like one. But I am counting, etc.

Your proposal pleases me and, believe me, I would not have my Head in the shop windows from any hand but yours—no, by Apelles! I will write Taylor and you shall hear from me.

Your's ever, *John Keats—*

1. Keats is replying to a letter he received from Haydon on January 19 about Taylor's proposal that Haydon make a drawing to be used as the frontispiece to *Endymion*.

To John Taylor
23 JANUARY 1818

Friday 23rd

My dear Taylor,

I have spoken to Haydon about the Drawing. He would do it with all his Art, and Heart too if so I will it, however he has written thus to me. But I must tell you first, he intends painting a finished picture from the Poem. Thus he writes:

"When I do anything for your poem, it must be effectual—an honor to both of us. To hurry up a sketch for the season won't do. I think an engraving from your head, from a Chalk drawing of mine, done with all my might, to which I would put my name, would answer Taylor's Idea more than the other—indeed, I am sure of it. This I will do and this will be effectual, and as I have not done it for any other human being it will have an effect."[1]

What think you of this? Let me hear. I shall have my second book in readiness forthwith.

Your's most sincerely
John Keats—

If Reynolds calls, tell him three lines would be acceptable for I am squat at Hampstead.

1. Haydon never drew Keats's portrait, and the book appeared without illustrations.

To Benjamin Bailey
23 JANUARY 1818

Friday, Jan. 23rd

My dear Bailey,

Twelve days have pass'd since your last reached me. What has gone through the myriads of human Minds since the 12th? We talk of the immense number of Books, the Volumes ranged thousands by thousands, but perhaps more goes through the human intelligence in 12 days than ever was written. How has that unfortunate Family lived through the twelve? One saying of yours I shall never forget—you may not recollect it—it being perhaps said when you were looking on the surface and seeming of Humanity alone, without a thought of the past or the future or the deeps of good and evil. You were at the moment estranged from speculation and I think you have arguments ready for the Man who would utter it to you. This is a formidable preface for a simple thing; merely you said, *"Why should Woman suffer?"* Aye. Why should she? "By heavens I'd coin my very Soul and drop my Blood for Drachmas!"[1] These things are, and he who feels how incompetent the most skyey Knight errantry is to heal this bruised fairness is like a sensitive leaf on the hot hand of thought. Your tearing, my dear friend, a spiritless and gloomy Letter up to rewrite to me is what I shall never forget; it was to me a real thing. Things have happen'd lately of great Perplexity. You must have heard of them. Reynolds and Haydon retorting and recriminating, and parting forever. The same thing has happened between Haydon and Hunt. It is unfortunate. Men should bear with each other. There lives not the Man who may not be cut up, aye, hashed to pieces on his weakest side. The best of Men have but a portion of good in them, a kind of spiritual yeast in their frames which creates the ferment of existence, by which a Man is propell'd to act and strive and buffet with Circumstance. The sure way, Bailey, is first to know a Man's faults, and then be passive. If after that he insensibly draws you towards him then you have no Power to break the link. Before I felt interested in either Reynolds or Haydon, I was well read in their faults. Yet knowing them I have been cementing gradually with both. I have an affection for them both for reasons almost opposite, and to both must I of necessity cling, supported always by the hope that when a little time, a few years shall have tried me more fully in their esteem, I may be able to bring them together. The time must come because they have both hearts and they will recollect the best parts of each other when this gust is overblown. I had a Message from you through a Letter to Jane,[2] I think about Cripps. There can be no idea of binding[3] till a sufficient sum is sure for him, and even then the thing should be maturely consider'd by all his helpers. I shall try my luck upon as many fat-purses as I can meet with. Cripps is improving very fast. I have the greater hopes of him because he is so slow in development. A Man of great executing Powers at 20 with a look and a speech almost stupid is sure to do something. I have just look'd through the second side of your Letter. I feel a great content at it. I was at Hunt's the other day, and he surprised me with a real authenticated Lock of *Milton's Hair.* I know you would like what I wrote thereon, so here it is, *as they say of a Sheep in a Nur*sery Book.

On seeing a Lock of Milton's Hair
Ode

Chief of organic Numbers!
    Old scholar of the spheres!
Thy spirit never slumbers,
    But rolls about our ears
For ever and for ever.

O, what a mad endeavour
        Worketh he
Who, to thy sacred and enobled hearse,
Would offer a burnt sacrifice of verse
        And Melody!

How heavenward thou soundedst
        Live Temple of sweet noise;
And discord unconfoundedst:
        Giving delight new joys,
And Pleasure nobler pinions.
O where are thy Dominions!
        Lend thine ear
To a young delian oath; aye, by thy soul,
By all that from thy mortal Lips did roll;
And by the kernel of thine earthly Love,
Beauty, in things on earth and things above,
        When every childish fashion
                Has vanish'd from my rhyme
        Will I grey-gone in passion,
                Give to an after-time
                Hymning and harmony
Of thee, and of thy Works and of thy Life:
But vain is now the burning and the strife;
Pangs are in vain, until I grow high-rife
        With Old Philosophy
And mad with glimpses at futurity!
For many years my offerings must be hush'd:
When I do speak I'll think upon this hour,
Because I feel my forehead hot and flush'd,
Even at the simplest vassal of thy Power,
        A Lock of thy bright hair!
                Sudden it came,

And I was startled when I heard thy name
    Coupled so unaware;
Yet, at the moment, temperate was my blood:
Methought I had beheld it from the flood.

Jan. 21st

This I did at Hunt's at his request. Perhaps I should have done something better alone and at home. I have sent my first book to the Press and this afternoon shall begin preparing the second. My visit to you will be a great spur to quicken the Proceeding. I have not had your Sermon returned. I long to make it the subject of a Letter to you. What do they say at Oxford?

I trust you and Gleig pass much fine time together. Remember me to him and Whitehead. My Brother Tom is getting stronger, but his Spitting of blood continues. I sat down to read King Lear yesterday and felt the greatness of the thing up to the writing of a Sonnet preparatory thereto; in my next you shall have it. There were some miserable reports of Rice's health. I went and lo! Master Jemmy had been to the play the night before and was out at the time. He always comes on his Legs like a Cat. I have seen a good deal of Wordsworth. Hazlitt is lecturing on Poetry at the Surrey institution. I shall be there next Tuesday.

Your most affectionate Friend
John Keats—

1. *Julius Caesar,* IV.iii.72f.
2. Jane Reynolds.
3. That is, of apprenticing him to Haydon.

To George and Tom Keats
23, 24 JANUARY 1818

Friday 23rd January 1818

My dear Brothers,

I was thinking what hindered me from writing so long, for I have many things to say to you and know not where to begin. It shall be upon a thing most interesting to you, my Poem. Well! I have given the 1st book to Taylor; he seemed more than satisfied with it, and to my surprise proposed publishing it in Quarto, if Haydon would make a drawing of some event therein, for a Frontispiece. I called on Haydon. He said he would do anything I liked, but said he would rather paint a finished picture from it, which he seems eager to do. This in a year or two will be a glorious thing for us and it will be, for Haydon is struck with the 1st Book. I left Haydon and the next day received a letter from him, proposing to make, as he says with all his might, a finished chalk sketch of my head to be engraved in the first style and put at the head of my Poem, saying at the same time he had never done the thing for any human being and that it must have considerable effect as he will put the name to it. I begin today to copy my 2nd Book, "thus far into the bowels of the Land."[1] You shall hear whether it will be Quarto or non Quarto, picture or non Picture. Leigh Hunt I showed my 1st Book to. He allows it not much merit as a whole, says it is unnatural and made ten objections to it in the mere skimming over. He says the conversation is unnatural and too high-flown for the Brother and Sister. Says it should be simple, forgetting do ye mind that they are both overshadowed by a Supernatural Power, and of force could not speak like Franchesca in the Rimini. He must first prove that Caliban's poetry is unnatural. This with me completely overturns his objections. The fact is he and Shelley are hurt and perhaps justly, at my not having showed them the affair officiously and from several hints I have had they appear much disposed to dissect and anatomize any trip or slip I may have made. But who's afraid? Ay! Tom! demme if I am.[2] I went last tuesday, an hour too late, to Hazlitt's Lecture on poetry, got there just as they were coming out, when all these pounced upon me. Hazlitt, John Hunt and son, Wells, Bewick, all the Landseers, Bob Harris, Rox of the Burrough, Aye and more. The Landseers enquired after you particularly. I know not whether Wordsworth has left town. But sunday I dined with Hazlitt and Haydon, also that I took Haslam with me. I dined with Brown lately. Dilke, having taken the Champion Theatricals, was obliged to be in Town. Fanny has returned to Walthamstow. Mr. Abbey appeared very glum the last time I went to see her and said in an indirect way that I had no business there. Rice has been ill, but has been mending much lately. I think a little change has taken place in my intellect lately. I cannot bear to be uninterested or unemployed, I, who for so long a time have been addicted to passiveness. Nothing is finer for the purposes of great productions than a very gradual ripening of the intellectual powers. As an instance of this, observe, I sat down yesterday to read King Lear once again. The thing appeared to demand the prologue of a Sonnet. I wrote it and began to read. (I know you would like to see it):

"On sitting down to King Lear once Again"

O golden-tongued Romance with serene Lute!
Fair-plumed syren! Queen of far away!
Leave melodizing on this wintry day,
Shut up thine olden volume and be mute.
Adieu! for once again the fierce dispute,
Betwixt Hell torment and impassioned Clay
Must I burn through; once more assay
The bitter sweet of this Shakespeareian fruit
Chief Poet! and ye clouds of Albion.
Begettors of our deep eternal theme,
When I am through the old oak forest gone
Let me not wander in a barren dream
But when I am consumed with the Fire
Give me new Pheonix-wings to fly at my desire.

So you see I am getting at it, with a sort of determination and strength, though verily I do not feel it at this moment. This is my fourth letter this morning and I feel rather tired and my head rather swimming, so I will leave it open till tomorrow's post.

I am in the habit of taking my papers to Dilke's and copying there, so I chat and proceed at the same time. I have been there at my work this evening and the walk over the Heath takes off all sleep, so I will even proceed with you. I left off short in my last, just as I began an account of a private theatrical. Well, it was of the lowest order, all greasy and oily, insomuch that if they had lived in olden times, when signs were hung over the doors, the only appropriate one for that oily place would have been a guttered Candle. They played John Bull, The Review, and it was to conclude with Bombastes Furioso. I saw from a Box the 1st Act of John Bull, then I went to Drury and did not return till it was over. When by Wells' interest we got behind the scenes, there was not a yard wide all the way round for actors, scene-shifters and interlopers to move in. For "Note Bene," the Green Room was under the stage and there was I threatened over and over again to be turned out by the oily scene-shifters. There did I hear a little painted Trollop own, very candidly, that she had failed in Mary, with a "damned if she'd play a serious part again, as long as she lived," and at the same time she was habited as the Quaker in the Review. There was a quarrel and a fat, good-natured looking girl in soldiers Clothes wished she had only been a man for Tom's sake. One fellow began a song but an unlucky finger-point from the Gallery sent him off like a shot. One chap was dressed to kill for the King in Bombastes and he stood at the edge of the scene in the very sweat of anxiety to show himself, but Alas the thing was not played. The sweetest morsel of the night, moreover, was that the musicians began pegging and fagging away at an overture. Never did you see faces more in earnest. Three times did they play it over, dropping all kinds of correctness and still did not the curtain draw up. Well, then they went into a country-dance, then into a region they well knew, into their old boonsome Pothouse. And then to see how pompous o' the sudden they turned; how they looked about and chatted; how they did not care a Damn was a great treat. I hope I have not tired you by this filling up of the dash in my last.

Constable the Bookseller has offered Reynolds ten guineas a sheet to write
for his magazine. It is an Edinburgh one which Blackwood's started up in
opposition to. Hunt said he was nearly sure that the "Cockney School" was
written by Scott,[3] so you are right, Tom! There are no more little bits of
news I can remember at present. I remain

> My dear Brothers Your very affectionate Brother
> (signed) *John*

1. *Richard III,* V.ii.3.
2. Keats is quoting from Horace Smith's *Nehemiah Muggs,* which he had read in
   manuscript, "Pooh! Nonsense! Damme! Who's afraid."
3. In his edition of Keats's letters, Robert Gittings argues that "the article on the
   Cockney School of Poetry, *Blackwood's,* October 1817, was written by J. G. Lockhart (1794–1854), and not John Scott, whom Tom Keats had met in Paris."

To George and Tom Keats
30 JANUARY 1818

Hampstead

My dear Brothers,

You shall have the Papers.[1] I lent the last to Dilke and he has not returned it, or rather I have been in Town two days gelding[2] the first Book
which is, I think, going to the Press today. It will not be in Quarto, nor
shall I have my head therein.[3] Taylor on looking attentively through it has
changed his Mind. I have got five pounds but these I owe him Brown and
have been delaying these two or three days to give it him; I must owe him
still. Perhaps this will do till Haslam sends you some. £10 to Mrs. Bentley,
£10 to Cripps and the £5 to Brown nearly swallowed up the Balance Mr. A[4]
gave me. I understand about Mr. Fry and will speak to Mr. A about it. I am
convinced now that my Poem will not sell. Hope, they say, so I will wait
about three Months before I make my determination—either to get some

employment at Home or abroad or to retire to a very cheap way of living in the Country. Haydon will take my Likeness all the same, but I think he will keep it; however we can get it engraved.

Horace Twiss dined the other day with Horace Smith. Now Horace Twiss has an affectation of repeating extempore verses, which however he writes at home. After dinner Horace T. was to recite some verses, and before he did he went aside to pretend to make on the spot verses composed before hand. While H. T. was out of the Room, H. S. wrote the following and handed it about, when H. Twiss had done his spouting.

What precious extempore verses are Twiss's
Which he makes ere he waters, and vows as he pisses,
'Twould puzzle the Sages of greece to unriddle
Which flows out the fastest his verse or his piddle,
And 'twould pose them as much to know whether or not
His Piss or his Poems go quickest to Pot!

I wrote the following which has pleased Reynolds and Dilke beyond anything I ever did. I was thinking of Ben Jonson, Beaumont and Fletcher and the rest who used to meet at the Mermaid in days of yore and to finish did this.

Souls of Poets dead and gone
What Elysium have ye known,
Happy field, or mossy cavern
Fairer than the Mermaid Tavern?
    Have ye tippled drink more fine
Than mine host's canary wine;
Or are fruits of Paradise
Richer than those dainty pies
Of venison. Oh! generous food!
Dress'd as though bold Robin Hood
Would, with his Maid Marian,
Sup and bouze from Horn and Can.
    I have heard that on a day

Mine Host's sign board flew away,
Nobody knew whither till
An Astrologer's old Quill
To a Sheepskin gave the story:
Says he saw ye in your glory
Underneath a new old sign
Sipping beverage divine,
And pledging with contented smack
The Mermaid in the Zodiac!
   Souls of Poets dead and gone
   Are the Winds a sweeter home,
   Richer is uncellar'd Cavern
  Than the merry mermaid Tavern?

May the £5 do and this please you. Trust to the Spring and farewell my dear Tom and George.

Your affectionate Brother
John—

1. Containing Keats's reviews of plays.
2. To cut out portions of a book, or to mutilate a book by excising objectionable or obscene passages.
3. An engraving of a chalk portrait of Keats done by Haydon.
4. Mr. Abbey.

To John Taylor
30 JANUARY 1818

Friday

My dear Taylor,

These Lines, as they now stand, about Happiness have rung in my ears like a "chime a mending." See here,

Behold

Wherein Lies happiness Peona? Fold—

This appears to me the very contrary of blessed. I hope this will appear to you more eligible.

> Wherein lies Happiness? In that which becks
> Our ready Minds to fellowship divine;
> A fellowship with essence, till we shine
> Full alchymized and free of space. Behold
> The clear Religion of heaven—fold etc.[1]

You must indulge me by putting this in for setting aside the badness of the other. Such a preface is necessary to the Subject. The whole thing must, I think, have appeared to you, who are a consequitive Man, as a thing almost of mere words, but I assure you that when I wrote it, it was a regular stepping of the Imagination towards a Truth. My having written that Argument will perhaps be of the greatest Service to me of anything I ever did. It set before me at once the gradations of Happiness even like a kind of Pleasure Thermometer, and is my first Step towards the chief Attempt in the Drama, the playing of different Natures with Joy and Sorrow.

Do me this favor and believe Me,

Your sincere friend
John Keats

I hope your next Work will be of a more general Interest. I suppose you
cogitate a little about it now and then.

1. *Endymion*, I.777–781.

To J. H. Reynolds
3 FEBRUARY 1818

Hampstead Tuesday

My dear Reynolds,

I thank you for your dish of Filberts—Would I could get a basket of
them by way of dessert every day for the sum of two pence.[1] Would we
were a sort of ethereal Pigs and turn'd loose to feed upon spiritual Mast and
Acorns, which would be merely being a squirrel and feeding upon filberts,
for what is a squirrel but an airy pig, or a filbert but a sort of archangelical
acorn. About the nuts being worth cracking, all I can say is that where there
are a throng of delightful Images ready drawn, simplicity is the only thing.
The first is the best on account of the first line, and the "arrow—foil'd of its
antler'd food"[2]—and moreover (and this is the only word or two I find fault
with, the more because I have had so much reason to shun it as a quick-
sand), the last has "tender and true."[3] We must cut this, and not be
rattlesnaked into any more of the like. It may be said that we ought to read
our Contemporaries, that Wordsworth etc. should have their due from us,
but for the sake of a few fine imaginative or domestic passages, are we to be
bullied into a certain Philosophy engendered in the whims of an Egotist?
Every man has his speculations, but every man does not brood and peacock
over them till he makes a false coinage and deceives himself. Many a man
can travel to the very borne of Heaven and yet want confidence to put
down his half-seeing. Sancho will invent a Journey heavenward as well as
anybody. We hate poetry that has a palpable design upon us—and if we do

not agree, seems to put its hand in its breeches pocket. Poetry should be great and unobtrusive, a thing which enters into one's soul and does not startle it or amaze it with itself but with its subject. How beautiful are the retired flowers! How would they lose their beauty were they to throng into the highway crying out, "admire me I am a violet! Dote upon me I am a primrose!" Modern poets differ from the Elizabethans in this. Each of the moderns like an Elector of Hanover governs his petty state and knows how many straws are swept daily from the Causeways in all his dominions and has a continual itching that all the Housewives should have their coppers well scoured. The antients were Emperors of vast Provinces; they had only heard of the remote ones and scarcely cared to visit them. I will cut all this. I will have no more of Wordsworth or Hunt in particular. Why should we be of the tribe of Manasseh, when we can wander with Esau?[4] Why should we kick against the Pricks[5] when we can walk on Roses? Why should we be owls, when we can be Eagles? Why be teased with "nice-Eyed wagtails,"[6] when we have in sight "the Cherub Contemplation"?[7] Why with Wordsworth's "Matthew with a bough of wilding in his hand"[8] when we can have Jacques "under an oak etc."[9] The secret of the Bough of Wilding will run through your head faster than I can write it. Old Matthew spoke to him some years ago on some nothing, and because he happens in an Evening Walk to imagine the figure of the old man, he must stamp it down in black and white and it is henceforth sacred. I don't mean to deny Wordsworth's grandeur and Hunt's merit, but I mean to say we need not be teased with grandeur and merit when we can have them uncontaminated and unobtrusive. Let us have the old Poets, and robin Hood. Your letter and its sonnets gave me more pleasure than will the 4th Book of Childe Harold[10] and the whole of anybody's life and opinions. In return for your dish of filberts, I have gathered a few Catkins. I hope they'll look pretty.

> To J.H.R. In answer to his Robin Hood Sonnets.
> "No those days are gone away etc."—   See Coll: p. 58[11]

I hope you will like them; they are at least written in the Spirit of Outlawry. Here are the Mermaid lines

> "Souls of Poets dead and gone, etc."—   ib. p. 61.

I will call on you at 4 tomorrow, and we will trudge together, for it is not the thing to be a stranger in the Land of Harpsicols.[12] I hope also to bring you my 2nd book.[13] In the hope that these Scribblings will be some amusement for you this Evening, I remain copying on the Hill

Your sincere friend and Co-scribbler
John Keats

1. Two sonnets by Reynolds on Robin Hood, sent to Keats by the twopenny post.
2. Sonnet 1, line 5.
3. Sonnet 2, line 8.
4. Keats refers to Genesis and to Judges vi.15, vii.23, etc.
5. Acts ix.5, xxvi.14.
6. Hunt, *Foliage* (1818), p. xxxiii.
7. Milton, "Il Penseroso," line 54.
8. Wordsworth, "The Two April Mornings," lines 59f.
9. *As You Like It,* II.i.31.
10. Byron's fourth canto was published in April 1818.
11. The copyist set down only the first lines of these two poems by Keats.
12. Archaic form of "harpsichord."
13. Of *Endymion.*

To George and Tom Keats
14 (?) FEBRUARY 1818

Hampstead, Saturday Night

My dear Brothers,

When once a man delays a letter beyond the proper time, he delays it longer for one or two reasons; first because he must begin in a very commonplace style, that is to say, with an excuse; and secondly, things and circumstances become so jumbled in his mind, that he knows not what, or what not, he has said in his last. I shall visit you as soon as I have copied my poem all out. I am now much beforehand with the printer; they have done none yet and I am half afraid they will let half the season by before the printing. I am determined they shall not trouble me when I have copied it all. Horace Smith has lent me his manuscript, called "Nehemiah Muggs, an exposure of the Methodists"; perhaps I may send you a few extracts. Hazlitt's last Lecture was on Thompson,[1] Cowper and Crabbe. He praised Cowper and Thompson, but he gave Crabbe an unmerciful licking. I think Hunt's article of Fazio, no it was not, but I saw Fazio the first night;[2] it hung rather heavily on me. I am in the high way of being introduced to a squad of people, Peter Pindar, Mrs. Opie,[3] Mrs. Scott.[4] Mr. Robinson,[5] a great friend of Coleridge's, called on me. Richards tells me that my Poems are known in the west country and that he saw a very clever copy of verses, headed with a Motto from my Sonnet to George. Honors rush so thickly upon me that I shall not be able to bear up against them. What think you, am I to be crowned in the Capitol, am I to be made a Mandarin? No! I am to be invited, Mrs. Hunt tells me, to a party at Ollier's to keep Shakespeare's birthday. Shakespeare would stare to see me there. The Wednesday before last Shelley, Hunt and I wrote each a Sonnet on the River Nile. Some day you shall read them all. I saw a sheet of Endymion and have all reason to suppose they will soon get it done. There shall be nothing wanting on my part. I have been writing at intervals many songs and Sonnets and I long to be at Teignmouth to read them over to you: however, I think I had better wait till this Book is off my mind. It will not be long first.

Reynolds has been writing two very capital articles in the Yellow Dwarf on popular Preachers. All the talk here is about Dr. Croft, the Duke of Devon, etc.[6]

Your most affectionate Brother
(signed) John

(The following Extracts from Horace Smith's Manuscript are on a loose
   sheet enclosed in the previous letter of date Hampstead, February 16th)[7]

Poem. Nehemiah Muggs: An Exposure of the Methodists

> Muggs had long wished to be a father
> And told his wish without succeeding

At length Rose brought him two together
And there I think she show'd her breeding.

Behold them in the Holy place
With others all agog for Grace
Where a perspiring preacher vexes
Sundry old women of both sexes

Thumping as though his zeal were pushing
To make a convert of the cushion.

But in their hurry to proceed
Each reached the door at the same minute
Where as they scuffled for the lead
Both struggling stuck together in it

Shouting rampant amorous hymns
Under pretext of singing Psalms.

He shudder'd and withdrew his eye
Perk'd up his head some inches higher
Drew his chair nearer to the fire
And hummed as if he would have said
Pooh! Nonsense! Damme! Who's afraid
Or sought by bustling up his frame
To make his courage do the same
Thus would some blushing trembling Elves
Conceal their terrors from themselves
By their own cheering wax the bolder
And pat themselves upon the shoulder.

A Saint's a sort of human Mill
That labours when the body's still
And gathers grist with inward groans
And creaking melancholy moans
By waving heavenward o'er his head
His arms and working them for bread.

Is it that addled brains perchance
When the skull's dark with ignorance
Like rotten eggs surveyed at night
Emit a temporary light?
Or is it that a heated brain
When it is rubbed against the grain,
Like a Cat's back though black as charcoal
Will in the gloom appear to sparkle?

New Missions sent
To make the Antipodes relent
Turn the Anthropophagetic race
To sucking lambs and babes of grace
Or tempt the hairy Hebrew rogues
To cut their beards and Synagogues.

This grave advertisement was seen
"Wanted a serious Shopman, who
To Gospel principles is true
Whose voice for Hymns is not too gruff
Who can grind brick dust, mix up snuff
And has an undisputed Nack in
Fearing the Lord and making Blacking.

(The above in all probability is published but they are copied to show
    John Keats's Choice in the selection of Extracts).

1. James Thomson (1700–1748), author of *The Seasons*.
2. *Fazio* by Henry Hart Milman (1791–1868) was presented at Covent Garden on 5 February.
3. Amelia Opie (1769–1853), novelist and poet.
4. Caroline Colnaghi (Mrs. John) Scott, who admired Keats's work as early as July 1817.
5. Henry Crabb Robinson (1775–1867), diarist, who fails to mention the visit in his published or unpublished journals.
6. Sir Richard Croft (1762–1818) had just shot himself after being accused of negligence over the death of Princess Charlotte in childbirth. His suicide revived the old

rumor that he had connived at an exchange of infants in the duke of Devonshire's
family.
7. This caption and the lines that follow it are in the hand of John Jeffrey, the second
husband of Georgiana Wylie Keats.

To J. H. Reynolds
19 FEBRUARY 1818

My dear Reynolds,

I have an idea that a Man might pass a very pleasant life in this manner:
let him on any certain day read a certain Page of full Poesy or distilled Prose
and let him wander with it, and muse upon it, and reflect from it, and
bring home to it, and prophesy upon it, and dream upon it until it becomes stale. But when will it do so? Never. When Man has arrived at a certain ripeness in intellect, any one grand and spiritual passage serves him as a
starting post towards all "the two-and-thirty Palaces." How happy is such
a "voyage of conception," what delicious diligent Indolence! A doze upon a
Sofa does not hinder it, and a nap upon Clover engenders ethereal finger-
pointings. The prattle of a child gives it wings, and the converse of middle
age a strength to beat them. A strain of musick conducts to "an odd angle
of the Isle,"[1] and when the leaves whisper it puts a "girdle round the earth."[2]
Nor will this sparing touch of noble Books be any irreverence to their
Writers, for perhaps the honors paid by Man to Man are trifles in comparison to the Benefit done by great Works to the "Spirit and pulse of good"[3]
by their mere passive existence. Memory should not be called knowledge.
Many have original Minds who do not think it; they are led away by Custom. Now it appears to me that almost any Man may like the Spider spin
from his own inwards his own airy Citadel. The points of leaves and twigs
on which the Spider begins her work are few and she fills the Air with a
beautiful circuiting. Man should be content with as few points to tip with
the fine Webb of his Soul and weave a tapestry empyrean, full of Symbols
for his spiritual eye, of softness for his spiritual touch, of space for his wan-

dering, of distinctness for his Luxury. But the Minds of Mortals are so different and bent on such diverse Journeys that it may at first appear impossible for any common taste and fellowship to exist between two or three under these suppositions. It is, however, quite the contrary. Minds would leave each other in contrary directions, traverse each other in Numberless points, and at last greet each other at the Journey's end. An old Man and a child would talk together and the old Man be led on his Path, and the child left thinking. Man should not dispute or assert, but whisper results to his neighbour, and thus by every germ of Spirit sucking the Sap from mould ethereal, every human might become great, and Humanity, instead of being a wide heath of Furse and Briars with here and there a remote Oak or Pine, would become a grand democracy of Forest Trees. It has been an old Comparison for our urging on—the Bee hive—however, it seems to me that we should rather be the flower than the Bee, for it is a false notion that more is gained by receiving than giving. No, the receiver and the giver are equal in their benefits. The flower, I doubt not, receives a fair guerdon from the Bee. Its leaves blush deeper in the next spring, and who shall say between Man and Woman which is the most delighted? Now it is more noble to sit like Jove than to fly like Mercury. Let us not therefore go hurrying about and collecting honey-bee like, buzzing here and there impatiently from a knowledge of what is to be arrived at; but let us open our leaves like a flower and be passive and receptive, budding patiently under the eye of Apollo and taking hints from every noble insect that favors us with a visit. Sap will be given us for Meat and dew for drink. I was led into these thoughts, my dear Reynolds, by the beauty of the morning operating on a sense of Idleness. I have not read any Books. The Morning said I was right. I had no Idea but of the Morning, and the Thrush said I was right, seeming to say:

> "O thou whose face hath felt the Winter's wind,
> Whose eye has seen the Snow clouds hung in Mist
> And the black-elm tops 'mong the freezing Stars;
> To thee the Spring will be a harvest-time.
> O thou whose only book has been the light
> Of supreme darkness which thou feddest on

Night after night, when Phoebus was away;
To thee the Spring shall be a triple[4] morn.
O fret not after knowledge—I have none
And yet my song comes native with the warmth.
O fret not after knowledge—I have none
And yet the Evening listens. He who saddens
At thought of Idleness cannot be idle,
And he's awake who thinks himself asleep."

Now I am sensible all this is a mere sophistication—however it may neighbour to any truths—to excuse my own indolence. So I will not deceive myself that Man should be equal with Jove, but think himself very well off as a sort of scullion-Mercury or even a humble Bee. It is no matter whether I am right or wrong, either one way or another, if there is sufficient to lift a little time from your Shoulders.

Your affectionate friend
John Keats—

1. *The Tempest,* I.ii.223.
2. *A Midsummer Night's Dream,* II.i.175.
3. Wordsworth, "The Old Cumberland Beggar," line 77.
4. Spelled "tripple."

To George and Tom Keats
21 FEBRUARY 1818

Hampstead, Saturday—

My dear Brothers,

I am extremely sorry to have given you so much uneasiness by not writing; however, you know good news is no news, or vice versa. I do not like to write a short Letter to you or you would have had one long before. The Weather although boisterous today has been very much milder and I think

Devonshire is not the last place to receive a temperate change. The occasion of my writing today is the enclosed Letter by the Post Mark from Miss Wylie.[1] Does she expect you in town, George? I have been abominably idle since you left, but have just turned over a new leaf and used as a marker a Letter of excuse to an invitation from Horace Smith. I received a Letter from Haydon the other day in which he says his essays on the elgin Marbles are being translated into italian, the which he superintends. I did not mention that I had seen the British Gallery. There are some nice things by Stark and Bathsheba by Wilkie which is condemned. I could not bear Leslie's Uriel.[2] Reynolds has been very ill for some time—confined to the house—and had Leeches applied to the chest. When I saw him on Wednesday he was much the same and he is in the worst place in the world for amendment—among the strife of women's tongues in a hot and parch'd room. I wish he would move to Butler's[3] for a short time. The Thrushes and Blackbirds have been singing me into an idea that it was spring, and almost that Leaves were on the trees, so that black clouds and boisterous winds seem to have muster'd and collected to full Divan for the purpose of convincing me to the contrary. I have not been to Edmonton all this While, and there is not a day but Le Mesurier's image reproaches me for it. And I suppose the Haughtons think us dead.[4] I will shortly go and set matters to rights thereabouts. Taylor says my Poem shall be out in a Month. I think he'll be out before it. The Thrushes are singing now, as if they would speak to the Winds because their big brother Jack, the spring, wasn't far off. I am reading Voltaire and Gibbon, although I wrote to Reynolds the other day to prove reading of no use. I have not seen Hunt since. I am a good deal with Dilke and Brown; we are very thick. They are very kind to me; they are well. I don't think I could stop in Hampstead but for their neighborhood. I hear Hazlitt's Lectures regularly. His last was on Grey, Collins, Young, etc. and he gave a very fine piece of discriminating criticism on Swift, Voltaire, and Rabelais. I was very disappointed at his treatment of Chatterton. I generally meet with many I know there. Lord Byron's 4th Canto[5] is expected out, and I heard somewhere that Walter Scott has a new Poem in readiness. I am sorry that Wordsworth has left a bad impression wherever he visited in Town—by his egotism, Vanity and bigotry—yet he is a great Poet if not a Philosopher. I have not yet read Shelley's poem.[6] I don't suppose you have it at the Teignmouth Libraries. These double Letters must come rather heavy. I hope you have a moderate portion of Cash, but don't fret at all if you have not. Lord, I intend to play at cut and run as well as Falstaff, that is to say before he got so lusty. I have not time for chequer work this Letter for I should like to be sure of the 4 o'Clock Post. So I remain praying for your health, my dear Brothers, your affectionate Brother

John—

1. Georgiana Wylie, afterwards George's wife.
2. Keats knew Charles Robert Leslie (1794–1859) and confused him with his teacher Washington Allston (1779–1843).
3. Charles Butler entered Guy's Hospital as a student a day before Keats (30 September 1815), and passed the examination at Apothecaries' Hall along with him on 25 July 1816.
4. According to Gittings, Le Mesurier was a close neighbor of Keats's grandmother in Church Street, Edmonton. The Haughtons have not been identified.
5. Of *Childe Harold.*
6. *Laon and Cythna.*

To John Taylor

27 FEBRUARY 1818

Hampstead, 27 Feb.

My dear Taylor,

Your alteration strikes me as being a great improvement; the page looks much better. And now I will attend to the Punctuations you speak of. The comma should be at *soberly,* and in the other passage the comma should follow *quiet.*[1] I am extremely indebted to you for this attention and also for your after admonitions. It is a sorry thing for me that anyone should have to overcome Prejudices in reading my Verses—that affects me more than any hypercriticism on any particular Passage. In *Endymion* I have most likely but moved into the Go-cart from the leading strings. In Poetry I have a few Axioms, and you will see how far I am from their Centre. First, I think Poetry should surprise by a fine excess and not by Singularity; it should strike the Reader as a wording of his own highest thoughts, and appear almost a Remembrance. Second, its touches of Beauty should never be half way, thereby making the reader breathless instead of content. The rise, the progress, the setting of imagery should like the Sun come natural to him, shine over him and set soberly, although in magnificence, leaving him in the Luxury of twilight. But it is easier to think what Poetry should be than to write it, and this leads me on to another axiom. That if Poetry comes not as naturally as the Leaves to a tree it had better not come at all. However it may be with me I cannot help looking into new countries with "O for a Muse of fire to ascend!"[2] If Endymion serves me as a Pioneer, perhaps I ought to be content. I have great reason to be content, for thank God I can read and perhaps understand Shakespeare to his depths and I have, I am sure, many friends who if I fail will attribute any change in my Life and Temper to Humbleness rather than to Pride, to a cowering under the Wings of great Poets rather than to a Bitterness that I am not appreciated. I am anxious to get Endymion printed that I may forget it and proceed. I have copied the 3rd Book and have begun the 4th. On running my Eye over the Proofs, I saw one Mistake. I will notice it presently and also any others if there be any. There should be no comma in "the raft branch down sweeping from a tall Ash top."[3] I have besides made one or two alterations and also altered the 13th Line, Page 32, to make sense of it as you will see. I will take care the Printer shall not trip up my Heels. There should be no dash after Dryope in the Line, "Dryope's lone lulling of her Child."[4] Remember me to Percy Street.

Your sincere and obliged friend

John Keats—

P.S. You shall have a short *Preface* in good time.

1. *Endymion,* I.149 and 247.
2. *Henry V,* Prologue, line 1.
3. *Endymion,* I.334f.
4. *Endymion,* I.495.

To Benjamin Bailey
13 MARCH 1818

Teignmouth, Friday

My dear Bailey,

When a poor devil is drowning, it is said he comes thrice to the surface
ere he makes his final sink. If, however, even at the third rise, he can manage to catch hold of a piece of weed or rock, he stands a fair chance, as I
hope I do now, of being saved. I have sunk twice in our Correspondence,
have risen twice and been too idle, or something worse, to extricate myself.
I have sunk the third time and just now risen again at this two of the Clock
P.M. and saved myself from utter perdition by beginning this, all drench'd as
I am and fresh from the Water. And I would rather endure the present
inconvenience of a Wet Jacket than you should keep a laced one in store for
me. Why did I not stop at Oxford in my Way? How can you ask such a
Question? Why did I not promise to do so? Did I not in a Letter to you
make a promise to do so? Then how can you be so unreasonable as to ask
me why I did not? This is the thing (for I have been rubbing up my invention, trying several sleights): I first polish'd a cold, felt it in my fingers, tried
it on the table, but could not pocket it. I tried Chilblains, Rheumatism,
Gout, tight Boots, nothing of that sort would do, so this is, as I was going
to say, the thing. I had a Letter from Tom saying how much better he had
got, and thinking he had better stop, I went down to prevent his coming
up. Will not this do? Turn it which way you like, it is selvaged all round. I
have used it these three last days to keep out the abominable Devonshire
Weather. By the by, you may say what you will of devonshire, the truth
is it is a splashy, rainy, misty snowy, foggy, haily floody, muddy, slipshod
County. The hills are very beautiful, when you get a sight of 'em. The
Primroses are out, but then you are in. The Cliffs are of a fine deep Colour,
but then the Clouds are continually vying with them. The Women like

your London People in a sort of negative way because the native men are the poorest creatures in England because Government never have thought it worthwhile to send a recruiting party among them. When I think of Wordsworth's Sonnet "Vanguard of Liberty! Ye Men of Kent!", the degenerated race about me are Pulvis Ipecac. Simplex[1] a strong dose. Were I a Corsair I'd make a descent on the South Coast of Devon, if I did not run the chance of having Cowardice imputed to me. As for the Men, they'd run away into the methodist meeting houses, and the Women would be glad of it. Had England been a large devonshire we should not have won the Battle of Waterloo. There are knotted oaks, there are lusty rivulets, there are Meadows such as are not, there are valleys of femminine Climate, but there are no thews and Sinews. Moor's Almanack is here a curiosity. Arms, Neck and shoulders may at least be seen there, and The Ladies read it as some out of the way romance. Such a quelling Power have these thoughts over me, that I fancy the very Air of a deteriorating quality. I fancy the flowers, all precocious, have an Acrasian[2] spell about them. I feel able to beat off the devonshire waves like soap froth. I think it well for the honor of Britain that Julius Caesar did not first land in this County. A Devonshirer standing on his native hills is not a distinct object. He does not show against the light. A wolf or two would dispossess him. I like, I love England; I like its strong Men. Give me a "long brown plain" for my Morning so I may meet with some of Edmond Iron side's descendants. Give me a barren mould so I may meet with some shadowing of Alfred in the shape of a Gipsy, a Huntsman or a Shepherd. Scenery is fine, but human nature is finer. The Sward is richer for the tread of a real, nervous, english foot. The eagle's nest is finer for the Mountaineer has look'd into it. Are these facts or prejudices? Whatever they are, for them I shall never be able to relish entirely any devonshire scenery. Homer is very fine, Achilles is fine, Diomed is fine, Shakespeare is fine, Hamlet is fine, Lear is fine, but dwindled englishmen are not fine. Where too the Women are so passable, and have such english names, such as Ophelia, Cordelia, etc., that they should have such Paramours or rather Imparamours. As for them I cannot in thought help wishing as did the cruel Emperor, that they had but one head and I might cut it off to deliver them from any horrible Courtesy they may do their undeserving Countrymen. I wonder I meet with no born Monsters. O, Devonshire, last night I thought the Moon had dwindled in heaven.

I have never had your Sermon from Wordsworth, but Mrs. Dilke lent it me. You know my ideas about Religion. I do not think myself more in the right than other people and that nothing in this world is proveable. I wish I could enter into all your feelings on the subject merely for one short 10 Minutes and give you a Page or two to your liking. I am sometimes so very sceptical as to think Poetry itself a mere Jack-a-lantern to amuse whoever may chance to be struck with its brilliance. As Tradesmen say, everything is worth what it will fetch, so probably every mental pursuit takes its reality and worth from the ardour of the pursuer—being in itself a nothing. Ethereal things may at least be thus real, divided under three heads: Things real, things semi-real, and no things. Things real—such as existences of Sun, Moon and Stars and passages of Shakespeare—Things semi-real, such as Love, the Clouds, etc., which require a greeting of the Spirit to make them wholly exist, and Nothings, which are made Great and dignified by an ardent pursuit, which by the by stamps the burgundy mark on the bottles of our Minds, insomuch as they are able to *"consecrate whate'er they look upon."* I have written a Sonnet here of a somewhat collateral nature, so don't imagine it an apropos des bottes:

> Four Seasons fill the Measure of the year;
> > Four Seasons are there in the mind of Man.
> He hath his lusty spring when fancy clear
> > Takes in all beauty with an easy span:
> He hath his Summer, when luxuriously
> > He chews the honied cud of fair spring thoughts,
> Till, in his Soul dissolv'd they come to be
> > Part of himself. He hath his Autumn ports
> And Havens of repose, when his tired wings
> > Are folded up, and he content to look
> On Mists in idleness; to let fair things
> > Pass by unheeded as a threshold brook.
> > > He hath his Winter too of pale Misfeature,
> > > Or else he would forget his mortal nature.

Aye, this may be carried, but what am I talking of? It is an old maxim of mine and of course must be well known that every point of thought is the centre of an intellectual world. The two uppermost thoughts in a Man's mind are the two poles of his World. He revolves on them and everything is southward or northward to him through their means. We take but three steps from feathers to iron. Now, my dear fellow, I must once for all tell you I have not one Idea of the truth of any of my speculations. I shall never be a Reasoner because I care not to be in the right, when retired from bickering and in a proper philosophical temper. So you must not stare if in any future letter I endeavour to prove that Apollo as he had a cat gut string to his Lyre used a cat's paw as a Pecten, and further from said Pecten's reiterated and continual teasing came the term Hen-peck'd. My Brother Tom desires to be remember'd to you. He has just this moment had a spitting of blood, poor fellow. Remember me to Gleig and Whitehead.

Your affectionate friend

John Keats—

1. "Pure powder of Ipecac." The period after "Ipecac" indicates an abbreviation of the word *Ipecacuanha,* a South American plant that works as an emetic. In effect, Keats is saying that the degenerated race around him makes him want to throw up vigorously.
2. Disordered. For Acrasia, see *The Faerie Queen,* II.i.51–55, xii.69, III.i.2.

To J. H. Reynolds
14 MARCH 1818

Teignmouth, Saturday

Dear Reynolds,

I escaped being blown over and blown under and trees and houses being toppled on me.[1] I have since, hearing of Brown's accident, had an aversion to a dose of parapet and being also a lover of antiquities, I would sooner have a harmless piece of herculaneum sent me quietly as a present, than ever so modern a chimney pot tumbled onto my head. Being agog to see some Devonshire, I would have taken a walk the first day, but the rain would not let me; and the second, but the rain would not let me; and the third; but the rain forbade it; Ditto 4; ditto 5; ditto. So I made up my Mind to stop in doors and catch a sight flying between the showers; and behold I saw a pretty valley—pretty cliffs, pretty Brooks, pretty Meadows, pretty trees, both standing as they were created, and blown down as they are uncreated. The green is beautiful, as they say, and pity it is that it is amphibious. Mais! But alas! The flowers here wait as naturally for the rain twice a day as the Mussels[2] do for the Tide. So we look upon a brook in these parts as you look upon a dash in your Country. There must be something to support this, aye fog, hail, snow, rain—Mist—blanketing up three parts of the year. This devonshire is like Lydia Languish,[3] very entertaining when at smiles, but cursedly subject to sympathetic moisture. You have the sensation of walking under one great Lamplighter and you can't go on the other side of the ladder to keep your frock clean, and cosset your superstition. Buy a girdle, put a pebble in your Mouth, loosen your Braces, for I am going among Scenery whence I intend to tip you the Damosel Radcliffe.[4] I'll cavern you, and grotto you, and waterfall you, and wood you, and water you, and immense-rock you, and tremendous sound you, and solitude you. I'll make a lodgment on your glacis by a row of Pines, and storm your covered way with bramble Bushes. I'll have at you with hip and haw smallshot, and cannonade you with Shingles. I'll be witty upon salt fish and impede your cavalry with clotted cream. But, ah Coward! to talk at this rate to a sick man, or I hope to one that was sick, for I hope by this you stand on your right foot. If you are not, that's all. I intend to cut all sick people if they do not make up their minds to cut sickness. A fellow to whom I have a complete aversion, and who strange to say is harboured and countenanced in several houses where I visit—he is sitting now quite impudent between me and Tom. He insults me at poor Jem Rice's and you have seated him before now between us at the Theatre, where I thought he look'd with a longing eye at poor Kean. I shall say, once for all, to my friends generally and severally, cut that fellow, or I cut you. I went to the

Theatre here the other night, which I forgot to tell George, and got insulted, which I ought to remember to forget to tell any Body; for I did not fight, and as yet have had no redress. "Lie thou there, sweetheart!" I wrote to Bailey yesterday, obliged to speak in a high way, and a damme who's afraid, for I had owed him so long; however, he shall see I will be better in future. Is he in Town yet? I have directed to Oxford as the better chance. I have copied my fourth Book[5] and shall write the preface soon. I wish it was all done, for I want to forget it and make my mind free for something new. Atkins the Coachman, Bartlet the Surgeon, Simmons the Barber, and the Girls over at the Bonnet shop say we shall now have a Month of seasonable Weather: warm, witty, and full of invention. Write to me and tell me you are well or thereabouts, or by the holy Beaucoeur, which I suppose is the virgin Mary, or the repented Magdalen (beautiful name, that Magdalen), I'll take to my Wings and fly away to anywhere but old or Nova Scotia. I wish I had a little innocent bit of Metaphysic in my head, to criss-cross this letter: but you know a favorite tune is hardest to be remembered when one wants it most and you, I know, have long ere this taken it for granted that I never have any speculations without associating you in them, where they are of a pleasant nature and you know enough of me to tell the places where I haunt most, so that if you think for five minutes after having read this you will find it a long letter and see written in the Air above you,

Your most affectionate friend

John Keats

Remember me to all. Tom's remembrances to you.

1. He refers to the terrific storm of 4 March and his trip to Exeter.
2. Keats spelled this word "muscles."
3. The sentimental heroine of Sheridan's play *The Rivals*.
4. A reference to Ann Radcliffe (1764–1823), whose gothic novels he then parodies.
5. Of *Endymion*.

To James Rice

24 MARCH 1818

Teignmouth, Tuesday

My dear Rice,

Being in the midst of your favorite Devon, I should not by rights pen one word but it should contain a vast portion of Wit, Wisdom, and learning, for I have heard that Milton ere he wrote his Answer to Salmasius[1] came into these parts and for one whole Month rolled himself for three whole hours in a certain meadow hard by us, where the mark of his nose at equidistances is still shown. The exhibitor of said Meadow further saith that after these rollings not a nettle sprang up in all the seven acres for seven years and that from said time a new sort of plant was made from the white thorn, of a thornless nature very much used by the Bucks of the present day to rap their Boots withall. This account made me very naturally suppose that the nettles and thorns etherealized by the Scholar's rotatory motion and garner'd in his head, thence flew after a new fermentation against the luckless Salmasius and occasioned his well known and unhappy end. What a happy thing it would be if we could settle our thoughts, make our minds up on any matter in five Minutes and remain content; that is, to build a sort of mental Cottage of feelings quiet and pleasant, to have a sort of Philosophical Back Garden and cheerful holiday-keeping front one. But Alas! this never can be, for as the material Cottager knows there are such places as france and Italy and the Andes and the Burning Mountains, so the spiritual Cottager has knowledge of the terra semi-incognita of things unearthly and cannot for his Life keep in the check rein—Or I should stop here quiet and comfortable in my theory of Nettles. You will see, however, I am obliged to run wild, being attracted by the Loadstone Concatenation. No sooner had I settled the knotty point of Salmasius than the Devil put this whim into my head in the likeness of one of Pythagora's questionings:

"Did Milton do more good or harm to the world?" He wrote, let me inform you (for I have it from a friend, who had it of ——), he wrote Lycidas, Comus, Paradise Lost and other Poems, with much delectable prose. He was, moreover, an active friend to Man all his Life and has been since his death. Very good, but my dear fellow I must let you know that as there is ever the same quantity of matter constituting this habitable globe, as the ocean notwithstanding the enormous changes and revolutions taking place in some or other of its demesnes, notwithstanding Waterspouts, whirlpools and mighty Rivers emptying themselves into it, it still is made up of the same bulk nor ever varies the number of its Atoms. And as a certain bulk of Water was instituted at the Creation, so very likely a certain portion of intellect was spun forth into the thin Air for the Brains of Man to prey upon it. You will see my drift without any unnecessary parenthesis. That which is contained in the Pacific can't lie in the hollow of the Caspian; that which was in Milton's head could not find Room in Charles the second's. He like a Moon attracted Intellect to its flow. It has not ebbed yet, but has left the shore pebble all bare, I mean all Bucks, Authors of Hengist[2] and Castlereaghs of the present day who without Milton's gormandizing might have been all wise Men. Now, for as much as I was very predisposed to a Country I had heard you speak so highly of, I took particular notice of everything during my journey and have bought some folio asses skin for Memorandums. I have seen everything but the wind and that, they say, becomes visible by taking a dose of Acorns or sleeping one night in a hog trough with your tail to the Sow Sow west. Some of the little Barmaids look'd at me as if I knew Jem Rice, but when I took a glass of Brandy they were quite convinced. One asked whether you preserved a secret she gave you on the nail; another how many buttons of your Coat were buttoned in general. I told her it used to be four, but since you had become acquainted with one Martin, you had reduced it to three and had been turning this third one in your Mind and would do so with finger and thumb, only you had taken to snuff. I have met with a Brace or twain of little Long heads— not a bit o' the german—all in the neatest little dresses, and avoiding all the puddles, but very fond of peppermint drops, laming ducks, and seeing little Girls' affairs. Well I can't tell! I hope you are showing poor Reynolds the way to get well. Send me a good account of him and if I can I'll send you one of Tom. Oh! for a day and all well! I went yesterday to dawlish fair

> Over the hill and over the dale,
> And over the bourn to Dawlish,
> Where Gingerbread Wives have a scanty sale
> And gingerbred nuts are smallish.
>
> Rantipole Betty she ran down a hill
> And kick'd up her petticoats fairly
> Says I, I'll be Jack if you will be Gill,
> So she sat on the Grass debonairly.
>
> Here's somebody coming, here's somebody coming!
> Says I, 'tis the Wind at a parley
> So without any fuss, any hawing and humming
> She lay on the grass debonairly.
>
> Here's somebody here and here's somebody *there!*
> Say's I, hold your tongue you young Gypsy.
> So she held her tongue and lay plump and fair
> And dead as a Venus tipsy.
>
> O who wouldn't hie to Dawlish fair
> O who wouldn't stop in a Meadow,
> O would not rumple the daisies there
> And make the wild fern for a bed do.

Tom's Remembrances and mine to all.

Your sincere friend
John Keats

---

1. Claudius Salmasius (1588–1653) attacked the Commonwealth at the request of the exiled Charles II. Milton demolished him in *Pro Populo Anglicano Defensio* (1651).
2. Charles Bucke (1781–1846), minor dramatist. *Hengist, Or The Fifth Century, An Historical Melodrama* (1816) was an anonymous play.

To J. H. Reynolds

25 MARCH 1818

Dear Reynolds, as last night I lay in bed,
There came before my eyes that wonted thread
Of Shapes, and Shadows and Remembrances,
That every other minute vex and please:
Things all disjointed come from North and south,
Two witch's eyes above a cherub's mouth,
Voltaire with casque and shield and Habergeon,
And Alexander with his night-cap on—
Old Socrates a-tying his cravat;
And Hazlitt playing with Miss Edgworth's cat;
And Junius Brutus[1] pretty well so-so,
Making the best of 's way towards Soho.

    Few are there who escape these visitings—
Perhaps one or two, whose lives have pat[i]ent wings;
And through whose curtains peeps no hellish nose,
No wild boar tusks, and no Mermaid's toes:
But flowers bursting out with lusty pride;
And young Eolian harps personified,
Some, Titian colours touch'd into real life—
The sacrifice goes on; the pontiff knife
Gleams in the sun, the milk-white heifer lows,
The pipes go shrilly, the libation flows:
A white sail shows above the green-head cliff,
Moves round the point, and throws her anchor stiff.
The Mariners join hymn with those on land.
You know the Enchanted Castle,[2] it doth stand
Upon a Rock on the Border of a Lake

Nested in Trees, which all do seem to shake
From some old Magic like Urganda's[3] sword.
O Phoebus, that I had thy sacred word
To show this Castle in fair dreaming-wise
Unto my friend, while sick and ill he lies.
        You know it well enough, where it doth seem
A mossy place, a Merlin's Hall, a dream.
You know the clear lake, and the little Isles,
The Mountains blue, and cold near neighbour rills—
All which elsewhere are but half animate.
Here do they look alive to love and hate;
To smiles and frowns; they seem a lifted mound
Above some giant, pulsing underground.
        Part of the building was a chosen See
Built by a banish'd santon[4] of Chaldee:
The other part two thousand years from him
Was built by Cuthbert de Saint Aldebrim.
Then there's a little wing, far from the sun,
Built by a Lapland Witch turn'd maudlin nun—
And many other juts of aged stone
Founded with many a mason-devil's groan.
        The doors all look as if they oped themselves,
The windows as if latch'd by fays and elves;
And from them comes a silver flash of light,
As from the Westward of a summer's night;
Or like a beauteous woman's large blue eyes
Gone mad through olden songs and Poesies.
        See what is coming from the distance dim!
A golden galley all in silken trim!
Three rows of oars are lightening moment-whiles
Into the verdurous bosoms of those Isles.
Towards the shade under the Castle Wall
It comes in silence—now 'tis hidden all.
The clarion sounds; and from a postern grate

An echo of sweet music doth create
A fear in the poor herdsman who doth bring
His beasts to trouble the enchanted spring.
He tells of the sweet music and the spot
To all his friends, and they believe him not.
    O that our dreamings all of sleep or wake
Would all their colours from the sunset take,
From something of material sublime
Rather than shadow our own Soul's daytime
In the dark void of Night. For in the world
We jostle—but my flag is not unfurl'd
On the Admiral staff—and to philosophize
I dare not yet! Oh, never will the prize,
High reason, and the lore of good and ill
Be my award. Things cannot to the will
Be settled, but they tease us out of thought.
Or is it that Imagination brought
Beyond its proper bound, yet still confined—
Lost in a sort of Purgatory blind,
Cannot refer to any standard law
Of either earth or heaven?—It is a flaw
In happiness to see beyond our bourn—
It forces us in Summer skies to mourn:
It spoils the singing of the Nightingale.
    Dear Reynolds. I have a mysterious tale
And cannot speak it. The first page I read
Upon a Lampit Rock of green seaweed
Among the breakers—'Twas a quiet Eve;
The rocks were silent—the wide sea did weave
An untumultuous fringe of silver foam
Along the flat brown sand. I was at home,
And should have been most happy, but I saw
Too far into the sea where every maw
The greater on the less feeds evermore;

But I saw too distinct into the core
Of an eternal fierce destruction,
And so from Happiness I far was gone.
Still am I sick of it, and though today
I've gathered young spring-leaves, and flowers gay
Of Periwinkle and wild strawberry,
Still do I that most fierce destruction see,
The shark at savage prey—the hawk at pounce,
The gentle Robin, like a pard or ounce,
Ravening a worm. Away ye horrid moods,
Moods of one's mind![5] You know I hate them well,
You know I'd sooner be a clapping bell
To some Kamschatkan missionary church,
Than with these horrid moods be left in lurch.
Do you get health—and Tom the same—I'll dance,
And from detested moods in new Romance
Take refuge—Of bad lines a Centaine dose
Is sure enough—and so "here follows prose."[6]

My Dear Reynolds,

In hopes of cheering you through a Minute or two I was determined nill-he will-he to send you some lines, so you will excuse the unconnected subject and careless verse. You know, I am sure, Claude's Enchanted Castle and I wish you may be pleased with my remembrance of it. The Rain is Come on again. I think with me Devonshire stands a very poor chance. I shall damn it up hill and down dale if it keeps up to the average of 6 fine days in three weeks. Let me have better news of you.

Your affectionate friend
John Keats

Tom's Remembrances to you. Remb. us to all—

1. Junius Brutus Booth (1796–1852), actor. "So-so" is slang for drunk.
2. A painting by Claude, probably known to Keats through an engraving by Vivares and Woollett.

3. Urganda the Unknown, a leading character in the fifteenth-century romance *Amadis of Gaul*.
4. A kind of dervish or priest, regarded as a saint.
5. A subtitle used by Wordsworth in his *Poems in Two Volumes* (1807).
6. *Twelfth Night*, II.v.154.

To B. R. Haydon
8 APRIL 1818

Wednesday—

My dear Haydon,

I am glad you were pleased with my nonsense[1] and if it so happen that the humour takes me when I have set down to prose to you I will not gainsay it. I should be (god forgive me) ready to swear because I cannot make use of your assistance in going through Devon if I was not in my own Mind determined to visit it thoroughly at some more favorable time of the year. But now Tom (who is getting greatly better) is anxious to be in Town, therefore I put off my threading the County. I purpose within a Month to put my knapsack at my back and make a pedestrian tour through the North of England and part of Scotland, to make a sort of Prologue to the Life I intend to pursue; that is, to write, to study and to see all Europe at the lowest expense. I will clamber through the Clouds and exist. I will get such an accumulation of stupendous recollections that as I walk through the suburbs of London I may not see them. I will stand upon Mount Blanc and remember this coming Summer when I intend to straddle ben Lomond—with my Soul!—galligaskins are out of the Question. I am nearer myself to hear your Christ is being tinted into immortality. Believe me, Haydon, your picture is a part of myself. I have ever been too sensible of the labyrinthian path to eminence in Art (judging from Poetry) ever to think I understood the emphasis of Painting, the innumerable compositions and decompositions which take place between the intellect and its thousand materials before it arrives at that trembling delicate and snail-horn perception of Beauty. I know not your many havens of intenseness, nor ever can know them, but for this I hope nought you atchieve is lost upon me: for when a Schoolboy the abstract Idea I had of an heroic painting was what I cannot describe. I saw it somewhat sideways, large, prominent, round and colour'd with magnificence, somewhat like the feel I have of Anthony and Cleopatra. Or of Alcibiades, leaning on his Crimson Couch in his Galley, his broad shoulders imperceptibly heaving with the Sea. That passage in Shakespeare is finer than this:

"See how the surly Warwick mans the Wall"[2]

I like your consignment of Corneille. That's the humor of it. They shall be called your Posthumous Works. I don't understand your bit of Italian.[3] I hope she will awake from her dream and flourish fair. My respects to her. The Hedges by this time are beginning to leaf. Cats are becoming more vociferous. Young Ladies that wear Watches are always looking at them. Women about forty-five think the Season very backward. Lady's Mares have but half an allowance of food. It rains here again, has been doing so for three days, however as I told you I'll take a trial in June, July, or August next year.

I am afraid Wordsworth went rather huff'd out of Town. I am sorry for it. He cannot expect his fireside Divan to be infallible; he cannot expect but that every Man of worth is as proud as himself. O, that he had not fit with a Warrener,[4] that is din'd at Kingston's. I shall be in town in about a fortnight and then we will have a day or so now and then before I set out on my northern expedition. We will have no more abominable Rows, for they leave one in a fearful silence. Having settled the Methodists let us be rational—not upon compulsion—no, if it will out, let it, but I will not play the Bassoon any more deliberately. Remember me to Hazlitt and Bewick. Your affectionate friend

John Keats—

1. A previous letter, not included here, largely consisting of light verse.
2. *3 Henry VI*, V.i.17.

3. Haydon had described Mrs. John Scott "con occhi neri" (with black eyes).
4. *The Merry Wives of Windsor,* I.iv.28, "He hath fought with a warrener." Perhaps a
   dig at the set of John Warren, who published some volumes of verse by Reynolds
   and others.

To J. H. Reynolds
9 APRIL 1818

Thurs. Morn.

My dear Reynolds,

Since you all agree that the thing[1] is bad, it must be so, though I am not
aware there is anything like Hunt in it (and if there is, it is my natural way,
and I have something in common with Hunt). Look it over again and examine into the motives, the seeds from which any one sentence sprung. I
have not the slightest feel of humility towards the Public or to anything in
existence but the eternal Being, the Principle of Beauty and the Memory of
great Men. When I am writing for myself for the mere sake of the Moment's enjoyment perhaps nature has its course with me, but a Preface is
written to the Public, a thing I cannot help looking upon as an Enemy and
which I cannot address without feelings of Hostility. If I write a Preface in a
supple or subdued style, it will not be in character with me as a public
speaker. I would be subdued before my friends and thank them for subdu-
ing me, but among Multitudes of Men I have no feel of stooping. I hate the
idea of humility to them.

I never wrote one single Line of Poetry with the least Shadow of public
thought.

Forgive me for vexing you and making a Trojan Horse of such a Trifle,
both with respect to the matter in Question and myself, but it eases me to
tell you. I could not live without the love of my friends. I would jump
down Aetna for any great Public good, but I hate a Mawkish Popularity. I

cannot be subdued before them. My glory would be to daunt and dazzle the thousand jabberers about Pictures and Books. I see swarms of Porcupines with their Quills erect "like lime-twigs set to catch my Winged Book,"[2] and I would fright 'em away with a torch. You will say my preface is not much of a Torch. It would have been too insulting "to begin from Jove" and I could not set a golden head upon a thing of clay. If there is any fault in the preface it is not affectation, but an undersong of disrespect to the Public. If I write another preface it must be done without a thought of those people. I will think about it. If it should not reach you in four or five days, tell Taylor to publish it without a preface and let the dedication simply stand "inscribed to the memory of Thomas Chatterton." I had resolved last night to write to you this morning. I wish it had been about something else, something to greet you towards the close of your long illness. I have had one or two intimations of your going to Hampstead for a space; and I regret to see your confounded Rheumatism keeps you in Little Britain where I am sure the air is too confined. Devonshire continues rainy. As the drops beat against the window, they give me the same sensation as a quart of cold water offered to revive a half-drowned devil; no feel of the clouds dropping fatness, but as if the roots of the Earth were rotten, cold and drench'd. I have not been able to go to Kents Cave[3] at Babbicun, however on one very beautiful day I had a fine Clamber over the rocks all along as far as that place. I shall be in Town in about Ten days. We go by way of Bath on purpose to call on Bailey. I hope soon to be writing to you about the things of the north, purposing to wayfare all over those parts. I have settled my accoutrements in my own mind, and will go to gorge wonders. However, we'll have some days together before I set out.

I have many reasons for going wonder-ways: to make my winter chair free from spleen, to enlarge my vision, to escape disquisitions on Poetry and Kingston Criticism, to promote digestion and economise shoe leather. I'll have leather buttons and belt, and if Brown holds his mind, over the Hills we go. If my Books will help me to it, thus will I take all Europe in turn, and see the Kingdoms of the Earth and the glory of them. Tom is getting better; he hopes you may meet him at the top o' the hill. My Love to your nurses.[4] I am ever

Your affectionate Friend
John Keats

1. The original preface to *Endymion*.
2. *2 Henry VI*, III.iii.16, "Like lime-twigs set to catch my winged soul."
3. Kents Cavern in Babbacombe, Torquay, famous for the bones and flint implements it provided for the British Museum.
4. Reynolds's sisters.

To J. H. Reynolds
17 APRIL 1818

Friday

My dear Reynolds,

I am anxious you should find this Preface[1] tolerable. If there is an affectation in it, 'tis natural to me. Do let the Printer's Devil cook it and "let me be as the casing air."[2]

You are too good in this Matter. Were I in your state, I am certain I should have no thought but of discontent and illness. I might tho' be taught patience. I had an idea of giving no Preface; however, don't you think this had better go? O, let it. One should not be too timid of committing faults.

The Climate here weighs us down completely. Tom is quite low-spirited. It is impossible to live in a country which is continually under hatches. Who would live in the region of Mists, Game Laws, indemnity Bills, etc. when there is such a place as Italy? It is said this England from its Clime produces a Spleen able to engender the finest Sentiment, and covers the whole face of the Isle with Green.[3] So it aught, I'm sure. I should still like the Dedication simply, as I said in my last.

I wanted to send you a few songs written in your favorite Devon. It cannot be—Rain! Rain! Rain! I am going this morning to take a facsimile of a Letter of Nelson's, very much to his honor. You will be greatly pleased when you see it in about a Week. What a spite it is; one cannot get out. The little way I went yesterday I found a lane bank'd on each side with store of Primroses, while the earlier bushes are beginning to leaf.

I shall hear a good Account of you soon.

Your affectionate Friend
John Keats

My Love to all and remember me to Taylor.

1. It was published with *Endymion.*
2. *Macbeth,* III.iv.23.
3. A reference to Matthew Green (1696–1737), author of *The Spleen* (1737).

To John Taylor
24 APRIL 1818

Teignmouth, Friday
My dear Taylor,

I think I did very wrong to leave you to all the trouble of Endymion, but I could not help it then; another time I shall be more bent to all sort of troubles and disagreeables. Young Men for some time have an idea that such a thing as happiness is to be had and therefore are extremely impatient under any unpleasant restraining. In time, however, of such stuff is the world about them they know better and instead of striving from Uneasiness greet it as an habitual sensation, a pannier which is to weigh upon them through life.

And in proportion to my disgust at the task is my sense of your kindness and anxiety. The book[1] pleased me much; it is very free from faults, and although there are one or two words I should wish replaced, I see in many places an improvement greatly to the purpose.

I think those speeches which are related—those parts where the speaker repeats a speech, such as Glaucus' repetition of Circe's words—should have inverted commas to every line. In this there is a little confusion. If we divide the speeches into *identical* and *related,* and to the former put merely one inverted comma at the beginning and another at the end, and to the latter inverted commas before every line, the book will be better understood at the first glance. Look at pages 126 and 127: you will find in the 3rd line the beginning of a *related* speech marked thus: "Ah! art awake," while at the same time in the next page the continuation of the *identical speech* is mark'd in the same manner, "Young Man of Latmos." You will find on the other side all the parts which should have inverted commas to every line.

I was purposing to travel over the north this Summer. There is but one thing to prevent me: I know nothing, I have read nothing and I mean to follow Solomon's directions of "get Wisdom—get understanding."[2] I find cavalier days are gone by. I find that I can have no enjoyment in the World but continual drinking of Knowledge. I find there is no worthy pursuit but the idea of doing some good for the world: some do it with their society, some with their wit, some with their benevolence, some with a sort of power of conferring pleasure and good humour on all they meet and in a thousand ways all equally dutiful to the command of Great Nature. There is but one way for me; the road lies through application, study and thought. I will pursue it and to that end purpose retiring for some years. I have been hovering for some time between an exquisite sense of the luxurious and a love for Philosophy; were I calculated for the former I should be glad, but as I am not I shall turn all my soul to the latter. My Brother Tom is getting better and I hope I shall see both him and Reynolds well before I retire from the World. I shall see you soon and have some talk about what Books I shall take with me.

Your very sincere friend
John Keats

Remember me to Hessey, Woodhouse and Percy Street.

I cannot discover any other error. The preface is well without those things you have left out. Adieu.[3]

   1. An advance copy of *Endymion*.
   2. Proverbs iv.5.
   3. Keats adds this postscript to a list of errata and corrections which is omitted here.

❧

To J. H. Reynolds
27 APRIL 1818

Teignmouth, Monday

My dear Reynolds,

   It is an awful while since you have heard from me. I hope I may not be punished when I see you well, and so anxious as you always are for me, with the remembrance of my so seldom writing when you were so horribly confined. The most unhappy hours in our lives are those in which we recollect times past to our own blushing. If we are immortal that must be the Hell. If I must be immortal, I hope it will be after having taken a little of "that watery labyrinth"[1] in order to forget some of my schoolboy days and others since those.

   I have heard from George at different times how slowly you were recovering. It is a tedious thing, but all Medical Men will tell you how far a very gradual amendment is preferable; you will be strong after this, never fear. We are here still enveloped in clouds. I lay awake last night listening to the

Rain with a sense of being drown'd and rotted like a grain of wheat. There is a continual courtesy between the Heavens and the Earth. The heavens rain down their unwelcomeness, and the Earth sends it up again to be returned tomorrow. Tom has taken a fancy to a Physician here, Dr. Turton,[2] and I think is getting better; therefore I shall perhaps remain here some Months. I have written to George for some Books, shall learn Greek, and very likely Italian and in other ways prepare myself to ask Hazlitt in about a year's time the best metaphysical road I can take. For although I take poetry to be Chief, there is something else wanting to one who passes his life among Books and thoughts on Books. I long to feast upon old Homer as we have upon Shakespeare and as I have lately upon Milton. If you understood Greek, and would read me passages now and then explaining their meaning, 'twould be, from its mistiness, perhaps a greater luxury than reading the thing one's self. I shall be happy when I can do the same for you. I have written for my folio Shakespeare, in which there is the first few stanzas of my "Pot of Basil." I have the rest here finish'd and will copy the whole out fair shortly and George will bring it to you. The Compliment is paid by us to Boccace, whether we publish or not[3]: so there is content in this world. Mine is short. You must be deliberate about yours: you must not think of it till many months after you are quite well; then put your passion to it and I shall be bound up with you in the shadows of mind, as we are in our matters of human life. Perhaps a Stanza or two will not be too foreign to your Sickness:

> "Were they unhappy then? It cannot be:
> Too many tears, etc., etc.

2 stanzas[4]

> But for the general award of love, etc.

> She wept alone for Pleasures, etc., etc.

1 stanza

The 5th line ran thus: "What might have been too plainly did she see."
    I heard from Rice this morning—very witty—and have just written to

Bailey. Don't you think I am brushing up in the letter way? And being in for it, you shall hear again from me very shortly, if you will promise not to put hand to paper for me until you can do it with a tolerable ease of health, except it be a line or two. Give my Love to your Mother and Sisters. Remember me to the Butlers, not forgetting Sarah.

Your affectionate friend
John Keats

1. *Paradise Lost,* II.584f.
2. William Turton (1762–1835), M.B., conchologist, author of various medical and scientific books.
3. Keats and Reynolds had planned to issue jointly a volume containing poems based on Boccaccio.
4. See "Isabella," stanzas 12, 13 (which were given in full in the original letter).

To J. H. Reynolds
3 MAY 1818

Teignmouth, May 3rd

My dear Reynolds,

What I complain of is that I have been in so an uneasy a state of Mind as not to be fit to write to an invalid. I cannot write to any length under a disguised feeling. I should have loaded you with an addition of gloom, which I am sure you do not want. I am now, thank God, in a humour to give you a good groat's worth, for Tom after a Night without a Wink of sleep and overburdened with fever, has got up after a refreshing day sleep and is better than he has been for a long time; and you, I trust, have been again round the Common without any effect but refreshment. As to the Matter, I hope I can say with Sir Andrew "I have matter enough in my head"[1] in your favor. And now, in the second place, for I reckon that I have finished my Imprimis, I am glad you blow up the weather. All through your letter there is a leaning towards a climate-curse and you know what a delicate satisfaction there is in having a vexation anathematized: one would think there has been growing up for these last four thousand years a grandchild Scion of the old forbidden tree, and that some modern Eve had just violated it, and that there was come with double charge, "Notus and Afer black with thunderous clouds from Sierra-leona."[2] I shall breathe worsted stockings[3] sooner than I thought for Tom wants to be in Town. We will have some such days upon the heath like that of last summer and why not with the same book: or what say you to a black Letter Chaucer printed in 1596: aye, I've got one huzza! I shall have it bounden gothique, a nice sombre binding; it will go a little way to unmodernize. And also I see no reason, because I have been away this last month, why I should not have a peep at your Spencerian,[4] notwithstanding you speak of your office, in my thought a little too early, for I do not see why a Mind like yours is not capable of harbouring and digesting the whole Mystery of Law as easily as Parson Hugh does Pepin's, which did not hinder him from his poetic Canary. Were I to study physic or rather Medicine again, I feel it would not make the least difference in my Poetry. When the Mind is in its infancy a Bias is in reality a Bias, but when we have acquired more strength, a Bias becomes no Bias. Every department of knowledge we see excellent and calculated towards a great whole. I am so convinced of this that I am glad at not having given away my medical Books, which I shall again look over to keep alive the little I know thitherwards; and moreover, intend through you and Rice to become a sort of Pipcivilian.[5] An extensive knowlege is needful to thinking people; it takes away the heat and fever and helps, by widening speculation, to ease the Burden of the Mystery,[6] a thing I begin to understand a little and which weighed upon you in the most gloomy and true sentence in your Letter. The difference of high Sensations with and without knowledge appears to me this: in the latter case we are falling continually ten thousand fathoms deep and being blown up again without wings and with all the horror of a bare-shouldered Creature. In the former case, our shoulders are fledged, and we go thro' the same air and space without fear. This is running one's rigs on the score of abstracted benefit. When we come to human Life and the affections, it is impossible how a parallel of breast and head can be drawn (you will forgive me for thus privately treading out of my depth and take it for treading as schoolboys tread the water), it is impossible to know how far knowledge will console us for the death of a friend and the ill "that flesh is heir to."[7] With respect to the affections and Poetry, you must know by a sympathy my thoughts that way, and I dare say these few lines will be but a ratification. I wrote them on May-day and intend to finish the ode all in good time.

> Mother of Hermes! and still youthful Maia!
>   May I sing to thee
> As thou wast hymned on the shores of Baiae?
>   Or may I woo thee
> In earlier Sicilian? or thy smiles
> Seek as they once were sought, in Grecian isles,
> By Bards who died content in pleasant sward,
> Leaving great verse unto a little clan?
> O give me their old vigour, and unheard,
> Save of the quiet Primrose, and the span
> Of Heaven and few [y]ears; rounded by thee
> My song should die away content as theirs,
> Rich in the simple worship of a day.

You may be anxious to know for fact to what sentence in your Letter I allude. You say, "I fear there is little chance of anything else in this life." You seem by that to have been going through with a more painful and acute zest the same labyrinth that I have. I have come to the same conclusion thus far. My Branchings out therefrom have been numerous: one of them is the consideration of Wordsworth's genius and as a help, in the manner of gold being the meridian Line of worldly wealth, how he differs from Milton. And here I have nothing but surmises, from an uncertainty whether Milton's apparently less anxiety for Humanity proceeds from his seeing further or no than Wordsworth, and whether Wordsworth has in truth epic passion, and martyrs himself to the human heart, the main region of his song. In regard to his genius alone, we find what he says true as far as we have experienced, and we can judge no further but by larger experience, for axioms in philosophy are not axioms until they are proved upon our pulses. We read fine things but never feel them to the full until we have gone the same steps as the Author. I know this is not plain; you will know exactly my meaning when I say that now I shall relish Hamlet more than I ever have done, or better. You are sensible no man can set down Venery as a bestial or joyless thing until he is sick of it, and therefore all philosophizing on it would be mere wording. Until we are sick, we understand not; in fine, as Byron says, "Knowledge is Sorrow,"[8] and I go on to say that "Sorrow is Wisdom," and further, for aught we can know for certainty! "Wisdom is folly." So you see how I have run away from Wordsworth and Milton and shall still run away from what was in my head to observe that some kind of letters are good squares, others handsome ovals, and others some orbicular, others spheroid. And why should there not be another species with two rough edges like a Rat-trap? I hope you will find all my long letters of that species, and all will be well, for by merely touching the spring delicately and etherially, the rough-edged will fly immediately into a proper compactness, and thus you may make a good wholesome loaf with your own leven in it of my frag-ments, if you cannot find this said Rat-trap sufficiently tractable—alas for me, it being an impossibility in grain for my ink to stain otherwise. If I scribble long letters I must play my vagaries. I must be too heavy, or too light, for whole pages. I must be quaint and free of Tropes and figures. I must play my draughts as I please, and for my advantage and your erudi-tion, crown a white with a black, or a black with a white, and move into black or white, far and near as I please. I must go from Hazlitt to Patmore and make Wordsworth and Coleman[9] play at leap-frog, or keep one of them down a whole half holiday at fly the garter, "from Gray to Gay, from Little[10] to Shakespeare." Also, as a long cause requires two or more sittings of the Court, so a long letter will require two or more sittings of the Breech, wherefore I shall resume after dinner.

Have you not seen a Gull, an orc, a sea Mew, or anything to bring this Line to a proper length and also fill up this clear part, that like the Gull I may *dip*[11]—I hope, not out of sight—and also, like a Gull, I hope to be lucky in a good-sized fish. This crossing a letter is not without its as-sociation, for chequer work leads us naturally to a Milkmaid, a Milkmaid to Hogarth, Hogarth to Shakespeare, Shakespeare to Hazlitt, Hazlitt to Shakespeare, and thus by merely pulling an apron string we set a pretty peal of Chimes at work. Let them chime on while, with your patience, I will return to Wordsworth, whether or no he has an extended vision or a circumscribed grandeur, whether he is an eagle in his nest or on the wing. And to be more explicit, and to show you how tall I stand by the giant, I will put down a simile of human life as far as I now perceive it; that is, to the point to which I say we both have arrived at. Well, I compare human life to a large Mansion of Many Apartments, two of which I can only describe, the doors of the rest being as yet shut upon me. The first we step into we call the infant or thoughtless Chamber, in which we remain as long as we do not think. We remain there a long while, and notwithstanding the doors of the second Chamber remain wide open showing a bright appearance, we care not to hasten to it, but are at length imperceptibly impelled by the awakening of the thinking principle within us. We no sooner get into the second Chamber, which I shall call the Chamber of Maiden-Thought, than we become intoxicated with the light and the atmosphere, we see nothing but pleasant wonders and think of delaying there forever in delight. However, among the effects this breathing is father of is that tremendous one of sharpening one's vision into the heart and nature of Man, of convincing one's nerves that the World is full of Misery and Heartbreak, Pain, Sickness and oppression, whereby This Chamber of Maiden Thought becomes gradually darken'd and at the same time on all sides of it many doors are set open, but all dark, all leading to dark passages. We see not the balance of good and evil. We are in a Mist. *We* are now in that state. We feel the "burden of the Mystery." To this point was Wordsworth come, as far as I can conceive, when he wrote "Tintern Abbey," and it seems to me that his Genius is explorative of those dark Passages. Now if we live, and go on thinking, we too shall explore them. He is a Genius and superior to us, in so far as he can, more than we, make discoveries and shed a light in them. Here I must think Wordsworth is deeper than Milton, though I think it has depended more upon the general and gregarious advance of intellect than individual greatness of Mind. From the Paradise Lost and the other Works of Milton, I hope it is not too presuming, even between ourselves, to say his

Philosophy, human and divine, may be tolerably understood by one not much advanced in years. In his time englishmen were just emancipated from a great superstition and Men had got hold of certain points and resting places in reasoning which were too newly born to be doubted, and too much opposed by the Mass of Europe not to be thought etherial and authentically divine. Who could gainsay his ideas on virtue, vice, and Chastity in Comus, just at the time of the dismissal of Cod-pieces and a hundred other disgraces? Who would not rest satisfied with his hintings at good and evil in the Paradise Lost, when just free from the inquisition and burning in Smithfield? The Reformation produced such immediate and great benefits that Protestantism was considered under the immediate eye of heaven, and its own remaining Dogmas and superstitions, then, as it were, regenerated, constituted those resting places and seeming sure points of Reasoning. From that I have mentioned, Milton, whatever he may have thought in the sequel, appears to have been content with these by his writings. He did not think into the human heart, as Wordsworth has done. Yet Milton as a Philosopher had sure as great powers as Wordsworth. What is then to be inferr'd? O, many things: It proves there is really a grand march of intellect. It proves that a mighty providence subdues the mightiest Minds to the service of the time being, whether it be in human Knowledge or Religion. I have often pitied a Tutor who has to hear "Nomᵉ: Musa"¹² so often dinn'd into his ears. I hope you may not have the same pain in this scribbling. I may have read these things before, but I never had even a thus dim perception of them; and moreover, I like to say my lesson to one who will endure my tediousness for my own sake. After all, there is certainly something real in the World. Moore's present to Hazlitt is real. I like that Moore, and am glad that I saw him at the Theatre just before I left Town. Tom has spit a little blood this afternoon, and that is rather a damper—but I know—the truth is there is something real in the World. Your third Chamber of Life shall be a lucky and a gentle one, stored with the wine of love and the Bread of Friendship. When you see George, if he should not have received a letter from me, tell him he will find one at home most likely. Tell Bailey I hope soon to see him. Remember me to all. The leaves have been out here for MONY a day. I have written to George for the first stanzas of my Isabel. I shall have them soon and will copy the whole out for you.

Your affectionate friend
John Keats

1. *The Merry Wives of Windsor,* I.i.127f.
2. *Paradise Lost,* X.702f.
3. That is, return to the house of the postman, Benjamin Bentley, and his noisy children.
4. "The Romance of Youth," later published in Reynolds's *Garden of Florence* (1821), pp. 29–92.
5. An amateur or undistinguished lawyer.
6. Wordsworth, "Tintern Abbey," line 38.
7. *Hamlet,* III.i.63.
8. *Manfred,* I.i.10, "Sorrow is knowledge."
9. Peter George Patmore (1786–1855), author, intimate friend of Hazlitt and Lamb, father of Victorian poet Coventry Patmore. George Colman the younger (1762–1836), playwright.
10. Pseudonym of Thomas Moore.
11. Woodhouse, who copied this letter, remarks that at this point "the first page of the letter is crossed and the two first lines . . . after 'Gull I may' are written in the clear space left as a margin—and the word 'dip' is the first word that *dips* into the former writing."
12. "Noun: Muse." The beginning of the grammatical and syntactical description of a word, the schoolboy's dreaded "parse."

To Benjamin Bailey
21, 25 MAY 1818

Hampstead, Thursday—
My dear Bailey,

I should have answered your letter on the moment, if I could have said yes to your invitation. What hinders me is insuperable. I will tell it at a little length. You know my Brother George has been out of employ for some time. It has weighed very much upon him and driven him to scheme and

turn over things in his Mind. The result has been his resolution to emigrate
to the back settlements of America, become farmer, and work with his own
hands after purchasing 1400 hundred Acres of the American Government.
This for many reasons has met with my entire consent, and the chief one is
this: he is of too independent and liberal a Mind to get on in trade in this
Country in which a generous Man with a scanty recourse must be ruined. I
would sooner he should till the ground than bow to a Customer. There is
no choice with him. He could not bring himself to the latter. I would not
consent to his going alone, no, but that objection is done away with. He
will marry before he sets sail a young Lady he has known some years of a
nature liberal and high-spirited enough to follow him to the Banks of the
Mississippi. He will set off in a month or six weeks, and you will see how I
should wish to pass that time with him—and then I must set out on a journey of my own. Brown and I are going a pedestrian tour through the north
of England and Scotland as far as John o' Grots. I have this morning such a
Lethargy that I cannot write. The reason of my delaying is oftentimes from
this feeling. I wait for a proper temper. Now you ask for an immediate answer. I do not like to wait even till tomorrow. However I am now so depressed that I have not an Idea to put to paper. My hand feels like lead, and
yet it is an unpleasant numbness. It does not take away the pain of existence. I don't know what to write.

Monday. You see how I have delayed, and even now I have but a confused idea of what I should be about. My intellect must be in a degenerat-
ing state; it must be, for when I should be writing about god knows what I
am troubling you with Moods of my own Mind, or rather body, for Mind
there is none. I am in that temper that if I were under Water I would
scarcely kick to come to the top. I know very well 'tis all nonsense. In a
short time I hope I shall be in a temper to feel sensibly your mention of my
Book. In vain have I waited till Monday to have any interest in that or in
anything else. I feel no spur at my Brother's going to America and am almost stony-hearted about his wedding. All this will blow over; all I am
sorry for is having to write to you in such a time, but I cannot force my letters in a hot bed. I could not feel comfortable in making sentences for you.
I am your debtor, I must ever remain so, nor do I wish to be clear of my
rational[1] debt. There is a comfort in throwing oneself on the charity of

one's friends. 'Tis like the albatross sleeping on its wings. I will be to you wine in the cellar and the more modestly or rather indolently I retire into the backward Bin, the more falerne will I be at the drinking. There is one thing I must mention. My Brother talks of sailing in a fortnight; if so I will most probably be with you a week before I set out for Scotland. The middle of your first page should be sufficient to rouse me. What I said is true and I have dreamt of your mention of it, and my not answering it has weighed on me since. If I come, I will bring your Letter and hear more fully your sentiments on one or two points. I will call about the Lectures at Taylor's and at Little Britain tomorrow. Yesterday I dined with Hazlitt, Barnes[2] and Wilkie at Haydon's. The topic was the Duke of Wellington very amusingly pro and con'd. Reynolds has been getting much better, and Rice may begin to crow for he got a little so so at a Party of his and was none the worse for it the next morning. I hope I shall soon see you for we must have many new thoughts and feelings to analyze, and to discover whether a little more knowledge has not made us more ignorant.

Your's affectionately *John Keats*—

1. The italicized *r* marks a pun on "national."
2. Thomas Barnes (1785–1841), friend of Hazlitt, Hunt, and Lamb, editor of *The Times* (1817–1841).

To Benjamin Bailey
10 JUNE 1818

London—

My dear Bailey,

I have been very much gratified and very much hurt by your Letters in the Oxford Paper[1] because independent of that unlawful and mortal feeling of pleasure at praise, there is a glory in enthusiasm, and because the world is malignant enough to chuckle at the most honorable Simplicity. Yes, on my

Soul, my dear Bailey, you are too simple for the World, and that Idea makes
me sick of it. How is it that by extreme opposites we have as it were got discontented nerves? You have all your Life (I think so) believed every Body. I
have suspected every Body, and although you have been so deceived you
make a simple appeal. The world has something else to do and I am glad of
it. Were it in my choice I would reject a petrarchal coronation, on account
of my dying day and because women have Cancers. I should not by rights
speak in this tone to you for it is an incendiary spirit that would do so. Yet I
am not old enough or magnanimous enough to annihilate self and it would
perhaps be paying you an ill compliment. I was in hopes some little time
back to be able to relieve your dullness by my spirits, to point out things in
the world worth your enjoyment, and now I am never alone without rejoicing that there is such a thing as death, without placing my ultimate in the
glory of dying for a great human purpose. Perhaps if my affairs were in a
different state I should not have written the above. You shall judge. I have
two Brothers, one is driven by the "burden of Society" to America, the
other, with an exquisite love of Life, is in a lingering state. My Love for my
Brothers from the early loss of our parents and even for earlier Misfortunes
has grown into an affection "passing the Love of Women."[2] I have been ill
temper'd with them, I have vex'd them, but the thought of them has always
stifled the impression that any woman might otherwise have made upon
me. I have a Sister[3] too and may not follow them, either to America or to
the Grave. Life must be undergone, and I certainly derive a consolation
from the thought of writing one or two more Poems before it ceases. I have
heard some hints of your retiring to scotland. I should like to know your
feeling on it. It seems rather remote. Perhaps Gleig will have a duty near
you. I am not certain whether I shall be able to go on my Journey on account of my Brother Tom and a little indisposition of my own. If I do not
you shall see me soon; if not on my return, or I'll quarter myself upon you
in Scotland next Winter. I had known my sister in Law some time before
she was my Sister and was very fond of her. I like her better and better. She
is the most disinterested woman I ever knew, that is to say, she goes beyond
degree in it. To see an entirely disinterested Girl quite happy is the most
pleasant and extraordinary thing in the world; it depends upon a thousand
Circumstances. On my word, 'tis extraordinary. Women must want Imagi-

nation and they may thank God for it, and so may we that a delicate being can feel happy without any sense of crime. It puzzles me and I have no sort of Logic to comfort me. I shall think it over. I am not at home and your letter being there I cannot look it over to answer any particular. Only I must say I felt that passage of Dante. If I take any book with me it shall be those minute volumes of carey,[4] for they will go into the aptest corner. Reynolds is getting, I may say, robust; his illness has been of service to him. Like anyone just recovered he is high-spirited. I hear also good accounts of Rice. With respect to domestic Literature, the Endinburgh Magasine in another blow up against Hunt calls me "the amiable Mister Keats"[5] and I have more than a Laurel from the Quarterly Reviewers for they have *smothered* me in "Foliage." I want to read you my "Pot of Basil." If you go to scotland I should much like to read it there to you among the Snows of next Winter. My Brothers' remembrances to you.

Your affectionate friend
John Keats—

1. *Oxford University & City Herald,* 30 May and 6 June 1818, in which Bailey reviewed *Endymion.*
2. 2 Samuel i.26.
3. His sister-in-law, Georgiana Keats.
4. H. F. Carey, translator of Dante's *Divine Comedy,* recently republished in a portable 32mo, three-volume edition.
5. J. G. Lockhart, "Letter from Z. to Leigh Hunt," *Blackwood's,* May 1818 (III:197).

To Tom Keats
25–27 JUNE 1818

Here beginneth my journal, this Thursday, the 25th day of June, Anno Domini 1818.[1] This morning we arose at 4, and set off in a Scotch mist; put up once under a tree, and in fine, have walked wet and dry to this place, called in the vulgar tongue Endmoor, 17 miles; we have not been incommoded by our knapsacks; they serve capitally, and we shall go on very well.

June 26. I merely put *pro forma*, for there is no such thing as time and space, which by the way came forcibly upon me on seeing for the first hour the Lake and Mountains of Winander. I cannot describe them; they surpass my expectation: beautiful water, shores and islands green to the marge, mountains all round up to the clouds. We set out from Endmoor this morning, breakfasted at Kendal with a soldier who had been in all the wars for the last seventeen years, then we have walked to Bowness to dinner (said Bowness situated on the Lake where we have just dined), and I am writing at this present. I took an oar to one of the islands to take up some trout for dinner, which they keep in porous boxes. I enquired of the waiter for Wordsworth. He said he knew him, and that he had been here a few days ago, canvassing for the Lowthers. What think you of that—Wordsworth versus Brougham!![2] Sad—sad—sad—and yet the family has been his friend always. What can we say? We are now about seven miles from Rydal,[3] and expect to see him tomorrow. You shall hear all about our visit.

There are many disfigurements to this Lake—not in the way of land or water. No, the two views we have had of it are of the most noble tenderness. They can never fade away; they make one forget the divisions of life—age, youth, poverty, and riches—and refine one's sensual vision into a sort of north star which can never cease to be open-lidded and steadfast over the wonders of the great Power. The disfigurement I mean is the miasma of London. I do suppose it contaminated with bucks and soldiers, and women of fashion—and hat-band ignorance. The border inhabitants are quite out of keeping with the romance about them, from a continual intercourse with London rank and fashion. But why should I grumble? They let me have a prime glass of soda water. O, they are as good as their neighbours. But Lord Wordsworth, instead of being in retirement, has himself and his house full in the thick of fashionable visitors quite convenient to be pointed at all the summer long. When we had gone about half this morning, we began to get among the hills and to see the mountains grow up before us; the other half brought us to Winandermere,[4] 14 miles to dinner. The weather is capital for the views, but is now rather misty, and we are in doubt whether to walk to Ambleside to tea; it is five miles along the borders of the Lake. Loughrigg will swell up before us all the way. I have an amazing partiality for mountains in the clouds. There is nothing in Devon like this, and Brown says there is nothing in Wales to be compared to it. I must tell you, that in going through Cheshire and Lancashire, I saw the Welsh mountains at a distance. We have passed the two castles, Lancaster and Kendal.

27th—We walked here to Ambleside yesterday along the border of Winandermere, all beautiful with wooded shores and Islands. Our road was a winding lane, wooded on each side, and green overhead, full of Foxgloves—every now and then a glimpse of the Lake, and all the while Kirkstone and other large hills nestled together in a sort of grey black mist. Ambleside is at the northern extremity of the Lake. We arose this morning at six, because we call it a day of rest, having to call on Wordsworth who lives only two miles hence. Before breakfast we went to see the Ambleside waterfall. The morning beautiful, the walk easy among the hills. We, I may say fortunately, missed the direct path, and after wandering a little, found it out by the noise; for, mark you, it is buried in trees, in the bottom of the valley. The stream itself is interesting throughout with "mazy error over pendant shades."[5] Milton meant a smooth river—this is buffeting all the way on a rocky bed ever various—but the waterfall itself, which I came suddenly upon, gave me a pleasant twinge. First we stood a little below the head about halfway down the first fall, buried deep in trees, and saw it streaming down two more descents to the depth of near fifty feet. Then we went on a jut of rock nearly level with the second fall-head, where the first fall was above us, and the third below our feet still. At the same time we saw that the water was divided by a sort of cataract island on whose other side burst out a glorious stream—then the thunder and the freshness. At the same time the different falls have as different characters; the first darting down the slate rock like an arrow; the second spreading out like a fan; the third dashed into a mist, and the one on the other side of the rock a sort of mixture of all these. We afterwards moved away a space, and saw nearly the whole more mild, streaming silverly through the trees. What astonishes me more than anything is the tone, the coloring, the slate, the stone, the moss,

Map of Keats's 1818 walking tour.
By permission of Yale University Press.

the rockweed; or, if I may so say, the intellect, the countenance of such places. The space, the magnitude of mountains and waterfalls are well imagined before one sees them; but this countenance or intellectual tone must surpass every imagination and defy any remembrance. I shall learn poetry here and shall henceforth write, more than ever, for the abstract endeavour of being able to add a mite to that mass of beauty which is harvested from these grand materials, by the finest spirits, and put into etherial existence for the relish of one's fellows. I cannot think with Hazlitt that these scenes make man appear little.[6] I never forgot my stature so completely; I live in the eye, and my imagination, surpassed, is at rest. We shall see another waterfall near Rydal, to which we shall proceed after having put these letters in the post office. I long to be at Carlisle, as I expect there a letter from George and one from you. Let any of my friends see my letters. They may not be interested in descriptions—descriptions are bad at all times—I did not intend to give you any, but how can I help it? I am anxious you should taste a little of our pleasure; it may not be an unpleasant thing, as you have not the fatigue. I am well in health. Direct henceforth to Portpatrick till the 12th July. Content that probably three or four pairs of eyes whose owners I am rather partial to will run over these lines, I remain, and moreover that I am

Your affectionate brother

John

1. Keats and Brown left London on 22 June, reached Liverpool the next afternoon, and early on the morning of 24 June took a coach for Lancaster, where they spent the night.
2. William Lowther (1787–1872), the Whig candidate, was elected M.P. for Westmorland after a bitter contest with Henry Brougham (1778–1868), the Tory whose cause Wordsworth was supporting.
3. Wordsworth lived at Rydal Mount, Westmorland, from 1817 till his death in 1850.
4. Windermere was formerly called Winandermere.
5. *Paradise Lost*, IV.239.
6. William Hazlitt said this in an 1814 review of Wordsworth's *Excursion* in the *Examiner*.

To George and Georgiana Keats
27, 28 JUNE 1818

Foot of Helvellyn, June 27

My dear George,

We have passed from Lancaster to Burton, from Burton to Endmoor, from Endmoor to Kendal, from Kendal to Bowness, on turning down to which place there burst upon us the most beautiful and rich view of Winandermere and the surrounding Mountains. We dined at Bowness on Trout, which I took an oar to fetch from some Box preserves close on one of the little green Islands. After dinner we walked to Ambleside down a beautiful shady Lane along the Borders of the Lake with ample opportunity for Glimpses all the way. We slept at Ambleside not above two Miles from Rydal, the Residence of Wordsworth. We arose not very early on account of having marked this day for a day of rest. Before breakfast we visited the first waterfall I ever saw, and certainly, small as it is, it surpassed my expectation in what I have mentioned in my letter to Tom, in its tone and intellect, its light, shade, slaty Rock, Moss and Rock weed, but you will see finer ones; I will not describe by comparison a teapot spout. We ate a Monstrous Breakfast on our return (which by the way I do every morning) and after it proceeded to Wordsworth's. He was not at home, nor was any Member of his family. I was much disappointed. I wrote a note for him and stuck it up over what I knew must be Miss Wordsworth's Portrait and set forth again, and we visited two Waterfalls in the neighbourhood, and then went along by Rydal Water and Grasmere through its beautiful Vale; then through a defile in the Mountains into Cumberland and So to the foot of Helvellyn, whose summit is out of sight, four Miles off, rise above rise. I have seen Kirkstone, Loughrigg, and Silver How, and discovered without a hint "that ancient woman seated on Helm Crag."[1] This is the summary of what I have written to Tom and dispatched from Ambleside. I have had a great confidence in your being well able to support the fatigue of your Journey since

I have felt how much new Objects contribute to keep off a sense of Ennui
and fatigue. Fourteen Miles here is not so much as the 4 from Hampstead
to London. You will have an inexhaustible astonishment; with that and
such a Companion, you will be cheered on from day to day. I hope you will
not have sail'd before this Letter reaches you, yet I do not know, for I will
have my Series to Tom copied and sent to you by the first Packet you have
from England. God send you both as good Health as I have now. Ha! my
dear Sister George, I wish I knew what humour you were in that I might
accommodate myself to any one of your Amiabilities. Shall it be a Sonnet
or a Pun or an Acrostic, a Riddle or a Ballad—"perhaps it may turn out a
Sang, and perhaps turn out a Sermon."² I'll write you on my word the first
and most likely the last I ever shall do, because it has struck me—what shall
it be about?

> Give me your patience, Sister, while I frame
> Enitials verse-wise of your golden name:
> Or sue the fair Apollo and he will
> Rouse from his Slumber heavy and instill
> Great Love in me for thee and Poesy.
> Imagine not that greatest Mastery
> And kingdom over all the realms of verse
> Nears more to heaven in aught than when we nurse
> And surety give to Love and Brotherhood.
>
> Anthropophagi in Othello's Mood,
> Ulysses stormed, and his enchanted Belt
> Glow with the Muse, but they are never felt
> Unbosom'd so and so eternal made,
> Such self-same incense in their Laurel shade,
> To all the regent sisters of the Nine,
> As this poor offering to thee, Sister mine.
>
> Kind Sister ! aye, this third name says you are;
> Enhanced has it been the Lord knows where.
> Ah ! may it taste to you like good old wine,

Take you to real happiness and give
Sons, daughters, and a Home like honied hive.

June 28th—I have slept and walked eight miles to Breakfast at Keswick on derwent water. We could not mount Helvellyn for the mist, so gave it up with hopes of Skiddaw, which we shall try tomorrow if it be fine. Today we shall walk round Derwent water, and in our Way see the Falls of Lodore. The Approach to derwent water is rich and magnificent beyond any means of conception—the Mountains all round sublime and graceful and rich in colour—Woods and wooded Islands here and there; at the same time in the distance among Mountains of another aspect we see Bassenthwaite. I shall drop like a Hawk on the Post Office at Carlisle to ask for some Letters from you and Tom.

Sweet, sweet is the greeting of eyes,
And sweet is the voice in its greeting,
When Adieux have grown old and good-byes
Fade away where old time is retreating.

Warm the nerve of a welcoming hand,
And earnest a kiss on the Brow,
When we meet over sea and o'er Land
Where furrows are new to the Plough.

This is all [. . .] in the m[. . .] please a[. . .] Letters as possi[bly . . .].[3] We will, before many Years are over, have written many folio volumes which as a Matter of self-defence to one whom you understand intends to be immortal in the best points and let all his Sins and peccadillos die away; I mean to say that the Booksellers will rather decline printing ten folio volumes of Correspondence printed as close as the Apostles' creed in a Watch paper. I have been looking out, my dear Georgy, for a joke or a Pun for you; there is none but the Names of romantic Misses on the Inn window Panes. You will of course have given me directions, brother George, where to direct on the other side of the Water. I have not had time to write to Henry,[4] for I have a journal to keep for Tom nearly enough to employ all my leisure. I am a day behindhand with him; I scarcely know how I shall manage

Fanny and two or three others I have promised. We expect to be in Scotland in at most three days, so you must, if this should catch you before you set sail, give me a line to Portpatrick.

God bless you, my dear Brother and Sister.

John——

1. A rock formation at the head of Grasmere Vale. Keats is quoting Wordsworth's "To Joanna," line 56.
2. Robert Burns, "Epistle to a Young Friend," lines 7–8.
3. The brackets and dots represent damage to the manuscript.
4. Henry Wylie, Georgiana Keats's brother.

To Tom Keats

29 JUNE, 1, 2 JULY 1818

Keswick, June 29th, 1818

My dear Tom,

I cannot make my Journal as distinct and actual as I could wish, from having been engaged in writing to George. And therefore I must tell you without circumstance that we proceeded from Ambleside to Rydal, saw the Waterfalls there, and called on Wordsworth, who was not at home, nor was any one of his family. I wrote a note and left it on the Mantelpiece. Thence on we came to the foot of Helvellyn, where we slept, but could not ascend it for the mist. I must mention that from Rydal we passed Thirlswater,[1] and a fine pass in the Mountains. From Helvellyn we came to Keswick on Derwent Water. The approach to Derwent Water surpassed Winandermere; it is richly wooded and shut in with rich-toned Mountains. From Helvellyn to Keswick was eight miles to Breakfast, After which we took a complete circuit of the Lake, going about ten miles and seeing on our way the Fall of

Lodore. I had an easy climb among the streams, about the fragments of Rocks, and should have got I think to the summit, but unfortunately I was damped by slipping one leg into a squashy hole. There is no great body of water, but the accompaniment is delightful; for it oozes out from a cleft in perpendicular Rocks, all fledged with Ash and other beautiful trees. It is a strange thing how they got there. At the south end of the Lake, the Mountains of Borrowdale are perhaps as fine as anything we have seen. On our return from this circuit, we ordered dinner, and set forth about a mile and a half on the Penrith road, to see the Druid temple.[2] We had a fag uphill, rather too near dinner-time, which was rendered void by the gratification of seeing those aged stones, on a gentle rise in the midst of Mountains, which at that time darkened all round, except at the fresh opening of the vale of St. John. We went to bed rather fatigued, but not so much so as to hinder us getting up this morning, to mount Skiddaw. It promised all along to be fair, and we had fagged and tugged nearly to the top, when at half past six there came a mist upon us and shut out the view. We did not, however, lose anything by it; we were high enough without mist to see the coast of Scotland, the Irish sea, the hills beyond Lancaster, and nearly all the large ones of Cumberland and Westmorland, particularly Helvellyn and Scafell. It grew colder and colder as we ascended, and we were glad at about three parts of the way to taste a little rum which the Guide brought with him, mixed, mind ye, with mountain water; I took two glasses going and one returning. It is about six miles from where I am writing to the top, so we have walked ten miles before Breakfast today. We went up with two others, very good sort of fellows. All felt, on arising into the cold air, that same elevation which a cold bath gives one. I felt as if I were going to a Tournament. Wordsworth's house is situated just on the rise of the foot of mount Rydal; his parlor window looks directly down Winandermere. I do not think I told you how fine the vale of Grasmere is, and how I discovered "the ancient woman seated on Helm Crag." We shall proceed immediately to Carlisle, intending to enter Scotland on the 1st of July via——

July 1st—We are this morning at Carlisle. After Skiddaw, we walked to Ireby, the oldest market town in Cumberland, where we were greatly amused by a country dancing school, holden at the Sun; it was indeed "no new cotillion fresh from France."[3] No, they kickit and jumpit with mettle extraordinary, and whiskit, and fleckit, and toe'd it, and go'd it, and twirl'd it, and wheel'd it, and stampt it, and sweated it, tattooing the floor like mad. The difference between our country dances and these scotch figures is about the same as leisurely stirring a cup o' Tea and beating up a batter pudding. I was extremely gratified to think, that if I had pleasures they knew nothing of, they had also some into which I could not possibly enter. I hope I shall not return without having got the Highland fling. There was as fine a row of boys and girls as you ever saw, some beautiful faces, and one exquisite mouth. I never felt so near the glory of Patriotism, the glory of making by any means a country happier. This is what I like better than scenery. I fear our continued moving from place to place will prevent our becoming learned in village affairs; we are mere creatures of Rivers, Lakes, and mountains. Our yesterday's journey was from Ireby to Wigton, and from Wigton to Carlisle. The Cathedral does not appear very fine; the Castle is very Ancient, and of Brick. The City is very various: old whitewashed narrow streets, broad red brick ones more modern. I will tell you anon whether the inside of the Cathedral is worth looking at. It is built of a sandy red stone or Brick. We have now walked 114 miles and are merely a little tired in the thighs, and a little blistered. We shall ride 38 miles to Dumfries, where we shall linger a while, about Nithsdale and Galloway. I have written two letters to Liverpool. I found a letter from sister George— very delightful indeed. I shall preserve it in the bottom of my knapsack for you.

On Visiting the Tomb of Burns

The Town, the churchyard, and the setting sun,
The Clouds, the trees, the rounded hills all seem,
Though beautiful, Cold—strange—as in a dream
I dreamed long ago. Now new begun,
The short-lived, paly summer is but won
From winter's ague, for one hour's gleam;
Though sapphire warm, their stars do never beam;

> All is cold Beauty; pain is never done
> For who has mind to relish, Minos-wise,
> The real of Beauty, free from that dead hue
> Sickly imagination and sick pride
> Cast wan upon it! Burns! with honour due
> I have oft honoured thee. Great shadow, hide
> Thy face—I sin against thy native skies.

You will see by this sonnet that I am at Dumfries; we have dined in Scotland. Burns' tomb is in the Churchyard corner, not very much to my taste, though on a scale large enough to show they wanted to honour him. Mrs. Burns lives in this place; most likely we shall see her tomorrow. This Sonnet I have written in a strange mood, half asleep. I know not how it is, the Clouds, the sky, the Houses, all seem anti-Grecian and anti-Charlemagnish. I will endeavour to get rid of my prejudices, and tell you fairly about the Scotch.

July 2nd—In Devonshire they say, "Well where be yee going." Here it is, "How is it all wi yoursel." A man on the Coach said the horses took a Hellish heap o' drivin; the same fellow pointed out Burns' tomb with a deal of life, "There de ye see it, amang the trees; white, wi a roond tap." The first well-dressed Scotchman we had any conversation with, to our surprise confessed himself a Deist. The careful manner of his delivering his opinions, not before he had received several encouraging hints from us, was very amusing. Yesterday was an immense Horse fair at Dumfries, so that we met numbers of men and women on the road, the women nearly all barefoot, with their shoes and clean stockings in hand, ready to put on and look smart in the Towns. There are plenty of wretched Cottages, where smoke has no outlet but by the door. We have now begun upon whiskey, called here *whuskey*—very smart stuff it is—mixed like our liquors with sugar and water, 'tis called toddy, very pretty drink, and much praised by Burns.

---

1. Thirlmere, or Wythburn Water, five miles southeast of Keswick.
2. The Druid Circle, two miles east of Keswick.
3. Burns, "Tam o' Shanter," line 116, "Nae cotillion, brent new frae France."

To Fanny Keats

2, 3, 5 JULY 1818

Dumfries, July 2nd

My dear Fanny,

I intended to have written to you from Kirkcudbright, the town I shall be in tomorrow, but I will write now because my knapsack has worn my coat in the Seams, my coat has gone to the Taylors, and I have but one Coat to my back in these parts. I must tell you how I went to Liverpool with George and our new Sister and the Gentleman my fellow traveller through the Summer and Autumn. We had a tolerable journey to Liverpool, which I left the next morning, before George was up, for Lancaster. Then we set off from Lancaster on foot with our knapsacks on, and have walked a Little zigzag through the mountains and Lakes of Cumberland and Westmorland. We came from Carlisle yesterday to this place. We are employed in going up Mountains, looking at Strange towns, prying into old ruins, and eating very hearty breakfasts. Here we are full in the Midst of broad Scotch "How is it a' wi yoursel." The Girls are walking about barefooted, and in the worst cottages the Smoke finds its way out of the door. I shall come home full of news for you, and for fear I should choke you by too great a dose at once I must make you used to it by a letter or two. We have been taken for travelling Jewelers, Razor sellers, and Spectacle vendors because friend Brown wears a pair. The first place we stopped at with our knapsacks contained one Richard Bradshaw, a notorious tippler. He stood in the shape of a 3 and balanced himself as well as he could, saying with his nose right in Mr. Brown's face, "Do you sell Spec-ta-cles?" Mr. Abbey says we are Don Quixotes; tell him we are more generally taken for Pedlars. All I hope is that we may not be taken for excisemen in this whiskey country. We are generally up about 5 walking before breakfast, and we complete our 20 Miles before dinner. Yesterday we visited Burns's Tomb and this morning the fine Ruins of Lincluden.

I had done thus far when my coat came back fortified at all points. So as we lose no time, we set forth again through Galloway—all very pleasant and pretty with no fatigue when one is used to it. We are in the midst of Meg Merrilies' country, of whom I suppose you have heard.

> Old Meg she was a Gypsy,
>   And liv'd upon the Moors;
> Her bed it was the brown heath turf,
>   And her house was out of doors.
>
> Her apples were swart blackberries,
>   Her currants pods o' broom,
> Her wine was dew o' the wild white rose,
>   Her book a churchyard tomb.
>
> Her Brothers were the craggy hills,
>   Her Sisters larchen trees,
> Alone with her great family
>   She liv'd as she did please.
>
> No breakfast had she many a morn,
>   No dinner many a noon,
> And 'stead of supper she would stare
>   Full hard against the Moon.
>
> But every morn of woodbine fresh
>   She made her garlanding,
> And every night the dark glen Yew
>   She wove and she would sing.
>
> And with her fingers old and brown
>   She plaited Mats o' Rushes,
> And gave them to the Cottagers
>   She met among the Bushes.
>
> Old Meg was brave as Margaret Queen
>   And tall as Amazon:

An old red blanket cloak she wore;
   A chip hat had she on.
God rest her aged bones somewhere,
   She died full long agone!

If you like these sort of Ballads I will now and then scribble one for you; if I send any to Tom I'll tell him to send them to you. I have so many interruptions that I cannot manage to fill a Letter in one day. Since I scribbled the Song we have walked through a beautiful Country to Kirkcudbright, at which place I will write you a song about myself—

There was a naughty Boy
   A naughty boy was he
He would not stop at home
   He could not quiet be.
      He took
      In his knapsack
      A Book
      Full of vowels
      And a shirt
      With some towels,
      A slight cap
      For nightcap,
      A hair brush
      Comb ditto,
      New Stockings
      For old ones
      Would split O!
      This knapsack
      Tight at 's back
      He riveted close
      And follow'd his Nose
      To the North
      To the North

And follow'd his nose
    To the North.

There was a naughty boy
    And a naughty boy was he
For nothing would he do
    But scribble poetry.
        He took
        An inkstand
        In his hand
        And a Pen
        Big as ten
        In the other
        And away
        In a Pother
        He ran
        To the mountains
        And fountains
        And ghostes
        And Postes
        And witches
        And ditches
        And wrote
        In his coat
        When the weather
        Was cool
        Fear of gout
        And without
        When the weather
        Was warm—
        Och the charm
        When we choose
        To follow one's nose

To the north
To the north
To follow one's nose to the north!

There was a naughty boy
    And a naughty boy was he
He kept little fishes
    In washing tubs three
        In spite
        Of the might
        Of the Maid
        Nor afraid
        Of his Granny-good,
        He often would
        Hurly burly
        Get up early
        And go
        By hook or crook
        To the brook
        And bring home
        Miller's thumb
        Tittlebat
        Not over fat
        Minnows small
        As the stall
        Of a glove
        Not above
        The size
        Of a nice
        Little Baby's
        Little finger.
        O he made
        'Twas his trade
        Of Fish a pretty kettle

A kettle—a kettle
Of Fish a pretty kettle
A kettle!

There was a naughty Boy
    And a naughty Boy was he
He ran away to Scotland
    The people for to see.
        There he found
        That the ground
        Was as hard
        That a yard
        Was as long,
        That a song
        Was as merry
        That a cherry
        Was as red,
        That lead
        Was as weighty
        That fourscore
        Was as eighty
        That a door
        Was as wooden
        As in england.
        So he stood in
        His shoes
        And he wonder'd
        He wonder'd,
        He stood in his
        Shoes and he wonder'd.

My dear Fanny, I am ashamed of writing you such stuff, nor would I if it
were not for being tired after my day's walking, and ready to tumble into
bed so fatigued that when I am asleep you might sew my nose to my great
toe and trundle me round the town like a Hoop without waking me. Then

I get so hungry—a Ham goes but a very little way, and fowls are like Larks to me; a Batch of Bread I make no more ado with than a sheet of parliament; and I can eat a Bull's head as easily as I used to do Bull's eyes. I take a whole string of Pork Sausages down as easily as a Pen'orth of Lady's fingers. Oh dear, I must soon be contented with an acre or two of oaten cake, a hogshead of Milk, and a Clothesbasket of Eggs morning, noon, and night when I get among the Highlanders. Before we see them we shall pass into Ireland and have a chat with the Paddies, and look at the Giant's Causeway, which you must have heard of. I have not time to tell you particularly, for I have to send a Journal to Tom, of whom you shall hear all particulars or from me when I return. Since I began this we have walked sixty miles to newton-stewart, at which place I put in this Letter. Tonight we sleep at Glenluce, tomorrow at Portpatrick, and the next day we shall cross in the passage boat to Ireland. I hope Miss Abbey has quite recovered. Present my respects to her and to Mr. and Mrs. Abbey. God bless you—

Your affectionate Brother John—

Do write me a Letter directed to *Inverness,* Scotland.

❧

To Tom Keats

3, 5, 7, 9 JULY 1818

Auchencairn, July 3rd

My dear Tom,

    I have not been able to keep up my journal completely on account of other letters to George and one which I am writing to Fanny, from which I have turned to lose no time whilst Brown is copying a song about Meg Merrilies which I have just written for her. We are now in Meg Merrilies country and have this morning passed through some parts exactly suited to her. Kirkcudbright County is very beautiful, very wild with craggy hills somewhat in the westmorland fashion. We have come down from Dumfries to the seacoast part of it. The song I mention you would have from Dilke, but perhaps you would like it here.[1]

Now I will return to Fanny—it rains. I may have time to go on here presently.

July 5—You see I have missed a day from fanny's letter. Yesterday was passed in Kirkcudbright. The Country is very rich, very fine, and with a little of Devon. I am now writing at Newton-Stewart six Miles into Wigton. Our Landlady of yesterday said very few Southrens passed these ways. The children jabber away as in a foreign Language. The barefooted Girls look very much in keeping, I mean with the Scenery about them. Brown praises their cleanliness and appearance of comfort, the neatness of their cottages, etc. It may be. They are very squat among trees and fern and heaths and broom, on levels, slopes, and heights. They are very pleasant because they are very primitive, but I wish they were as snug as those up the Devonshire valleys. We are lodged and entertained in great varieties. We dined yesterday on dirty bacon, dirtier eggs, and dirtiest Potatoes with a slice of Salmon. We breakfast this morning in a nice carpeted Room with Sofa, hair-bottomed chairs, and green-baized mehogany. A spring by the roadside is always welcome; we drink water for dinner diluted with a Gill of whiskey.

July 7th—Yesterday Morning we set out from Glenluce going some distance round to see some Ruins;[2] they were scarcely worth the while. We went on towards Stranraer in a burning sun and had gone about six Miles when the Mail overtook us. We got up, were at Portpatrick in a jiffy, and I am writing now in little Ireland. The dialect on the neighbouring shores of Scotland and Ireland is much the same, yet I can perceive a great difference in the nations from the Chambermaid at this nate Inn kept by Mr. Kelly. She is fair, kind, and ready to laugh, because she is out of the horrible dominion of the Scotch kirk. A Scotch Girl stands in terrible awe of the Elders, poor little Susannas. They will scarcely laugh. They are greatly to be pitied, and the kirk is greatly to be damn'd. These kirkmen have done scotland good (Query?): they have made Men, Women, Old Men, Young Men, old Women, young women, boys, girls, and infants all careful, so that they are formed into regular Phalanges of savers and gainers. Such a thrifty army cannot fail to enrich their Country and give it a greater appearance of comfort than that of their poor irish neighbours. These kirkmen have done Scotland harm; they have banished puns and laughing and kissing (except in cases where the very danger and crime must make it very fine and gustful). I shall make a full stop at kissing, for after that there should be a better paren*t*-thesis, and go on to remind you of the fate of Burns. Poor unfortunate fellow; his disposition was southern. How sad it is when a luxurious imagination is obliged in self-defence to deaden its delicacy in vulgarity, and riot in things attainable that it may not have leisure to go mad after things which are not. No Man in such matters will be content with the experience of others. It is true that out of sufferance there is no greatness, no dignity; that in the most abstracted Pleasure there is no lasting happiness: yet who would not like to discover over again that Cleopatra was a Gypsy, Helen a Rogue, and Ruth a deep one? I have not sufficient reasoning faculty to settle the doctrine of thrift—as it is consistent with the dignity of human Society—with the happiness of Cottagers. All I can do is by plump contrasts: Were the fingers made to squeeze a guinea or a white hand? Were the Lips made to hold a pen or a kiss? And yet in Cities Man is shut out from his fellows if he is poor, the Cottager must be dirty and very wretched if she be not thrifty. The present state of society demands this, and this convinces me that the world is very young and in a very ignorant state. We live in a barbarous age. I would sooner be a wild deer than a Girl under the dominion of the kirk, and I would sooner be a wild hog than be the occasion of a Poor Creature's penance before those execrable elders.

It is not so far to the Giant's Causeway as we supposed; we thought it 70 and hear it is only 48 Miles. So we shall leave one of our knapsacks here at Donaghadee, take our immediate wants, and be back in a week, when we shall proceed to the County of Ayr. In the Packet Yesterday we heard some Ballads from two old Men. One was a romance which seemed very poor; then there was the Battle of the Boyne; then Robin Huid, as they call him: "Before the king you shall go, go, go, before the king you shall go." There were no Letters for me at Portpatrick, so I am behindhand with you I dare say in news from George. Direct to Glasgow till the 17th of this month.

9th—We stopped very little in Ireland, and that you may not have leisure to marvel at our speedy return to Portpatrick I will tell you that it is as dear living in Ireland as at the Hummums,³ thrice the expence of Scotland; it would have cost us £15 before our return. Moreover we found those 48 Miles to be irish ones, which reach to 70 english. So having walked to Belfast one day and back to Donaghadee the next, we left Ireland with a fair breeze. We slept last night at Portpatrick, where I was gratified by a letter from you. On our walk in Ireland we had too much opportunity to see the worse than nakedness, the rags, the dirt and misery of the poor common Irish. A Scotch cottage, though in that sometimes the Smoke has no exit but at the door, is a palace to an irish one. We could observe that impetiosity in Man and boy and Woman. We had the pleasure of finding our way through a Peat-Bog—three miles long at least—dreary, black, dank, flat, and spongy. Here and there were poor dirty creatures and a few strong men cutting or carting peat. We heard on passing into Belfast through a most wretched suburb that most disgusting of all noises, worse than the Bagpipe, the laugh of a Monkey, the chatter of women *solus,* the scream of a Macaw, I mean the sound of the Shuttle. What a tremendous difficulty is the improvement of the condition of such people. I cannot conceive how a mind "with child"⁴ of Philantrophy could grasp at possibility; with me it is absolute despair. At a miserable house of entertainment halfway between Donaghadee and Belfast were two Men Sitting at Whiskey, one a Laborer and the other I took to be a drunken Weaver. The Laborer took me for a Frenchman and the other hinted at Bounty Money, saying he was ready to take it. On calling for the Letters at Portpatrick the man snapp'd out, "what Regiment?" On our return from Belfast we met a Sedan—the Duchess of Dunghill. It is no laughing matter tho. Imagine the worst dog kennel you ever saw placed upon two poles from a mouldy fencing. In such a wretched thing sat a squalid old Woman squat like an ape half starved from a scarcity of Biscuit in its passage from Madagascar to the cape, with a pipe in her mouth and looking out with a round-eyed skinny-lidded inanity—with a sort of horizontal idiotic movement of her head—squat and lean she sat and puff'd out the smoke while two ragged tattered Girls carried her along. What a thing would be a history of her Life and sensations. I shall endeavour, when I know more and have thought a little more, to give you my ideas of the difference between the scotch and irish. The two Irishmen I mentioned were speaking of their treatment in England when the Weaver said, "Ah you were a civil Man but I was a drinker." Remember me to all. I intend writing to Haslam, but don't tell him for fear I should delay. We left a notice at Portpatrick that our Letters should be thence forwarded to Glasgow. Our quick return from Ireland will occasion our passing Glasgow sooner than we thought, so till further notice you must direct to Inverness.

Your most affectionate Brother
John—

Remember me to the Bentleys.

1. Here Keats again copies out "Meg Merrilies."
2. The ruins of Glenluce Abbey (1190), a mile and a half northwest on Luce Water.
3. An expensive hotel in Covent Garden, London.
4. *The Faerie Queen,* IV.i; Sidney, *Astrophel and Stella,* Sonnet 1, line 12.

To J. H. Reynolds
11, 13 JULY 1818

Maybole, July 11
My dear Reynolds,

I'll not run over the Ground we have passed. That would be nearly as bad as telling a dream, unless perhaps I do it in the manner of the Laputan printing press;[1] that is, I put down Mountains, Rivers, Lakes, dells, glens, Rocks, and Clouds, With beautiful, enchanting, gothic, picturesque, fine, delightful, enchanting, Grand, sublime—a few Blisters, etc.—and now you have our journey thus far: where I begin a letter to you because I am approaching Burns's Cottage very fast. We have made continual enquiries from the time we saw his Tomb at Dumfries. His name of course is known all about; his great reputation among the plodding people is "that he wrote a good *mony* sensible things." One of the pleasantest means of annulling self is approaching such a shrine as the Cottage of Burns; we need not think of his misery—that is all gone—bad luck to it. I shall look upon it hereafter with unmixed pleasure as I do upon my Stratford-on-Avon day with Bailey. I shall fill this sheet for you in the Bardie's Country, going no further than this till I get into the Town of Ayr, which will be a 9 miles' walk to Tea.

We were talking on different and indifferent things, when on a sudden we turned a corner upon the immediate County of Air.[2] The Sight was as rich as possible. I had no Conception that the native place of Burns was so beautiful; the Idea I had was more desolate, his rigs of Barley seemed always to me but a few strips of Green on a cold hill. O prejudice! it was rich as Devon. I endeavour'd to drink in the Prospect, that I might spin it out to you as the silkworm makes silk from Mulberry leaves. I cannot recollect it. Besides all the Beauty, there were the Mountains of Arran Isle, black and huge over the Sea. We came down upon everything suddenly; there were, in our way, the "bonny Doon,"[3] with the Brig that Tam o' Shanter cross'd, Kirk Alloway, Burns's Cottage, and then the Brigs of Ayr. First we stood upon the Bridge across the Doon, surrounded by every Phantasy of Green in tree, Meadow, and Hill. The Stream of the Doon, as a Farmer told us, is covered with trees from head to foot—you know those beautiful heaths so fresh against the weather of a summer's evening—there was one stretching along behind the trees.

I wish I knew always the humour my friends would be in at opening a letter of mine, to suit it to them nearly as possible. I could always find an eggshell for Melancholy, and as for Merriment a Witty humour will turn anything to Account. My head is sometimes in such a whirl in considering the million likings and antipathies of our Moments, that I can get into no settled strain in my Letters. My Wig! Burns and sentimentality coming across you and frank Floodgate[4] in the office. O scenery that thou shouldst be crush'd between two Puns. As for them I venture the rascalliest in the Scotch Region. I hope Brown does not put them punctually in his journal. If he does I must sit on the cutty-stool all next winter. We Went to Kirk

Allow'y; "a Prophet is no Prophet in his own Country."⁵ We went to the Cottage and took some Whiskey. I wrote a sonnet⁶ for the mere sake of writing some lines under the roof; they are so bad I cannot transcribe them. The Man at the Cottage was a great Bore with his Anecdotes. I hate the rascal. His Life consists in fuzz, fuzzy, fuzziest. He drinks glasses five for the Quarter and twelve for the hour. He is a mahogany-faced old Jackass who knew Burns. He ought to be kicked for having spoken to him. He calls himself "a curious old Bitch,"⁷ but he is a flat old Dog. I should like to employ Caliph Vathek⁸ to kick him. O the flummery of a birthplace! Cant! Cant! Cant! It is enough to give a spirit the guts-ache. Many a true word they say is spoken in jest; this may be because his gab hindered my sublimity. The flat dog made me write a flat sonnet. My dear Reynolds, I cannot write about scenery and visitings. Fancy is indeed less than a present palpable reality, but it is greater than remembrance; you would lift your eyes from Homer only to see close before you the real Isle of Tenedos; you would rather read Homer afterwards than remember yourself. One song of Burns's is of more worth to you than all I could think for a whole year in his native country. His Misery is a dead weight upon the nimbleness of one's quill. I tried to forget it—to drink Toddy without any Care—to write a merry Sonnet—it won't do. He talked with Bitches, he drank with Blackguards, he was miserable. We can see horribly clear in the works of such a man his whole life, as if we were God's spies. What were his addresses to Jean⁹ in the latter part of his life. I should not speak so to you, yet why not; you are not in the same case, you are in the right path, and you shall not be deceived. I have spoken to you against Marriage, but it was general. The Prospect in those matters has been to me so blank, that I have not been unwilling to die. I would not now, for I have inducements to Life. I must see my little Nephews in America, and I must see you marry your lovely Wife. My sensations are sometimes deadened for weeks together, but believe me, I have more than once yearned for the time of your happiness to come, as much as I could for myself after the lips of Juliet. From the tenor of my occasional rodomontade in chitchat, you might have been deceived concerning me in these points; upon my soul, I have been getting more and more

close to you every day, ever since I knew you, and now one of the first pleasures I look to is your happy Marriage[10]—the more, since I have felt the
pleasure of loving a sister in Law. I did not think it possible to become so
much attached in so short a time. Things like these, and they are real, have
made me resolve to have a care of my health; you must be as careful. The
rain has stopped us today at the end of a dozen Miles, yet we hope to see
Loch Lomond the day after tomorrow. I will piddle out my information, as
Rice says, next Winter at any time when a substitute is wanted for Vingt-
un. We bear the fatigue very well—20 Miles a day in general. A cloud came
over us in getting up Skiddaw; I hope to be more lucky in Ben Lomond,
and more lucky still in Ben Nevis. What I think you would enjoy is pok-
ing about Ruins—sometimes Abbey, sometimes Castle. The short stay we
made in Ireland has left few remembrances, but an old woman in a dog-
kennel Sedan with a pipe in her Mouth is what I can never forget. I wish I
may be able to give you an idea of her. Remember me to your Mother and
Sisters, and tell your Mother how I hope she will pardon me for having a
scrap of paper pasted in the Book sent to her. I was driven on all sides and
had not time to call on Taylor. So Bailey is coming to Cumberland; well, if
you'll let me know where at Inverness, I will call on my return and pass a
little time with him. I am glad 'tis not scotland. Tell my friends I do all I
can for them, that is, drink their healths in Toddy. Perhaps I may have
some lines by and by to send you fresh on your own Letter. Tom has a few
to shew you.

Your affectionate friend
John Keats

1. *Gulliver's Travels,* part III, chapter 5.
2. That is, "Ayr."
3. A reference to Burns's "The Banks o' Doon," lines 1, 13.
4. Francis Fladgate, Jr. (1799–1892). Reynolds was studying law with him in the office
   of Frank's father.
5. Mark vi.4, Luke iv.24, John iv.44.
6. The sonnet, beginning "This mortal body of a thousand days," is known only from
   a printed text of 1848 based on a now lost transcript made by Brown.

7. See Burns's "On a Noisey Polemic," line 3, "such a bleth'rin bitch."
8. In the gothic novel *Vathek* by William Beckford (1759–1844).
9. Burns's wife.
10. To Eliza Drewe, which was postponed till 31 August 1822.

To Tom Keats

10, 11, 13, 14 JULY 1818

Ah! ken ye what I met the day
    Out owre the Mountains,
A-coming down by craggis grey
    An' mossie fountains?
Ah goud hair'd Marie, yeve I pray
    Ane minute's guessing,
For that I met upon the way
    Is past expressing.
As I stood where a rocky brig
    A torrent crosses,
I spied upon a misty rig
    A troupe o' Horses.
And as they trotted down the glen
    I sped to meet them,
To see if I might know the Men,
    To stop and greet them.
First Willie on his sleek mare came
    At canting gallop,
His long hair rustled like a flame
    On board a shallop.
Then came his brother Rab and then
    Young Peggy's Mither,

And Peggy too, adown the glen
    They went togither.
I saw her wrappit in her hood
    Fra wind and raining;
Her cheek was flush wi' timid blood
    'Twixt growth and waning.
She turn'd her dazed head full oft,
    For thence her Brithers
Came riding with her Bridegroom soft
    An' mony ithers.
Young Tam came up an' eyed me quick
    With reddened cheek;
Braw Tom was daffed like a chick,
    He could na speak.
Ah Marie, they are all gone hame
    Through blustring weather,
An' every heart is full on flame
    An' light as feather.
Ah! Marie, they are all gone hame
    Fra happy wedding,
Whilst I—Ah is it not a shame?
    Sad tears am shedding.

                          Ballantrae, July 10

My dear Tom,

    The reason for my writing these lines was that Brown wanted to impose a galloway song upon dilke—but it won't do. The subject I got from meeting a wedding just as we came down into this place, where I am afraid we shall be imprisoned awhile by the weather. Yesterday we came 27 Miles from Stranraer, entered Ayrshire a little beyond Cairn, and had our path through a delightful Country. I shall endeavour that you may follow our steps in this walk; it would be uninteresting in a Book of Travels; it cannot be interesting but by my having gone through it. When we left Cairn our

Road lay halfway up the sides of a green mountainous shore, full of Clefts of verdure and eternally varying, sometimes up, sometimes down, and over little Bridges going across green chasms of moss rock and trees, winding about everywhere. After two or three Miles of this we turned suddenly into a magnificent glen finely wooded in Parts—seven Miles long—with a Mountain Stream winding down the Midst, full of cottages in the most happy Situations—the sides of the Hills covered with sheep; the effect of cattle lowing I never had so finely. At the end we had a gradual ascent and got among the tops of the Mountains whence in a little time I descried in the Sea Ailsa Rock, 940 feet high. It was 15 Miles distant and seemed close upon us. The effect of ailsa with the peculiar perspective of the Sea in connection with the ground we stood on, and the misty rain then falling, gave me a complete Idea of a deluge. Ailsa struck me very suddenly; really I was a little alarmed.

Thus far had I written before we set out this morning. Now we are at Girvan, 13 Miles north of Ballantrae. Our Walk has been along a more grand shore today than yesterday, Ailsa beside us all the way. From the heights we could see quite at home Kintyre and the large Mountains of Arran, one of the Hebrides. We are in comfortable Quarters. The Rain we feared held up bravely and it has been "fu fine this day."[1] Tomorrow we shall be at Ayr.

To Ailsa Rock

Hearken, thou craggy ocean pyramid,
    Give answer by thy voice, the Sea fowls' screams!
    When were thy shoulders mantled in huge Streams?
When from the Sun was thy broad forehead hid?
How long is't since the mighty Power bid
    Thee heave to airy sleep from fathom dreams,
    Sleep in the Lap of Thunder or Sunbeams,
Or when grey clouds are thy cold Coverlid?
Thou answer'st not, for thou art dead asleep;
    Thy Life is but two dead eternities,

The last in Air, the former in the deep:
    First with the Whales, last with the eagle skies;
Drown'd wast thou till an Earthquake made thee steep,
    Another cannot wake thy giant Size!

This is the only Sonnet of any worth I have of late written; I hope you will like it. 'Tis now the 11th of July and we have come 8 Miles to Breakfast to Kirkoswald. I hope the next Kirk will be Kirk Alloway. I have nothing of consequence to say now concerning our Journey, so I will speak as far as I can judge on the irish and Scotch. I know nothing of the higher Classes. Yet I have a persuasion that there the Irish are victorious. As to the "profanum vulgus"[2] I must incline to the scotch. They never laugh, but they are always comparatively neat and clean. Their constitutions are not so remote and puzzling as the irish. The Scotchman will never give a decision on any point; he will never commit himself in a sentence which may be referred to as a meridian in his notions of things—so that you do not know him—and yet you may come in nigher neighborhood to him than to the irishman, who commits himself in so many places that it dazes your head. A Scotchman's motive is more easily discovered than an irishman's. A Scotchman will go wisely about to deceive you, an irishman cunningly. An Irishman would bluster out of any discovery to his disadvantage; a Scotchman would retire perhaps without much desire of revenge. An Irishman likes to be thought a gallous fellow; a scotchman is contented with himself. It seems to me they are both sensible of the Character they hold in England and act accordingly to Englishmen. Thus the Scotchman will become over-grave and over-decent and the Irishman over-impetuous. I like a Scotchman best because he is less of a bore. I like the Irishman best because he ought to be more comfortable. The Scotchman has made up his Mind within himself in a sort of snail-shell wisdom. The Irishman is full of strong-headed instinct. The Scotchman is farther in Humanity than the Irishman; there he will stick perhaps when the Irishman shall be refined beyond him; for the former thinks he cannot be improved, the latter would grasp at it forever, place but the good plain before him.

Maybole. Since breakfast we have come only four Miles to dinner, not merely, for we have examined in the way two Ruins, one of them very fine called Crossraguel Abbey. There is a winding Staircase to the top of a little Watch Tower.

July 13. *Kingswells.* I have been writing to Reynolds, therefore any particulars since Kirkoswald have escaped me. From said kirk we went to Maybole to dinner; then we set forward to Burns's town Ayr. The Approach to it is extremely fine—quite outwent my expectations—richly meadowed, wooded, heathed, and rivuleted with a grand Sea view terminated by the black Mountains of the isle of Arran. As soon as I saw them so nearly I said to myself, "How is it they did not beckon Burns to some grand attempt at Epic?" The bonny Doon is the sweetest river I ever saw, overhung with fine trees as far as we could see. We stood some time on the Brig across it, over which Tam o' shanter fled. We took a pinch of snuff on the keystone. Then we proceeded to "auld Kirk Alloway." As we were looking at it a Farmer pointed out the spots where "Mungo's Mither hang'd hersel" and "drunken Charlie brake's neck's bane."[3] Then we proceeded to the Cottage he was born in. There was a board to that effect by the door Side; it had the same effect as the same sort of memorial at Stratford-on-Avon. We drank some Toddy to Burns's Memory with an old Man who knew Burns. Damn him, and damn his Anecdotes. He was a great bore. It was impossible for a Southern to understand above 5 words in a hundred. There was something good in his description of Burns's melancholy the last time he saw him. I was determined to write a sonnet in the Cottage. I did, but it is so bad I cannot venture it here. Next we walked into Ayr Town and before we went to Tea saw the new Brig and the Auld Brig and wallace tower. Yesterday we dined with a Traveler. We were talking about Kean. He said he had seen him at Glasgow "in Othello in the Jew, I mean er, er, er, the Jew in Shylock." He got bother'd completely in vague ideas of the Jew in Othello, Shylock in the Jew, Shylock in Othello, Othello in Shylock, the Jew in Othello, etc., etc., etc. He left himself in a mess at last. Still satisfied with himself, he went to the Window and gave an abortive whistle of some tune or other; it might have been Handel. There is no end to these Mistakes: he'll go and tell people how he has seen "Malvolio in the Count-ess," "Twelfth night in Midsummer night's dream"—Bottom in much ado about Nothing—Viola in Barrymore—Antony in Cleopatra—Falstaff in the mouse Trap.

July 14. We enter'd Glasgow last Evening under the most oppressive Stare a body could feel. When we had crossed the Bridge, Brown look'd back and said its whole population had turned to wonder at us. We came on till a drunken Man came up to me. I put him off with my Arm; he re-turned all up in Arms, saying aloud that "he had seen all foreigners bu-u-u t he never saw the like o' me." I was obliged to mention the word Officer and Police before he would desist. The City of Glasgow I take to be a very fine one. I was astonished to hear it was twice the size of Edinburgh. It is built of Stone and has a much more solid appearance than London. We shall see the Cathedral this morning; they have devilled it into a "High Kirk." I want very much to know the name of the Ship George is gone in, also what port he will land in. I know nothing about it. I hope you are leading a quiet Life and gradually improving. Make a long lounge of the whole Summer; by the time the Leaves fall I shall be near you with plenty of confab. There are a thousand things I cannot write. Take care of yourself—I mean in not being vexed or bothered at anything. God bless you!

John—

1. Adapted from the refrain of Burns's "The Holy Fair."
2. Horace, *Odes,* III.i.i, "the uninitiated crowd."
3. The three quotations are from "Tam o' Shanter," lines 32, 96, and 92.

To Tom Keats
17, 18, 20, 21 JULY 1818

Cairn-something,[1] July 17th

My dear Tom,

Here's Brown going on so that I cannot bring to Mind how the two last days have vanished; for example he says, "The Lady of the Lake went to Rock herself to sleep on Arthur's seat and the Lord of the Isles coming to Press a Piece and seeing her Assleap remembered their last meeting at Cony stone Water; so touching her with one hand on the Vallis Lucis while the other un-Derwent her Whitehaven, Ireby stifled her clack man on, that he might her Anglesea and give her a Buchanan and said." I told you last how we were stared at in Glasgow; we are not out of the Crowd yet. Steam Boats on Loch Lomond and Barouches on its sides take a little from the Pleasure of such romantic chaps as Brown and I. The Banks of the Clyde are extremely beautiful—the north End of Loch Lomond grand in excess—the entrance at the lower end to the narrow part from a little distance is precious good. The Evening was beautiful; nothing could surpass our fortune in the weather, yet was I worldly enough to wish for a fleet of chivalry Barges with Trumpets and Banners just to die away before me into that blue place among the mountains. I must give you an outline as well as I can.[2] Nota B—the Water was a fine Blue-silver'd and the Mountains a dark purple, the Sun setting aslant behind them; meantime the head of ben Lomond was covered with a rich Pink Cloud. We did not ascend Ben Lomond, the price being very high and a half a day of rest being quite acceptable. We were up at 4 this morning and have walked to breakfast 15 Miles through two tremendous Glens. At the end of the first there is a place called rest and be thankful, which we took for an Inn. It was nothing but a Stone, and so we were cheated into 5 more Miles to Breakfast. I have just been bathing in Loch fyne, a saltwater Lake opposite the Window, quite

pat and fresh but for the cursed Gadflies. Damn 'em, they have been at me
ever since I left the Swan and two necks.

All gentle folks who owe a grudge
    To any living thing,
Open your ears and stay your trudge
    Whilst I in dudgeon sing.

The gadfly he hath stung me sore,
    O may he ne'er sting you!
But we have many a horrid bore
    He may sting black and blue.

Has any here an old grey Mare
    With three Legs all her store?
O put it to her Buttocks bare
    And Straight she'll run on four.

Has any here a Lawyer suit
    Of 1743?
Take Lawyer's nose and put it to 't
    And you the end will see.

Is there a Man in Parliament
    Dumfounder'd in his speech?
O let his neighbour make a rent
    And put one in his breech.

O Lowther, how much better thou
    Hadst figur'd t'other day,
When to the folks thou mad'st a bow
    And hadst no more to say,

If lucky gadfly had but ta'en
    His seat upon thine A——e,
And put thee to a little pain
    To save thee from a worse.

Better than Southey it had been,
　　Better than Mr. D——,
Better than Wordsworth too, I ween,
　　Better than Mr. V——.

Forgive me pray, good people all,
　　For deviating so;
In spirit sure I had a call,
　　And now I on will go.

Has any here a daughter fair
　　Too fond of reading novels,
Too apt to fall in love with care
　　And charming Mister Lovels?[3]

O put a gadfly to that thing
　　She keeps so white and pert;
I mean the finger for the ring,
　　And it will breed a Wart.

Has any here a pious spouse
　　Who seven times a day
Scolds as King David pray'd, to chouse
　　And have her holy way?

O let a Gadfly's little sting
　　Persuade her sacred tongue
That noises are a common thing
　　But that her bell has rung.

And as this is the summum bo-
　　Num of all conquering,
I leave withouten wordes mo'
　　The Gadfly's little sting.

Last Evening we came round the End of Loch Fyne to Inverary. The Duke of Argyll's Castle is very modern magnificent, and more so from the place it is in; the woods seem old enough to remember two or three changes in the Crags about them. The Lake was beautiful and there was a Band at a distance by the Castle. I must say I enjoyed two or three common tunes, but nothing could stifle the horrors of a solo on the Bag-pipe. I thought the Beast would never have done, yet was I doomed to hear another. On entering Inverary we saw a Play Bill. Brown was knock'd up from new shoes, so I went to the Barn alone, where I saw The Stranger[4] accompanied by a Bag-pipe. There they went on about "interesting creaters" and "human nater," till the Curtain fell and then Came the Bag-pipe. When Mrs. Haller fainted, down went the Curtain and out came the Bag-pipe. At the heart-rending, shoe-mending reconciliation the Piper blew amain. I never read or saw this play before; not the Bag-pipe nor the wretched players themselves were little in comparison with it. Thank heaven it has been scoffed at lately almost to a fashion.

> Of late two dainties were before me plac'd,
>> Sweet, holy, pure, sacred, and innocent,
>> From the ninth sphere to me benignly sent
> That Gods might know my own particular taste.
> First the soft bag-pipe mourn'd with zealous haste;
>> The Stranger next with head on bosom bent
>> Sigh'd; rueful again the piteous bag-pipe went;
> Again the Stranger sighings fresh did waste.
> O Bag-pipe, thou didst steal my heart away;
>> O Stranger, thou my nerves from Pipe didst charm;
> O Bag-pipe, thou didst reassert thy sway;
>> Again thou Stranger gav'st me fresh alarm—
> Alas! I could not choose. Ah ! my poor heart,
> Mumchance art thou with both obliged to part.

I think we are the luckiest fellows in Christendom. Brown could not proceed this morning on account of his feet, and lo there is thunder and rain.

July 20th. For these two days past we have been so badly accommodated more particularly in coarse food that I have not been at all in cue to write. Last night poor Brown with his feet blistered and scarcely able to walk, after a trudge of 20 Miles down the Side of Loch Awe, had no supper but Eggs and Oat Cake; we have lost the sight of white bread entirely. Now we had eaten nothing but Eggs all day, about 10 apiece and they had become sickening. Today we have fared rather better, but no oat Cake wanting. We had a small Chicken and even a good bottle of Port, but altogether the fare is too coarse. I feel it a little; another week will break us in. I forgot to tell you that when we came through Glen Croe it was early in the morning and we were pleased with the noise of Shepherds, Sheep, and dogs in the misty heights close above us; we saw none of them for some time, till two came in sight creeping among the Crags like Emmets, yet their voices came quite plainly to us. The Approach to Loch Awe was very solemn towards night-fall; the first glance was a streak of water deep in the Bases of large black Mountains. We had come along a complete mountain road, where if one listened there was not a sound but that of Mountain Streams. We walked 20 Miles by the side of Loch Awe, every ten steps creating a new and beau-tiful picture, sometimes through little wood. There are two islands on the Lake, each with a beautiful ruin, one of them rich in ivy.

We are detained this morning by the rain. I will tell you exactly where we are. We are between Loch Craignish and the Sea just opposite Long Is-land. Yesterday our walk was of this description: the near Hills were not very lofty but many of their Steeps beautifully wooded; the distant Moun-tains in the Hebrides very grand, the Saltwater Lakes coming up between Crags and Islands full-tided and scarcely ruffled, sometimes appearing as one large Lake, sometimes as three distinct ones in different directions. At one point we saw afar off a rocky opening into the main Sea. We have also seen an Eagle or two. They move about without the least motion of Wings when in an indolent fit. I am for the first time in a country where a foreign Language is spoken. They gabble away Gaelic at a vast rate; numbers of them speak English. There are not many Kilts in Argyllshire. At Fort Wil-liam they say a Man is not admitted into Society without one; the Ladies there have a horror at the indecency of Breeches. I cannot give you a better idea of Highland Life than by describing the place we are in. The Inn or public is by far the best house in the immediate neighbourhood. It has a white front with tolerable windows. The table I am writing on surprises me as being a nice flapped Mehogany one; at the same time the place has no water-closet nor anything like it. You may if you peep see through the floor chinks into the ground rooms. The old Grandmother of the house seems intelligent, though not over clean. N.B. No snuff being to be had in the village, she made us some. The Guid Man is a rough looking hardy stout Man who I think does not speak so much English as the Guid wife, who is very obliging and sensible and moreover, though stockingless, has a pair of old Shoes. Last night some Whiskey Men sat up clattering Gaelic till I am sure one o' Clock to our great annoyance. There is a Gaelic testament on the Drawers in the next room. White and blue China ware has crept all about here. Yesterday there passed a Donkey laden with tin pots. Opposite the Window there are hills in a Mist, a few Ash trees and a mountain stream at a little distance. They possess a few head of Cattle. If you had gone round to the back of the House just now, you would have seen more hills in a Mist, some dozen wretched black Cottages scented of peat smoke, which finds its way by the door or a hole in the roof, a girl here and there barefoot. There was one little thing driving Cows down a slope like a mad thing; there was another standing at the cow-house door rather pretty fac'd, all up to the ankles in dirt.

We have walk'd 15 Miles in a soaking rain to Oban, opposite the Isle of Mull, which is so near Staffa we had thought to pass to it; but the expence is 7 Guineas and those rather extorted. Staffa, you see, is a fashionable place, and therefore everyone concerned with it either in this town or the Island are what you call up; 'tis like paying sixpence for an apple at the playhouse. This irritated me, and Brown was not best pleased. We have therefore resolved to set northward for fort William tomorrow morning. I fell upon a bit of white Bread today like a Sparrow—it was very fine—I cannot manage the cursed Oatcake. Remember me to all and let me hear a good account of you at Inverness. I am sorry Georgy had not those Lines. Good-bye.

Your affectionate Brother
John—

1. Keats is writing from Cairndow.
2. A rough pen sketch is given here.

3. The hero of Walter Scott's *The Antiquary.*
4. A play by Augustus von Kotzebue. Mrs. Haller is its heroine.

To Benjamin Bailey
18, 22 JULY 1818

Inverary, July 18th

My dear Bailey,

The only day I have had a chance of seeing you when you were last in London I took every advantage of; some devil led you out of the way. Now I have written to Reynolds to tell me where you will be in Cumberland, so that I cannot miss you. And when I see you the first thing I shall do will be to read that about Milton and Ceres and Proserpine,[1] for though I am not going after you to John o' Groats,[2] it will be but poetical to say so. And here, Bailey, I will say a few words written in a sane and sober Mind, a very scarce thing with me, for they may hereafter save you a great deal of trouble about me, which you do not deserve, and for which I ought to be bastinadoed. I carry all matters to an extreme, so that when I have any little vexation it grows in five Minutes into a theme for Sophocles. Then and in that temper if I write to any friend I have so little self-possession that I give him matter for grieving at the very time perhaps when I am laughing at a Pun. Your last Letter made me blush for the pain I had given you. I know my own disposition so well that I am certain of writing many times hereafter in the same strain to you. Now you know how far to believe in them; you must allow for imagination. I know I shall not be able to help it. I am sorry you are grieved at my not continuing my visits to little Britain,[3] yet I think I have as far as a Man can do who has Books to read and subjects to think upon. For that reason I have been nowhere else except to Wentworth place so nigh at hand. Moreover I have been too often in a state of health that made me think it prudent not to hazard the night Air. Yet further, I will confess to you that I cannot enjoy Society small or numerous. I am cer-

tain that our fair friends[4] are glad I should come for the
coming; but I am certain I bring with me a Vexation they ˌ
out. If I can possibly at any time feel my temper coming upon
even from a promised visit. I am certain I have not a right feeli
Women; at this moment I am striving to be just to them, but I cai   ˌt
because they fall so far beneath my Boyish imagination? When ˌ was a
Schoolboy I thought a fair Woman a pure Goddess; my mind was a soft
nest in which some one of them slept, though she knew it not. I have no
right to expect more than their reality. I thought them ethereal above Men;
I find them perhaps equal. Great by comparison is very small. Insult may
be inflicted in more ways than by Word or action; one who is tender of being insulted does not like to think an insult against another. I do not like to
think insults in a Lady's Company; I commit a Crime with her which absence would have not known. Is it not extraordinary? When among Men I
have no evil thoughts, no malice, no spleen; I feel free to speak or to be silent. I can listen and from everyone I can learn; my hands are in my pockets, I am free from all suspicion and comfortable. When I am among
Women I have evil thoughts, malice, spleen. I cannot speak or be silent. I
am full of Suspicions and therefore listen to nothing; I am in a hurry to be
gone. You must be charitable and put all this perversity to my being disappointed since Boyhood. Yet with such feelings I am happier alone among
Crowds of men, by myself or with a friend or two. With all this trust me,
Bailey, I have not the least idea that Men of different feelings and inclinations are more short-sighted than myself. I never rejoiced more than at my
Brother's Marriage and shall do so at that of any of my friends. I must abso-
lutely get over this, but how? The only way is to find the root of evil, and so
cure it "with backward mutters of dissevering Power."[5] That is a difficult
thing; for an obstinate Prejudice can seldom be produced but from a
gordian complication of feelings, which must take time to unravel and care
to keep unraveled. I could say a good deal about this but I will leave it in
hopes of better and more worthy dispositions and also content that I am
wronging no one, for after all I do think better of Womankind than to suppose they care whether Mister John Keats five feet high likes them or not.
You appeared to wish to avoid any words on this subject; don't think it a

ɔore, my dear fellow. It shall be my Amen. I should not have consented to myself these four Months tramping in the highlands but that I thought it would give me more experience, rub off more Prejudice, use me to more hardship, identify finer scenes, load me with grander Mountains, and strengthen more my reach in Poetry, than would stopping at home among Books even though I should reach Homer. By this time I am comparatively a mountaineer. I have been among wilds and Mountains too much to break out much about their Grandeur. I have fed upon Oat cake, not long enough to be very much attached to it. The first Mountains I saw, though not so large as some I have since seen, weighed very solemnly upon me. The effect is wearing away, yet I like them mainly.

We have come this evening with a Guide—for without was impossible—into the middle of the Isle of Mull, pursuing our cheap journey to Iona and perhaps staffa. We would not follow the common and fashionable mode from the great imposition of expence. We have come over heath and rock and river and bog to what in England would be called a horrid place. Yet it belongs to a Shepherd pretty well off perhaps. The family speak not a word but gaelic, and we have not yet seen their faces for the smoke, which after visiting every cranny (not excepting my eyes, very much incommoded for writing), finds its way out at the door. I am more comfortable than I could have imagined in such a place, and so is Brown. The People are all very kind. We lost our way a little yesterday and enquiring at a Cottage, a young Woman without a word threw on her cloak and walked a Mile in a mizzling rain and splashy way to put us right again. I could not have had a greater pleasure in these parts than your mention of my Sister. She is very much prisoned from me. I am afraid it will be some time before I can take her to many places I wish. I trust we shall see you ere long in Cumberland, at least I hope I shall before my visit to America more than once. I intend to pass a whole year with George if I live to the completion of the three next. My sister's welfare and the hopes of such a stay in America will make me observe your advice; I shall be prudent and more careful of my health than I have been. I hope you will be about paying your first visit to Town after settling when we come into Cumberland. Cumberland however will be no distance to me after my present journey; I shall spin to you in a min-

ute. I begin to get rather a contempt for distances. I hope you will have a
nice convenient room for a Library. Now you are so well in health, do keep
it up by never missing your dinner, by not reading hard, and by taking
proper exercise. You'll have a horse, I suppose, so you must make a point of
sweating him. You say I must study Dante; well, the only Books I have with
me are those three little Volumes. I read that fine passage you mention a
few days ago. Your Letter followed me from Hampstead to Portpatrick and
thence to Glasgow; you must think me by this time a very pretty fellow.
One of the pleasantest bouts we have had was our walk to Burns's Cottage,
over the Doon and past Kirk Alloway. I had determined to write a Sonnet
in the Cottage. I did, but lawk it was so wretched I destroyed it. However
in a few days afterwards I wrote some lines cousin-german to the Circumstance, which I will transcribe or rather cross-scribe[6] in the front of this.
Reynolds's illness has made him a new Man; he will be stronger than ever.
Before I left London he was really getting a fat face. Brown keeps on writing volumes of adventures to Dilke. When we get in of an evening and I
have perhaps taken my rest on a couple of Chairs, he affronts my indolence
and Luxury by pulling out of his knapsack 1st his paper, 2nd his pens, and
last his ink. Now I would not care if he would change about a little; I say
now, why not, Bailey, take out his pens first sometimes? But I might as well
tell a hen to hold up her head before she drinks instead of afterwards. Your
affectionate friend

John Keats—

There is a joy in footing slow across a silent plain,
Where Patriot Battle has been fought, when Glory had the gain;
There is a pleasure on the heath where Druids old have been,
Where Mantles grey have rustled by and swept the nettles green:
There is a joy in every spot made known by times of old,
New to the feet, although the tale a hundred times be told:
There is a deeper joy than all, more solemn in the heart,
More parching to the tongue than all, of more divine a smart,
When weary feet forget themselves upon a pleasant turf,

Upon hot sand, or flinty road, or Sea shore iron scurf,
Toward the Castle or the Cot where long ago was born
One who was great through mortal days and died of fame
    unshorn.
Light Heather-bells may tremble then, but they are far away;
Woodlark may sing from sandy fern, the Sun may hear his Lay;
Runnels may kiss the grass on shelves and shallows clear,
But their low voices are not heard, though come on travels drear;
Blood-red the sun may set behind black mountain peaks;
Blue tides may sluice and drench their time in Caves and weedy
    creeks;
Eagles may seem to sleep wing-wide upon the Air;
Ring doves may fly convuls'd across to some high cedar'd lair;
But the forgotten eye is still fast wedded to the ground,
As Palmer's that with weariness mid-desert shrine hath found.
At such a time the Soul's a Child, in Childhood is the brain;
Forgotten is the worldly heart; alone, it beats in vain.
Aye, if a Madman could have leave to pass a healthful day,
To tell his forehead's swoon and faint when first began decay,
He might make tremble many a Man whose Spirit had gone forth
To find a Bard's low Cradle place, about the silent north.
Scanty the hour and few the steps beyond the Bourn of Care,
Beyond the sweet and bitter world, beyond it unaware;
Scanty the hour and few the steps, because a longer stay
Would bar return and make a Man forget his mortal way.
O horrible! to lose the sight of well remember'd face,
Of Brother's eyes, of Sister's Brow, constant to every place;
Filling the Air, as on we move, with Portraiture intense,
More warm than those heroic tints that fill a Painter's sense,
When Shapes of old come striding by and visages of old,
Locks shining black, hair scanty grey, and passions manifold.
No, No, that horror cannot be, for at the Cable's length
Man feels the gentle Anchor pull and gladdens in its strength.
One hour, half idiot, he stands by mossy waterfall,

But in the very next he reads his Soul's memorial:
He reads it on the Mountain's height, where chance he may sit
    down
Upon rough marble diadem, that Hill's eternal crown.
Yet be the Anchor e'er so fast, room is there for a prayer
That Man may never lose his Mind on Mountains bleak and bare;
That he may stray league after League some great Birthplace to
    find,
And keep his vision clear from speck, his inward sight unblind.

1. *Paradise Lost,* IV.268–272.
2. The northern extremity of Scotland's mainland.
3. The home of J. H. Reynolds, his parents, and his four sisters. Bailey had proposed
   to the second sister, Mariane.
4. The Reynolds girls, whom Keats soon came to dislike.
5. Milton, *Comus,* line 817.
6. To write sideways across lines already written on the page. The practice—referred
   to again in the next two letters as "chequer work" and "crossing"—was a common
   way of getting more writing on a sheet and thus saving on postage.

To Tom Keats
23, 26 JULY 1818

Dun an cullen[1]

My dear Tom,

Just after my last had gone to the Post in came one of the Men with
whom we endeavoured to agree about going to Staffa. He said what a pity it
was we should turn aside and not see the Curiosities. So we had a little talk
and finally agreed that he should be our guide across the Isle of Mull. We
set out, crossed two ferries, one to the isle of Kerrera of little distance, the
other from Kerrera to Mull, 9 Miles across. We did it in forty minutes with
a fine Breeze. The road through the Island, or rather the track, is the most

dreary you can think of, between dreary Mountains, over bog and rock and river with our Breeches tucked up and our Stockings in hand. About eight o' Clock we arrived at a shepherd's Hut, into which we could scarcely get for the Smoke through a door lower than my shoulders. We found our way into a little compartment with the rafters and turf thatch blackened with smoke, the earth floor full of Hills and Dales. We had some white Bread with us, made a good Supper, and slept in our Clothes in some Blankets; our Guide snored on another little bed about an Arm's length off. This morning we came about six² Miles to Breakfast by rather a better path, and we are now in by comparison a Mansion. Our Guide is I think a very obliging fellow—in the way this morning he sang us two Gaelic songs—one made by a Mrs. Brown on her husband's being drowned, the other a jacobin one on Charles Stuart. For some days Brown has been enquiring out his Genealogy here. He thinks his Grandfather came from long Island. He got a parcel of people about him at a Cottage door last Evening, chatted with ane who had been a Miss Brown and who I think from a likeness must have been a Relation. He jawed with the old Woman, flattered a young one, kissed a child who was afraid of his Spectacles, and finally drank a pint of Milk. They handle his Spectacles as we do a sensitive leaf.

July 26th. Well, we had a most wretched walk of 37 Miles across the Island of Mull and then we crossed to Iona or Icolmkill. From Icolmkill we took a boat at a bargain to take us to Staffa and land us at the head of Loch Nakgal,³ whence we should only have to walk half the distance to Oban again and on a better road. All this is well pass'd and done with this singular piece of Luck, that there was an intermission in the bad Weather just as we saw Staffa, at which it is impossible to land but in a tolerable Calm Sea. But I will first mention Icolmkill. I know not whether you have heard much about this Island. I never did before I came nigh it. It is rich in the most interesting Antiquities. Who would expect to find the ruins of a fine Cathedral Church, of Cloisters, Colleges, Monasteries and Nunneries in so remote an Island? The Beginning of these things was in the sixth Century under the superstition of a would-be Bishop-saint who landed from Ireland and chose the spot from its Beauty, for at that time the now treeless place was covered with magnificent Woods. Columba in the Gaelic is Colm signifying Dove; Kill signifies church and I is as good as Island; so I-colm-kill means the Island of Saint Columba's Church. Now this Saint Columba became the Dominic of the barbarian Christians of the north and was famed also far south, but more especially was reverenced by the Scots, the Picts, the Norwegians, the Irish. In a course of years perhaps the Island was considered the most holy ground of the north, and the old kings of the aforementioned nations chose it for their burial place. We were shown a spot in the Churchyard where they say 61 kings are buried—48 Scotch from Fergus 2nd to Macbeth, 8 Irish, 4 Norwegian and 1 french. They lie in rows compact. Then we were shown other matters of later date but still very ancient: many tombs of Highland Chieftains, their effigies in complete armour face upwards, black and moss-covered, Abbots and Bishops of the island, always of one of the chief Clans. There were plenty Macleans and Macdonalds, among these latter the famous Macdonald Lord of the Isles.[4] There have been 300 Crosses in the Island but the Presbyterians destroyed all but two, one of which is a very fine one and completely covered with a shaggy coarse Moss. The old Schoolmaster, an ignorant little man but reckoned very clever, showed us these things. He is a Maclean and as much above 4 foot as he is under 4 foot 3 inches. He stops at one glass of whiskey unless you press another, and at the second unless you press a third. I am puzzled how to give you an Idea of Staffa. It can only be represented by a first-rate drawing. One may compare the surface of the Island to a roof; this roof is supported by grand pillars of basalt standing together as thick as honeycombs. The finest thing is Fingal's Cave; it is entirely a hollowing out of Basalt Pillars. Suppose now the Giants who rebelled against Jove had taken a whole Mass of black Columns and bound them together like bunches of matches, and then with immense Axes had made a cavern in the body of these columns; of course the roof and floor must be composed of the broken ends of the Columns. Such is fingal's Cave except that the Sea has done the work of excavations and is continually dashing there, so that we walk along the sides of the cave on the pillars which are left as if for convenient Stairs. The roof is arched somewhat gothic-wise and the length of some of the entire side pillars is 50 feet. About the island you might seat an army of Men each on a pillar. The length of the Cave is 120 feet and from its extremity the view into the sea through the large Arch at the entrance; the colour of the columns is a sort of black with a lurking gloom of purple therein. For solemnity and grandeur it far surpasses the finest Cathedral. At the extremity of the Cave there is a small perforation into another cave, at which, the waters meeting and buffeting each other, there is sometimes produced a report as of a cannon heard as far as Iona, which must be 12 Miles. As we approached in the boat there was such a fine swell of the sea that the pillars appeared rising immediately out of the crystal. But it is impossible to describe it—

Not Aladdin magian
Ever such a work began;
Not the Wizard of the dee
Ever such a dream could see;
Not St. John in Patmos' isle,
In the passion of his toil,
When he saw the churches seven,
Golden-aisled, built up in heaven,
Gazed at such a rugged wonder.
As I stood its roofing under,
Lo! I saw one sleeping there
On the marble cold and bare,
While the surges washed his feet
And his garments white did beat
Drench'd about the sombre rocks;
On his neck his well-grown locks,
Lifted dry above the Main,
Were upon the curl again.
"What is this and what art thou?"
Whisper'd I and touch'd his brow.
"What art thou and what is this?"
Whisper'd I and strove to kiss
The Spirit's hand to wake his eyes.
Up he started in a trice.
"I am Lycidas," said he,

"Fam'd in funeral Minstrelsy.
This was architected thus
By the great Oceanus;
Here his mighty waters play
Hollow Organs all the day;
Here by turns his dolphins all,
Finny palmers great and small,
Come to pay devotion due,
Each a mouth of pearls must strew.
Many a Mortal of these days
Dares to pass our sacred ways,
Dares to touch audaciously
This Cathedral of the Sea.
I have been the Pontiff priest
Where the Waters never rest,
Where a fledgy sea-bird choir
Soars forever; holy fire
I have hid from Mortal Man;
Proteus is my Sacristan.
But the stupid eye of Mortal
Hath pass'd beyond the Rocky portal;
So for ever will I leave
Such a taint, and soon unweave
All the magic of the place.
'Tis now free to stupid face,
To cutters and to fashion boats,
To cravats and to Petticoats.
The great Sea shall war it down,
For its fame shall not be blown
At every farthing quadrille dance."
So saying with a Spirit's glance
He dived—

I am sorry I am so indolent as to write such stuff as this; it can't be help'd.
The western coast of Scotland is a most strange place. It is composed of

rocks, Mountains, mountainous and rocky Islands intersected by Lochs. You can go but a small distance anywhere from salt water in the highlands.

I have a slight sore throat and think it best to stay a day or two at Oban. Then we shall proceed to Fort William and Inverness, where I am anxious to be on account of a Letter from you. Brown in his Letters puts down every little circumstance. I should like to do the same but I confess myself too indolent, and besides next winter everything will come up in prime order as we verge on such and such things. Have you heard in any way of George? I should think by this time he must have landed. I in my carelessness never thought of knowing where a letter would find him on the other side—I think Baltimore but I am afraid of directing to the wrong place. I shall begin some chequer work for him directly, and it will be ripe for the post by the time I hear from you next after this. I assure you I often long for a seat and a Cup o' tea at well Walk, especially now that mountains, castles, and Lakes are becoming common to me. Yet I would rather summer it out, for on the whole I am happier than when I have time to be glum; perhaps it may cure me. Immediately on my return I shall begin studying hard with a peep at the theatre now and then and depend upon it I shall be very luxurious. With respect to Women I think I shall be able to conquer my passions hereafter better than I have yet done. You will help me to talk of george next winter and we will go now and then to see Fanny. Let me hear a good account of your health and comfort, telling me truly how you do alone.

Remember me to all including Mr. and Mrs. Bentley.

Your most affectionate Brother
John—

1. Keats's approximation of Derry-na-Cullen.
2. Keats actually wrote "sax" and may have intended a Scottish spelling of the word.
3. Loch na Keal.
4. Donald Macdonald (d. 1420?), second Lord of the Isles.

To Tom Keats

3, 6 AUGUST 1818

Letter Findlay, August 3rd

My dear Tom,   Ah mio Ben.

We have made but poor progress Lately—chiefly from bad weather, for my throat is in a fair way of getting quite well—so I have had nothing of consequence to tell you till yesterday, when we went up Ben Nevis, the highest Mountain in Great Britain. On that account I will never ascend another in this empire. Skiddaw is nothing to it either in height or in difficulty. It is above 4300 feet from the Sea level, and Fort William stands at the head of a Salt water Lake; consequently we took it completely from that level. I am heartily glad it is done; it is almost like a fly crawling up a wainscot. Imagine the task of mounting 10 Saint Pauls without the convenience of Staircases. We set out about five in the morning with a Guide in the Tartan and Cap and soon arrived at the foot of the first ascent, which we immediately began upon. After much fag and tug and a rest and a glass of whiskey apiece we gained the top of the first rise and saw then a tremendous chap above us which the guide said was still far from the top. After the first Rise our way lay along a heath valley in which there was a Loch. After about a Mile in this Valley we began upon the next ascent, more formidable by far than the last, and kept mounting with short intervals of rest until we got above all vegetation, among nothing but loose Stones, which lasted us to the very top. The Guide said we had three Miles of a stony ascent. We gained the first tolerable level after the valley to the height of what in the Valley we had thought the top, and saw still above us another huge crag which still the Guide said was not the top. To that we made with an obstinate fag and, having gained it, there came on a Mist, so that from that part to the very top we walked in a Mist. The whole immense head of the Mountain is composed of large loose stones, thousands of acres. Before we had got halfway up we passed large patches of snow, and near the top there is a chasm some hundred feet deep completely glutted with it. Talking of chasms, they are the finest wonder of the whole. They appear great rents in the very heart of the mountain, though they are not, being at the side of it, but other huge crags arising round it give the appearance to Nevis of a shattered heart or Core in itself. These Chasms are 1500 feet in depth and are the most tremendous places I have ever seen; they turn one giddy if you choose to give way to it. We tumbled in large stones and set the echoes at work in fine style. Sometimes these chasms are tolerably clear, sometimes there is a misty cloud which seems to steam up, and sometimes they are entirely smothered with clouds.

After a little time the Mist cleared away, but still there were large Clouds about attracted by old Ben to a certain distance so as to form, as it appeared, large dome curtains which kept sailing about, opening and shutting at intervals here and there and everywhere; so that although we did not see one vast wide extent of prospect all round, we saw something perhaps finer: these cloud-veils opening with a dissolving motion and showing us the mountainous region beneath as through a loophole—these Mouldy loopholes ever varying and discovering fresh prospect east, west, north, and South. Then it was misty again, and again it was fair; then puff came a cold breeze of wind and bared a craggy chap we had not yet seen, though in close neighbourhood. Every now and then we had overhead blue Sky clear and the sun pretty warm. I do not know whether I can give you an Idea of the prospect from a large Mountain top. You are on a stony plain, which of course makes you forget you are on any but low ground. The horizon or rather edges of this plain, being above 4000 feet above the Sea, hide all the Country immediately beneath you, so that the next objects you see all round next to the edges of the flat top are the Summits of Mountains of some distance off. As you move about, on all sides you see more or less of the near neighbour country according as the Mountain you stand upon is in different parts steep or rounded. But the most new thing of all is the sudden leap of the eye from the extremity of what appears a plain into so vast a distance. On one part of the top there is a handsome pile of stones done

pointedly by some soldiers of artillery. I climbed onto them and so got a little higher than old Ben himself. It was not so cold as I expected, yet cold
enough for a glass of Whiskey now and then. There is not a more fickle
thing than the top of a Mountain. What would a Lady give to change her
head-dress as often and with as little trouble! There are a good many red
deer upon Ben Nevis. We did not see one. The dog we had with us kept a
very sharp lookout and really languished for a bit of a worry. I have said
nothing yet of our getting on among the loose stones large and small,
sometimes on two, sometimes on three, sometimes four legs; sometimes
two and stick, sometimes three and stick, then four again, then two, then a
jump, so that we kept on ringing changes on foot, hand, Stick, jump, bog-
gle, stumble, foot, hand, foot (very gingerly), stick again, and then again a
game at all fours. After all there was one Mrs. Cameron of 50 years of age
and the fattest woman in all inverness-shire, who got up this Mountain
some few years ago. True she had her servants, but then she had herself. She
ought to have hired Sisyphus: "Up the high hill he heaves a huge round—
Mrs. Cameron."[1] 'Tis said a little conversation took place between the
mountain and the Lady. After taking a glass of Whiskey, as she was tolerably seated at ease she thus begun:

Mrs. C——

Upon my Life, Sir Nevis, I am pique'd
That I have so far panted, tugg'd, and reek'd
To do an honor to your old bald pate
And now am sitting on you just to bate,
Without your paying me one compliment.
Alas, 'tis so with all, when our intent
Is plain, and in the eye of all Mankind
We fair ones show a preference, too blind!
You Gentlemen immediately turn tail—
O let me then my hapless fate bewail!
Ungrateful Baldpate, have I not disdain'd
The pleasant Valleys—have I not, mad-brain'd,

Deserted all my Pickles and preserves,
My China closet too—with wretched Nerves
To boot—say, wretched ingrate, have I not
Left my soft cushion chair and candle pot?
'Tis true I had no corns—no! thank the fates,
My Shoemaker was always Mr. Bates.
And if not Mr. Bates, why I'm not old!
Still dumb, ungrateful Nevis—still so cold!

(Here the Lady took some more whiskey and was putting even more to her lips when she dashed it to the Ground, for the Mountain began to grumble, which continued for a few Minutes before he thus began):

Ben Nevis

What whining bit of tongue and Mouth thus dares
Disturb my Slumber of a thousand years?
Even so long my sleep has been secure,
And to be so awaked I'll not endure.
Oh pain, for since the Eagle's earliest scream
I've had a damn'd confounded ugly dream,
A Nightmare sure. What, Madam, was it you?
It cannot be! My old eyes are not true!
Red-Crag,* my Spectacles! Now let me see!
Good Heavens, Lady, how the gemini
Did you get here? O I shall split my Sides!
I shall earthquake.

Mrs. C——

Sweet Nevis, do not quake, for though I love
Your honest Countenance all things above,
Truly I should not like to be convey'd

---

*A domestic of Ben's.

So far into your Bosom; gentle Maid
Loves not too rough a treatment, gentle sir;
Pray thee be calm and do not quake nor stir,
No, not a Stone, or I shall go in fits.

Ben Nevis

I must—I shall—I meet not such titbits,
I meet not such sweet creatures every day.
By my old nightcap, nightcap night and day,
I must have one sweet Buss—I must and shall!
Red-Crag! What, Madam, can you then repent
Of all the toil and vigour you have spent
To see Ben Nevis and to touch his nose?
Red-Crag, I say! O I must have you close!
Red-crag, there lies beneath my farthest toe
A vein of Sulphur—go, dear Red-Crag, go—
And rub your flinty back against it—budge!
Dear Madam, I must kiss you, faith I must!
I must Embrace you with my dearest gust!
Blockhead,* d'ye hear, Blockhead, I'll make her feel.
There lies beneath my east leg's northern heel
A cave of young earth dragons; well, my boy,
Go thither quick and so complete my joy.
Take you a bundle of the largest pines,
And where the sun on fiercest Phosphor shines
Fire them and ram them in the Dragons' nest;
Then will the dragons fry and fizz their best,
Until ten thousand now no bigger than
Poor Alligators, poor things of one span,
Will each one swell to twice ten times the size

---

*Another domestic of Ben's.

Of northern whale—then for the tender prize—
The moment then, for then will red-Crag rub
His flinty back, and I shall kiss and snub
And press my dainty morsel to my breast.
Blockhead, make haste!
        O Muses, weep the rest;
The Lady fainted and he thought her dead,
So pulled the clouds again about his head
And went to sleep again. Soon she was rous'd
By her affrighted Servants. Next day, hous'd
Safe on the lowly ground, she bless'd her fate
That fainting fit was not delayed too late.

But what surprises me above all is how this Lady got down again. I felt it horribly. 'Twas the most vile descent, shook me all to pieces.

Overleaf you will find a Sonnet I wrote on the top of Ben Nevis. We have just entered Inverness. I have three Letters from you and one from Fanny and one from Dilke. I would set about crossing this all over for you but I will first write to Fanny and Mrs. Wylie, then I will begin another to you and not before, because I think it better you should have this as soon as possible. My Sore throat is not quite well and I intend stopping here a few days.

Read me a Lesson, muse, and speak it loud
Upon the top of Nevis, blind in Mist!
I look into the Chasms, and a Shroud
Vaprous doth hide them; just so much I wist
Mankind do know of Hell: I look o'erhead,
    And there is sullen Mist; even so much
Mankind can tell of Heaven: Mist is spread
    Before the Earth beneath me; even such,
Even so vague is Man's sight of himself.
    Here are the craggy Stones beneath my feet;
Thus much I know, that a poor witless elf,

> I tread on them; that all my eye doth meet
> Is mist and Crag—not only on this height,
> But in the World of thought and mental might.

Good-bye till tomorrow.

Your most affectionate Brother
John—

1. From Pope's translation of Homer's *Odyssey,* XI.736.

To Mrs. James Wylie
6 AUGUST 1818

Inverness, 6th August 1818

My dear Madam,

It was a great regret to me that I should leave all my friends, just at the moment when I might have helped to soften away the time for them. I wanted not to leave my Brother Tom, but more especially, believe me, I should like to have remained near you, were it but for an atom of consolation, after parting with so dear a daughter. My brother George has ever been more than a brother to me; he has been my greatest friend, and I can never forget the sacrifice you have made for his happiness. As I walk along the Mountains here, I am full of these things, and lay in wait, as it were, for the pleasure of seeing you immediately on my return to town. I wish, above all things, to say a word of Comfort to you, but I know not how. It is impossible to prove that black is white, it is impossible to make out that sorrow is joy or joy is sorrow.

Tom tells me that you called on Mr. Haslam with a Newspaper giving an account of a Gentleman in a Fur cap falling over a precipice in

Kirkcudbrightshire. If it was me, I did it in a dream, or in some magic interval between the first and second cup of tea; which is nothing extraordinary, when we hear that Mahomet, in getting out of Bed, upset a jug of water, and whilst it was falling, took a fortnight's trip as it seemed to Heaven,
yet was back in time to save one drop of water being spilt. As for Fur caps, I
do not remember one beside my own, except at Carlisle; this was a very
good Fur cap I met in the High Street, and I dare say was the unfortunate
one. I dare say that the fates, seeing but two Fur caps in the North, thought
it too extraordinary, and so threw the Dies[1] which of them should be
drowned. The lot fell upon Jonas; I dare say his name was Jonas. All I hope
is, that the gaunt Ladies said not a word about hanging; if they did, I shall
one day regret that I was not half drowned in Kirkcudbright. Stop! Let me
see! Being half-drowned by falling from a precipice is a very romantic affair;
why should I not take it to myself? Keep my secret and I will. How glorious
to be introduced in a drawing room to a Lady who reads Novels, with "Mr.
so and so—Miss so and so—Miss so and so, this is Mr. so and so who fell
off a precipice and was half-drowned." Now I refer it to you whether I
should lose so fine an opportunity of making my fortune; no romance lady
could resist me—None—Being run under a Wagon, side-lamed at a playhouse, Apoplectic through Brandy, and a thousand other tolerably decent
things for badness would be nothing; but being tumbled over a precipice
into the sea—Oh, it would make my fortune—especially if you could continue to hint, from this bulletin's authority, that I was not upset on my own
account, but that I dashed into the waves after Jessy of Dumblane[2] and
pulled her out by the hair—But that, Alas! she was dead or she would have
made me happy with her hand. However, in this you may use your own
discretion.

But I must leave joking and seriously aver that I have been *werry* romantic indeed, among these Mountains and Lakes. I have got wet through day
after day, eaten oat cake, and drank whiskey, walked up to my knees in Bog,
got a sore throat, gone to see Icolmkill and Staffa, met with wholesome
food, just here and there as it happened; went up Ben Nevis, and N.B.
came down again. Sometimes when I am rather tired, I lean rather lan-
guishingly on a Rock, and long for some famous Beauty to get down

from her Palfrey in passing, approach me with—her saddle-bags—and give me—a dozen or two capital roast beef sandwiches.

When I come into a large town, you know there is no putting one's Knapsack into one's fob; so the people stare. We have been taken for Spectacle vendors, Razor sellers, Jewelers, travelling linen-drapers, Spies, Excisemen, and many things else I have no idea of. When I asked for letters at the Post Office, Portpatrick, the man asked what Regiment? I have had a peep also at little Ireland. Tell Henry I have not Camped quite on the bare Earth yet, but nearly as bad in walking through Mull, for the Shepherds' huts you can scarcely breathe in, for the smoke, which they seem to endeavour to preserve for smoking on a large scale. Besides riding about 400, we have walked above 600 Miles, and may therefore reckon ourselves as set out.

I wish, my dear Madam, that one of the greatest pleasures I shall have on my return will be seeing you and that I shall ever be

Yours with the greatest Respect and sincerity
John Keats—

1. Dice.
2. A reference to "Jessie, The Flow'r o' Dumblane" by Robert Tannahill (1774–1810), in his *Poems & Songs* (1817), pp. 137f.

To Fanny Keats
19 AUGUST 1818

Hampstead, August 18th
My dear Fanny,

I am afraid you will think *me* very negligent in not having answered your Letter; I see it is dated June 12. I did not arrive at Inverness till the 8th of this Month so I am very much concerned at your being disappointed so long a time. I did not intend to have returned to London so soon but have a bad sore throat from a cold I caught in the island of Mull. Therefore I thought it best to get home as soon as possible and went on board the Smack from Cromarty. We had a nine day's passage and were landed at London Bridge yesterday. I shall have a good deal to tell you about Scotland; I would begin here but I have a confounded toothache. Tom has not been getting better since I left London and for the last fortnight has been worse than ever; he has been getting a little better for these two or three days. I shall ask Mr. Abbey to let me bring you to Hampstead. If Mr. A should see this Letter tell him that he still must, if he pleases, forward the Post Bill to Perth, as I have empowered my fellow traveller to receive it. I have a few scotch pebbles for you from the Island of Icolmkill; I am afraid they are rather shabby. I did not go near the Mountain of Cairn Gorm. I do not know the Name of George's ship; the Name of the Port he has gone to is Philadelphia whence he will travel to the Settlement[1] across the Country. I will tell you all about this when I see you. The Title of my last Book is "Endymion." You shall have one soon. I would not advise you to play on the Flageolet, however I will get you one if you please. I will speak to Mr. Abbey on what you say concerning school.[2] I am sorry for your poor Canary. You shall have another volume of my first Book. My tooth Ache keeps on so that I cannot write with any pleasure; all I can say now is that your Letter is a very nice one without fault and that you will hear from or see in a few days if his throat will let him,

Your affectionate Brother
John

1. Morris Birkbeck's Albion, Illinois, colony. Birkbeck (1764–1825) bought sixteen thousand acres of land in Illinois, where he founded the town of Albion.
2. Mr. Abbey soon removed her from school in spite of Keats's efforts.

To C. W. Dilke

20, 21 SEPTEMBER 1818

My dear Dilke,

According to the Wentworth place Bulletin you have left Brighton much improved; therefore now a few lines will be more of a pleasure than a bore. I have a few things to say to you and would fain begin upon them in this fourth line, but I have a Mind too well-regulated to proceed upon anything without due preliminary remarks. You may perhaps have observed that in the simple process of eating radishes I never begin at the root but constantly dip the little green head in the salt, that in the Game of Whist if I have an ace I constantly play it first. So how can I with any face begin without a dissertation on letter writing? Yet when I consider that a sheet of paper contains room only for three pages and a half, how can I do justice to such a pregnant subject? However, as you have seen the history of the world stamped as it were by a diminishing glass in the form of a chronological Map, so will I "with retractile claws"[1] draw this in to the form of a table whereby it will occupy merely the remainder of this first page:

Folio	Parsons, Lawyers, Statesmen, Physicians out of place— Ut—Eustace[2]—Thornton[3]—out of practice or on their travels.
Fools cap	1 superfine! rich or noble poets—ut Byron. Two common ut egomet.
Quarto	Projectors, Patentees, Presidents, Potato-growers.
Bath	Boarding schools, and suburbans in general.
Gilt edge	Dandies in general, male, female and literary.
Octavo or tears	All who make use of a lascivious seal.
Duodec	May be found for the most part on Milliners and Dressmakers' Parlour tables.

Strip	At the Playhouse doors, or anywhere.
Slip	Being but a variation.
Snip	So-called from its size being disguised by a twist.

I suppose you will have heard that Hazlitt has on foot a prosecution against Blackwood. I dined with him a few days since at Hessey's; there was not a word said about it, though I understand he is excessively vexed. Reynolds, by what I hear, is almost over happy and Rice is in town. I have not seen him nor shall I for some time as my throat has become worse after getting well, and I am determined to stop at home till I am quite well. I was going to Town tomorrow with Mrs. D. but I thought it best to ask her excuse this morning. I wish I could say Tom was any better. His identity presses upon me so all day that I am obliged to go out, and although I intended to have given some time to study alone, I am obliged to write, and plunge into abstract images to ease myself of his countenance, his voice and feebleness— so that I live now in a continual fever. It must be poisonous to life, although I feel well. Imagine "the hateful siege of contraries."[4] If I think of fame, of poetry, it seems a crime to me, and yet I must do so or suffer. I am sorry to give you pain; I am almost resolv'd to burn this, but I really have not self possession and magnanimity enough to manage the thing otherwise; after all, it may be a nervousness proceeding from the Mercury.

Bailey, I hear, is gaining his Spirits and he will yet be what I once thought impossible: a cheerful Man. I think he is not quite so much spoken of in Little Britain. I forgot to ask Mrs. Dilke if she had anything she wanted to say immediately to you. This morning look'd so unpromising that I did not think she would have gone, but I find she has on sending for some volumes of Gibbon. I was in a little funk yesterday, for I sent an unseal'd note of sham abuse, until I recollected from what I had heard Charles say, that the servant could neither read nor write—not even to her Mother as Charles observed. I have just had a Letter from Reynolds; he is going on gloriously. The following is a translation of a Line of Ronsard—

"Love poured her Beauty into my warm veins."[5]

You have passed your Romance and I never gave into it or else I think this line a feast for one of your Lovers. How goes it with Brown?

Your sincere friend
John Keats—

1. Dante's *Inferno* (Cary's translation), XVII.101.
2. J. C. Eustace (1762?–1815), *A Classical Tour through Italy* (1817).
3. Thomas Thornton (d. 1814), *The Present State of Turkey* (1807).
4. *Paradise Lost*, IX.121f.
5. Sonnet II in *Les amours de Cassandre*, line 12.

To J. H. Reynolds
22 (?) SEPTEMBER 1818

My dear Reynolds,

Believe me I have rather rejoiced in your happiness than fretted at your silence. Indeed I am grieved on your account that I am not at the same time happy. But I conjure you to think at Present of nothing but pleasure, "Gather the rose, etc." Gorge the honey of life. I pity you as much that it cannot last forever, as I do myself now drinking bitters. Give yourself up to it; you cannot help it, and I have a Consolation in thinking so. I never was in love, yet the voice and the shape of a woman[1] has haunted me these two days at such a time when the relief, the feverous relief of Poetry seems a much less crime. This morning Poetry has conquered. I have relapsed into those abstractions which are my only life. I feel escaped from a new, strange and threatening sorrow, and I am thankful for it. There is an awful warmth about my heart like a load of Immortality.

Poor Tom. That woman, and Poetry were ringing changes in my senses. Now I am in comparison happy. I am sensible this will distress you; you must forgive me. Had I known you would have set out so soon I could have sent you the "Pot of Basil" for I had copied it out ready. Here is a free translation of a Sonnet of Ronsard, which I think will please you. I have the loan of his works; they have great Beauties.

Nature withheld Cassandra in the skies, etc., etc.[2]

I had not the original by me when I wrote it, and did not recollect the purport of the last lines. I should have seen Rice ere this, but I am confined by Sawrey's mandate in the house now, and have as yet only gone out in fear of the damp night; you know what an undangerous matter it is. I shall soon be quite recovered. Your offer I shall remember as though it had even now taken place in fact. I think it can not be. Tom is not up yet; I cannot say he is better. I have not heard from George.

Your affectionate friend *John Keats*

1. "Charmian," or Jane Cox.
2. Woodhouse, the copyist, notes: "here follow the 1ˢᵗ 12 lines of the sonnet, then 2 strokes are drawn for the last lines."

To J. A. Hessey
8 OCTOBER 1818

My dear Hessey,

You are very good in sending me the letter from the Chronicle, and I am very bad in not acknowledging such a kindness sooner. Pray forgive me; it has so chanced that I have had that paper everyday. I have seen today's. I cannot but feel indebted to those Gentlemen who have taken my part. As for the rest, I begin to get a little acquainted with my own strength and weakness. Praise or blame has but a momentary effect on the man whose love of beauty in the abstract makes him a severe critic on his own Works. My own domestic criticism has given me pain without comparison beyond what Blackwood or the Quarterly could possibly inflict, and also when I feel I am right no external praise can give me such a glow as my own solitary reperception and ratification of what is fine. J.S. is perfectly right in regard to the slipshod Endymion. That it is so is no fault of mine—No!—though it may sound a little paradoxical. It is as good as I had power to make it—by myself—Had I been nervous about its being a perfect piece and with that view asked advice and trembled over every page, it would not have been written; for it is not in my nature to fumble. I will write independently. I have written independently *without Judgment*. I may write independently *and with judgment* hereafter. The Genius of Poetry must work out its own salvation in a man: It cannot be matured by law and precept, but by sensation and watchfulness in itself. That which is creative must create itself. In Endymion, I leaped headlong into the Sea, and thereby have become better acquainted with the Soundings, the quicksands, and the rocks, than if I had stayed upon the green shore, and piped a silly pipe, and took tea and comfortable advice. I was never afraid of failure; for I would sooner fail than not be among the greatest. But I am nigh getting into a rant. So, with remembrances to Taylor and Woodhouse, etc. I am

Yours very sincerely
John Keats

To Fanny Keats
26 OCTOBER 1818

My dear Fanny,

I called on Mr. Abbey in the beginning of last Week when he seemed averse to letting you come again from having heard that you had been to other places besides Well Walk. I do not mean to say you did wrongly in speaking of it, for there should rightly be no objection to such things, but you know with what People we are obliged in the course of Childhood to

associate, whose conduct forces us into duplicity and falshood to them. To
the worst of People we should be openhearted, but it is as well as things are
to be prudent in making any communication to anyone that may throw an
impediment in the way of any of the little pleasures you may have. I do not
recommend duplicity but prudence with such people. Perhaps I am talking
too deeply for you. If you do not now, you will understand what I mean in
the course of a few years. I think poor Tom is a little Better. He sends his
love to you. I shall call on Mr. Abbey tomorrow when I hope to settle when
to see you again. Mrs. Dilke has been for some time at Brighton. She is expected home in a day or two. She will be pleased I am sure with your present. I will try for permission for you to remain here all Night should Mrs.
D. return in time.[1]

Your affectionate Brother
John—

1. Fanny was not allowed to visit her brothers after the beginning of October.

❀
———

To Richard Woodhouse
27 OCTOBER 1818

My dear Woodhouse,

Your Letter gave me a great satisfaction, more on account of its friendliness than any relish of that matter in it which is accounted so acceptable in
the "genus irritabile."[1] The best answer I can give you is in a clerk-like manner to make some observations on two principle points, which seem to
point like indices into the midst of the whole pro and con about genius,
and views, and atchievements, and ambition, and coetera. 1st As to the poetical Character itself (I mean that sort of which, if I am anything, I am a
Member; that sort distinguished from the wordsworthian or egotistical sublime, which is a thing per se and stands alone),[2] it is not itself—it has no

self—it is everything and nothing—It has no character—it
shade; it lives in gusto, be it foul or fair, high or low, rich or
elevated. It has as much delight in conceiving an Iago as an Im.
shocks the virtuous philosopher, delights the camelion Poet. ɪ
harm from its relish of the dark side of things any more than from ɪaste
for the bright one; because they both end in speculation. A Poet is the most
unpoetical of anything in existence because he has no Identity; he is continually in for and filling some other Body. The Sun, the Moon, the Sea and
Men and Women who are creatures of impulse are poetical and have about
them an unchangeable attribute. The poet has none; no identity. He is certainly the most unpoetical of all God's Creatures. If then he has no self, and
if I am a Poet, where is the Wonder that I should say I would write no
more? Might I not at that very instant have been cogitating on the Characters of saturn and Ops?³ It is a wretched thing to confess but is a very fact
that not one word I ever utter can be taken for granted as an opinion growing out of my identical nature. How can it, when I have no nature? When I
am in a room with People, if I ever am free from speculating on creations of
my own brain, then not myself goes home to myself, but the identity of everyone in the room begins to press upon me that I am in a very little time
annihilated. Not only among Men; it would be the same in a Nursery of
children. I know not whether I make myself wholly understood; I hope
enough so to let you see that no dependence is to be placed on what I said
that day.

In the second place I will speak of my views, and of the life I purpose to
myself. I am ambitious of doing the world some good. If I should be
spared, that may be the work of maturer years. In the interval I will assay to
reach to as high a summit in Poetry as the nerve bestowed upon me will
suffer. The faint conceptions I have of Poems to come brings the blood frequently into my forehead. All I hope is that I may not lose all interest in
human affairs, that the solitary indifference I feel for applause even from
the finest Spirits will not blunt any acuteness of vision I may have. I do not
think it will. I feel assured I should write from the mere yearning and fond-
ness I have for the Beautiful even if my night's labours should be burnt every morning and no eye ever shine upon them. But even now I am perhaps

1ot speaking from myself but from some character in whose soul I now live. I am sure however that this next sentence is from myself. I feel your anxiety, good opinion and friendliness in the highest degree, and am

Your's most sincerely
John Keats

1. Horace, *Epistles,* II.ii.102.
2. *Troilus and Cressida,* I.ii.15f., "he is a very man *per se, /* And stands alone."
3. Characters in Keats's *Hyperion.*

To George and Georgiana Keats
14, 16, 21, 24, 31 OCTOBER 1818

My dear George,

There was a part in your Letter which gave me a great deal of pain, that where you lament not receiving Letters from England. I intended to have written immediately on my return from Scotland (which was two Months earlier than I had intended on account of my own as well as Tom's health) but then I was told by Mrs. Wylie that you had said you would not wish anyone to write till we had heard from you. This I thought odd and now I see that it could not have been so; yet at the time I suffered my unreflecting head to be satisfied and went on in that sort of abstract careless and restless Life with which you are well acquainted. This sentence, should it give you any uneasiness, do not let it last for before I finish it will be explained away to your satisfaction.

I am grieved to say that I am not sorry you had not Letters at Philadelphia; you could have had no good news of Tom, and I have been withheld on his account from beginning these many days. I could not bring myself to say the truth, that he is no better, but much worse; however, it must be told, and you must, my dear Brother and Sister, take example from me and bear up against any Calamity for my sake as I do for your's. Our's are ties which independent of their own Sentiment are sent us by providence to prevent the deleterious effects of one great, solitary grief. I have Fanny and I have you: three people whose Happiness to me is sacred, and it does annul that selfish sorrow which I should otherwise fall into, living as I do with poor Tom who looks upon me as his only comfort. The tears will come into your Eyes—let them—and embrace each other. Thank heaven for what happiness you have, and after thinking a moment or two that you suffer in common with all Mankind, hold it not a sin to regain your cheerfulness. I will relieve you of one uneasiness of overleaf. I returned, I said, on account of my health. I am now well from a bad sore throat which came of bog trotting in the Island of Mull—of which you shall hear by the copies I shall make from my Scotch Letters. Your content in each other is a delight to me which I cannot express. The Moon is now shining full and brilliant. She is the same to me in Matter what you are to me in Spirit. If you were here, my dear Sister, I could not pronounce the words which I can write to you from a distance. I have a tenderness for you, and an admiration which I feel to be as great and more chaste than I can have for any woman in the world. You will mention Fanny. Her character is not formed; her identity does not press upon me as yours does. I hope from the bottom of my heart that I may one day feel as much for her as I do for you. I know not how it is, but I have never made any acquaintance of my own—nearly all through your medium, my dear Brother—through you I know not only a Sister but a glorious human being. And now I am talking of those to whom you have made me known I cannot forbear mentioning Haslam as a most kind and obliging and constant friend. His behaviour to Tom during my absence and since my return has endeared him to me forever, besides his anxiety about you. Tomorrow I shall call on your Mother and exchange information with her. On Tom's account I have not been able to pass so much time with her as I would otherwise have done. I have seen her but twice—once I dined with her and Charles. She was well, in good Spirits and I kept her laughing at my bad jokes. We went to tea at Mrs. Millar's and in going were particularly struck with the light and shade through the Gateway at the Horse Guards. I intend to write you such Volumes that it will be impossible

for me to keep any order or method in what I write: that will come first
which is uppermost in my Mind, not that which is uppermost in my heart;
besides, I should wish to give you a picture of our Lives here whenever by a
touch I can do it, even as you must see by the last sentence our walk past
Whitehall all in good health and spirits. This I am certain of, because I felt
so much pleasure from the simple idea of your playing a game at Cricket.
At Mrs. Millar's I saw Henry quite well. There was Miss Keasle, and the
goodnatured Miss Waldegrave.[1] Mrs. Millar began a long story and you
know it is her Daughter's way to help her on as though her tongue were ill
of the gout. Mrs. M. certainly tells a Story as though she had been taught
her Alphabet in Crutched Friars. Dilke has been very unwell; I found him
very ailing on my return. He was under Medical care for some time, and
then went to the Sea Side whence he has returned well. Poor little Mrs. D.
has had another gallstone attack. She was well ere I returned; she is now at
Brighton. Dilke was greatly pleased to hear from you and will write a Letter
for me to enclose. He seems greatly desirous of hearing from you of the Settlement itself. I came by ship from Inverness and was nine days at Sea without being sick. A little Qualm now and then put me in mind of you; however as soon as you touch the shore all the horrors of sickness are soon
forgotten, as was the case with a Lady on board who could not hold her
head up all the way. We had not been in the Thames an hour before her
tongue began to some tune, paying off, as it was fit she should, all old
scores. I was the only Englishman on board. There was a downright Scotchman who hearing that there had been a bad crop of Potatoes in England
had brought some triumphant Specimens from Scotland. These he exhibited with national pride to all the Lightermen and Watermen from the
Nore to the Bridge. I fed upon beef all the way, not being able to eat the
thick Porridge which the Ladies managed to manage with large awkward
horn spoons into the bargain. Severn has had a narrow escape of his Life
from a Typhous fever; he is now gaining strength. Reynolds has returned
from a six weeks enjoyment in Devonshire. He is well and persuades me to
publish my pot of Basil as an answer to the attacks made on me in Blackwood's Magazine and the Quarterly Review. There have been two Letters in
my defense in the Chronicle and one in the Examiner, copied from the

Alfred Exeter paper and written by Reynolds. I do not know who wrote those in the Chronicle. This is a mere matter of the moment. I think I shall be among the English Poets after my death. Even as a Matter of present interest the attempt to crush me in the Quarterly has only brought me more into notice and it is a common expression among book men: "I wonder the Quarterly should cut its own throat."

It does me not the least harm in Society to make me appear little and rediculous.[2] I know when a Man is superior to me and give him all due respect. He will be the last to laugh at me and, as for the rest, I feel that I make an impression upon them which insures me personal respect while I am in sight whatever they may say when my back is turned. Poor Haydon's eyes will not suffer him to proceed with his picture. He has been in the Country. I have seen him but once since my return. I hurry matters together here because I do not know when the Mail sails. I shall enquire tomorrow and then shall know whether to be particular or general in my letter. You shall have at least two sheets a day till it does sail, whether it be three days or a fortnight, and then I will begin a fresh one for the next Month. The Miss Reynoldses are very kind to me, but they have lately displeased me much and in this way. Now I am becoming the Richardson. On my return, the first day I called they were in a sort of taking or bustle about a Cousin of theirs[3] who having fallen out with her Grandpapa in a serious manner was invited by Mrs. Reynolds to take Asylum in her house. She is an east indian and ought to be her Grandfather's Heir. At the time I called, Mrs. R. was in conference with her upstairs and the young Ladies were warm in her praises downstairs, calling her genteel, interesting and a thousand other pretty things to which I gave no heed, not being partial to 9 days wonders. Now all is completely changed. They hate her, and from what I hear she is not without faults of a real kind, but she has others which are more apt to make women of inferior charms hate her. She is not a Cleopatra, but she is at least a Charmian. She has a rich eastern look; she has fine eyes and fine manners. When she comes into a room she makes an impression the same as the Beauty of a Leopardess. She is too fine and too conscious of her Self to repulse any Man who may address her; from habit she thinks that nothing *particular.* I always find myself more at ease with such a ıan; the picture before me always gives me a life and animation which I ᴗ ınot possibly feel with anything inferior. I am at such times too much occupied in admiring to be awkward or on a tremble. I forget myself entirely because I live in her. You will by this time think I am in love with her, so before I go any further I will tell you I am not. She kept me awake one Night as a tune of Mozart's might do. I speak of the thing as a passtime and an amuzement than which I can feel none deeper than a conversation with an imperial woman the very "yes" and "no" of whose Lips is to me a Banquet. I don't cry to take the moon home with me in my Pocket, nor do I fret to leave her behind me. I like her and her like because one has no *sensations;* what we both are is taken for granted. You will suppose I have by this had much talk with her—no such thing—there are the Miss Reynoldses on the look out. They think I don't admire her because I did not stare at her. They call her a flirt to me. What a want of knowledge! She walks across a room in such a manner that a Man is drawn towards her with a magnetic Power. This they call flirting! They do not know things. They do not know what a Woman is. I believe tho' she has faults, the same as Charmian and Cleopatra might have had; yet she is a fine thing speaking in a worldly way, for there are two distinct tempers of mind in which we judge of things: the worldly, theatrical and pantomimical, and the unearthly, spiritual and ethereal. In the former Buonaparte, Lord Byron and this Charmian hold the first place in our Minds; in the latter John Howard, Bishop Hooker rocking his child's cradle[4] and you my dear Sister are the conquering feelings. As a Man in the world I love the rich talk of a Charmian; as an eternal Being I love the thought of you. I should like her to ruin me, and I should like you to save me. Do not think, my dear Brother, from this that my Passions are headlong or likely to be ever of any pain to you—no,

> "I am free from Men of Pleasure's cares
> By dint of feelings far more deep than theirs."

This is Lord Byron[5] and is one of the finest things he has said. I have no town talk for you, as I have not been much among people. As for Politics, they are in my opinion only sleepy because they will soon be too wide awake. Perhaps not, for the long and continued Peace of England itself has

given us notions of personal safety which are likely to prevent the reestablishment of our national Honesty. There is of a truth nothing manly or
sterling in any part of the Government. There are many Madmen in the
Country, I have no doubt, who would like to be beheaded on tower Hill
merely for the sake of eclat; there are many Men like Hunt who from a
principle of taste would like to see things go on better; there are many like
Sir F. Burdett[6] who like to sit at the head of political dinners, but there are
none prepared to suffer in obscurity for their Country. The motives of our
worst Men are interest and of our best Vanity. We have no Milton, no
Algernon Sidney.[7] Governers in these days lose the title of Man in exchange
for that of Diplomat and Minister. We breathe in a sort of Officinal Atmosphere. All the departments of Government have strayed far from Simplicity which is the greatest of Strength. There is as much difference in this respect between the present Government and oliver Cromwell's, as there is
between the 12 Tables of Rome and the volumes of Civil Law which were
digested by Justinian. A Man now entitled Chancellor has the same honour
paid to him whether he be a Hog or a Lord Bacon. No sensation is created
by Greatness but by the number of orders a Man has at his Button holes,
Notwithstanding the part which the Liberals take in the Cause of Napoleon. I cannot but think he has done more harm to the life of Liberty than
anyone else could have done; not that the divine right Gentlemen have
done or intend to do any good—no, they have taken a Lesson of him and
will do all the further harm he would have done without any of the good.
The worst thing he has done is that he has taught them how to organize
their monstrous armies. The Emperor Alexander, it is said, intends to divide
his Empire as did Diocletian, creating two Czars besides himself and continuing the supreme Monarch of the whole. Should he do this and they for
a series of Years keep peaceable among themselves Russia may spread her
conquest even to China. I think a very likely thing that China itself may
fall, Turkey certainly will. Meanwhile european north Russia will hold its
horns against the rest of Europe, intriguing constantly with France. Dilke,
whom you know to be a Godwin perfectibility Man,[8] pleases himself with
the idea that America will be the country to take up the human intellect
where england leaves off. I differ there with him greatly. A country like the

united states whose greatest Men are Franklins and Washingtons will never do that. They are great Men doubtless, but how are they to be compared to those our countrymen Milton and the two Sidneys. The one is a philosophical Quaker full of mean and thrifty maxims, the other sold the very Charger who had taken him through all his Battles. Those Americans are great but they are not sublime Man; the humanity of the United States can never reach the sublime. Birkbeck's[9] mind is too much in the American Style; you must endeavour to infuse a little Spirit of another sort into the Settlement, always with great caution, for thereby you may do your descendents more good than you may imagine. If I had a prayer to make for any great good, next to Tom's recovery, it should be that one of your Children should be the first American Poet. I have a great mind to make a prophecy and they say prophecies work out their own fullfillment.

> 'Tis "the witching time of night"[10]
> Orbed is the Moon and bright
> And the Stars they glisten, glisten
> Seeming with bright eyes to listen;
> For what listen they?
> For a song and for a charm,
> See they glisten in alarm
> And the Moon is waxing warm
> To hear what I shall say.
> Moon keep wide thy golden ears
> Hearken Stars, and hearken Spheres,
> Hearken thou eternal Sky
> I sing an infant's lullaby,
> A pretty Lullaby!
> Listen, Listen, listen, listen,
> Glisten, glisten, glisten, glisten,
> And hear my lullaby?
> Though the Rushes that will make
> Its cradle still are in the lake:
> Though the linnen that will be
> Its swathe is on the cotton tree;

Though the wollen that will keep
It warm, is on the silly sheep;
Listen Stars light, listen, listen,
Glisten, Glisten, glisten, glisten,
And hear my lullaby!
Child! I see thee! Child I've found thee
Midst of the quiet all around thee!
Child I see thee! Child I spy thee
And thy mother sweet is nigh thee!
Child I know thee! Child no more
But a Poet *ever*more.
See, See the Lyre, the Lyre
In a flame of fire
Upon the little cradle's top
Flaring, flaring, flaring.
Past the eyesight's bearing,
Awake it from its sleep
And see if it can keep
Its eyes upon the blaze.
Amaze, Amaze!
It stares, it stares, it stares,
It dares what no one dares,
It lifts its little hand into the flame
Unharm'd, and on the strings
Paddles a little tune and sings
With dumb endeavour sweetly!
Bard art thou completely!
Little Child
O' the western wild
Bard art thou completely!
Sweetly, with dumb endeavour,
A Poet now or never!
Little Child
O' the western wild
A Poet now or never!

This is friday, I know not what day of the Month. I will enquire tomorrow for it is fit you should know the time I am writing. I went to Town yesterday, and calling at Mrs. Millar's was told that your Mother would not be
found at home. I met Henry as I turned the corner. I had no leisure to return, so I left the letters with him. He was looking very well. Poor Tom is
no better tonight; I am afraid to ask him what Message I shall send from
him. And here I could go on complaining of my Misery, but I will keep
myself cheerful for your Sakes. With a great deal of trouble I have succeeded in getting Fanny to Hampstead. She has been several times. Mr.
Lewis has been very kind to Tom; all the Summer there has scarce a day
passed but he has visited him, and not one day without bringing or sending
some fruit of the nicest kind. He has been very assiduous in his enquiries
after you. It would give the old Gentleman a great pleasure if you would
send him a Sheet enclosed in the next parcel to me, after you receive this—
how long it will be first. Why did I not write to Philadelphia? Really, I am
sorry for that neglect. I wish to go on writing ad infinitum to you. I wish
for interesting matter, and a pen as swift as the wind, but the fact is I go so
little into the Crowd now that I have nothing fresh and fresh everyday to
speculate upon, except my own Whims and Theories. I have been but once
to Haydon's, once to Hunt's, once to Rice's, once to Hessey's. I have not
seen Taylor; I have not been to the Theatre. Now if I had been many times
to all these and was still in the habit of going I could on my return at night
have each day something new to tell you of without any stop. But now I
have such a dearth that when I get to the end of this sentence and to the
bottom of this page I must wait till I can find something interesting to you
before I begin another. After all it is not much matter what it may be about,
for the very words from such a distance penned by this hand will be grateful to you, even though I were to copy out the tale of Mother Hubbard or
Little Red Riding Hood. I have been over to Dilke's this evening. There
with Brown we have been talking of different and indifferent Matters: of
Euclid, of Metaphysics, of the Bible, of Shakespeare, of the horrid System
and consequences of the fagging at great Schools. I know not yet how large
a parcel I can send, I mean by way of Letters. I hope there can be no objection to my dowling up a quire made into a small compass; that is the man-

ner in which I shall write. I shall send you more than Letters—I mean a
tale—which I must begin on account of the activity of my Mind, of its inability to remain at rest. It must be prose and not very exciting. I must do
this because in the way I am at present situated I have too many interruptions to a train of feeling to be able to write Poetry. So I shall write this Tale
and if I think it worthwhile get a duplicate made before I send it off to you.

This is a fresh beginning, the 21st October. Charles and Henry were with
us on Sunday and they brought me your Letter to your Mother. We agreed
to get a Packet off to you as soon as possible. I shall dine with your Mother
tomorrow, when they have promised to have their Letters ready. I shall send
as soon as possible without thinking of the little you may have from me in
the first parcel, as I intend, as I said before, to begin another Letter of more
regular information. Here I want to communicate so largely in a little time
that I am puzzled where to direct my attention. Haslam has promised to let
me know from Capper and Hazlewood.[11] For want of something better I
shall proceed to give you some extracts from my Scotch Letters. Yet now I
think on it why not send you the letters themselves. I have three of them at
present; I believe Haydon has two which I will get in time. I dined with
your Mother and Henry at Mrs. Millar's on thursday when they gave me
their Letters. Charles's I have not yet; he has promised to send it. The
thought of sending my scotch Letters has determined me to enclose a few
more which I have received and which will give you the best cue to how I
am going on better than you could otherwise know. Your Mother was well
and was sorry I could not stop later. I called on Hunt yesterday. It has been
always my fate to meet Ollier there. On thursday I walked with Hazlitt as
far as covent Garden; he was going to play Rackets. I think Tom has been
rather better these few last days; he has been less nervous. I expect Reynolds
tomorrow. Since I wrote thus far I have met with that same Lady again[12]
whom I saw at Hastings and whom I met when we were going to the English Opera. It was in a street which goes from Bedford Row to Lamb's Conduit Street. I passed her and turned back. She seemed glad of it, glad to see
me and not offended at my passing her before. We walked on towards
Islington where we called on a friend of her's who keeps a Boarding School.
She has always been an enigma to me. She has been in a Room with you

and with Reynolds and wishes we should be acquainted without any of our common acquaintance knowing it. As we went along, some times through shabby, sometimes through decent Streets, I had my guessing at work, not knowing what it would be and prepared to meet any surprise. First it ended at this House at Islington, on parting from which I pressed to attend her home. She consented and then again my thoughts were at work what it might lead to, tho' now they had received a sort of genteel hint from the Boarding School. Our Walk ended in 34 Gloucester Street, Queen Square. Not exactly so, for we went upstairs into her sitting room, a very tasty sort of place with Books, Pictures, a bronze statue of Buonaparte, Music, aeolian Harp, a Parrot, a Linnet, a Case of choice Liquers, etc., etc. and she behaved in the kindest manner; made me take home a Grouse for Tom's dinner, asked for my address for the purpose of sending more game. As I had warmed with her before and kissed her, I thought it would be living backwards not to do so again. She had a better taste. She perceived how much a thing of course it was and shrunk from it, not in a prudish way but in, as I say, a good taste. She contrived to disappoint me in a way which made me feel more pleasure than a simple kiss could do. She said I should please her much more if I would only press her hand and go away. Whether she was in a different disposition when I saw her before, or whether I have in fancy wrong'd her, I cannot tell. I expect to pass some pleasant hours with her now and then, in which I feel I shall be of service to her in matters of knowledge and taste. If I can, I will. I have no libidinous thought about her; she and your George are the only women à peu près de mon age[13] whom I would be content to know for their mind and friendship alone. I shall in a short time write you as far as I know how I intend to pass my Life. I cannot think of those things now Tom is so unwell and weak. Notwithstanding your Happiness and your recommendation I hope I shall never marry. Though the most beautiful Creature were waiting for me at the end of a Journey or a Walk; though the carpet were of Silk, the Curtains of the morning Clouds, the chairs and Sofa stuffed with Cygnet's down, the food Manna, the Wine beyond Claret, the Window opening on Winandermere, I should not feel, or rather my Happiness would not be so fine as my Solitude is sublime. Then instead of what I have described, there is a Sublimity to welcome me home. The roaring of the wind is my wife and the Stars through the window pane are my Children. The mighty abstract Idea I have of Beauty in all things stifles the more divided and minute domestic happiness. An amiable wife and sweet Children I contemplate as a part of that Beauty, but I must have a thousand of those beautiful particles to fill up my heart. I feel more and more every day, as my imagination strengthens, that I do not live in this world alone but in a thousand worlds. No sooner am I alone than shapes of epic greatness are stationed around me and serve my Spirit the office which is equivalent to a king's bodyguard— then "Tragedy, with scepter'd pall, comes sweeping by."[14] According to my state of mind, I am with Achilles shouting in the Trenches[15] or with Theocritus in the Vales of Sicily. Or I throw my whole being into Troilus and repeating those lines, "I wander, like a lost soul upon the stygian Banks staying for waftage,"[16] I melt into the air with a voluptuousness so delicate that I am content to be alone. These things combined with the opinion I have of the generality of women—who appear to me as children to whom I would rather give a Sugar Plum than my time—form a barrier against Matrimony which I rejoice in. I have written this that you might see I have my share of the highest pleasures and that though I may choose to pass my days alone I shall be no Solitary. You see there is nothing spleenical in all this. The only thing that can ever affect me personally for more than one short passing day is any doubt about my powers for poetry. I seldom have any, and I look with hope to the nighing time when I shall have none. I am as happy as a Man can be; that is, in myself I should be happy if Tom was well, and I knew you were passing pleasant days. Then I should be most enviable, with the yearning Passion I have for the beautiful connected and made one with the ambition of my intellect. Think of my Pleasure in Solitude, in comparison of my commerce with the world. There I am a child; there they do not know me, not even my most intimate acquaintance. I give into their feelings as though I were refraining from irritating a little child. Some think me middling, others silly, others foolish. Everyone thinks he sees my weak side against my will, when in truth it is with my will. I am content to be thought all this because I have in my own breast so great a resource. This is one great reason why they like me so; because they can all show to advantage in a room, and eclipse from a certain tact one who is reckoned to be a good Poet. I hope I am not here playing tricks "to make the angels weep."[17] I think not, for I have not the least contempt for my species, and though it may sound paradoxical, my greatest elevations of soul leave me every time more humbled. Enough of this, though in your Love for me you will not think it enough.

Haslam has been here this morning, and has taken all the Letters except this sheet, which I shall send him by the Twopenny, as he will put the Parcel in the Boston post Bag by the advice of Capper and Hazlewood, who assure him of the safety and expedition that way. The Parcel will be forwarded to Warder and thence to you all the same. There will not be a Philadelphia Ship for these six weeks; by that time I shall have another Letter to you. Mind you I mark this Letter A. By the time you will receive this you will have, I trust, passed through the greatest of your fatigues. As it was with your Sea sickness I shall not hear of them till they are past. Do not set to your occupation with too great an anxiety—take it calmly—and let your health be the prime consideration. I hope you will have a Son, and it is one of my first wishes to have him in my Arms, which I will do, please God, before he cuts one double tooth. Tom is rather more easy than he has been, but is still so nervous that I can not speak to him of these Matters; indeed it is the care I have had to keep his Mind aloof from feelings too acute that has made this Letter so short a one. I did not like to write before him a Letter he knew was to reach your hands. I cannot even now ask him for any Message; his heart speaks to you. Be as happy as you can. Think of me and for my sake be cheerful. Believe me, my dear Brother and sister,

Your anxious and affectionate Brother
John—

This day is my Birthday. All our friends have been anxious in their
enquiries and all send their remembrances.

1. Henry Wylie appears to have lived with his aunt, Mrs. Millar. Apparently Miss Keasle and Miss Waldegrave were lodgers.
2. Keats's own suggestive misspelling of "ridiculous," which he often repeats.

3. Jane Cox.
4. Howard (1726?–1790), famous philanthropist and reformer. Richard Hooker (1554?–1600) was not a bishop.
5. Actually Leigh Hunt in *Story of Rimini*, III.121f.
6. Sir Francis Burdett (1770–1844), politician.
7. Sidney (1622–1683), republican.
8. Keats had read Godwin's *Political Justice* as well as at least three of his novels.
9. Morris Birkbeck, founder of the colony in Albion, Illinois.
10. *Hamlet*, III.ii.406.
11. Stockbrokers.
12. Mrs. Isabella Jones.
13. "Close to my age."
14. Adapted from Milton's "Il Penseroso," lines 97f.
15. See the *Iliad*, XVIII.228.
16. *Troilus and Cressida*, III.ii.9–11.
17. *Measure for Measure*, II.ii.121f.

To James Rice
24 NOVEMBER 1818

Well Walk—Nov. 24—

My dear Rice,

Your amende honorable, I must call "un surcroit d'amitié,"[1] for I am not at all sensible of anything but that you were unfortunately engaged and I was unfortunately in a hurry. I completely understand your feeling in this mistake, and find in it that balance of comfort which remains after regretting your uneasiness. I have long made up my Mind to take for granted the genuine heartedness of my friends, notwithstanding any temporary ambiguousness in their behaviour or their tongues—nothing of which, however, I had the least scent of this morning. I say completely understand, for I am everlastingly getting my mind into such like painful trammels, and am even at this moment suffering under them in the case of a friend of ours. I will tell you. Two most unfortunate and parallel slips. It seems downright preintention. A friend says to me, "Keats, I shall go and see Severn this Week."

"Ah," says I, "You want him to take your Portrait." And again, "Keats," says a friend, "When will you come to town again?" "I will," says I, "let you have the Mss. next week." In both these I appeared to attribute an interested motive to each of my friends' questions. The first made him flush; the second made him look angry. And yet I am innocent. In both cases my Mind leapt over every interval to what I saw was per se a pleasant subject with him. You see I have no allowances to make. You see how far I am from supposing you could show me any neglect. I very much regret the long time I have been obliged to exile from you, for I have had one or two rather pleasant occasions to confer upon with you. What I have heard from George is favorable. I expect soon a Letter from the Settlement itself.

Your sincere friend
John Keats

I cannot give any good news of Tom—

1. "An excess of friendship or kindness."

To B. R. Haydon
22 DECEMBER 1818

Tuesday, Wentworth Place—

My dear Haydon,

Upon my Soul I never felt your going out of the room at all, and believe me I never rhodomontade anywhere but in your Company. My general Life in Society is silence. I feel in myself all the vices of a Poet—irritability, love of effect and admiration—and influenced by such devils I may at times say more rediculous things than I am aware of. But I will put a stop to that in a manner I have long resolved upon. I will buy a gold ring and put it on my finger, and from that time a Man of superior head shall never have occasion to pity me, or one of inferior Nunskull to chuckle at me. I am certainly more for greatness in a Shade than in the open day; I am speaking as a mortal. I should say I value more the Privilege of seeing great things in loneliness than the fame of a Prophet. Yet here I am sinning so I will turn to a thing I have thought on more, I mean your means till your Picture be finished: not only now but for this year and half have I thought of it. Believe me Haydon I have that sort of fire in my Heart that would sacrifice everything I have to your service. I speak without any reserve. I know you would do so for me. I open my heart to you in a few words. I will do this sooner than you shall be distressed, but let me be the last stay. Ask the rich lovers of art first; I'll tell you why. I have a little money which may enable me to study and to travel three or four years. I never expect to get anything by my Books and moreover I wish to avoid publishing. I admire Human Nature but I do not like *Men*. I should like to compose things honourable to Man, but not fingerable over by *Men*. So I am anxious to exist without troubling the printer's devil or drawing upon Men's and Women's admiration; in which great solitude I hope God will give me strength to rejoice. Try the long purses, but do not sell your drawing or I shall consider it a breach of friendship. I am sorry I was not at home when Salmon[1] called. Do write and let me know all your present why's and wherefore's.

Your's most faithfully
John Keats

1. Corporal John Salmon, Haydon's model.

1819

To George and Georgiana Keats

16–18, 22, 29 (?), 31 DECEMBER 1818, 2–4 JANUARY 1819

B[1]   My dear Brother and Sister,

You will have been prepared before this reaches you for the worst news you could have, nay if Haslam's letter arrives in proper time, I have a consolation in thinking the first shock will be past before you receive this. The last days of poor Tom were of the most distressing nature, but his last moments were not so painful, and his very last was without a pang. I will not enter into any parsonic comments on death, yet the common observations of the commonest people on death are as true as their proverbs. I have scarce a doubt of immortality of some nature or other; neither had Tom. My friends have been exceedingly kind to me every one of them. Brown detained me at his House. I suppose no one could have had their time made smoother than mine has been. During poor Tom's illness I was not able to write and since his death the task of beginning has been a hindrance to me. Within this last Week I have been everywhere, and I will tell you as nearly as possible how all goes on. With Dilke and Brown I am quite thick,[2] with Brown indeed I am going to domesticate, that is, we shall keep house together. I Shall have the front parlour and he the back one, by which I shall avoid the noise of Bentley's Children and be the better able to go on with my Studies, which ave[3] been greatly interrupted lately, so that I have not the Shadow of an idea of a book in my head and my pen seems to have grown too goutty for verse. How are you going on now? The goings on of the world make me dizzy. There you are with Birkbeck; here I am with brown. Sometimes I fancy an immense separation, and sometimes, as at present, a direct communication of spirit with you. That will be one of the grandeurs of immortality; there will be no space and consequently the only commerce between spirits will be by their intelligence of each other—when they will completely understand each other—while we in this world merely comprehend each other in different degrees. The higher the degree of good so higher is our Love and friendship. I have been so little used to writing lately that I am afraid you will not smoke my meaning, so I will give an example. Suppose Brown or Haslam or anyone whom I understand in the nether degree to what I do you, were in America, they would be so much the farther from me in proportion as their identity was less impressed upon me. Now the reason why I do not feel at the present moment so far from you is that I remember your Ways and Manners and actions. I know your manner of thinking, your manner of feeling. I know what shape your joy or your sorrow would take; I know the manner of your walking, standing, sauntering, sitting down, laughing, punning, and every action so truly that you seem near to me. You will remember me in the same manner, and the more when I tell you that I shall read a passage of Shakespeare every Sunday at ten o' Clock; you read one at the same time and we shall be as near each other as blind bodies can be in the same room. I saw your Mother the day before yesterday, and intend now frequently to pass half a day with her. She seem'd tolerably well. I called in Henrietta Street and so was speaking with your Mother about Miss Millar. We had a chat about Heiresses. She told me I think of 7 or 8 dying Swains. Charles was not at home. I think I have heard a little more talk about Miss Keasle; all I know of her is she had a new sort of shoe on of bright leather like our Knapsacks. Miss Millar gave me one of her confounded pinches. N.B. did not like it. Mrs. Dilke went with me to see Fanny last week, and Haslam went with me last Sunday. She was well. She gets a little plumper and had a little Colour. On Sunday I brought from her a present of facescreens and a work bag for Mrs. D. They were really very pretty. From walthamstow we walked to Bethnal green,[4] where I felt so tired from my long walk that I was obliged to go to Bed at ten. Mr. and Mrs. {. . .}[5] were there. Haslam has been excessively kind and his anxiety about you is great. I never meet him but we have some chat thereon. He is always doing me some good turn; he gave me this thin paper for the purpose of writing to you. I have been passing an hour this morning with

Mr. Lewis. He wants news of you very much. Haydon was here yesterday; he amused us much by speaking of young Hopner who went with Capt. Ross on a voyage of discovery to the Poles.[6] The Ship was sometimes entirely surrounded with vast mountains and crags of ice and in a few Minutes not a particle was to be seen all round the Horizon. Once they met with so vast a Mass that they gave themselves over for lost; their last recourse was in meeting it with the Bowspit, which they did, and split it asunder and glided through it as it parted for a great distance—one Mile and more. Their eyes were so fatigued with the eternal dazzle and whiteness that they lay down on their backs upon deck to relieve their sight on the blue Sky. Hopner describes his dreadful weariness at the continual day, the sun ever moving in a circle round above their heads, so pressing upon him that he could not rid himself of the sensation even in the dark Hold of the Ship. The Esquimaux are described as the most wretched of Beings; they float from the Summer to their winter residences and back again like white Bears on the ice floats. They seem never to have washed, and so when their features move, the red skin shows beneath the cracking peal of dirt. They had no notion of any inhabitants in the World but themselves. The sailors who had not seen a Star for some time, when they came again southwards, on the hailing of the first revision of one all ran upon deck with feelings of the most joyful nature. Haydon's eyes will not suffer him to proceed with his Picture. His Physician tells him he must remain two months more inactive. Hunt keeps on in his old way. I am completely tired of it all. He has lately publish'd a Pocket-Book call'd the literary Pocket-Book, full of the most sickening stuff you can imagine. Reynolds is well; he has become an edinburgh Reviewer. I have not heard from Bailey. Rice I have seen very little of lately, and I am very sorry for it. The Miss R's are all as usual. Archer[7] above all people called on me one day; he wanted some information, by my means, from Hunt and Haydon, concerning some Man they knew. I got him what he wanted, but know none of the why's and wherefore's. Poor Kirkman[8] left wentworth place one evening about half past eight and was stopped, beaten and robbed of his Watch in Pond Street. I saw him a few days since; he had not recovered from his bruise. I called on Hazlitt the day I went to Romney Street. I gave John Hunt extracts from your Letters; he has taken no notice. I have seen Lamb lately. Brown and I were taken by Hunt to Novello's; there we were devastated and excruciated with bad and repeated puns. Brown don't want to go again. We went the other evening to see Brutus, a new Tragedy by Howard Payne, an American.[9] Kean was excellent; the play was very bad. It is the first time I have been since I went with you to the Lyceum.

Mrs. Brawne who took Brown's house for the Summer, still resides in Hampstead. She is a very nice woman and her daughter senior[10] is I think beautiful and elegant, graceful, silly, fashionable and strange. We have a little tiff now and then and she behaves a little better, or I must have sheered off. I find by a sidelong report from your Mother that I am to be invited to Miss Millar's birthday dance. Shall I dance with Miss Waldegrave? Eh! I shall be obliged to shirk a good many there—I shall be the only Dandy there—and indeed I merely comply with the invitation that the party may not be entirely destitute of a specimen of that Race. I shall appear in a complete dress of purple Hat and all with a list of the beauties I have conquered embroidered round my Calves.

Thursday. This morning[11] is so very fine I should have walked over to Walthamstow if I had thought of it yesterday. What are you doing this morning? Have you a clear hard frost as we have? How do you come on with the gun? Have you shot a Buffalo? Have you met with any Pheasants? My Thoughts are very frequently in a foreign Country. I live more out of England than in it. The Mountains of Tartary are a favourite lounge, if I happen to miss the Allegany ridge, or have no whim for Savoy. There must be great pleasure in pursuing game—pointing your gun. No, it won't do, now, no. Rabbit it—now bang—smoke and feathers—where is it? Shall you be able to get a good pointer or so? Have you seen Mr. Trimmer? He is an acquaintance of Peachey's. Now I am not addressing myself to G. minor, and yet I am, for you are one. Have you some warm furs? By your next Letters I shall expect to hear exactly how you go on; smother nothing, let us have all, fair and foul all plain. Will the little bairn have made his entrance before you have this? Kiss it for me, and when it can first know a cheese from a Caterpillar show it my picture twice a Week. You will be glad to hear that Gifford's[12] attack upon me has done me service; it has got my

Book among several *Sets*. Nor must I forget to mention once more, what I suppose Haslam has told you, the present of a £25 note I had anonymously sent me. I have many things to tell you; the best way will be to make copies of my correspondence, and I must not forget the Sonnet I received with the Note. Last Week I received the following from Woodhouse, whom you must recollect: "My dear Keats, I send enclosed a Letter which, when read take the trouble to return to me. The History of its reaching me is this. My Cousin, Miss Frogley of Hounslow, borrowed my copy of Endymion for a specified time. Before she had time to look into it she and my friend Mr. Harry Neville of Esher, who was house Surgeon to the late Princess Charlotte, insisted upon having it to read for a day or two, and undertook to make my Cousin's peace with me on account of the extra delay. Neville told me that one of the Misses Porter[13] (of romance Celebrity) had seen it on his table, dipped into it, and expressed a wish to read it. I desired he would keep it as long, and lend it to as many, as he pleased, provided it was not allowed to slumber on anyone's shelf. I learned subsequently from Miss Frogley that these Ladies had requested of Mr. Neville, if he was acquainted with the Author the Pleasure of an introduction. About a week back the enclosed was transmitted by Mr. Neville to my Cousin, as a species of apology for keeping her so long without the Book. And she sent it to me, knowing it would give me Pleasure. I forward it to you for somewhat the same reason, but principally because it gives me the opportunity of naming to you (which it would have been fruitless to do before) the opening there is for an introduction to a class of society, from which you may possibly derive advantage as well as gratification, if you think proper to avail yourself of it. In such case I should be very happy to further your Wishes. But do just as you please. The whole is entirely entre nous—Your's, etc., R.W." Well, now this is Miss Porter's Letter to Neville: "Dear Sir, as my Mother is sending a Messenger to Esher, I cannot but make the same the bearer of my regrets for not having had the pleasure of seeing you, the morning you called at the gate. I had given orders to be denied: I was so very unwell with my still adhesive cold; but had I known it was you I should have taken off the interdict for a few minutes, to say, how very much I am delighted with Endymion. I had just finished the Poem, and have done as you permitted

lent it to Miss Fitzgerald. I regret you are not personally acquainted with
the Author, for I should have been happy to have acknowledged to him,
through the advantage of your Communication the very rare delight my
Sister and myself have enjoyed from this first fruits of Genius. I hope the
ill-natured Review will not have damaged (or damped) such true Parnassian
fire; it ought not for when Life is granted, etc." And so she goes on. Now I
feel more obliged than flattered by this, so obliged that I will not at present
give you an extravaganza of a Lady Romancer. I will be introduced to them
if it be merely for the pleasure of writing to you about it. I shall certainly
see a new race of People. I shall more certainly have no time for them.
Hunt has asked me to meet Tom Moore some day, so you shall hear of him.
The night we went to Novello's there was a complete set to of Mozart and
punning. I was so completely tired of it that if I were to follow my own inclinations I should never meet anyone of that set again, not even Hunt,
who is certainly a pleasant fellow in the main when you are with him, but
in reality he is vain, egotistical and disgusting in matters of taste and in
morals. He understands many a beautiful thing; but then, instead of giving
other minds credit for the same degree of perception as he himself pos-
sesses, he begins an explanation in such a curious manner that our taste and
self-love is offended continually. Hunt does one harm by making fine
things petty and beautiful things hateful. Through him I am indifferent to
Mozart, I care not for white Busts, and many a glorious thing when associ-
ated with him becomes a nothing. This distorts one's mind, makes one's
thoughts bizarre, perplexes one in the standard of Beauty. Martin is very
much irritated against Blackwood for printing some Letters in his Magazine which were Martin's property; he always found excuses for Blackwood
till he himself was injured and now he is enraged. I have been several times
thinking whether or not I should send you the examiners, as Birkbeck no
doubt has all the good periodical Publications. I will save them at all events.
I must not forget to mention how attentive and useful Mrs. Bentley has
been. I am sorry to leave her, but I must, and I hope she will not be much a
loser by it. Bentley is very well. He has just brought me a clothes basket of
Books. Brown has gone to town today to take his Nephews who are on a
visit here to see the Lions. I am passing a Quiet day, which I have not done

a long while, and if I do continue so I must again begin with my poetry, for if I am not in action mind or Body I am in pain, and from that I suffer greatly by going into parties where from the rules of society and a natural pride I am obliged to smother my Spirit and look like an Idiot, because I feel my impulses given way to would too much amaze them. I live under an everlasting restraint never relieved except when I am composing, so I will write away.

Friday.[14] I think you knew before you left England that my next subject would be "the fall of Hyperion." I went on a little with it last night, but it will take some time to get into the vein again. I will not give you any extracts because I wish the whole to make an impression. I have however a few Poems which you will like and I will copy out on the next sheet. I shall dine with Haydon on Sunday and go over to Walthamstow on Monday if the frost hold. I think also of going into Hampshire this Christmas to Mr. Snook's.[15] They say I shall be very much amused, but I don't know. I think I am in too huge a Mind for study; I must do it. I must wait at home, and let those who wish come to see me. I cannot always be (how do you spell it?) trapsing. Here I must tell you that I have not been able to keep the journal or write the Tale I promised. Now I shall be able to do so. I will write to Haslam this morning to know when the Packet sails and till it does I will write something every day. After that my journal shall go on like clockwork and you must not complain of its dullness, for what I wish is to write a quantity to you, knowing well that dullness itself will from me be interesting to you. You may conceive how this not having been done has weighed upon me. I shall be able to judge from your next what sort of information will be of most service or amusement to you. Perhaps as you were fond of giving me sketches of character you may like a little picnic of scandal even across the Atlantic. But now I must speak particularly to you, my dear Sister, for I know you love a little quizzing better than a great bit of apple dumpling. Do you know Uncle Redall? He is a little Man with an innocent, powdered, upright head. He lisps with a protruded under lip; he has two Nieces, each one would weigh three of him—one for height and the other for breadth. He knew Barttolozzi.[16] He gave a supper and ranged his bottles of wine all up the kitchen and cellar stairs, quite ignorant of what ht be drank. It might have been a good joke to pour on the sly bottle after bottle into a washing tub and roar for more. If you were to trip him up it would discompose a Pigtail and bring his under lip nearer to his nose. He never had the good luck to lose a silk Handkerchief in a Crowd and therefore has only one topic of conversation—Bartolozzi.

Shall I give you Miss Brawn? She is about my height, with a fine style of countenance of the lengthen'd sort. She wants sentiment in every feature. She manages to make her hair look well; her nostrils are fine, though a little painful. Her mouth is bad and good; her Profile is better than her full-face which indeed is not full but pale and thin without showing any bone. Her shape is very graceful and so are her movements. Her Arms are good, her hands baddish, her feet tolerable. She is not seventeen,[17] but she is ignorant, monstrous in her behaviour, flying out in all directions, calling people such names that I was forced lately to make use of the term *Minx*. This is I think not from any innate vice but from a penchant she has for acting stylishly. I am however tired of such style and shall decline any more of it. She had a friend to visit her lately—you have known plenty such—her face is raw as if she was standing out in a frost, her lips raw and seem always ready for a Pullet. She plays the Music without one sensation but the feel of the ivory at her fingers. She is a downright Miss without one set off. We hated her and smoked her and baited her, and I think drove her away. Miss B——— thinks her a Paragon of fashion, and says she is the only woman she would change persons with. What a Stupe. She is superior as a Rose to a Dandelion. When we went to bed Brown observed as he put out the Taper what an ugly old woman that Miss Robinson[18] would make, at which I must have groan'd aloud for I'm sure ten minutes. I have not seen the thing Kingston again; George will describe him to you. I shall insinuate some of these Creatures into a Comedy some day and perhaps have Hunt among them. Scene, a little Parlour. Enter Hunt—Gattie[19]—Hazlitt—Mrs. Novello—Ollier. Gattie: Ha! Hunt! Got into your new house? Ha! Mr. Novello, seen Altam and his Wife?[20] Mrs. N: Yes, (with a grin) *its* Mr. Hunt's isn't it? Gattie: Hunts' no ha! Mr. Ollier: I congratulate you upon the highest compliment I ever heard paid to the Book. Mr. Hazlitt, I hope you are well (Hazlitt: yes Sir, no Sir). Mr. Hunt (at the Music) La Biondina,

Silhouette of Fanny Brawne,
by August Edouart.
Keats House, Hampstead. By permission of the
London Metropolitan Archives.

etc.: Mr. Hazlitt, did you ever hear this, La Biondina, etc.? Hazlitt: O, no Sir, I never. Ollier: Do Hunt, give it us over again—divino. Gattie: Divino. Hunt, when does your Pocket Book come out? Hunt: What is this absorbs me quite? O, we are spinning on a little, we shall floridize soon I hope. Such a thing was very much wanting; people think of nothing but money-getting. Now for me I am rather inclined to the liberal side of things, but I am reckoned lax in my christian principles, etc., etc.

It is some days since I wrote the last page[21] and what have I been about since I have no Idea. I dined at Haslam's on sunday, with Haydon yesterday, and saw Fanny in the morning. She was well. Just now I took out my poem[22] to go on with it, but the thought of my writing so little to you came upon me and I could not get on, so I have began at random and I have not a word to say, and yet my thoughts are so full of you that I can do nothing else. I shall be confined at Hampstead a few days on account of a sore throat. The first thing I do will be to visit your Mother again. The last time I saw Henry he show'd me his first engraving which I thought capital. Mr. Lewis called this morning and brought some american Papers. I have not look'd into them. I think we ought to have heard of you before this. I am in daily expectation of Letters. Nil desperandum.[23] Mr. Abbey wishes to take Fanny from School. I shall strive all I can against that. There has happened great Misfortune in the Drewe Family. Old Drewe[24] has been dead some time and lately George Drewe expired in a fit, on which account Reynolds has gone into Devonshire. He dined a few days since at Horace Twisse's[25] with Liston and Charles Kemble.[26] I see very little of him now, as I seldom go to little Britain because the Ennui always seizes me there, and John Reynolds is very dull at home. Nor have I seen Rice. How you are now going on is a Mystery to me. I hope a few days will clear it up.

I never know the day of the Month. It is very fine here today, though I expect a Thundercloud or rather a snow cloud in less than an hour. I am at present alone at Wentworth place, Brown being at Chichester and Mr. and Mrs. Dilke making a little stay in Town. I know not what I should do without a Sunshiny morning now and then; it clears up one's spirits. Dilke and I frequently have some chat about you. I have now and then some doubts but he seems to have a great confidence. I think there will soon be perceptible a change in the fashionable slang literature of the day. It seems to me that Reviews have had their day, that the public have been surfeited. There will soon be some new folly to keep the Parlours in talk. What it is I care not. We have seen three literary kings in our Time—Scott, Byron, and then the scotch novels.[27] All now appears to be dead, or I may mistake. Literary Bodies may still keep up the Bustle which I do not hear. Haydon show'd me a letter he had received from Tripoli. Ritchey was well and in good Spirits, among Camels, Turbans, Palm Trees and sands. You may remember I promised to send him an Endymion which I did not; however he has one, you have one; one is in the Wilds of america, the other is on a Camel's back in the plains of Egypt. I am looking into a Book of Dubois's. He has written directions to the Players; one of them is very good: "In singing never mind the music—observe what time you please. It would be a pretty degradation indeed if you were obliged to confine your genius to the dull regularity of a fiddler—horse hair and cat's guts—no, let him keep *your* time and play *your* tune—*dodge him.*" I will now copy out the Letter and Sonnet I have spoken of. The outside cover was thus directed: "Messrs. Taylor and Hessey (Booksellers), No. 93 Fleet Street, London" and it contained this: "Messrs. Taylor and Hessey are requested to forward the enclosed letter by some *safe* mode of conveyance to the Author of Endymion, who is not known at Teignmouth: or if they have not his address, they will return the letter by post, directed as below, within *a fortnight:* "Mr P. Fenbank,[28] P. O. Teignmouth" 9th Nov. 1818. In this sheet was enclosed the following with a superscription, "Mr. John Keats, Teignmouth." Then came Sonnet to John Keats, which I would not copy for any in the world but you, who know that I scout "mild light and loveliness" or any such nonsense in myself.

> Star of high promise! not to this dark age
>   Do thy mild light and loveliness belong;
>   For it is blind intolerant and wrong;
> Dead to empyreal soarings, and the rage
> Of scoffing spirits bitter war doth wage
>   With all that hold integrity of song.
>   Yet thy clear beam shall shine through ages strong
> To ripest times a light and heritage.
> And there breathe now who dote upon thy fame,
>   Whom thy wild numbers wrap beyond their being,
>   Who love the freedom of thy Lays, their aim
>   Above the scope of a dull tribe unseeing.

And there is one whose hand will never scant
From his poor store of fruits all *thou* can'st want.

November, 1818   turn over

I turn'd over and found a £25 note. Now this appears to me all very
proper. If I had refused it, I should have behaved in a very bragadochio
dunderheaded manner and yet the present galls me a little and I do not
know whether I shall not return it if I ever meet with the donor, after
whom to no purpose I have written. I have your Miniature on the Table,
George the great; it's very like, though not quite about the upper lip. I wish
we had a better of you, little George. I must not forget to tell you that a few
days since I went with Dilke a-shooting on the heath and shot a Tomtit.
There were as many guns abroad as Birds. I intended to have been at
Chichester this Wednesday, but on account of this sore throat I wrote him
(Brown) my excuse yesterday.

Thursday (I will date when I finish). I received a Note from Haslam yesterday asking if my letter is ready. Now this is only the second sheet, notwithstanding all my promises, but you must reflect what hindrances I have
had. However, on sealing this I shall have nothing to prevent my proceeding in a gradual journal which will increase in a Month to a considerable
size. I will insert any little pieces I may write, though I will not give any extracts from my large poem[29] which is scarce began. I want to hear very
much whether Poetry and literature in general has gained or lost interest
with you, and what sort of writing is of the highest gust with you now.
With what sensation do you read Fielding? And do not Hogarth's pictures
seem an old thing to you? Yet you are very little more removed from general
association than I am. Recollect that no Man can live but in one society at a
time. His enjoyment in the different states of human society must depend
upon the Powers of his Mind; that is, you can imagine a roman triumph, or
an olympic game as well as I can. We with our bodily eyes see but the fashion and Manners of one country for one age, and then we die. Now to me
manners and customs long since passed whether among the Babylonians or
the Bactrians are as real, or even more real than those among which I now
live. My thoughts have turned lately this way. The more we know the more

inadequacy we discover in the world to satisfy us. This is an old observation, but I have made up my Mind never to take anything for granted but even to examine the truth of the commonest proverbs. This however is true: Mrs. Tighe and Beattie[30] once delighted me; now I see through them and can find nothing in them but weakness, and yet how many they still delight! Perhaps a superior being may look upon Shakespeare in the same light; is it possible? No. This same inadequacy is discovered (forgive me, little George, you know I don't mean to put you in the mess) in Women with few exceptions: the Dress Maker, the blue Stocking and the most charming sentimentalist differ but in a Slight degree and are equally smokeable. But I'll go no further—I may be speaking sacrilegiously—and on my word I have thought so little that I have not one opinion upon anything except in matters of taste. I never can feel certain of any truth but from a clear perception of its Beauty, and I find myself very young-minded even in that perceptive power, which I hope will increase. A year ago I could not understand in the slightest degree Raphael's cartoons; now I begin to read them a little, and how did I learn to do so? By seeing something done in quite an opposite spirit; I mean a picture of Guido's in which all the Saints, instead of that heroic simplicity and unaffected grandeur which they inherit from Raphael, had each of them both in countenance and gesture all the canting, solemn melodramatic mawkishness of Mackenzie's father Nicholas.[31] When I was last at Haydon's I looked over a Book of Prints taken from the fresco of the Church at Milan, the name of which I forget.[32] In it are comprised Specimens of the first and second age of art in Italy. I do not think I ever had a greater treat out of Shakespeare. Full of Romance and the most tender feeling, magnificence of draperies beyond any I ever saw not excepting Raphael's, but Grotesque to a curious pitch, yet still making up a fine whole, even finer to me than more accomplish'd works, as there was left so much room for Imagination. I have not heard one of this last course of Hazlitt's lecture's. They were upon "Wit and Humour," the english comic writers.

Saturday, Jan. 2nd. Yesterday Mr. and Mrs. D and myself dined at Mrs. Brawne's; nothing particular passed. I never intend hereafter to spend any time with Ladies unless they are handsome; you lose time to no purpose.

For that reason I shall beg leave to decline going again to Redall's or Butler's or any Squad where a fine feature cannot be mustered among them all, and where all the evening's amusement consists in saying your good health, *your* good health, and YOUR good health, and (O, I beg your pardon) your's Miss ———, and such things not even dull enough to keep one awake. With respect to amiable speaking I can read; let my eyes be fed or I'll never go out to dinner anywhere. Perhaps you may have heard of the dinner given to Thomas Moore in Dublin, because I have the account here by me in the Philadelphia democratic paper. The most pleasant thing that occurred was the speech Mr. Tom made on his Father's health being drank. I am afraid a great part of my Letters are filled up with promises and what I will do rather than any great deal written; but here I say once for all that circumstances prevented me from keeping my promise in my last, but now I affirm that as there will be nothing to hinder me I will keep a journal for you. That I have not yet done so you would forgive if you knew how many hours I have been repenting of my neglect. For I have no thought pervading me so constantly and frequently as that of you. My Poem cannot frequently drive it away; you will retard it much more than You could by taking up my time if you were in England. I never forget you except after seeing now and then some beautiful woman, but that is a fever. The thought of you both is a passion with me but for the most part a calm one. I asked Dilke for a few lines for you; he has promised them. I shall send what I have written to Haslam on Monday Morning. What I can get into another sheet tomorrow I will; there are one or two little poems you might like. I have given up snuff very nearly quite. Dilke has promised to sit with me this evening. I wish he would come this minute for I want a pinch of snuff very much just now. I have none though in my own snuff box. My sore throat is much better today; I think I might venture on a crust. Here are the Poems. They will explain themselves, as all poems should do without any comment.

> Ever let the Fancy roam,
> Pleasure never is at home.
> At a touch sweet pleasure melteth

Like to bubbles when rain pelteth:
Then let winged fancy wander
Towards heaven still spread beyond her.
Open wide the mind's cage door
She'll dart forth and cloudward soar.
O sweet Fancy, let her loose!
Summer's joys are spoilt by use,
And the enjoying of the spring
Fades as doth its blossoming:
Autumn's red-lipp'd fruitage too
Blushing through the mist and dew
Cloys with kissing. What do then?
Sit thee in an ingle when
The sear faggot blazes bright,
Spirit of a winter night;
When the soundless earth is muffled,
And the caked snow is shuffled
From the Ploughboy's heavy shoon:
When the night doth meet the noon
In a dark conspiracy
To banish vesper from the sky.
Sit thee then and send abroad
With a Mind self-overaw'd
Fancy high commission'd; send her,
She'll have vassals to attend her,
She will bring thee, spite of frost,
Beauties that the Earth has lost;
She will bring thee all together
All delights of summer weather;
All the faery buds of May
On spring turf or scented spray;
All the heaped Autumn's wealth
With a still, mysterious stealth;
She will mix these pleasures up,

Like three fit wines in a cup
And thou shalt quaff it; Thou shalt hear
Distant harvest carols clear,
Rustle of the reaped corn
Sweet Birds antheming the Morn;
And in the same moment hark
To the early April lark,
And the rooks with busy caw
Foraging for sticks and straw.
Thou shalt at one glance behold
The daisy and the marigold;
White-plumed lillies and the first
Hedgerow primrose that hath burst;
Shaded Hyacinth alway
Sapphire Queen of the Mid-may;
And every leaf and every flower
Pearled with the same soft shower.
Thou shalt see the fieldmouse creep
Meagre from its celled sleep,
And the snake all winter shrank
Cast its skin on sunny bank;
Freckled nest eggs shalt thou see
Hatching in the hawthorn tree;
When the hen bird's wing doth rest
Quiet on its mossy nest,
Then the hurry and alarm
When the Beehive casts its swarm,
Acorn's ripe down pattering
While the autumn breezes sing,
For the same sleek-throated mouse
To store up in its winter house.
    O sweet Fancy, let her loose!
Every joy is spoilt by use,
Every pleasure, every joy,

Not a Mistress but doth cloy.
Where's the cheek that doth not fade
Too much gaz'd at? Where's the Maid
Whose lip mature is ever new?
Where's the eye however blue
Doth not weary? Where's the face
One would meet in every place?
Where's the voice however soft
One would hear too oft and oft?
At a touch sweet pleasure melteth
Like to bubbles when rain pelteth.
Let then winged fancy find
Thee a Mistress to thy mind.
Dulcet-eyed as Cere's daughter
Ere the God of torment taught her
How to frown and how to chide:
With a waist, and with a side
White as Hebe's when her Zone
Slipp'd its golden clasp, and down
Fell her kirtle to her feet,
While she held the goblet sweet,
And Jove grew languid. Mistress fair,
Thou shalt have that tressed hair
Adonis tangled all for spite;
And the mouth he would not kiss,
And the treasure he would miss,
And the hand he would not press,
And the warmth he would distress,
          O the Ravishment, the Bliss!
Fancy has her there she is,
Never fulsome, ever new,
There she steps! And tell me who
Has a Mistress so divine?
Be the palate ne'er so fine

> She cannot sicken.
>   Break the Mesh
> Of the Fancy's silken leash
> Where she's tether'd to the heart,
> Quickly break her prison string
> And such joys as these she'll bring
> Let the winged fancy roam
> Pleasure never is at home.

I did not think this had been so long a Poem. I have another not so long, but as it will more conveniently be copied on the other side I will just put down here some observations on Caleb Williams by Hazlitt. I meant to say St. Leon, for although he has mentioned all the Novels of Godwin very finely, I do not quote them, but this only on account of its being a specimen of his usual abrupt manner and fiery laconicism. He says of St. Leon, "He is a limb torn off from Society. In possession of eternal youth and beauty, he can feel no love; surrounded, tantalized and tormented with riches, he can do no good. The faces of Men pass before him as in a speculum, but he is attached to them by no common tie of sympathy or suffering. He is thrown back into himself and his own thoughts. He lives in the solitude of his own breast, without wife or child or friend or Enemy in the world. *His is the solitude of the Soul, not of woods or trees or mountains,* but the desert of society, the waste and oblivion of the heart. He is himself alone. His existence is purely intellectual and is therefore intolerable to one who has felt the rapture of affection, or the anguish of woe." As I am about it I might as well give you his character of Godwin as a Romancer: "Whoever else is, it is pretty clear that the author of Caleb Williams is not the Author of waverly. Nothing can be more distinct or excellent in their several ways than these two writers. If the one owes almost everything to external observation and traditional character, the other owes everything to internal conception and contemplation of the possible workings of the human Mind. There is little knowledge of the world, little variety, neither an eye for the picturesque, nor a talent for the humourous in Caleb Williams, for instance, but you can not doubt for a moment of the originality of the work and the force of the conception. The impression made upon the reader is the exact measure of the strength of the author's genius. For the effect both in Caleb Williams and St. Leon is entirely made out, not by facts nor dates, by blackletter or magazine learning, by transcript nor record, but by intense and patient study of the human heart, and by an imagination projecting itself into certain situations, and capable of working up its imaginary feelings to the height of reality."[33] This appears to me quite correct. Now I will copy the other Poem. It is on the double immortality of Poets.

> Bards of Passion and of Mirth
> Ye have left your souls on earth,
> Have ye souls in heaven too,
> Double-liv'd in regions new?
> Yes, and those of heaven commune
> With the spheres of Sun and Moon;
> With the noise of fountains wondrous,
> And the parle of voices thundrous;
> With the Whisper of heaven's trees,
> And one another's, in soft ease
> Seated on elysian Lawns,
> Browsed by none but Dian's fawns;
> Underneath large bluebells tented
> Where the daisies are rose scented
> And the rose herself has got
> Perfume that on Earth is not.
> Where the nightingale doth sing
> Not a senseless tranced thing;
> But melodious truth divine
> Philosophic numbers fine;
> Tales and golden histories
> Of Heaven and its Mysteries.
>   Thus ye live on Earth and then
> On the Earth ye live again;
> And the souls ye left behind you

Teach us here the way to find you,
Where your other Souls are joying
Never slumber'd, never cloying.
Here your earth born souls still speak
To mortals of the little week
They must sojourn with their cares;
Of their sorrows and delights,
Of their Passions and their spites;
Of their glory and their shame,
What doth strengthen and what maim.
Thus ye teach us every day
Wisdom though fled far away.
  Bards of Passion and of Mirth
Ye have left your Souls on Earth,
Ye have souls in heaven too,
Double-liv'd in Regions new!

These are specimens of a sort of rondeau which I think I shall become partial to because you have one idea amplified with greater ease and more delight and freedom than in the sonnet. It is my intention to wait a few years before I publish any minor poems and then I hope to have a volume of some worth, and which those people will realish who cannot bear the burthen of a long poem. In my journal I intend to copy the poems I write the days they are written. There is just room I see in this page to copy a little thing I wrote off to some Music as it was playing.

I had a dove and the sweet dove died,
  And I have thought it died of grieving:
O what could it mourn for? It was tied
  With a silken thread of my own hands weaving.
Sweet little red-feet why did you die?
Why would you leave me, sweet dove, why?
You live'd alone on the forest tree
Why pretty thing could you not live with me?

I kiss'd you oft, and I gave you white peas,
Why not live sweetly as in the green trees?

Sunday.[34]

I have been dining with Dilke today. He is up to his Ears in Walpole's letters. Mr. Manker[35] is there; I have come round to see if I can conjure up anything for you. Kirkman came down to see me this morning; his family has been very badly off lately. He told me of a villainous trick of his Uncle William in Newgate Street who became sole Creditor to his father under pretence of serving him, and put an execution on his own Sister's goods. He went into the family at Portsmouth, conversed with them, went out and sent in the Sheriff's officer. He tells me too of abominable behaviour of Archer to Caroline Mathew. Archer has lived nearly at the Mathews these two years; he has been amusing Caroline all this time and now he has written a Letter to Mrs. M, declining on pretence of inability to support a wife as he would wish, all thoughts of marriage. What is the worst is Caroline is 27 year's old. It is an abominable matter. He has called upon me twice lately. I was out both times. What can it be for? There is a letter today in the Examiner to the Electors of westminster on Mr. Hobhouse's account. In it there is a good Character of Cobbet. I have not the paper by me or I would copy it. I do not think I have mentioned the Discovery of an african kingdom. The account is much the same as the first accounts of Mexico—all magnificence. There is a Book being written about it.[36] I will read it and give you the cream in my next. The ramance we have heard upon it runs thus: they have window frames of gold, 100,000 infantry, human sacrifices. The Gentleman who is the adventurer has his wife with him; she I am told is a beautiful little sylphid woman. Her husband was to have been sacrificed to their Gods and was led through a Chamber filled with different instruments of torture with privilege to choose what death he would die, without their having a thought of his aversion to such a death, they considering it a supreme distinction. However he was let off and became a favorite with the King, who at last openly patronised him, though at first on account of the Jealousy of his Ministers he was wont to hold conversations with his Majesty in the dark middle of the night. All this sounds a little Bluebeardish, but I hope it is true. There is another thing I must mention of the momentous kind, but I must mind my periods in it.

Mrs. Dilke has two Cats—a Mother and a Daughter. Now the Mother is a tabby and the daughter a black and white like the spotted child. Now it appears ominous to me for the doors of both houses are opened frequently, so that there is a complete thoroughfare for both Cats (there being no board up to the contrary). They may one and several of them come into my room ad libitum. But no. The Tabby only comes, whether from sympathy from ann the maid or me I can not tell, or whether Brown has left behind him any atmospheric spirit of Maidenhood I can not tell. The Cat is not an old Maid herself; her daughter is a proof of it. I have questioned her. I have look'd at the lines of her paw. I have felt her pulse—to no purpose. Why should the *old* Cat come to me? I ask myself, and myself has not a word to answer. It may come to light some day; if it does you shall hear of it. Kirkman this morning promised to write a few lines for you and send them to Haslam. I do not think I have anything to say in the Business way. You will let me know what you would wish done with your property in England— What things you would wish sent out—but I am quite in the dark about what you are doing. If I do not hear soon I shall put on my Wings and be after you. I will in my next, and after I have seen your next letter, tell you my own particular idea of America. Your next letter will be the key by which I shall open your hearts and see what spaces want filling with any particular information. Whether the affairs of Europe are more or less interesting to you, whether you would like to hear of the Theatres, of the bear Garden, of the Boxers, the Painters, The Lecturers, the Dress, The Progress of Dandyism, The Progress of Courtship, or the fate of Mary Millar, being a full true and très particular account of Miss M's ten Suitors. How the first tried the effect of swearing; the second of stammering; the third of whispering; the fourth of sonnets; the fifth of spanish leather boots; the sixth of flattering her body; the seventh of flattering her mind; the eighth of flattering himself; the ninth stuck to the Mother; the tenth kissed the Chambermaid and told her to tell her Mistress, but he was soon discharged. His reading led him into an error; he could not sport the Sir

Lucius[37] to any advantage. And now for this time I bid you good bye. I have been thinking of these sheets so long that I appear in closing them to take my leave of you, but that is not it. I shall immediately as I send this off begin my journal, when some days I shall write no more than 10 lines and others 10 times as much. Mrs. Dilke is knocking at the wall for Tea is ready. I will tell you what sort of a tea it is and then bid you Good bye.

This is monday morning.[38] Nothing particular happened yesterday evening, except that just when the tray came up Mrs. Dilke and I had a battle with celery stalks. She sends her love to you. I shall close this and send it immediately to Haslam. Remaining ever

My dearest brother and sister
Your most affectionate Brother
John—

1. He had designated the previous letter to them "A."
2. Who lived in a "double house," Wentworth Place.
3. A Cockneyism for "have"?
4. Where Haslam lived with his parents in Virginia Row.
5. Manuscript torn.
6. Sir John Ross (1777–1856) commanded the whaler *Isabella,* while Lieutenant Henry Hoppner (1795–1833) was on the *Alexander,* which Lieutenant W. E. Parry commanded.
7. Archibald Archer, historical and portrait painter.
8. Gittings thinks that this is probably George B. Kirkman, stationer, a relative of George Felton Mathew.
9. John Howard Payne (1791–1852), *Brutus, Or, The Fall of Tarquin.*
10. The first mention of Fanny Brawne.
11. December 17.
12. Or rather Croker's.
13. Jane Porter (1776–1850) and her sister Anna Maria (1780–1832), authors of romances. (Gittings)
14. That is, 18 December.
15. John Snook, Dilke's brother-in-law.
16. Francesco Bartolozzi (1727–1815), Italian engraver.
17. Actually, she was eighteen in August 1818.
18. Caroline Robinson, who became the mother of Robinson Ellis, the great Latinist. (Gittings)
19. John Byng Gattie (1788–1828) of the Treasury; relative of the Olliers.
20. A "domestic tale" (1818) by Charles Ollier.
21. He is now writing on 22 December, a very foggy day.

22. *Hyperion.*
23. Horace, *Odes,* I.vii.27, "One must not lose hope."
24. To whose daughter Reynolds was engaged.
25. Twisse (1787–1849), wit, author, politician.
26. John Liston (1776?–1846) and Charles Kemble (1775–1854) were both actors.
27. He means Scott and Byron as poets and then Scott as a novelist.
28. Evidently a pseudonym, which may represent Woodhouse.
29. *Hyperion.*
30. Mary Tighe (1772–1810), whose poem *Psyche, or The Legend of Love* (1805) reached a fifth edition. James Beattie (1735–1803), Scottish poet.
31. Henry Mackenzie (1745–1831), whose "Father Nicholas" appeared in the Edinburgh *Lounger.*
32. Conte Carlo Lasinio's *Pitture a fresco del Campo Santo di Pisa, intagliate* (Florence, 1812).
33. Keats copied both excerpts from the *Examiner* (1818), pp. 825–826.
34. That is, 3 January 1819.
35. Possibly John Mancur, hosier, a friend of Charles Brown.
36. Thomas Edward Bowditch (1791–1824), *Mission from Cape Coast Castle to Ashantee* (1819).
37. In Sheridan's *The Rivals.*
38. That is, 4 January.

To B. R. Haydon
10 (?) JANUARY 1819

Wentworth place

My dear Haydon,

We are very unlucky. I should have stopped to dine with you, but I knew I should not have been able to leave you in time for my plaguy sore throat, which is getting well. I shall have a little trouble in procuring the Money and a great ordeal to go through. No trouble indeed to anyone else, or ordeal either. I mean I shall have to go to town some thrice, and stand in the Bank an hour or two, to me worse than anything in Dante. I should have less chance with the people around me than Orpheus had with the Stones. I have been writing a little now and then lately, but nothing to speak of being discontented and as it were moulting. Yet I do not think I shall ever come to the rope or the Pistol, for after a day or two's melancholy, although I smoke[1] more and more my own insufficiency, I see by little and little more of what is to be done, and how it is to be done, should I ever be able to do it. On my Soul there should be some reward for that continual "agonie ennuiyeuse." I was thinking of going into Hampshire for a few days: I have been delaying it longer than I intended. You shall see me soon and do not be at all anxious, for *this* time I really will do what I never did before in my life: business in good time and properly. With respect to the Bond; it may be a satisfaction to you to let me have it, but as you love me do not let there be any mention of interest, although we are mortal men and bind ourselves for fear of death.

Your's forever
John Keats—

1. "Discern."

To Fanny Keats
11 FEBRUARY 1819

Wentworth Place—
Feb.—Thursday—

My dear Fanny,

Your Letter to me at Bedhampton hurt me very much. What objection can there be to your receiving a Letter from me? At Bedhampton I was unwell and did not go out of the Garden Gate but twice or thrice during the fortnight I was there. Since I came back I have been taking care of myself. I have been obliged to do so, and am now in hopes that by this care I shall get rid of a sore throat which has haunted me at intervals nearly a twelve-month. I had always a presentiment of not being able to succeed in persuading Mr. Abbey to let you remain longer at School. I am very sorry that he will not consent.[1] I recommend you to keep up all that you know and to learn more by yourself however little. The time will come when you will be more pleased with Life; look forward to that time and, though it may appear a trifle, be careful not to let the idle and retired Life you lead fix any awkward habit or behaviour on you. Whether you Sit or walk, endeavour to let it be in a seemly and if possible a graceful manner. We have been very little together: but you have not the less been with me in thought. You have no one in the world besides me who would sacrifice anything for you; I feel myself the only Protector you have. In all your little troubles think of me with the thought that there is at least one person in England who, if he could, would help you out of them. I live in hopes of being able to make you happy. I should not perhaps write in this manner, if it were not for the fear of not being able to see you often, or long together. I am in hopes Mr. Abbey will not object any more to your receiving a letter now and then from me. How unreasonable! I want a few more lines from you for George. There are some young Men, acquaintances of a School-fellow of mine,[2] going out to Birkbeck's at the latter end of this Month. I am in expectation every day of hearing from George. I begin to fear his last letters Miscarried. I shall be in town tomorrow. If you should not be in town, I shall send this little parcel by the Walthamstow Coach. I think you will like Goldsmith.[3] Write me soon.

Your affectionate Brother
John—

Mrs. Dilke has not been very well; she has gone a walk to town today for exercise.

1. Abbey had removed her from the school before Christmas.
2. James Peachey.
3. Oliver Goldsmith's *Poems, and Essays* (1817).

To B. R. Haydon
18 (?) FEBRUARY 1819

Wentworth Place—

My dear Haydon,

My throat has not suffered me yet to expose myself to the night air. However, I have been to town in the day time, have had several interviews with my guardian, have written him a rather plain-spoken Letter—which has had its effect—and he now seems inclined to put no stumbling block in my way, so that I see a good prospect of performing my promise. What I should have lent you ere this if I could have got it was belonging to poor Tom, and the difficulty is whether I am to inherit it before my Sister is of age, a period of six years. Should it be so, I must incontinently take to Corderoy Trowsers. But I am nearly confident 'tis all a Bam.[1] I shall see you soon, but do let me have a line today or tomorrow concerning your health and spirits.

Your sincere friend
John Keats

---

1. Perhaps an abbreviation of *bamboozle;* thus, "to hoax, practise on the credulity of, deceive." *(OED)*

To Fanny Keats
27 FEBRUARY 1819

Wentworth Place, Saturday Morn—

My dear Fanny,

I intended to have not failed to do as you requested and write you as you say once a fortnight. On looking to your letter I find there is no date, and not knowing how long it is since I received it I do not precisely know how great a sinner I am. I am getting quite well, and Mrs. Dilke is getting on pretty well. You must pay no attention to Mrs. Abbey's unfeeling and ignorant gabble. You can't stop an old woman's crying more than you can a Child's. The old woman is the greatest nuisance because she is too old for the rod. Many people live opposite a Blacksmith's till they cannot hear the hammer. I have been in Town for two or three days and came back last night. I have been a little concerned at not hearing from George. I continue in daily expectation. Keep on reading and play as much on the music and the grassplot as you can. I should like to take possession of those Grassplots for a Month or so and send Mrs. A to Town to count coffee berries instead of currant Bunches, for I want you to teach me a few common dancing steps and I would buy a Watch box to practise them in by myself. I think I had better always pay the postage of these Letters. I shall send you another book the first time I am in Town early enough to book it with one of the morning Walthamstow Coaches. You did not say a word about your Chilblains. Write me directly and let me know about them. Your Letter shall be answered like an echo—

Your affectionate Brother
John—

To B. R. Haydon

8 MARCH 1819

My dear Haydon,

You must be wondering where I am and what I am about! I am mostly at Hampstead and about nothing, being in a sort of qui bono[1] temper, not exactly on the road to an epic poem. Nor must you think I have forgotten you. No, I have about every three days been to Abbey's and to the Lawyers.[2] Do let me know how you have been getting on, and in what spirits you are.

You got out gloriously in yesterday's Examiner.[3] What a set of little people we live amongst. I went the other day into an ironmonger's shop, without any change in my sensations; men and tin kettles are much the same in these days. They do not study like children at five and thirty, but they talk like men at twenty. Conversation is not a search after knowlege, but an endeavour at effect. In this respect two most opposite men, Wordsworth and Hunt, are the same. A friend of mine observed the other day that if Lord Bacon were to make any remark in a party of the present day, the conversation would stop on the sudden. I am convinced of this, and from this I have come to the resolution never to write for the sake of writing, or making a poem, but from running over with any little knowledge and experience which many years of reflection may perhaps give me; otherwise I will be dumb. What Imagination I have I shall enjoy, and greatly, for I have experienced the satisfaction of having great conceptions without the toil of sonnetteering. I will not spoil my love of gloom by writing an ode to darkness; and with respect to my livelihood I will not write for it, for I will not mix with that most vulgar of all crowds the literary. Such things I ratify by looking upon myself, and trying myself at lifting mental weights, as it were. I am three and twenty with little knowledge and middling intellect. It is true that in the height of enthusiasm I have been cheated into some fine passages, but that is nothing.

I have not been to see you because all my going out has been to town, and that has been a great deal. Write soon.

Yours constantly,
John Keats

1. "Cui bono" (Cicero, *Pro Milone,* 12), "Whose good?"
2. Keats spelled this word "Lawers."
3. In "Attacks on Mr. Haydon," *Examiner,* 7 March 1819, Haydon replies to critics of an exhibition of his pupils' drawings.

To Fanny Keats
13 MARCH 1819

Wentworth Place
March 13th

My dear Fanny,

I have been employed lately in writing to George. I do not send him very short letters, but keep on day after day. There were some young Men I think I told you of who were going to the Settlement. They have changed their minds, and I am disappointed in my expectation of sending Letters by them. I went lately to the only dance I have been to these twelve months or shall go to for twelve months again; it was to our Brother-in-law's cousin's.[1] She gave a dance for her Birthday and I went for the sake of Mrs. Wylie. I am waiting every day to hear from George. I trust there is no harm in the silence: other people are in the same expectation as we are. On looking at your seal I cannot tell whether it is done or not with a Tassi.[2] It seems to me to be paste. As I went through Leicester Square lately I was going to call and buy you some, but not knowing but you might have some I would not run the chance of buying duplicates. Tell me if you have any or if you would like any, and whether you would rather have motto ones like that with which I seal this letter,[3] or heads of great Men such as Shakespeare, Milton, etc., or fancy pieces of Art, such as Fame, Adonis, etc.—those gentry you read of at the end of the English Dictionary. Tell me also if you want any particular Book, or Pencils, or drawing paper—anything but live Stock—though I will not now be very severe on it, remembring how fond I used to be of Goldfinches, Tomtits, Minnows, Mice, Ticklebacks, Dace, Cock salmons and all the whole tribe of the Bushes and the Brooks. But verily they are better in the Trees and the water, though I must confess even now a partiality for a handsome Globe of goldfish; then I would have it hold 10 pails of water and be fed continually fresh through a cool pipe with another pipe to let through the floor. Well-ventilated, they would preserve all their beautiful silver and Crimson; then I would put it before a handsome painted window and shade it all round with myrtles and Japonicas. I should like the window to open onto the Lake of Geneva, and there I'd sit and read all day like the picture of somebody reading.

The weather now and then begins to feel like spring, and therefore I have begun my walks on the heath again. Mrs. Dilke is getting better than she has been as she has at length taken a Physician's advice. She ever and anon asks after you and always bids me remember her in my Letters to you. She is going to leave Hampstead for the sake of educating their Son Charles at the Westminster school. We (Mr. Brown and I) shall leave in the beginning of may. I do not know what I shall do or where be all the next Summer. Mrs. Reynolds has had a sick house, but they are all well now. You see what news I can send you I do. We all live one day like the other as well as you do. The only difference is being sick and well, with the variations of single and double knocks, and the story of a dreadful fire in the Newspapers. I mentioned Mr. Brown's name, yet I do not think I ever said a word about him to you. He is a friend of mine of two years standing with whom I walked through Scotland, who has been very kind to me in many things when I most wanted his assistance and with whom I keep house till the first of May. You will know him some day. The name of the young Man who came with me is William Haslam.

Ever, your affectionate Brother
John

1. The brothers-in-law were Henry and Charles Wylie; their cousin was Mary Millar.
2. As Gittings explains, the engraved enamel gems originated by James Tassie (1735–1799) had been widely popularized, and the range of their designs extended by his nephew William Tassie (1777–1860), whose shop was at 20 Leicester Square.
3. A lyre surrounded on three sides by the legend "Qui me néglige me désole" (He who neglects me devastates me).

To Joseph Severn
29 MARCH 1819

Wentworth Place—
Monday—aft.

My dear Severn,

Your note gave me some pain, not on my own account, but on yours. Of course I should never suffer any petty vanity of mine to hinder you in any wise; and therefore I should say, "put the miniature in the exhibition," if only myself was to be hurt. But will it not hurt you? What good can it do to any future picture? Even a large picture is lost in that canting place. What a drop of water in the ocean is a Miniature.[1] Those who might chance to see it for the most part, if they had ever heard of either of us and know what we were and of what years, would laugh at the puff of the one and the vanity of the other. I am however in these matters a very bad judge, and would advise you to act in a way that appears to yourself the best for your interest. As your Hermia and Helena is finished, send that without the prologue of a Miniature. I shall see you soon, if you do not pay me a visit sooner. There's a Bull for you.

Yours ever sincerely
John Keats—

1. Severn's famous miniature portrait of Keats and his picture *Hermia and Helena* were exhibited at the Royal Academy in May.

To Fanny Keats

31 MARCH 1819

Wednesday—

Dear Fanny,

I shall be going to town tomorrow and will call at the Nursery on the road for those roots and seeds you want, which I will send by the Walthamstow stage. The best way, I thought, for you to learn to answer those questions, is to read over the little book, which I sent from a Bookseller's in town, or you should have had a Letter with it. Tell me whether it will do. If not, I will put down the answers for you. I have not yet heard from George. Perhaps if I just give you the heads of the answers it may be better, though I think you will find them all in that little book.

Ansr. 1. It was instituted by John the Baptist when he baptised those people in the river Jordan who believed through him in the coming of Christ, and more particularly when he baptised christ himself.

2. It corresponds to the Jewish Circumscision.

3. The meaning is that we are confirmed members of Christ. It is not administered till 14 years of age because before that age the mind is not judged to be sufficiently mature and capable. The act of confirmation imposes on the Christian self circumspection, as by that ceremony the Christian duties of Godfathers and godmothers is annulled and put an end to, as you see in the catechism: "they promise and vow three things in my name." Confirmation absolves this obligation.

4. There are two Sacraments of our Church—Baptisim and the Lord's Supper. The Church of Rome has seven Sacraments. The church of Rome includes several ceremonies (I forget what they are) and the civil rite of marriage. I believe Confirmation is a Sacrament with them. Extreme unction or the anointing the extremities of dying persons with holy water. The reason why we have but two Sacraments is that it is proved from

the Scriptures by the great protestant reformers that only two are commanded by god. The rest adopted by the Church of Rome are human institutions.

5. You must here repeat your belief and say the question is too hard
for you.

6. Look in Isaiah for *"A virgin shall conceive,"* etc. Look in the Psalms for
"The Kings of the Earth set themselves and the Princes take counsel together"
and *"they parted my Garments among them, etc"* and *"My god, my god why has
thou forsaken me, etc."* In Jeremiah *"Comfort ye, comfort ye, etc."* In Daniel
The stone cut out of the mountain without hands that breaks the image in
pieces is a type of the Kingdom of Christ. Look at the 2nd Chap. Isaiah,
Chap. 7–9: *"For unto us a Child is born."* 11 Jeremiah, Chap. xxxi; Micah,
Chap. 5, Zechariah, Chap. 6 and Chap. 13, *verse 6.* Those I have marked
will be sufficient. You will remember their completion in the new testament.

7. The communion of saints is the fruition they enjoy in heaven among
one another and in the Divinity of Christ.

8. It was instituted on the night of the feast of the Passover at the Last
supper with the Twelve, the night Judas betrayed Christ and you may see in
the 26 Mathew. It corresponds to the "Feast of the Passover in the Jewish
Ritual."

9. They expected Christ to be a temporal Prince and being disappointed
rejected him.

10. Look to the Catechisim: "What is your duty towards God?"

11. The Prophecy to our first parents is this, Genesis 3 Chapter, verse 15:
"And I will put enmity between thee and the woman and between thy seed
and her seed; *it shall bruize thy head* and thou shall bruize his heel. Christ
the Son of David by dying on the Cross triumphed over death and the
grave from which he saved mankind, and in that way did he "bruize the
Serpent's head."

Your affectionate Parson

John—

To Fanny Keats
12 APRIL 1819

Wentworth Place

My dear Fanny,

I have been expecting a Letter from you about what the Parson said to your answers. I have thought also of writing to you often, and I am sorry to confess that my neglect of it has been but a small instance of my idleness of late, which has been growing upon me, so that it will require a great shake to get rid of it. I have written nothing, and almost read nothing, but I must turn over a new leaf. One most discouraging thing hinders me. We have no news yet from George, so that I cannot with any confidence continue the Letter I have been preparing for him. Many are in the same state with us and many have heard from the Settlement. They must be well however and we must consider this silence as good news. I ordered some bulbous roots for you at the Gardeners, and they sent me some, but they were all in bud and could not be sent, so I put them in our Garden. There are some beautiful heaths now in bloom in Pots. Either heaths or some seasonable plants I will send you instead, perhaps some that are not yet in bloom that you may see them come out. Tomorrow night I am going to a rout,[1] a thing I am not at all in love with. Mr. Dilke and his Family have left Hampstead. I shall dine with them today in Westminster where I think I told you they were going to reside for the sake of sending their Son Charles to the Westminster School. I think I mentioned the Death of Mr. Haslam's Father. Yesterday week the two Mr. Wylies dined with me. I hope you have good store of double violets. I think they are the Princesses of flowers and in a shower of rain almost as fine as barley sugar drops are to a schoolboy's tongue. I suppose this fine weather the lambs tails give a frisk or two extraordinary when a boy would cry "huzza" and a Girl, "O my!" A little Lamb frisks its tail. I have not been lately through Leicester Square; the first time I do I will re-member your Seals. I have thought it best to live in Town this Summer, chiefly for the sake of books, which cannot be had with any comfort in the Country. Besides my Scotch journey gave me a doze[2] of the Picturesque with which I ought to be contented for some time. Westminster is the place I have pitched upon. The City or any place very confined would soon turn me pale and thin, which is to be avoided. You must make up your mind to get Stout this summer; indeed, I have an idea we shall both be corpulent old folks with tripple[3] chins and stumpy thumbs.

Your affectionate Brother
John

1. "A fashionable gathering or assembly, a large evening party or reception." *(OED)*
2. Keats's spelling.
3. Keats's spelling.

To B. R. Haydon

13 APRIL 1819

Tuesday—

My dear Haydon,

When I offered you assistance I thought I had it in my hand; I thought I had nothing to do, but to do. The difficulties I met with arose from the alertness and suspicion of Abbey, and especially from the affairs being still in a Lawyer's[1] hand who has been draining our Property for the last 6 years of every charge he could make. I cannot do two things at once, and thus this affair has stopped my pursuits in every way, from the first prospect I had of difficulty. I assure you I have harassed myself 10 times more than if I alone had been concerned in so much gain or loss. I have also ever told you the exact particulars as well as and as literally as my hopes or fear could translate them, for it was only by parcels that I found all those petty obstacles which for my own sake should not exist a moment. And yet why not, for from my own imprudence and neglect all my accounts are entirely in my Guardian's Power. This has taught me a Lesson. Hereafter I will be more correct. I find myself possessed of much less than I thought for, and now if I had all on the table all I could do would be to take from it a moderate two years subsistence and lend you the rest; but I cannot say how soon I could become possessed of it. This would be no sacrifice nor any matter worth thinking of, much less than parting as I have more than once done with little sums which might have gradually formed a library to my taste. These sums amount together to nearly 200, which I have but a chance of ever being repaid or paid at a very distant period. I am humble enough to put this in writing from the sense I have of your struggling situation and the great desire that you should do me the justice to credit the unostentatious and willing state of my nerves on all such occasions. It has not been my fault. I am doubly hurt at the slightly reproachful tone of your note and at the occasion of it, for it must be some other disappointment. You seem'd so sure of some important help when I last saw you. Now you have maimed me again. I was whole. I had began reading again. When your note came I was engaged in a Book. I dread as much as a Plague the idle fever of two months more without any fruit. I will walk over the first fine day then see what aspect your affairs have taken, and if they should continue gloomy, walk into the City to Abbey and get his consent, for I am persuaded that to me alone he will not concede a jot.

* * *2

1. Keats wrote "Lawer's."
2. The letter is complete but the signature has been cut off.

To Fanny Keats
I MAY (?) 1819

Wentworth Place, Saturday—

My dear Fanny,

If it were but six o' Clock in the morning I would set off to see you to-day. If I should do so now I could not stop long enough for a how d'ye do; it is so long a walk through Hornsey and Tottenham. And as for Stage Coaching it, besides that it is very expensive, it is like going into the Boxes by way of the pit. I cannot go out on Sunday, but if on Monday it should promise as fair as today I will put on a pair of loose easy palatable boots and me rendre chez vous.[1] I continue increasing my letter to George to send it by one of Birkbeck's sons who is going out soon, so if you will let me have a few more lines, they will be in time. I am glad you got on so well with Monsr le Curè. Is he a nice Clergyman? A great deal depends upon a cock'd hat and powder; not gun powder, lord love us, but lady-meal, violet-smooth, dainty-scented, lily-white, feather-soft, wigsby-dressing, coat-col-lar-spoiling, whisker-reaching, pig-tail loving, swans down-puffing, parson-sweetening powder. I shall call in passing at the tottenham nursery and see if I can find some seasonable plants for you. That is the nearest place, or by our la' kin or lady kin, that is by the virgin Mary's kindred, is there not a twig-manufacturer in Walthamstow? Mr. and Mrs. Dilke are coming to dine with us today; they will enjoy the country after Westminster. O, there is nothing like fine weather, and health, and Books, and a fine country, and a contented Mind, and Diligent-habit of reading and thinking, and an am-ulet against the ennui—and, please heaven, a little claret-wine cool out of a cellar a mile deep—with a few or a good many ratafia cakes, a rocky basin to bathe in, a strawberry bed to say your prayers to Flora in, a pad nag to go you ten miles or so, two or three sensible people to chat with, two or three spiteful folks to spar with, two or three odd fishes to laugh at and two or three numskulls to argue with, instead of using dumb bells on a rainy day:

Two or three Posies
With two or three simples
Two or three Noses
With two or three pimples,
Two or three wise men
And two or three ninny's
Two or three purses
And two or three guineas
Two or three raps
At two or three doors
Two or three naps
Of two or three hours,
Two or three Cats
And two or three mice
Two or three sprats
At a very great price,
Two or three sandies
And two or three tabbies
Two or three dandies,
And two Mrs.——— mum!
Two or three Smiles
And two or three frowns
Two or three Miles
To two or three towns
Two or three pegs
For two or three bonnets
Two or three dove's eggs
To hatch into sonnets.

Good bye. I've an appointment; can't stop pon word; good bye. Now don't get up—open the door myself—go-o-o-d bye—see ye Monday.

J—K—

1. "Go to see you."

To George and Georgiana Keats

14, 19 FEBRUARY, 3 (?), 12, 13, 17, 19 MARCH, 15, 16, 21, 30 APRIL, 3, 4 MAY 1819

sunday Morn., Feb. 14—

Letter C—[1]

My dear Brother and Sister,

How is it we have not heard from you from the Settlement yet? The Letters must surely have miscarried. I am in expectation everyday. Peachey wrote me a few days ago saying some more acquaintances of his were preparing to set out for Birkbeck, therefore I shall take the opportunity of sending you what I can muster in a sheet or two. I am still at Wentworth Place; indeed, I have kept in doors lately, resolved if possible to rid myself of my sore throat. Consequently, I have not been to see your Mother since my return from Chichester, but my absence from her has been a great weight upon me. I say since my return from Chichester. I believe I told you I was going thither. I was nearly a fortnight at Mr. John Snook's and a few days at old Mr. Dilke's. Nothing worth speaking of happened at either place. I took down some of the thin paper and wrote on it a little Poem call'd "St. Agnes Eve" which you shall have as it is when I have finished the blank part of the rest for you. I went out twice at Chichester to old Dowager card parties. I see very little now, and very few Persons, being almost tired of Men and things. Brown and Dilke are very kind and considerate towards me. The Miss Reynoldses have been stopping next door lately, but all very dull. Miss Brawne and I have every now and then a chat and a tiff. Brown and Dilke are walking round their Garden hands in Pockets making observations. The Literary world I know nothing about. There is a Poem from Rogers dead born and another satire is expected from Byron call'd Don Giovanni.[2] Yesterday I went to town for the first time for these three weeks. I met people from all parts and of all sets: Mr. Towers, one of the

Holts, Mr. Domine Williams, Mr. Woodhouse, Mrs. Hazlitt and Son, Mrs. Webb, Mr. Septimus Brown.[3] Mr. Woodhouse was looking up at a Book-window in newgate street and being short-sighted twisted his Muscles into so queer a stupe that I stood by in doubt whether it was him or his brother, if he has one, and turning round saw Mrs. Hazlitt with that little Nero, her son. Woodhouse on his features subsiding proved to be Woodhouse and not his Brother. I have had a little business with Mr. Abbey. From time to time he has behaved to me with a little Brusquerie. This hurts me a little especially when I knew him to be the only Man in England who dared to say a thing to me I did not approve of without its being resented or at least noticed; so I wrote him about it and have made an alteration in my favor. I expect from this to see more of Fanny, who has been quite shut out from me. I see Cobbet has been attacking the Settlement, but I cannot tell what to believe and shall be all out at elbows till I hear from you. I am invited to Miss Millar's Birthday dance on the 19th. I am nearly sure I shall not be able to go; a Dance would injure my throat very much. I see very little of Reynolds. Hunt I hear is going on very badly, I mean in money Matters. I shall not be surprised to hear of the worst. Haydon too in consequence of his eyes is out at elbows. I live as prudently as it is possible for me to do. I have not seen Haslam lately. I have not seen Richards for this half year, Rice for three Months or C. C. C.[4] for god knows when. When I last called in Henrietta Street Mrs. Millar was very unwell, Miss Waldegrave as staid and self possessed as usual. Miss Millar was well. Henry was well. There are two new tragedies: one by the Apostate Man,[5] and one by Miss Jane Porter. Next week I am going to stop at Taylor's for a few days when I will see them both and tell you what they are. Mrs. and Mr. Bentley are well and all the young Carrots. I said nothing of consequence passed at Snook's—no more than this that I like the family very much. Mr. and Mrs. Snook were very kind. We used to have over a little Religion and politics together almost every evening, and sometimes about you. He proposed writing out for me all the best part of his experience in farming to send to you. If I should have an opportunity of talking to him about it I will get all I can at all events, but you may say in your answer to this what value you place upon such information. I have not seen Mr. Lewis lately for I have shrunk from going up the hill. Mr. Lewis went a few mornings ago to town with Mrs. Brawne. They talked about me, and I heard that Mr. L Said a thing I am not at all contented with; Says he, "O, he is quite the little Poet." Now this is abominable; you might as well say Buonaparte is quite the little Soldier. You see what it is to be under six foot and not a lord. There is a long fuzz today in the examiner about a young Man who delighted a young woman with a Valentine. I think it must be Ollier's.[6] Brown and I are thinking of passing the summer at Brussels; if we do we shall go about the first of May. We, i.e. Brown and I, sit opposite one another all day authorizing (N.B. an s instead of a z would give a different meaning). He is at present writing a Story of an old Woman who lived in a forest and to whom the Devil or one of his Aid de feus came one night very late and in disguise. The old Dame sets before him pudding after pudding, mess after mess, which he devours and moreover casts his eyes up at a side of Bacon hanging over his head and at the same time asks whether her Cat is a Rabbit. On going he leaves her three pips of eve's apple, and somehow she, having liv'd a virgin all her life, begins to repent of it and wishes herself beautiful enough to make all the world and even the other world fall in love with her. So it happens. She sets out from her smoaky Cottage in magnificent apparel; the first city She enters every one falls in love with her—from the Prince to the Blacksmith. A young gentleman on his way to the church to be married leaves his unfortunate Bride and follows this nonsuch. A whole regiment of soldiers are smitten at once and follow her. A whole convent of Monks in corpus christi procession join the Soldiers. The Mayor and Corporation follow the same road— Old and young, deaf and dumb—all but the blind are smitten and form an immense concourse of people who—what Brown will do with them I know not. The devil himself falls in love with her, flies away with her to a desert place, in consequence of which she lays an infinite number of Eggs. The Eggs being hatched from time to time fill the world with many nuisances such as John Knox, George Fox, Johanna Southcote, Gifford.

There have been within a fortnight eight failures of the highest consequence in London. Brown went a few evenings since to Davenport's and on his coming in he talk'd about bad news in the City with such a face, I began to think of a national Bankruptcy. I did not feel much surprised and was rather disappointed. Carlisle, a Bookseller on the *Hone* principle, has been issuing Pamphlets from his shop in fleet Street Called the Deist. He was conveyed to Newgate last Thursday. He intends making his own defence.[7] I was surprised to hear from Taylor the amount of Murray the Booksellers last sale. What think you of £25,000? He sold 4000 copies of Lord Byron. I am sitting opposite the Shakespeare I brought from the Isle of wight, and I never look at it but the silk tassels on it give me as much pleasure as the face of the Poet itself, except that I do not know how you are going on. In my next Packet, as this is one by the way, I shall send you the Pot of Basil, St. Agnes' eve, and if I should have finished it, a little thing call'd the "eve of St. Mark." You see what fine mother Radcliff names I have. It is not my fault; I did not search for them. I have not gone on with Hyperion, for to tell the truth I have not been in great cue for writing lately. I must wait for the spring to rouse me up a little. The only time I went out from Bedhampton was to see a Chapel consecrated. Brown, I and John Snook the boy went in a chaise behind a leaden horse Brown drove, but the horse did not mind him. This Chapel is built by a Mr. Way,[8] a great Jew converter, who in that line has spent one hundred thousand Pounds. He maintains a great number of poor Jews. Of course his communion plate was stolen. He spoke to the Clerk about it. The Clerk said he was very sorry adding, "I dare shay your honour its among ush." The Chapel is built in Mr. Way's park. The Consecration was—not amusing. There were numbers of carriages, and his house crammed with Clergy. They sanctified the Chapel and it being a wet day consecrated the burial ground through the vestry window. I begin to hate Parsons. They did not make me love them that day when I saw them in their proper colours. A Parson is a Lamb in a drawing room and a lion in a Vestry. The notions of Society will not permit a Parson to give way to his temper in any shape, so he festers in himself. His features get a peculiar diabolical self-sufficient iron stupid expression. He is continually acting. His mind is against every Man and every Man's mind is against him. He is an Hippocrite[9] to the Believer and a Coward to the unbeliever. He must be either a Knave or an Ideot, and there is no Man so much to be pitied as an ideot parson. The soldier who is cheated into an esprit du corps by a red coat, a Band and Colours for the purpose of nothing is not half so pitiable

as the Parson who is led by the nose by the Bench of Bishops and is smothered in absurdities, a poor necessary subaltern of the Church.

Friday Feb. 18. The day before yesterday I went to Romney Street. Your
Mother was not at home, but I have just written her that I shall see her on
wednesday. I call'd on Mr. Lewis this morning. He is very well and tells me
not to be uneasy about Letters, the chances being so arbitrary. He is going
on as usual among his favorite democrat papers. We had a chat as usual
about Cobbett and the westminster electors. Dilke has lately been very
much harrassed about the manner of educating his Son. He at length decided for a public school, and then he did not know what school. He at last
has decided for Westminster and as Charley is to be a day boy, Dilke will
remove to Westminster. We lead very quiet lives here. Dilke is at present in
greek histories and antiquities and talks of nothing but the electors of Westminster and the retreat of the ten-thousand. I never drink now above three
glasses of wine, and never any spirits and water. Though by the bye the
other day Woodhouse took me to his coffeehouse and ordered a Bottle of
Claret. Now I like Claret. Whenever I can have Claret I must drink it. 'Tis
the only palate affair that I am at all sensual in. Would it not be a good
Speck to send you some vine roots? Could it be done? I'll enquire. If you
could make some wine like Claret to drink on summer evenings in an ar-
bour! For really 'tis so fine. It fills the mouth, one's mouth with a gushing
freshness, then goes down cool and feverless. Then you do not feel it quar-
relling with your liver; no, it is rather a Peace maker and lies as quiet as it
did in the grape; then it is as fragrant as the Queen Bee and the more ethereal Part of it mounts into the brain, not assaulting the cerebral apartments
like a bully in a bad house looking for his trull and hurrying from door to
door bouncing against the wainscot, but rather walks like Aladdin about
his own enchanted palace so gently that you do not feel his step. Other
wines of a heavy and spirituous nature transform a Man to a Silenus; this
makes him a Hermes and gives a Woman the soul and immortality of
Ariadne for whom Bacchus always kept a good cellar of claret. And even of
that he could never persuade her to take above two cups. I said this same
Claret is the only palate-passion I have; I forgot game. I must plead guilty
to the breast of a Partridge, the back of a hare, the backbone of a grouse, the

wing and side of a Pheasant and a Woodcock *passim.* Talking of game (I wish I could make it) the Lady whom I met at Hastings and of whom I said something in my last I think, has lately made me many presents of game and enabled me to make as many. She made me take home a Pheasant the other day which I gave to Mrs. Dilke; on which, tomorrow, Rice, Reynolds and the Wentworthians will dine next door. The next I intend for your Mother. These moderate sheets of paper are much more pleasant to write upon than those large thin sheets which I hope you by this time have received, though that can't be now I think of it. I have not said in any Letter yet a word about my affairs; in a word I am in no despair about them. My poem has not at all succeeded. In the course of a year or so I think I shall try the public again. In a selfish point of view I should suffer my pride and my contempt of public opinion to hold me silent, but for your's and fanny's sake I will pluck up a spirit and try again. I have no doubt of success in a course of years if I persevere, but it must be patience for the Reviews have enervated and made indolent mens' minds; few think for themselves. These Reviews too are getting more and more powerful and especially the Quarterly. They are like a superstition which the more it prostrates the Crowd and the longer it continues the more powerful it becomes just in proportion to their increasing weakness. I was in hopes that when people saw, as they must do now, all the trickery and iniquity of these Plagues they would scout them, but no they are like the spectators at the Westminster cockpit—they like the battle and do not care who wins or who loses. Brown is going on this morning with the story of his old woman and the Devil. He makes but slow progress. The fact is, it is a Libel on the Devil and as that person is Brown's Muse, look ye, if he libels his own Muse how can he expect to write. Either Brown or his muse must turn tale. Yesterday was Charley Dilke's birthday. Brown and I were invited to tea. During the evening nothing passed worth notice but a little conversation between Mrs. Dilke and Mrs. Brawne. The subject was the watchman. It was ten o' Clock and Mrs. Brawne, who lived during the summer in Brown's house and now lives in the Road, recognized her old Watchman's voice and said that he came as far as her now. "Indeed," said Mrs. D., "does he turn the Corner?" There have been some Letters pass between me and Haslam, but I have not seen him lately. The day before yesterday, which I made a day of Business, I call'd upon him. He was out as usual. Brown has been walking up and down the room a-breeding; now at this moment he is being delivered of a couplet—and I dare say will be as well as can be expected. Gracious, he has twins!

I have a long Story to tell you about Bailey. I will say first the circumstances as plainly and as well as I can remember, and then I will make my comment. You know that Bailey was very much cut up about a little Jilt in the country somewhere. I thought he was in a dying state about it when at Oxford with him, little supposing as I have since heard, that he was at that very time making impatient Love to Marian Reynolds. And guess my astonishment at hearing after this that he had been trying at Miss Martin. So matters have been. So Matters stood when he got ordained and went to a Curacy near Carlisle where the family of the Gleigs reside. There his susceptible heart was conquered by Miss Gleig, and thereby all his connections in town have been annulled, both male and female. I do not now remember clearly the facts. These however I know. He showed his correspondence with Marian to Gleig, returned all her Letters and asked for his own. He also wrote very abrupt letters to Mrs. Reynolds. I do not know any more of the Martin affair than I have written above. No doubt his conduct has been very bad. The great thing to be considered is whether it is want of delicacy and principle or want of Knowledge and polite experience—and again Weakness. Yes, that is it—and the want of a Wife—yes, that is it. And then Marian made great Bones of him, although her Mother and sister have teased her very much about it. Her conduct has been very upright throughout the whole affair. She liked Bailey as a Brother, but not as a Husband, especially as he used to woo her with the Bible and Jeremy Taylor under his arm. They walked in no grove but Jeremy Taylor's.[10] Marian's obstinacy is some excuse, but his so quickly taking to Miss Gleig can have no excuse except that of a Ploughman's who wants a wife. The thing which sways me more against him than anything else is Rice's conduct on the occasion. Rice would not make an immature resolve. He was ardent in his friendship for Bailey; he examined the whole for and against minutely, and he has abandoned Bailey entirely. All this I am not supposed by the Reynoldses to have any hint of. It will be a good Lesson to the Mother and Daughters; nothing would serve but Bailey. If you mentioned the word Tea pot, some one of them came out with an apropos about Bailey. Noble fellow, fine fellow! was always in their mouths. This may teach them that the man who redicules romance is the most romantic of Men, that he who abuses women and slights them, loves them the most; that he who talks of roasting a Man alive would not do it when it came to the push, and above all that they are very shallow people who take everything literal. A Man's life of any worth is a continual allegory and very few eyes can see the Mystery of his life—a life like the scriptures, figurative—which such people can no more make out than they can the hebrew Bible. Lord Byron cuts a figure, but he is not figurative. Shakespeare led a life of Allegory; his works are the comments on it.

On Monday we had to dinner Severn and Cawthorn,[11] the Bookseller and print virtuoso; in the evening Severn went home to paint and we other three went to the play to see Shield's new tragedy ycleped Evadné. In the morning Severn and I took a turn round the Museum. There is a Sphinx there of a giant size and most voluptuous Egyptian expression. I had not seen it before. The play was bad even in comparison with *1818* the Augustan age of the Drama, "Comme on sait,"[12] as Voltaire says. The whole was made up of a virtuous young woman, an indignant brother, a suspecting lover, a libertine prince, a gratuitous villain, a street in Naples, a Cypress grove, lilies and roses, virtue and vice, a bloody sword, a spangled jacket, One Lady Olivia, One Miss O'Neil alias Evadné, alias Bellamira, alias— Alias—yea, and I say unto you a greater than Elias. There was Abbot, and talking of Abbot his name puts me in mind of a Spelling book lesson, descriptive of the whole Dramatis personae: Abbot—Abbess—Actor—Actress. The play is a fine amusement, as a friend of mine once said to me. "Do what you will," says he, "A poor gentleman who wants a guinea, cannot spend his two shillings better than at the playhouse." The pantomime was excellent, I had seen it before and enjoyed it again. Your Mother and I had some talk about Miss H. Says I, will Henry have that Miss H. a lath with a boddice? She who has been fine drawn, fit for nothing but to cut up into Cribbage pins to the tune of 15.2;[13] One who is all muslin; all feathers and bone. Once in travelling she was made use of as a lynch pin; I hope he will not have her, though it is no uncommon thing to be *smitten with a staff,* though she might be very useful as his walking stick, his fishing rod, his toothpick, his hat stick (she runs so much in his head). Let him turn farmer, she would cut into hurdles; let him write poetry she would be his turnstyle. Her gown is like a flag on a pole; she would do for him if he turn freemason. I hope she will prove a flag of truce. When she sits languishing with her one foot on a stool, and one elbow on the table, and her head inclined, she looks like the sign of the crooked billet, or the frontispiece to Cinderella, or a teapaper wood cut of Mother Shipton at her studies. She is a make-believe; she is bon a *s*ide, a thin young 'Oman, but this is mere talk of a fellow creature; yet pardie I would not that Henry have her—non volo ut eam possideat, nam[14]—for it would be a bam, for it would be a sham.

Don't think I am writing a petition to the Governors of St. Lukes;[15] no, that would be in another style. May it please your worships; forasmuch as the undersigned has committed, transferred, given up, made over, consigned, and aberrated himself, to the art and mystery of poetry; for as much as he hath cut, rebuffed, affronted, huffed, and shirked, and taken stint, at all other employments, arts, mysteries, and occupations honest, middling and dishonest; for as much as he hath at sundry times, and in diverse places, told truth unto the men of this generation, and eke to the women, moreover; for as much as he hath kept a pair of boots that did not fit, and doth not admire Sheild's play, Leigh Hunt, Tom Moore, Bob Southey and Mr. Rogers; and does admire Wm. Hazlitt. Moreover, for as more, as he liketh half of Wordsworth and none of Crabbe; moreover-est, for as most as he hath written this page of penmanship, he prayeth your Worships to give him a lodging. Witnessed by Richard Abbey and Co. cum familiaribus and Consanguiniis[16] (signed) Count de Cockaigne.

The nothing of the day is a machine called the Velocepede. It is a wheel-carriage to ride cock horse upon, sitting astride and pushing it along with the toes, a rudder wheel in hand. They will go seven miles an hour. A handsome gelding will come to eight guineas, however they will soon be cheaper, unless the army takes to them. I look back upon the last month and find nothing to write about, indeed I do not recollect one thing particular in it. It's all alike; we keep on breathing. The only amusement is a little scandal of however fine a shape, a laugh at a pun and then after all we wonder how we could enjoy the scandal, or laugh at the pun.

I have been at different times turning it in my head whether I should go to Edinburgh and study for a physician; I am afraid I should not take kindly to it. I am sure I could not take fees and yet I should like to do so; it is not worse than writing poems and hanging them up to be flyblown on the Reviewshambles. Everybody is in his own mess. Here is the parson at Hampstead quarreling with all the world; he is in the wrong by this same token. When the black Cloth was put up in the Church for the Queen's mourning, he asked the workmen to hang it the wrong side outwards, that it might be better when taken down, it being his perquisite. Parsons will always keep up their Character, but as it is said there are some animals the Ancients knew which we do not, let us hope our posterity will miss the black badger with tri-cornered hat. Who knows but some Reviser of Buffon or Pliny may put an account of the parson in the Appendix. No one will then believe it any more than we believe in the Phoenix. I think we may class the lawyer in the same natural history of Monsters—a green bag will hold as much as a lawn sleeve—the only difference is that the one is fustian and the other flimsy. I am not unwilling to read Church history at present and have Milnes[17] in my eye. His is reckoned a very good one.

March 12, Friday. I went to town yesterday chiefly for the purpose of seeing some young Men who were to take some Letters for us to you through the medium of Peachey. I was surprised and disappointed at hearing they had changed their minds and did not purpose going so far as Birkbeck's. I was much disappointed, for I had counted upon seeing some persons who were to see you, and upon your seeing some who had seen me. I have not only lost this opportunity, but the sail of the Post-Packet to new york or Philadelphia, by which last, your Brothers have sent some Letters. The weather in town yesterday was so stifling that I could not remain there though I wanted much to see Kean in Hotspur. I have by me at present Hazlitt's Letter to Gifford.[18] Perhaps you would like an extract or two from the high season'd parts. It begins thus: "Sir, you have an ugly trick of saying what is not true of anyone you do not like; and it will be the object of this

Letter to cure you of it. You say what you please of others; it is time you were told what you are. In doing this give me leave to borrow the familiarity of your style, for the fidelity of the picture I shall be answerable. You are a little person, but a considerable cat's paw; and so far worthy of notice. Your clandestine connection with persons high in office constantly influences your opinions, and alone gives importance to them. You are the government critic—a character nicely differing from that of a government spy—the invisible link, that connects literature with the Police." Again: "Your employers, Mr. Gifford, do not pay their hirelings for nothing, for condescending to notice weak and wicked sophistry; for pointing out to contempt what excites no admiration; for cautiously selecting a few specimens of bad taste and bad grammar where nothing else is to be found. They want your invincible pertness, your mercenary malice, your impenetrable dullness, your barefaced impudence, your pragmatical self-sufficiency, your hypocritical zeal, your pious frauds to stand in the gap of their Prejudices and pretensions, to fly blow and taint public opinion, to defeat independent efforts, to apply not the touch of the scorpion but the touch of the Torpedo to youthful hopes, to crawl and leave the slimy track of sophistry and lies over every work that does not 'dedicate its sweet leaves' to some Luminary of the treasury bench, or is not fostered in the hot bed of corruption. This is your office, 'this is what is look'd for at your hands and this you do not baulk'—to sacrifice what little honesty and prostitute what little intellect you possess to any dirty job you are commission'd to execute. 'They keep you as an ape does an apple in the corner of his jaw, first mouth'd to be at last swallow'd.' You are by appointment literary toad-eater to greatness and taster to the court. You have a natural aversion to whatever differs from your own pretensions, and an acquired one for what gives offence to your superiors. Your vanity panders to your interest, and your malice truckles only to your love of Power. If your instinctive or premeditated abuse of your enviable trust were found wanting in a single instance; if you were to make a single slip in getting up your select committee of enquiry and greenbag report of the state of Letters, your occupation would be gone. You would never after obtain a squeeze of the hand from a great man, or a smile from a Punk of Quality. The great and powerful (whom you call wise and good) do not like to have the privacy of their self love startled by the obtrusive and unmanageable claims of Literature and Philosophy, except through the intervention of people like you, whom if they have common penetration, they soon find out to be without any superiority of intellect; or if they do not whom they can despise for their meanness of soul. You 'have the office opposite to saint Peter.' You 'keep a corner in the public mind, for foul prejudice and corrupt power to knot and gender in'; you volunteer your services to people of quality to ease scruples of mind and qualms of conscience; you lay the flattering unction of venal prose and laurell'd verse to their souls. You persuade them that there is neither purity of morals, nor depth of understanding, except in themselves and their hangers on; and would prevent the unhallow'd names of Liberty and humanity from ever being whispered in ears polite! You, sir, do you not do all this? I cry you mercy then: I took you for the Editor of the Quarterly Review!" This is the sort of feu de joie[19] he keeps up. There is another extract or two, one especially which I will copy tomorrow for the candles are burnt down and I am using the wax taper, which has a long snuff on it. The fire is at its last click. I am sitting with my back to it with one foot rather askew upon the rug and the other with the heel a little elevated from the carpet. I am writing this on the Maid's tragedy which I have read since tea with Great pleasure. Besides this volume of Beaumont and Fletcher, there are on the table two volumes of chaucer and a new work of Tom Moore's call'd "Tom Cribb's memorial to Congress"; nothing in it. These are trifles, but I require nothing so much of you as that you will give me a like description of yourselves, however it may be when you are writing to me. Could I see the same thing done of any great Man long since dead it would be a great delight: as to know in what position Shakespeare sat when he began "To be or not to be." Such things become interesting from distance of time or place. I hope you are both now in that sweet sleep which no two beings deserve more than you do. I must fancy you so, and please myself in the fancy of speaking a prayer and a blessing over you and your lives. God bless you. I whisper good night in your ears and you will dream of me.

Saturday 13 March. I have written to Fanny this morning and received a note from Haslam. I was to have dined with him tomorrow: he gives me a bad account of his Father, who has not been in Town for 5 weeks, and is not well enough for company. Haslam is well, and from the prosperous state of some love affair he does not mind the double tides he has to work. I have been [for] a Walk past westend, and was going to call at Mr. Monkhouse's but I did not, not being in the humour. I know not why Poetry and I have been so distant lately; I must make some advances soon or she will cut me entirely. Hazlitt has this fine Passage in his Letter. Gifford, in his Review of Hazlitt's characters of Shakespeare's plays, attacks the Coriolanus critique. He says that Hazlitt has slandered Shakespeare in saying that he had a leaning to the arbitrary side of the question. Hazlitt thus defends himself: "My words are 'Coriolanus is a storehouse of political commonplaces. The Arguments for and against aristocracy and democracy, on the Privileges of the few and the claims of the many, on Liberty and slavery, power and the abuse of it, peace and war, are here very ably handled, with the spirit of a poet and the acuteness of a Philosopher. Shakespeare himself seems to have had a leaning to the arbitrary side of the question, perhaps from some feeling of contempt for his own origin, and to have spared no occasion of bating the rabble. *What he says of them is very true; what he says of their betters is also very true, though he dwells less upon it.'* I then proceed to account for this by showing how it is that 'the cause of the people is but little calculated for a subject for Poetry; or that the language of Poetry naturally falls in with the language of power.' I affirm, Sir, that Poetry, that the imagination, generally speaking, delights in power, in strong excitement, as well as in truth, in good, in right, whereas pure reason and the moral sense approve only of the true and good. I proceed to show that this general love or tendency to immediate excitement or theatrical effect, no matter how produced, gives a Bias to the imagination often consistent with the greatest good, that in Poetry it triumphs over Principle, and bribes the passions to make a sacrifice of common humanity. You say that it does not, that there is no such original Sin in Poetry, that it makes no such sacrifice or unworthy compromise between poetical effect and the still small voice of reason. And how do you prove that there is no such principle giving a bias to the imagination, and a false colouring to poetry? Why by asking in reply to the instances where this principle operates, and where no other can with much modesty and simplicity. 'But are these the only topics that afford delight in Poetry etc.?' No, but these objects do afford delight in poetry, and they afford it in proportion to their strong and often tragical effect, and not in proportion to their strong and often tragical effect, and not in proportion to the good produced, or their desireableness in a moral point of view. 'Do we read with more pleasure of the ravages of a beast of prey than of the Shepherd's pipe upon the Mountain?' No, but we do read with pleasure of the ravages of a beast of prey, and we do so on the principle I have stated, namely from the sense of power abstracted from the sense of good; and it is the same principle that makes us read with admiration and reconciles us in fact to the triumphant progress of the conquerors and mighty Hunters of mankind, who come to stop the shepherd's Pipe upon the Mountains and sweep away his listening flock. Do you mean to deny that there is anything imposing to the imagination in power, in grandeur, in outward show, in the accumulation of individual wealth and luxury, at the expense of equal justice and the commonweal? Do you deny that there is anything in the 'Pride, Pomp and Circumstance of glorious war, that makes ambition virtue' in the eyes of admiring multitudes? Is this a new theory of the Pleasures of the imagination, which says that the pleasures of the imagination do not take rise solely in the calculations of the understanding? Is it a paradox of my creating that 'one murder makes a villain, millions a Hero!' or is it not true that here, as in other cases, the enormity of the evil overpowers and makes a convert of the imagination by its very magnitude? You contradict my reasoning, because you know nothing of the question, and you think that no one has a right to understand what you do not. My offence against purity in the passage alluded to, 'which contains the concentrated venom of my malignity,' is, that I have admitted that there are tyrants and slaves abroad in the world; and you would hush the matter up, and pretend that there is no such thing in order that there may be nothing else. Farther I have explained the cause, the subtle sophistry of the human mind, that tolerates and pampers the evil in order to guard against its approaches; you would conceal the cause in order to prevent the cure, and to leave the proud flesh about the heart to harden and ossify into one impenetrable mass of selfishness and hypocrisy, that we may not 'sympathise in the distresses of suffering virtue' in any case in which they come in competition with the fictitious wants and 'imputed weaknesses of the great.' You ask 'are we gratified by the cruelties of Domitian or Nero?' No, not we. They were too petty and cowardly to strike the imagination at a distance; but the Roman senate tolerated them, addressed their perpetrators, exalted them into gods, the fathers of their people; they had pimps and scribblers of all sorts in their pay, their Senecas, etc. till a turbulent rabble thinking that there were no injuries to Society greater than the endurance of unlimited and wanton oppression, put an end to the farce and abated the nuisance as well as they could. Had you and I lived in those times we should have been what we are now, I 'a sour mal content,' and you 'a sweet courtier.'"

The manner in which this is managed, the force and innate power with which it yeasts and works up itself, the feeling for the costume of society is in a style of genius. He hath a demon as he himself says of Lord Byron. We are to have a party this evening. The Davenports from Church row—I don't think you know anything of them—they have paid me a good deal of attention. I like Davenport himself. The names of the rest are Miss Barnes, Miss Winter with the Children.

March 17th Wednesday. On sunday I went to Davenports where I dined and had a nap. I cannot bare a day anhilated in that manner. There is a great difference between an easy and an uneasy indolence. An indolent day—fill'd with speculations even of an unpleasant colour—is bearable and even pleasant alone, when one's thoughts cannot find out anything better in the world and experience has told us that locomotion is no change. But to have nothing to do, and to be surrounded with unpleasant human identities who press upon one just enough to prevent one getting into a lazy position and not enough to interest or rouse one is a capital punishment of a capital crime: for is not giving up, through good nature, one's time to people who have no light and shade a capital crime? Yet what can I do? They have been very kind and attentive to me. I do not know what I did on monday—nothing—nothing—nothing. I wish this was anything extraordinary. Yesterday I went to town. I called on Mr. Abbey; he began again (he has done it frequently lately) about that hat-making concern, saying he wish you had hearkened to it. He wants to make me a Hat-maker. I really believe 'tis all interested, for from the manner he spoke withal and the card he gave me I think he is concerned in hat-making himself. He speaks well of Fanny's health. Hodgkinson is married. From this I think he takes a little Latitude. Mr. A. was waiting very impatiently for his return to the counting house, and meanwhile observed how strange it was that Hodgkinson should have been not able to walk two months ago and that now he should be married. "I do not," says he, "think it will do him any good: I should not be surprised if he should die of a consumption in a year or two." I called at Taylor's and found that he and Hilton had set out to dine with me; so I followed them immediately back. I walk'd with them townwards again as far as Cambden Town and smoak'd home a Segar. This morning I have been reading the "*False one.*"[20] I have been up to Mrs. Bentley's. Shameful to say I was in bed at ten, I mean this morning. The Blackwood's review has committed themselves in a scandalous heresy. They have been putting up Hogg the ettrick shepherd against Burns—The senseless villains. I have not seen Reynolds, Rice or any of our set lately. Reynolds is completely limed in the law; he is not only reconcil'd to it but hobbyhorses upon it. Blackwood wanted very much to see him. The scotch cannot manage by themselves at all. They want imagination, and that is why they are so fond of Hogg, who has a little of it.

Friday 19th Yesterday I got a black eye, the first time I took a Cricket bat. Brown who is always one's friend in a disaster applied a leech to the eyelid, and there is no inflammation this morning, though the ball hit me directly on the sight. 'Twas a white ball. I am glad it was not a clout. This is the second black eye I have had since leaving school. During all my school days I never had one at all; we must eat a peck before we die. This morning I am in a sort of temper indolent and supremely careless: I long after a stanza or two of Thomson's Castle of indolence. My passions are all asleep from my having slumbered till nearly eleven and weakened the animal fibre all over me to a delightful sensation about three degrees on this side of faintness. If I had teeth of pearl and the breath of lilies I should call it langour, but as I am I must call it Laziness.† In this state of effeminacy the fibres of the brain

---

†especially as I have a black eye.

are relaxed in common with the rest of the body, and to such a happy degree that pleasure has no show of enticement and pain no unbearable frown. Neither Poetry, nor Ambition, nor Love have any alertness of countenance as they pass by me; they seem rather like three figures on a greek vase—a Man and two women—whom no one but myself could distinguish in their disguisement. This is the only happiness and is a rare instance of advantage in the body overpowering the Mind. I have this moment received a note from Haslam in which he expects the death of his Father who has been for some time in a state of insensibility. His mother bears up he says very well. I shall go to town tomorrow to see him. This is the world. Thus we cannot expect to give way many hours to pleasure. Circumstances are like Clouds continually gathering and bursting. While we are laughing the seed of some trouble is put into the wide arable land of events. While we are laughing it sprouts, it grows and suddenly bears a poison fruit which we must pluck. Even so we have leisure to reason on the misfortunes of our friends; our own touch us too nearly for words. Very few men have ever arrived at a complete disinterestedness of Mind. Very few have been influenced by a pure desire of the benefit of others. In the greater part of the Benefactors to Humanity some meretricious motive has sullied their greatness, some melodramatic scenery has fascinated them. From the manner in which I feel Haslam's misfortune I perceive how far I am from any humble standard of disinterestedness. Yet this feeling ought to be carried to its highest pitch, as there is no fear of its ever injuring society, which it would do I fear pushed to an extremity. For in wild nature the Hawk would lose his Breakfast of Robins and the Robin his of Worms. The Lion must starve as well as the swallow. The greater part of Men make their way with the same instinctiveness, the same unwandering eye from their purposes, the same animal eagerness as the Hawk. The Hawk wants a Mate, so does the Man. Look at them both; they set about it and procure one in the same manner. They want both a nest and they both set about one in the same manner; they get their food in the same manner. The noble animal Man for his amusement smokes his pipe; the Hawk balances about the Clouds—that is the only difference of their leisures. This it is that makes the Amusement of Life to a speculative Mind. I go among the Fields and catch a glimpse of a stoat or a field mouse peeping out of the withered grass. The creature hath a purpose and its eyes are bright with it. I go amongst the buildings of a city and I see a Man hurrying along—to what? The Creature has a purpose and his eyes are bright with it. But then as Wordsworth says, "we have all one human heart."[21] There is an ellectric fire in human nature tending to purify, so that among these human creatures there is continually some birth of new heroism. The pity is that we must wonder at it, as we should at finding a pearl in rubbish. I have no doubt that thousands of people never heard of have had hearts completely disinterested. I can remember but two—Socrates and Jesus—their Histories evince it. What I heard a little time ago Taylor observe with respect to Socrates, may be said of Jesus; that he was so great a man that though he transmitted no writing of his own to posterity, we have his Mind and his sayings and his greatness handed to us by others. It is to be lamented that the history of the latter was written and revised by Men interested in the pious frauds of Religion. Yet through all this I see his splendour. Even here, though I myself am pursuing the same instinctive course as the veriest human animal you can think of, I am however young writing at random, straining at particles of light in the midst of a great darkness without knowing the bearing of any one assertion of any one opinion. Yet may I not in this be free from sin? May there not be superior beings amused with any graceful, though instinctive attitude my mind may fall into, as I am entertained with the alertness of a Stoat or the anxiety of a Deer? Though a quarrel in the streets is a thing to be hated, the energies displayed in it are fine; the commonest Man shows a grace in his quarrel. By a superior being our reasonings may take the same tone; though erroneous, they may be fine. This is the very thing in which consists poetry, and if so it is not so fine a thing as philosophy for the same reason that an eagle is not so fine a thing as a truth. Give me this credit; do you not think I strive to know myself? Give me this credit and you will not think that on my own account I repeat Milton's lines

> "How charming is divine Philosophy
> Not harsh and crabbed as dull fools suppose
> But musical as is Apollo's lute."[22]

No—no for myself—feeling grateful as I do to have got into a state of mind to relish them properly. Nothing ever becomes real till it is experienced. Even a Proverb is no proverb to you till your Life has illustrated it. I am ever afraid that your anxiety for me will lead you to fear for the violence of my temperament continually smothered down. For that reason I did not intend to have sent you the following sonnet, but look over the two last pages and ask yourselves whether I have not that in me which will well bear the buffets of the world. It will be the best comment on my sonnet; it will show you that it was written with no Agony but that of ignorance; with no thirst of anything but knowledge when pushed to the point though the first steps to it were through my human passions. They went away, and I wrote with my Mind—and perhaps I must confess a little bit of my heart—

> Why did I laugh tonight? No voice will tell:
>   No God, no Deamon of severe response
> Deigns to reply from heaven or from Hell.
>   Then to my human heart I turn at once;
> Heart! thou and I are here sad and alone;
>   Say, wherefore did I laugh? O mortal pain!
> O Darkness! Darkness! ever must I moan
>   To question Heaven and Hell and Heart in vain!
> Why did I laugh? I know this being's lease
>   My fancy to its utmost blisses spreads:
> Yet could I on this very midnight cease,
>   And the world's gaudy ensigns see in shreds.
> Verse, fame and Beauty are intense indeed
> But Death intenser—Death is Life's high mead.

I went to bed and enjoyed an uninterrupted sleep. Sane I went to bed and sane I arose.

This is the 15th of April. You see what a time it is since I wrote. All that time I have been day by day expecting Letters from you. I write quite in the dark. In the hopes of a Letter daily I have deferred that I might write in the light. I was in town yesterday and at Taylor's heard that young Birkbeck had been in Town and was to set forward in six or seven days, so I shall dedicate that time to making up this parcel ready for him. I wish I could hear from you to make me "whole and general as the casing air." A few days after the 19th of april,[23] I received a note from Haslam containing the news of his father's death. The Family has all been well. Haslam has his father's situation. The Framptons have behaved well to him. The day before yesterday I went to a rout at Sawrey's. It was made pleasant by Reynolds being there, and our getting into conversation with one of the most beautiful Girls I ever saw. She gave a remarkable prettiness to all those commonplaces which most women who talk must utter. I liked Mrs. Sawrey very well. The Sunday before last your Brothers were to come by a long invitation, so long that for the time I forgot it when I promised Mrs. Brawne to dine with her on the same day. On recollecting my engagement with your Brothers I immediately excused myself with Mrs. Brawne, but she would not hear of it and insisted on my bringing my friends with me. So we all dined at Mrs. Brawne's. I have been to Mrs. Bentley's this morning and put all the Letters to and from you and poor Tom and me. I have found some of the correspondence between him and that degraded Wells and Amena.[24] It is a wretched business. I do not know the rights of it, but what I do know would, I am sure, affect you so much that I am in two Minds whether I will tell you anything about it. And yet I do not see why, for anything tho' it be unpleasant that calls to mind those we still love has a compensation in itself for the pain it occasions. So very likely tomorrow I may set about copying the whole of what I have about it with no sort of a Richardson self-satisfaction. I hate it to a sickness and I am afraid more from indolence of mind than anything else. I wonder how people exist with all their worries. I have not been to Westminster but once lately and that was to see Dilke in his new Lodgings. I think of living somewhere in the neighbourhood myself. Your mother was well by your Brothers' account. I shall see her perhaps tomorrow; yes I shall. We have had the Boys[25] here lately. They make a bit of a racket. I shall not be sorry when they go. I found also this morning in a note from George to you, my dear sister, a lock of your hair which I shall this moment put in the miniature case. A few days ago Hunt dined here and Brown invited Davenport to meet him. Davenport from a sense of weakness thought it incumbent on him to show off, and pursuant to that never ceased talking and boaring[26] all day, till I was completely fagged out. Brown grew melancholy, but Hunt perceiving what a complimentary tendency all this had bore it remarkably well. Brown grumbled about it for two or three days. I went with Hunt to Sir John Leicester's gallery. There I saw Northcote,[27] Hilton, Bewick and many more of great and Little note. Haydon's picture is of very little progress this last year; he talks about finishing it next year. Wordsworth is going to publish a Poem called Peter Bell. What a perverse fellow it is! Why wilt he talk about Peter Bells? I was told not to tell, but to you it will not be telling. Reynolds hearing that said Peter Bell was coming out, took it into his head to write a skit upon it call'd Peter Bell. He did it as soon as thought on. It is to be published this morning, and comes out before the real Peter Bell, with this admirable motto from the "Bold stroke for a Wife": "I am the real Simon Pure."[28] It would be just as well to trounce Lord Byron in the same manner. I am still at a stand in versifying. I cannot do it yet with any pleasure. I mean however to look round at my resources and means and see what I can do without poetry. To that end I shall live in Westminster. I have no doubt of making by some means a little to help on or I shall be left in the Lurch—with the burden of a little Pride—however I look in time. The Dilke's like their lodging in Westminster tolerably well. I cannot help thinking what a shame it is that poor Dilke should give up his comfortable house and garden for his Son, whom he will certainly ruin with too much care. The boy has nothing in his ears all day but himself and the importance of his education. Dilke has continually in his mouth "My Boy." This is what spoils princes; it may have the same effect with Commoners. Mrs. Dilke has been very well lately, but what a shameful thing it is that for that obstinate Boy Dilke should stifle himself in Town Lodgings and wear out his Life by his continual apprehension of his Boy's fate in Westminster school with the rest of the Boys and the Masters. Everyone has some wear and tear. One would think Dilke ought to be quiet and happy, but no, this one Boy makes his face pale, his society silent and his vigilance jealous. He would, I have no doubt, quarrel with anyone who snubb'd his Boy. With all this he has no notion how to manage him. O what a farce is our greatest cares! Yet one must be in the pother for the sake of Clothes, food and Lodging. There has been a squabble between Kean and one Mr. Bucke. There are faults on both sides. On Bucke's the faults are positive to the Question; Kean's fault is a want of genteel knowledge and high Policy. The former writes knavishly foolish and the other silly bombast. It was about a Tragedy written by said Mr. Bucke which it appears Mr. Kean kick'd at, it was so bad. After a little struggle of Mr. Bucke's against Kean, drury Lane had the Policy to bring it one and Kean the impolicy not to appear in it. It was damn'd. The people in the Pit had a favourite call on the night of "Buck, Buck, rise up" and "Buck, Buck, how many horns do I hold up?"[29]

Kotzebue the German Dramatist and traitor to his country was murdered lately by a young student whose name I forget. He stabbed himself immediately after crying out Germany! Germany![30] I was unfortunate to miss Richards the only time I have been for many months to see him. Shall I treat you with a little extempore?

When they were come unto the Faery's Court
They rang—no one at home—all gone to sport
And dance and kiss and love as faery's do
For Faeries be as humans lovers true;
Amid the woods they were so lone and wild
Where even the Robin feels himself exil'd
And where the very brooks as if afraid
Hurry along to some less magic shade.
"No one at home!" the fretful princess cry'd
"And all for nothing such a dreary ride
And all for nothing my new diamond cross
No one to see my persian feathers toss
No one to see my Ape, my Dwarf, my Fool
Or how I pace my otahaietan mule
Ape, Dwarf and Fool why stand you gaping there
Burst the door open, quick—or I declare
I'll switch you soundly and in pieces tear."
The Dwarf began to tremble and the Ape
Star'd at the Fool; the Fool was all agape

The Princess grasp'd her switch but just in time
The dwarf with piteous face began to rhyme.

"O mighty Princess did you never hear tell
What your poor servants know but too too well
Know you the three 'great crimes' in faery land
The first alas! poor Dwarf I understand
I made a whipstock of a faery's wand
The next is snoring in their company
The next, the last the direst of the three
Is making free when they are not at home
I was a Prince—a baby prince—my doom
You see, I made a whipstock of a wand
My top has henceforth slept in faery land.
He was a Prince, the Fool a grown up Prince
But he has never been a king's son since
He fell a-snoring at a faery Ball.
Your poor Ape was a Prince, and he poor thing
Picklock'd a faery's boudoir—now no King
But ape—so pray your highness stay awhile
'Tis sooth indeed We know it to our sorrow,
Persist and *you* may be an ape tomorrow.
While the Dwarf spake the Princess all for spite
Peal'd the brown hazel twig to lily white,
Clench'd her small teeth, and held her lips apart,
Try'd to look unconcern'd with beating heart
They saw her highness had made up her mind
A quavering like the reeds before the wind
And they had had it, but o happy chance
The Ape for very fear began to dance
And grin'd as all his ugliness did ache,
She staid her vixen fingers for his sake
He was so very ugly: then she took
Her pocket mirror and began to look

First at herself and at him and then
She smil'd at her own beauteous face again.
Yet for all this—for all her pretty face—
She took it in her head to see the place.
Women gain little from experience
Either in Lovers, husbands or expense
The more their beauty, the more fortune too
Beauty before the wide world never knew
So each Fair reasons, tho' it oft miscarries.
She thought *her* pretty face would please the faeries
"My darling Ape, I won't whip you today
Give me the Picklock sirrah and go play;
They all three wept, but counsel was as vain
As crying cup biddy to drops of rain.
Yet lingeringly did the sad Ape forth draw
The Picklock from the Pocket in his Jaw.
The Princess took it and dismounting straight
Trip'd in blue-silver'd slippers to the gate
And touch'd the wards; the Door full courteously
Opened. She enter'd with her servants three.
Again it clos'd and there was nothing seen
But the Mule grasing on the herbage green.

End of Canto xii

Canto the xiii

The Mule no sooner saw himself alone
Than he prick'd up his Ears and said "well done,
At least unhappy Prince I may be free,
No more a Princess shall sidesaddle me.
O king of Othaietè—tho' a Mule
"Aye every inch a king"[31]—tho'—"Fortune's fool"[32]
Well done, for by what Mr. Dwarfy said
I would not give a sixpence for her head."

Even as he spake he trotted in high glee
To the knotty side of an old Pollard tree
And rub'd his sides against the mossed bark
Till his Girths burst and left him naked stark
Except his Bridle. How get rid of that
Buckled and tied with many a twist and plait?
At last it struck him to pretend to sleep
And then the thievish Monkeys down would creep
And filch the unpleasant trammels quite away.
No sooner thought of than adown he lay
Shamm'd a good snore. The Monkey-men descended
And whom they thought to injure they befriended.
They hung his Bridle on a topmost bough
And off he went run, trot, or anyhow.

Brown is gone to bed and I am tired of rhyming. There is a north wind blowing, playing young gooseberry with the trees. I don't care so it helps even with a side wind a Letter to me, for I cannot put faith in any reports I hear of the Settlement. Some are good, some bad. Last Sunday I took a Walk towards highgate and in the lane that winds by the side of Lord Mansfield's park[33] I met Mr. Green, our Demonstrator at Guy's,[34] in conversation with Coleridge. I joined them, after enquiring by a look whether it would be agreeable. I walked with him at his alderman after-dinner pace for near two miles I suppose. In those two Miles he broached a thousand things. Let me see if I can give you a list: Nightingales, Poetry, on Poetical sensation, Metaphysics, Different genera and species of Dreams, Nightmare, a dream accompanied by a sense of touch, single and double touch, a dream related, First and second consciousness, the difference explained between will and Volition, so many metaphysicians from a want of smoking the second consciousness, Monsters, the Kraken, Mermaids, southey believes in them, southey's belief too much diluted, A Ghost story, Good morning. I heard his voice as he came towards me. I heard it as he moved away. I had heard it all the interval, if it may be called so. He was civil enough to ask me to call on him at Highgate. Good Night! It looks so much like rain I shall not go to town today, but put it off till tomorrow.

Brown this morning is writing some spenserian stanzas against Mrs. Miss Brawne and me, so I shall amuse myself with him a little. In the manner of Spenser:

> He is to weet a melancholy Carle
> Thin in the waist, with bushy head of hair
> As hath the seeded thistle when in parle
> It holds the Zephyr ere it sendeth fair
> Its light balloons into the summer air
> Thereto his beard had not began to bloom
> No brush had touch'd his chin or razor sheer
> No care had touch'd his cheek with mortal doom
> But new he was and bright as scarf from persian loom.

> Ne cared he for wine, or half and half[35]
> Ne cared he for fish or flesh or fowl
> And sauces held he worthless as the chaff
> He 'sdeign'd the swine herd at the wassail bowl.
> Ne with lewd ribbalds sat he cheek by jowl
> Ne with sly Lemans in the scorner's chair
> But after water brooks this Pilgrim's soul
> Panted, and all his food was woodland air
> Though he would ofttimes feast on gilliflowers rare.

> The slang of cities in no wise he knew
> *Tipping the wink* to him was hethen greek
> He sipp'd no olden Tom or ruin blue[36]
> Or nantz,[37] or cherry brandy drank full meek
> By many a Damsel hoarse and rouge of cheek
> Nor did he know each aged Watchman's beat,
> Nor in obscured perlieus would he seek
> For curled Jewesses with ankles neat
> Who as they walk abroad make tinkling with their feet.

This character would ensure him a situation in the establishment of patient Griselda. The servant has come for the little Browns this morning. They have been a toothache to me which I shall enjoy the riddance of. Their little voices are like wasps stings: "Sometimes am I all wound with Browns."[38] We had a claret feast some little while ago. There were Dilke, Reynolds, Skinner,[39] Mancur, John Brown, Martin, Brown and I. We all got a little tipsy, but pleasantly so. I enjoy Claret to a degree. I have been looking over the correspondence of the pretended Amena and Wells this evening. I now see the whole cruel deception. I think Wells must have had an accomplice in it. Amena's Letters are in a Man's language, and in a Man's hand imitating a woman's. The instigations to this diabolical scheme were vanity, and the love of intrigue. It was no thoughtless hoax, but a cruel deception on a sanguine Temperament with every show of friendship. I do not think death too bad for the villain. The world would look upon it in a different light should I expose it; they would call it a frolic, so I must be wary, but I consider it my duty to be prudently revengeful. I will hang over his head like a sword by a hair. I will be opium to his vanity, if I cannot injure his interests. He is a rat and he shall have ratsbane to his vanity. I will harm him all I possibly can. I have no doubt I shall be able to do so. Let us leave him to his misery alone except when we can throw in a little more.

The fifth canto of Dante pleases me more and more. It is that one in which he meets with Paulo and Francesca. I had passed many days in rather a low state of mind and in the midst of them I dreamt of being in that region of Hell. The dream was one of the most delightful enjoyments I ever had in my life. I floated about the whirling atmosphere as it is described with a beautiful figure to whose lips mine were joined as it seem'd for an age, and in the midst of all this cold and darkness I was warm. Even flowery tree tops sprung up and we rested on them sometimes with the lightness of a cloud till the wind blew us away again. I tried a Sonnet upon it. There are fourteen lines but nothing of what I felt in it. O that I could dream it every night.

> As Hermes once took to his feathers light
> When lulled Argus, baffled, swoon'd and slept
> So on a delphic reed my idle spright
> So play'd, so charm'd, so conquer'd, so bereft
> The dragon world of all its hundred eyes

And seeing it asleep so fled away,
Not to pure Ida with its snow-cold skies,
Nor unto Tempe where Jove grieved that day,
But to that second circle of sad hell,
Where in the gust, the whirlwind and the flaw
Of Rain and hailstones lovers need not tell
Their sorrows. Pale were the sweet lips I saw,
Pale were the lips I kiss'd and fair the form
I floated with about that melancholy storm.

I want very very much a little of your wit my dear sister, a Letter or two of yours just to bandy back a pun or two across the Atlantic and send a quibble over the Floridas. Now you have by this time crumpled up your large Bonnet; what do you wear—a cap! Do you put your hair in papers of a night? Do you pay the Miss Birkbeck's a morning visit? Have you any tea? Or do you milk and water with them? What place of Worship do you go to? The Quakers, the Moravians, the Unitarians, or the Methodists? Are there any flowers in bloom you like, any beautiful heaths? Any Streets full of Corset Makers? What sort of shoes have you to fit those pretty feet of yours? Do you desire Compliments to one another? Do you ride on Horseback? What do you have for breakfast, dinner and supper, without mentioning lunch and bever and wet[40] and snack and a bit to stay one's stomach? Do you get any spirits? Now you might easily distill some whiskey and going into the woods set up a whiskey shop for the Monkeys. Do you and the miss Birkbecks get groggy on anything, a little so so-ish so as to be obliged to be seen home with a Lantern? You may perhaps have a game at puss in the corner. Ladies are warranted to play at this game though they have not whiskers. Have you a fiddle in the Settlement, or at any rate a jew's harp which will play in spite of one's teeth? When you have nothing else to do for a whole day I tell you how you may employ it. First get up and when you are dress'd, as it would be pretty early, with a high wind in the woods give George a cold Pig[41] with my Complements. Then you may saunter into the nearest coffeehouse and after taking a dram and a look at the chronicle, go and frighten the wild boars upon the strength. You may as well bring one home for breakfast serving up the hoofs garnished with bristles and a grunt or two to accompany the singing of the kettle. Then if George is not up give him a colder Pig always with my Compliments. When you are both set down to breakfast I advise you to eat your full share, but leave off immediately on feeling yourself inclined to anything on the other side of the puffy. Avoid that for it does not become young women. After you have eaten your breakfast, keep your eye upon dinner. It is the safest way. You should keep a Hawk's eye over your dinner and keep hovering over it till due time, then pounce taking care not to break any plates. While you are hovering with your dinner in prospect you may do a thousand things: put a hedgehog into George's hat; pour a little water into his rifle; soak his boots in a pail of water; cut his jacket round into shreds like a Roman kilt or the back of my grandmother's stays; sow *off* his buttons.

Yesterday I could not write a line I was so fatigued, for the day before I went to town in the morning, called on your Mother and returned in time for a few friends we had to dinner. There were Taylor, Woodhouse, Reynolds. We began cards at about 9 o' Clock, and the night coming on and continuing dark and rainy they could not think of returning to town, so we played at Cards till very daylight and yesterday I was not worth a sixpence. Your mother was very well but anxious for a Letter. We had half an hour's talk and no more for I was obliged to be home. Mrs. and Miss Millar were well, and so was Miss Waldegrave. I have asked your Brothers here for next Sunday. When Reynolds was here on Monday he asked me to give Hunt a hint to take notice of his Peter Bell in the Examiner. The best thing I can do is to write a little notice of it myself which I will do here and copy it out if it should suit my Purpose: "*Peter-Bell.* There have been lately advertized two Books both Peter Bell by name. What stuff the one was made of might be seen by the motto, 'I am the real Simon Pure.' This false florimel[42] has hurried from the press and obtruded herself into public notice while for ought we know the real one may be still wandering about the woods and mountains. Let us hope she may soon appear and make good her right to the magic girdle. The Pamphleteering Archimage we can perceive has rather a splenetic love than a downright hatred to real florimels, if indeed they had been so christened, or had even a pretention to play at bob cherry with Barbara Lewthwaite.[43] But he has a fixed aversion to those three rhyming Graces Alice Fell, Susan Gale and Betty Foy,[44] and now at length especially to Peter Bell—fit Apollo. It may be seen from one or two Passages in this little skit, that the writer of it has felt the finer parts of Mr. Wordsworth and perhaps expatiated with his more remote and sublimer muse. This as far as it relates to Peter Bell is unlucky. The more he may love the sad embroidery of the Excursion, the more he will hate the coarse Samplers of Betty Foy and Alice Fell; and as they come from the same hand, the better will be able to imitate that which can be imitated—to wit, Peter Bell—as far as can be imagined from the obstinate Name. We repeat, it is very unlucky. This real Simon Pure is in parts the very Man. There is a pernicious likeness in the scenery, a 'pestilent humour' in the rhymes, and an inveterate cadence in some of the Stanzas that must be lamented. If we are one part amused at this, we are three parts sorry that an appreciator of Wordsworth should show so much temper at this really provoking name of Peter Bell!"

This will do well enough. I have copied it and enclosed it to Hunt. You will call it a little politic, seeing I keep clear of all parties. I say something for and against both parties and suit it to the tune of the examiner. I mean to say I do not unsuit it and I believe I think what I say, nay I am sure I do. I and my conscience are in luck today, which is an excellent thing. The other night I went to the Play with Rice, Reynolds and Martin. We saw a new dull and half-damned opera call'd "the heart of Mid Lothian"[45] that was on Saturday. I stopped at Taylor's on sunday with Woodhouse and passed a quiet sort of pleasant day. I have been very much pleased with the Panorama of the ships at the north Pole, with the icebergs, the Mountains, the Bears, the Walrus, the seals, the Penguins, and a large whale floating back above water. It is impossible to describe the place. Wednesday Evening.[46]

> La belle dame sans merci
>
> O what can ail thee knight-at-arms
> Alone and palely loitering?

The sedge has withered from the Lake
    And no birds sing!

O what can ail thee knight-at-arms
    So haggard and so woe begone?
The squirrel's granary is full
    And the harvest's done.

I see a lilly on thy brow
    With anguish moist and fever dew,
And on thy cheeks a fading rose
    Fast Withereth too.

I met a Lady in the Meads
    Full beautiful, a faery's child
Her hair was long, her foot was light
    And her eyes were wild.

I made a Garland for her head,
    And bracelets too, and fragrant Zone
She look'd at me as she did love
    And made sweet moan.

I set her on my pacing steed
    And nothing else saw all day long
For sidelong would she bend and sing
    A faery's song.

She found me roots of relish sweet
    And honey wild and manna dew
And sure in language strange she said
    I love thee true.

She took me to her elfin grot
    And there she wept and sigh'd full sore
And there I shut her wild wild eyes
    With kisses four.

And there she lulled me asleep
  And there I dream'd, Ah Woe betide!
The latest dream I ever dreamt
  On the cold hill side.

I saw pale kings and Princes too,
  Pale warriors, death pale were they all;
They cried, La belle dame sans merci
  Thee hath in thrall.

I saw their starv'd lips in the gloam
  With horrid warning gaped wide,
And I awoke and found me here
  On the cold hill's side.

And this is why I sojourn here
  Alone and palely loitering;
Though the sedge is wither'd frome the Lake
  And no birds sing.

Why four kisses, you will say? Why four because I wish to restrain the headlong impetuosity of my Muse. She would have fain said "score" without hurting the rhyme, but we must temper the Imagination, as the Critics say, with Judgment. I was obliged to choose an even number that both eyes might have fair play: and to speak truly I think two a-piece quite sufficient. Suppose I had said seven; there would have been three and a half a-piece; a very awkward affair and well got out of on my side.

Chorus of Faeries (4): Fire, air, earth and water.
  Salamander, Zephyr, Dusketha, Breama.

Sal.	Happy happy glowing fire!
Zep.	Fragrant air, delicious light!
Dusk.	Let me to my glooms retire
Bream	I to greenweed rivers bright.

Salam

Happy, happy glowing fire
Dazzling bowers of soft retire!
Ever let my nourish'd wing
Like a bats still wandering
Faintless fan your fiery spaces
Spirit sole in deadly places
In unhaunted roar and blaze
Open eyes that never daze
Let me see the myriad shapes
Of Men and Beasts and Fish and apes
Portray'd in many a fiery den,
And wrought by spumy bitumen
On the deep intenser roof
Arched every way aloof
Let me breathe upon my Skies
And anger their live tapestries
Free from cold and every care
Of chilly rain and shivring air.

Zephyr

Spright of fire—away, away!
Or your very roundelay
Will sear my plumeage newly budded
From its quilled sheath all studded
with the selfsame dews that fell
On the May-grown Asphodel.
Spright of fire, away, away!

Breama

Spright of fire, away, away!
Zephyr blue-eyed faery turn
And see my cool sedge shaded urn

Where it rests its mossy brim
Mid water mint and cresses dim
And the flowers in sweet troubles
Lift their eyes above the bubbles
Like our Queen when she would please
To sleep and Oberon will tease.
Love me blue-eyed Faery true
Soothly I am sick for you.

Zephyr

Gentle Brema by the first
Violet young nature nurst
I will bathe myself with thee
So you sometime follow me
To my home far, far in west
Far beyond the search and quest
Of the golden-browed sun.
Come with me o'er tops of trees
To my fragrant Palaces
Where they ever floating are
Beneath the cherish of a star
Call'd Vesper, who with silver veil
Ever hides his brilliance pale
Ever gently drows'd doth keep
Twilight of the Fays to sleep
Fear not that your watry hair
Will thirst in drouthy ringlets there.
Clouds of stored summer rains
Thou shalt taste before the stains
Of the mountain soil they take,
And too unlucent for thee make
    I love thee chrystal faery true,
    Sooth I am as sick for you

Salam

Out, ye agueish Faeries, out!
Chilly Lovers what a rout,
Keep ye with your frozen breath
Colder than the mortal death.
Adder-eyed Dusketha, speak
Shall we leave these and go seek
In the Earth's wide Entrails old
Couches warm as theirs is cold?
O for a fiery gloom and thee
Dusketha so enchantingly
        Freckle-wing'd and lizard-sided!

Dusketha

By thee, spright, will I be guided
I care not for cold or heat
Frost and Flame or sparks or sleet
To my essence are the same
But I honor more the flame.
Spright of fire I follow thee
Wheresoever it may be,
To the torrid spouts and fountains
Underneath earthquaked mountains
Or at thy supreme desire
Touch the very pulse of fire
With my bare unlidded eyes.

Salam

Sweet Dusketha, Paradise!
Off ye icy spirits, fly
Frosty creatures of sky.

Dusketha

Breathe upon them fiery spright

Zephyr Brema to each other
Away, Away to our delight!

Salam

Go feed on icicles while we
Bedded in tongued flames will be.

Dusketha

Lead me to those fevrous glooms,
Spright of fire.

Breana

   Me to the blooms
Blue-eyed Zephyr of those flowers
Far in the west where the May cloud lours
And the beams of still vesper, where winds are all wist
Are shed through the rain and the milder mist
And twilight your floating bowers.

I have been reading lately two very different books, Robertson's America and Voltaire's Siecle De Louis xiv.[47] It is like walking arm and arm between Pizarro and the great-little Monarch. In how lamentable a case do we see the great body of the people in both instances. In the first, where Men might seem to inherit quiet of Mind from unsophisticated senses, from uncontamination of civilisation, and especially from their being as it were estranged from the mutual helps of Society and its mutual injuries—and thereby more immediately under the Protection of Providence—even there they had mortal pains to bear as bad, or even worse than Baliffs, Debts and Poverties of civilised Life. The whole appears to resolve into this; that Man is originally "a poor forked creature"[48] subject to the same mischances as the beasts of the forest, destined to hardships and disquietude of some kind or other. If he improves by degrees his bodily accommodations and comforts, at each stage, at each accent there are waiting for him a fresh set of annoyances. He is mortal and there is still a heaven with its Stars above his head.

The most interesting question that can come before us is, How far by the persevering endeavours of a seldom appearing Socrates Mankind may be made happy. I can imagine such happiness carried to an extreme, but what must it end in? Death. And who could in such a case bear with death? The whole troubles of life which are now frittered away in a series of years, would then be accumulated for the last days of a being who instead of hailing its approach, would leave this world as Eve left Paradise. But in truth I do not at all believe in this sort of perfectibility. The nature of the world will not admit of it; the inhabitants of the world will correspond to itself. Let the fish philosophise the ice away from the Rivers in winter time and they shall be at continual play in the tepid delight of summer. Look at the Poles and at the sands of Africa, Whirlpools and volcanoes. Let men exterminate them and I will say that they may arrive at earthly Happiness. The point at which Man may arrive is as far as the parallel state in inanimate nature and no further. For instance, suppose a rose to have sensation; it blooms on a beautiful morning, it enjoys itself. But there comes a cold wind, a hot sun; it can not escape it, it cannot destroy its annoyances. They are as native to the world as itself. No more can man be happy in spite, the worldly elements will prey upon his nature. The common cognomen of this world among the misguided and superstitious is "a vale of tears" from which we are to be redeemed by a certain arbitrary interposition of God and taken to Heaven. What a little circumscribed straightened notion! Call the world if you Please "The vale of Soul-making." Then you will find out the use of the world (I am speaking now in the highest terms for human nature admitting it to be immortal, which I will here take for granted for the purpose of showing a thought which has struck me concerning it). I say *"Soul-making,"* Soul as distinguished from an Intelligence. There may be intelligences or sparks of the divinity in millions, but they are not Souls till they acquire identities, till each one is personally itself. Intelligences are atoms of perception; they know and they see and they are pure, in short they are God. How then are Souls to be made? How then are these sparks which are God to have identity given them so as ever to possess a bliss peculiar to each one's individual existence? How, but by the medium of a world like this? This point I sincerely wish to consider because I think it a grander system of salvation than the chrystain religion, or rather it is a system of Spirit-creation. This is effected by three grand materials acting the one upon the other for a series of years. These three Materials are the *Intelligence,* the *human heart* (as distinguished from intelligence or Mind) and the *World* or *Elemental space* suited for the proper action of *Mind and Heart* on each other for the purpose of forming the *Soul* or *Intelligence destined to possess the sense of Identity.* I can scarcely express what I but dimly perceive, and yet I think I perceive it. That you may judge the more clearly I will put it in the most homely form possible. I will call the *world* a School instituted for the purpose of teaching little children to read. I will call the *human heart* the *horn Book* used in that School, and I will call the *Child able to read, the Soul* made from that *school* and its *hornbook.* Do you not see how necessary a World of Pains and troubles is to school an Intelligence and make it a soul? A Place where the heart must feel and suffer in a thousand diverse ways! Not merely is the Heart a Hornbook; it is the Mind's Bible, it is the Mind's experience, it is the teat from which the Mind or intelligence sucks its identity. As various as the Lives of Men are, so various become their souls, and thus does God make individual beings, Souls, Identical Souls of the sparks of his own essence. This appears to me a faint sketch of a system of Salvation which does not affront our reason and humanity. I am convinced that many difficulties which christians labour under would vanish before it. There is one which even now Strikes me: the Salvation of Children. In them the Spark or intelligence returns to God without any identity, it having had no time to learn of, and be altered by, the heart or seat of the human Passions. It is pretty generally suspected that the christian scheme has been copied from the ancient persian and greek Philosophers. Why may they not have made this simple thing even more simple for common apprehension by introducing Mediators and Personages in the same manner as in the hethen mythology abstractions are personified? Seriously, I think it probable that this System of Soul-making may have been the Parent of all the more palpable and personal Schemes of Redemption, among the Zoroastrians, the Christians and the Hindoos. For as one part of the human species must have their carved Jupiter, so another part must have the palpable and named Mediatior and saviour, their Christ, their Oromanes[49] and their

Vishnu. If what I have said should not be plain enough, as I fear it may not be, I will put you in the place where I began in this series of thoughts; I mean, I began by seeing how man was formed by circumstances, and what are circumstances but touchstones of his heart? And what are touchstones but proovings of his heart? And what are proovings of his heart but fortifiers or alterers of his nature? And what is his altered nature but his soul? And what was his soul before it came into the world and had These provings and alterations and perfectionings? An intelligence—without Identity—and how is this Identity to be made? Through the medium of the Heart. And how is the heart to become this Medium but in a world of Circumstances? There, now I think what with Poetry and Theology you may thank your Stars that my pen is not very longwinded. Yesterday I received two Letters from your Mother and Henry which I shall send by young Birkbeck with this.

Friday, April 30th Brown has been rummaging up some of my old sins, that is to say sonnets. I do not think you remember them, so I will copy them out as well as two or three lately written. I have just written one on Fame which Brown is transcribing and he has his book and mine. I must employ myself perhaps in a sonnet on the same subject.

On Fame

"You cannot eat your cake and have it too"
—Proverb

How fever'd is that Man who cannot look
    Upon his mortal days with temperate blood,
Who vexes all the leaves of his Life's book
    And robs his fair name of its maidenhood.
It is as if the rose should pluck herself,
    Or the ripe plum finger its misty bloom,
As if a clear Lake meddling with itself
    Should cloud its pureness with a muddy gloom.
But the rose leaves herself upon the Briar
For winds to kiss and grateful Bees to feed,

And the ripe plumb still wears its dim attire.
  The undisturbed Lake has crystal space,
  Why then should Man, leasing the world for grace,
Spoil his salvation by a fierce miscreed?

Another on Fame

Fame like a wayward girl will still be coy
  To those who woo her with too slavish knees,
  But makes surrender to some thoughtless boy
And dotes the more upon a heart at ease.
She is a Gipsey will not speak to those
  Who have not learnt to be content without her;
A Jilt whose ear was never whisper'd close
  Who think they scandal her who talk about her.
A very Gipsey is she Nilus born,
Sister-in-law to jealous Potiphar.
Ye lovesick Bards, repay her scorn for scorn,
Ye lovelorn Artists, madmen that ye are,
Make your best bow to her and bid adieu,
Then if she likes it she will follow you.

To Sleep

O soft embalmer of the still midnight,
  Shutting with careful fingers and benign
Our gloom-pleas'd eyes, embowered from the light,
  Enshaded in forgetfulness divine.
O soothest sleep, if so it please thee close
  In midst of this thine hymn my willing eyes,
Or wait the amen, ere thy poppy throws
  Around my bed its dewy Charities.
Then save me or the passed day will shine
Upon my pillow breeding many woes.
Save me from curious conscience that still lords

Its strength for darkness, burrowing like a Mole.
Turn the key deftly in the oiled wards,
And seal the hushed Casket of my soul.

The following Poem—the last I have written—is the first and the only one with which I have taken even moderate pains. I have for the most part dash'd off my lines in a hurry. This I have done leisurely; I think it reads the more richly for it and will I hope encourage me to write other things in even a more peaceable and healthy spirit. You must recollect that Psyche was not embodied as a goddess before the time of Apulieus the Platonist who lived after the Augustan age, and consequently the Goddess was never worshipped or sacrificed to with any of the ancient fervour, and perhaps never thought of in the old religion. I am more orthodox than to let a hethen Goddess be so neglected.

Ode to Psyche

O Goddess hear these tuneless numbers, wrung
    By sweet enforcement, and remembrance dear,
And pardon that thy secrets should be sung
    Even into thine own soft-conched ear!
Surely I dreamt today, or did I see
The winged Psyche, with awaked eyes?
I wander'd in a forest thoughtlessly,
And on the sudden, fainting with surprise,
Saw two fair Creatures couched side by side
In deepest grass beneath the whisp'ring fan
Of leaves and trembled blossoms, where there ran
A Brooklet scarce espied.
'Mid hush'd, cool-rooted flowers, fragrant-eyed,
Blue, freckle-pink, and budded syrian
They lay, calm-breathing on the bedded grass.
Their arms embraced and their pinions too;
Their lips touch'd not, but had not bid adieu,
As if disjoined by soft-handed slumber,

And ready still past kisses to outnumber,
At tender eye-dawn of aurorian love.
The winged boy I knew:
But who wast thou, O happy, happy dove?
His Psyche true?

O latest born, and loveliest vision far
    Of all Olympus faded Hierarchy!
Fairer than Phoebe's sapphire-region'd star,
    Or Vesper amorous glow-worm of the sky;
Fairer than these though Temple thou hadst none,
    Nor Altar heap'd with flowers;
Nor virgin choir to make delicious moan
    Upon the midnight hours:
No voice, no lute, no pipe, no incense sweet
    From chain-swung Censer teeming,
No shrine, no grove, no Oracle, no heat
    Of pale-mouth'd Prophet dreaming!

O Bloomiest! though too late for antique vows;
    Too, too late for the fond believing Lyre,
When holy were the haunted forest boughs,
    Holy the air, the water and the fire:
Yet even in these days so far retir'd
From happy Pieties, thy lucent fans,
Fluttering among the faint Olympians,
I see, and sing by my own eyes inspired.
O let me be thy Choir and make a moan
Upon the midnight hours;
Thy voice, thy lute, thy pipe, thy incense sweet
From swinged Censer teeming;
Thy shrine, thy Grove, thy Oracle, thy heat
Of pale-mouth'd Prophet dreaming!
Yes, I will be thy Priest and build a fane
In some untrodden region of my Mind,

The last leaf of Keats's journal letter (recto) to George and Georgiana Keats,
14 February–4 May 1819 (Ms Keats 1.53).
By permission of the Houghton Library, Harvard University.

Wednesday May 4 - I went to Town this
morning and calling at Taylors they
told me that I must let young Birkbeck
have the Packet immediately - so I
shall seal it tonight and be in Town
early tomorrow morning - I hope I
shall see him - for the sake of his seeing you afterwards - I have been waiting for Taylor to perform his promise of
inviting young B. to meet me at his
House - I suppose he has had no opportunity. I have heard to day that the
Packets from Illionois had been robbed
and that accounts for my not having
received any Letters - Thb I have never
been very uneasy about it. and have
constantly kept your mother from any
despondence about it. Rice and Reynolds
came with me from Town and drank
Tea - they both desire particularly the
Remembrances. You must let me
know every thing - how parcels come
and go - what Papers Birkbecks has
and what news paper you want and
other things. God bless you, my dear
Brother & Sister. Your ever affectionate
Brother John Keats.

The last leaf of Keats's journal letter (verso).

Where branched thoughts new grown with pleasant pain,
Instead of pines shall murmur in the wind.
Far, far around shall those dark-cluster'd trees
Fledge the wild-ridged mountains steep by steep,
And there by Zephyrs, streams and birds and bees
The moss-lain Dryads shall be lull'd to sleep.
And in the midst of this wide-quietness
A rosy Sanctuary will I dress
With the wreath'd trellis of a working brain:
With buds and bells and stars without a name;
With all the gardener, fancy e'er could feign
Who breeding flowers will never breed the same.
And there shall be for thee all soft delight
That shadowy thought can win;
A bright torch, and a casement ope at night,
To let the warm Love in—

Here endethe ye Ode to Psyche

Incipit altera Sonneta.[50]

I have been endeavouring to discover a better sonnet stanza than we have. The legitimate does not suit the language over-well from the pouncing rhymes; the other kind appears too elegiac, and the couplet at the end of it has seldom a pleasing effect. I do not pretend to have succeeded. It will explain itself.

If by dull rhymes our english must be chain'd,
And, like Andromeda, the Sonnet sweet
Fetter'd in spite of pained Loveliness;
Let us find out, if we must be constrain'd,[51]
Sandals more interwoven and complete
To fit the naked foot of Poesy.
Let us inspect the Lyre, and weigh the stress
Of every chord, and see what may be gain'd

By ear industrious and attention meet.
Misers of sound and syllable no less
Than Midas of his coinage, let us be
Jealous of dead leaves in the bay wreath crown.
So if we may not let the Muse be free,
She will be bound with garlands of her own.

Here endeth the other Sonnet. This is the 3rd of May and everything is in delightful forwardness; the violets are not wither'd before the peeping of the first rose. Yesterday I walked to Walthamstow through the fields, through Highgate, Hornsey and Tottenham. I call'd in my way on the Haughtons. They were well and enquired after you. Fanny is as well, but she is grown so much lately as to be thin and I do not think very strong. Mrs. Abbey was ill, and Miss Abby look'd not much better. Fanny is very sensible in my mind. She does not grow very pretty. We took a walk in the Garden and about the Village. She complains about Mrs. Abbey's behaviour. I long to send her some Letters from you. I only want some Letters from you to make the spring in proper time.

Wednesday May 4. I went to Town this morning and calling at Taylors they told me that I must let young Birkbeck have the Packet immediately. So I shall seal it tonight and be in Town early tomorrow morning. I hope I shall see him, for the sake of his seeing you afterwards. I have been waiting for Taylor to perform his promise of inviting young B. to meet me at his House. I suppose he has had no opportunity. I have heard today that the Packets from Illoinois had been robbed and that accounts for my not having received any Letters, tho' I have never been very uneasy about it, and have constantly kept your mother from any despondence about it. Rice and Reynolds came with me from Town and drank Tea. They both desire particularly their Remembrances. You must let me know everything, how parcels come and go, what Papers Birkbecks has and what newspaper you want, and other things. God bless you, my dear Brother and Sister.

Your ever affectionate Brother
John Keats

1. Keats sent several large packets to his brother and sister-in-law which he designated "A," "B," "C," etc.

2. Samuel Rogers (1763–1855), *Human Life.* The first two cantos of *Don Juan* appeared without the author's or publisher's names in July 1819.

3. Mr. Towers was Charles Cowden Clarke's brother-in-law; Holt was a solicitor; Mrs. Septimus Brown was the wife of Charles Brown's brother.

4. Charles Cowden Clarke.

5. Richard Sheil (1791–1851), whose play *The Apostate* was presented at Covent Garden on 3 May 1817. His *Evadne* was produced there in February 1819.

6. Actually it was written by Charles Lamb.

7. Richard Carlile (1790–1843), publisher and freethinker, was arrested on 11 February, tried and found guilty on 13 and 14 October of republishing Paine's *Age of Reason* and Palmer's *Principles of Deism,* and in November sentenced to a fine of £1,500 and three years' imprisonment.

8. Lewis Way (1772–1840), philanthropist, of Stansted, near Bedhampton. (Gittings)

9. Keats's suggestive misspelling.

10. He refers to Jeremy Taylor (1613–1667), *The Golden Grove,* a devotional manual.

11. James Cawthorn (d. 1833) of the British Library.

12. "As we know."

13. A score in cribbage.

14. "I do not want him to have her, for . . ."

15. A hospital for lunatics.

16. "With members of his household and his kin."

17. The copyist's error for Joseph Milner (1744–1797), divine, dean of Carlisle, and professor of mathematics at Cambridge. With his brother Isaac he wrote *The History of the Church of Christ,* 5 vols. (1794–1809).

18. *A Letter to William Gifford, Esq. From William Hazlitt, Esq.* (1819).

19. "Bonfire."

20. Beaumont and Fletcher.

21. "The Old Cumberland Beggar," line 153.

22. *Comus,* lines 475–477.

23. An error for "March."

24. In 1816, probably as a joke, C. J. Wells sent Tom a series of letters signed "Amena Bellefila," a fictitious woman supposedly in love with him. Oddly enough, Tom was fooled, and when he discovered the truth his health, so his biographers report, suffered. Keats broke with Wells for good after this incident.

25. Brown's nephews.

26. Keats's own misspelling.

27. Sir John Leicester (1762–1827), later first Baron de Tabley; James Northcote (1746–1831), painter and author.

28. Simon Pure, a "quaking preacher" from Pennsylvania, is impersonated by Colonel Fainwell in this play by Susannah Centlivre (1667?–1723).

29. Charles Bucke, *The Italians; Or, The Fatal Accusation,* presented at Drury Lane on 3 and 12 April.

30. Kotzebue was murdered by Karl Ludwig Sand.

31. *King Lear,* IV.vi.109.

32. *Romeo and Juliet,* III.i.141.
33. Kenwood, the seat of William Murray, first earl of Mansfield (1705–1793), lord chief justice.
34. Joseph Henry Green (1791–1863), Coleridge's literary executor.
35. A drink of ale and beer, or ale and porter, in equal quantities.
36. Both names for gin.
37. Brandy.
38. Adapted from *The Tempest,* II.ii.12f.
39. Robert Skynner, Brown's solicitor.
40. "Bever": a small snack between meals; "wet": a drink.
41. A cold splash of water to wake him up.
42. The "snowy," or false, Florimell of *The Faerie Queene,* III.viii.5–20, IV.ii, iv, V.iii.
43. The heroine of Wordsworth's "The Pet Lamb."
44. Susan Gale and Betty Foy are characters in Wordsworth's "The Idiot Boy."
45. A musical drama by Daniel Terry (1780?–1829).
46. That is, 21 April.
47. William Robertson (1721–1793), *The History of America* (1777); Voltaire, *Le Siècle de Louis XIV.*
48. *King Lear,* III.iv.3f.
49. *Abudah; Or, The Talisman of Oromanes,* described on the program as "a new Oriental Fairy Tale, founded on one of the Tales of the Genii, in 2 Acts," was presented at Drury Lane in the spring of 1819.
50. "Another [properly a second] sonnet begins."
51. The last leaf of this letter begins with the word "Sandals" and is printed here for the first time. It was presented to the Houghton Library in 1995.

To Miss Jeffery

31 MAY 1819

C. Brown Esq.'s
Wentworth Place—Hampstead—

My dear Lady,

I was making a day or two ago a general conflagration of all old Letters and Memorandums, which had become of no interest to me. I made however, like the Barber-inquisitor in Don Quixote some reservations, among the rest your and your Sister's Letters. I assure you you had not entirely vanished from my Mind, or even become shadows in my remembrance; it only needed such a memento as your Letters to bring you back to me. Why have I not written before? Why did I not answer your Honiton Letter? I had no good news for you; every concern of ours, (ours I wish I could say) and still I must say *ours,* though George is in America and I have no Brother left. Though in the midst of my troubles I had no relation except my young sister, I have had excellent friends. Mr. B. at whose house I now am, invited me. I have been with him ever since. I could not make up my mind to let you know these things. Nor should I now, but see what a little interest will do. I want you to do me a Favor which I will first ask and then tell you the reasons. Enquire in the Villages round Teignmouth if there is any Lodging commodious for its cheapness; and let me know where it is and what price. I have the choice as it were of two Poisons (yet I ought not to call this a Poison): the one is voyaging to and from India for a few years; the other is leading a fevrous life alone with Poetry. This latter will suit me best, for I cannot resolve to give up my Studies. It strikes me it would not be quite so proper for you to make such inquiries, so give my love to your Mother and ask her to do it. Yes, I would rather conquer my indolence and strain my nerves at some grand Poem than be in a dunderheaded indiaman. Pray let no one in Teignmouth know anything of this. Fanny must by this time have altered her name. Perhaps you have also. Are you all alive? Give my Compliments to Mrs. ———, your Sister. I have had good news, (tho' 'tis a queerish world in which such things are call'd good) from George. He and his wife are well. I will tell you more soon. Especially don't let the Newfoundland fisherman know it, and especially no one else. I have been always till now almost as careless of the world as a fly; my troubles were all of the Imagination. My Brother George always stood between me and any dealings with the world. Now I find I must buffet it. I must take my stand upon some vantage ground and begin to fight. I must choose between despair and Energy. I choose the latter, though the world has taken on a quakerish look with me, which I once thought was impossible:

> "Nothing can bring back the hour
> Of splendour in the grass and glory in the flower."[1]

I once thought this a Melancholist's dream.

But why do I speak to you in this manner? No, believe me, I do not write for a mere selfish purpose. The manner in which I have written of myself will convince you. I do not do so to Strangers. I have not quite made up my mind. Write me on the receipt of this and again at your Leisure. Between whiles you shall hear from me again.

Your sincere friend
John Keats

1. Slightly misquoted from Wordsworth's "Ode: Intimations of Immortality," lines 181f.

To Miss Jeffery
9 JUNE 1819

Wentworth Place

My dear young Lady,

I am exceedingly obliged by your two Letters. Why I did not answer your first immediately was that I have had a little aversion to the South of Devon from the continual remembrance of my Brother Tom. On that account I do not return to my old Lodgings in Hampstead, though the people of the house have become friends of mine. This however I could think nothing of; it can do no more than keep one's thoughts employed for a day or two. I like your description of Bradley very much and I dare say shall be there in the course of the summer; it would be immediately but that a friend with ill health and to whom I am greatly attached[1] call'd on me yesterday and proposed my spending a Month with him at the back of the Isle of Wight. This is just the thing at present; the morrow will take care of itself. I do not like the name of Bishop's Teigntown. I hope the road from Teignmouth to Bradley does not lie that way. Your advice about the Indiaman is a very wise advice, because it just suits me, though you are a little in the wrong concerning its destroying the energies of Mind. On the contrary, it would be the finest thing in the world to strengthen them. To be thrown among people who care not for you, with whom you have no sympathies, forces the Mind upon its own resources and leaves it free to make its Speculations of the differences of human character and to class them with the calmness of a Botanist. An Indiaman is a little world. One of the great reasons that the english have produced the finest writers in the world is that the English world has ill-treated them during their lives and foster'd them after their deaths. They have in general been trampled aside into the byepaths of Life and seen the festerings of Society. They have not been treated like the Raphaels of Italy. And where is the Englishman and Poet who has given a magnificent Entertainment at the christening of one of his Hero's Horses as Boyardo did?[2] He had a Castle in the Appenine. He was a noble Poet of Romance, not a miserable and mighty Poet of the human Heart. The middle age of Shakespeare was all clouded over: his days were not more happy than Hamlet's who is perhaps more like Shakespeare himself in his common everyday Life than any other of his Characters. Ben Johnson was a common Soldier and in the Low countries, in the face of two armies, fought a single combat with a french Trooper and slew him. For all this I will not go on board an Indiaman, nor for example's sake run my head into dark alleys. I dare say my discipline is to come, and plenty of it too. I have been very idle lately, very averse to writing, both from the overpowering idea of our dead poets and from abatement of my love of fame. I hope I am a little more of a Philosopher than I was, consequently a little less of a versifying Pet-lamb.[3] I have put no more in Print or you should have had it. You will judge of my 1819 temper when I tell you that the thing I have most enjoyed this year has been writing an ode to Indolence. Why did not you make your long-haired Sister put her great brown hard fist to paper and cross your Letter? Tell her when you write again that I expect chequer work. My Friend Mr. Brown is sitting opposite me employed in writing a Life of David. He reads me passages as he writes them, stuffing my infidel mouth as though I were a young rook. Infidel Rooks do not provender with Elijah's Ravens. If he goes on as he has begun your new Church had better not proceed, for parsons will be superseeded, and of course the Clerks must follow. Give my love to your Mother with the assurance that I can never forget her anxiety for my Brother Tom. Believe also that I shall ever remember our leave-taking with *you.*

Ever sincerely yours
John Keats

1. James Rice.
2. Matteo Maria Boiardo (1434–1494), author of *Orlando Innamorato.*
3. See Keats's "Ode on Indolence," vi.4.

To Fanny Keats
9 JUNE 1819

Wentworth Place

My dear Fanny,

I shall be with you next monday at the farthest. I could not keep my promise of seeing you again in a week because I am in so unsettled a state of mind about what I am to do. I have given up the Idea of the Indiaman. I cannot resolve to give up my favorite studies, so I purpose to retire into the Country and set my Mind at work once more. A Friend of Mine who has an ill state of health called on me yesterday and proposed to spend a little time with him at the back of the Isle of Wight, where he said we might live very cheaply. I agreed to his proposal. I have taken a great dislike to Town. I never go there. Someone is always calling on me and as we have spare beds they often stop a couple of days. I have written lately to some Acquaintances in Devonshire concerning a cheap Lodging and they have been very kind in letting me know all I wanted. They have described a pleasant place which I think I shall eventually retire to. How came you on With my young Master Yorkshire Man? Did not Mrs. A. sport her Carriage and one? They really surprised me with super civility. How did Mrs. A. manage it? How is the old tadpole gardener and little Master next door? It is to be hop'd they will both die some of these days. Not having been to Town I have not heard whether Mr. A—— purposes to retire from business. Do let me know if you have heard anything more about it. If he should not I shall be very disappointed. If anyone deserves to be put to his shifts it is that Hodgkinson. As for the other, he would live a long time upon his fat and be none the worse for a good long lent. How came milidi to give one Lisbon wine? Had she drained the Gooseberry? Truly, I cannot delay making another visit—asked to take Lunch, whether I will have ale, wine, take sugar, objection to green, like cream, thin bread and butter, another cup, agreeable, enough sugar, little more cream, too weak 12 shilling, etc., etc., etc. Lord, I must come again.

    We are just going to Dinner. I must run with this to the Post.

Your affectionate Brother
John—

To B. R. Haydon
17 JUNE 1819

Wentworth Place,
Thursday Morning

My dear Haydon,

    I know you will not be quite prepared for this, because your Pocket must needs be very low having been at ebb tide so long, but what can I do? Mine is lower. I was the day before yesterday much in want of Money, but some news I had yesterday has driven me into necessity. I went to Abbey's for some Cash, and he put into my hand a Letter from my Aunt's Solicitor containing the pleasant information that she was about to file a Bill in Chancery against us. Now in case of a defeat Abbey will be very undeservedly in the wrong box; so I could not ask him for any more money, nor can I till the affair is decided; and if it goes against him I must in conscience make over to him what little he may have remaining. My purpose is now to make one more attempt in the Press. If that fail, "ye hear no more of me,"[1] as Chaucer says. Brown has lent me some money for the present. Do borrow or beg somehow what you can for me. Do not suppose I am at all uncomfortable about the matter in any other way than as it forces me to apply to the needy. I could not send you those lines, for I could not get the only copy of them before last Saturday evening. I sent them Mr. Elmes on Monday. I saw Monkhouse on sunday. He told me you were getting on with the Picture. I would have come over to you today, but I am fully employed.

Your's ever sincerely
John Keats—

1. *Legend of Good Women,* line 1557.

To Fanny Keats
17 JUNE 1819

Wentworth Place

My dear Fanny,

Still I cannot afford to spend money by Coachire and still my throat is not well enough to warrant my walking. I went yesterday to ask Mr. Abbey for some money, but I could not on account of a Letter he showed me from my Aunt's Solicitor. You do not understand the business. I trust it will not in the end be detrimental to you. I am going to try the Press once more and to that end shall retire to live cheaply in the country and compose myself and verses as well as I can. I have very good friends ready to help me, and I am the more bound to be careful of the money they lend me. It will all be well in the course of a year I hope. I am confident of it, so do not let it trouble you at all. Mr. Abbey showed me a Letter he had received from George containing the news of the birth of a Niece for us, and all doing well. He said he would take it to you, so I suppose today you will see it. I was preparing to enquire for a Situation with an Apothecary, but Mr. Brown persuades me to try the press once more—so I will with all my industry and ability. Mr. Rice, a friend of mine in ill health, has proposed retiring to the back of the isle of wight, which I hope will be cheap in the summer. I am sure it will in the winter. Thence you shall frequently hear from me and in the Letters I will copy those lines I may write which will be most pleasing to you, in the confidence you will show them to no one. I have not run quite aground yet I hope, having written this morning to several people to whom I have lent money, requesting repayment. I shall hencefore shake off my indolent fits, and among other reformation be more diligent in writing to you and mind you always answer me. I shall be obliged to go out of town on Saturday and shall have no money till tomorrow, so I am very sorry to think I shall not be able to come to Walthamstow. The Head Mr. Severn did of me is now too dear, but here inclosed is a very capital Profile done by Mr Brown. I will write again on Monday or Tuesday. Mr. and Mrs. Dilke are well.

Your affectionate Brother
John—

To Fanny Brawne
1 JULY 1819

Shanklin,
Isle of Wight, Thursday

My dearest Lady,

I am glad I had not an opportunity of sending off a Letter which I wrote for you on Tuesday night. 'Twas too much like one out of Rousseau's Heloise. I am more reasonable this morning. The morning is the only proper time for me to write to a beautiful Girl whom I love so much, for at night, when the lonely day has closed, and the lonely, silent, unmusical Chamber is waiting to receive me as into a Sepulchre, then believe me my passion gets entirely the sway, then I would not have you see those Rapsodies which I once thought it impossible I should ever give way to, and which I have often laughed at in another, for fear you should think me either too unhappy or perhaps a little mad. I am now at a very pleasant Cottage window, looking onto a beautiful hilly country with a glimpse of the sea; the morning is very fine. I do not know how elastic my spirit might be, what pleasure I might have in living here and breathing and wandering as free as a stag about this beautiful Coast if the remembrance of you did not weigh so upon me. I have never known any unalloy'd Happiness for many days together. The death or sickness of someone has always spoilt my hours, and now when none such troubles oppress me, it is you must confess very hard that another sort of pain should haunt me. Ask yourself, my love, whether you are not very cruel to have so entrammelled me, so destroyed my freedom. Will you confess this in the Letter you must write immediately and do all you can to console me in it? Make it rich as a draught of poppies to intoxicate me. Write the softest words and kiss them that I may at least touch my lips where yours have been. For myself I know not how to express my devotion to so fair a form: I want a brighter word than bright, a fairer word than fair. I almost wish we were butterflies and liv'd but three summer days. Three such days with you I could fill with more delight than fifty common years could ever contain. But however selfish I may feel, I am sure I could never act selfishly. As I told you a day or two before I left Hampstead, I will never return to London if my Fate does not turn up Pam or at least a Court-card.[1] Though I could centre my Happiness in you, I cannot expect to engross your heart so entirely; indeed, if I thought you felt as much for me as I do for you at this moment I do not think I could restrain myself from seeing you again tomorrow for the delight of one embrace. But no, I must live upon hope and Chance. In case of the worst that can happen, I shall still love you, but what hatred shall I have for another! Some lines I read the other day are continually ringing a peal in my ears:

> To see those eyes I prize above mine own
> Dart favors on another,

And those sweet lips (yielding immortal nectar)
Be gently press'd by any but myself.
Think, think, Francesca, what a cursed thing
It were beyond expression![2]

J.

Do write immediately. There is no Post from this Place, so you must
address Post Office, Newport, Isle of Wight. I know before night I shall
curse myself for having sent you so cold a Letter; yet it is better to do it
as much as in my senses as possible. Be as kind as the distance will
permit to your

J. Keats

Present my Compliments to your mother, my love to Margaret and best
remembrances to your Brother—if you please so.

---

1. That is, the knave of hearts, the highest trump in five-card loo, or at least a picture
   card.
2. Misquoted from Philip Massinger's *Duke of Milan*, I.iii.

To Fanny Keats
6 JULY 1819

Shanklin,
Isle of Wight
Tuesday July 6th—

My dear Fanny,

   I have just received another Letter from George full of as good news as
we can expect. I cannot enclose it to you as I could wish, because it contains matters of Business to which I must for a Week to come have an im-

mediate reference. I think I told you the purpose for which I retired to this place—to try the fortune of my Pen once more—and indeed I have some confidence in my success. But in every event, believe me my dear sister, I shall be sufficiently comfortable, as, if I cannot lead that life of competence and society I should wish, I have enough knowledge of my gallipots[1] to ensure me an employment and maintainance. The Place I am in now I visited once before and a very pretty place it is were it not for the bad Weather. Our window looks over housetops and Cliffs onto the Sea, so that when the Ships sail past the Cottage chimneys you may take them for Weathercocks. We have Hill and Dale, forest and Mead and plenty of Lobsters. I was on the Portsmouth Coach the Sunday before last in that heavy shower, and I may say I went to Portsmouth by water. I got a little cold and as it always flies to my throat I am a little out of sorts that way. There were on the Coach with me some common french people, but very well behaved. There was a woman amongst them to whom the poor Men in ragged coats were more gallant than ever I saw gentleman to Lady at a Ball. When we got down to walk up hill one of them pick'd a rose, and on remounting gave it to the woman with—"Ma'mselle—voila, une bell rose!"

I am so hard at work that perhaps I should not have written to you for a day or two if George's Letter had not diverted my attention to the interests and pleasure of those I love. And ever believe that when I do not behave punctually it is from a very necessary occupation, and that my silence is no proof of my not thinking of you, or that I want more than a gentle philip to bring your image with every claim before me. You have never seen mountains, or I might tell you that the hill at Steephill is I think almost of as much consequence as Mount Rydal on Lake Winander. Bonchurch too is a very delightful Place—as I can see by the Cottages all romantic—covered with creepers and honeysuckles,[2] with roses and eglantines peeping in at the windows. Fit abodes, for the People I guess live in them, romantic old maids fond of novels or soldiers, widows with a pretty jointure, or anybody's widows or aunts or anythings given to Poetry and a Piano forte—as far as in 'em lies—as people say. If I could play upon the Guitar I might make my fortune with an old song and get two blessings at once: a Lady's heart and the Rheumatism. But I am almost afraid to peep at those little windows, for a pretty window should show a pretty face, and as the world

311

es are against me. I am living with a very good fellow indeed, a
He is unfortunately labouring under a complaint which has for
so.. ars been a burthen to him. This is a pain to me. He has a greater
tact in speaking to people of the village than I have, and in those matters is
a great amusement as well as a good friend to me. He bought a ham the
other day, for say he "Keats, I don't think a Ham is a wrong thing to have in
a house." Write to me, Shanklin, Isle of Wight as soon as you can, for a Letter is a great treat to me here. Believing me

ever your affectionate Brother,
John—

1. A reference to the conclusion of Lockhart's "Cockney School" attack on him. A
   gallipot is a small earthen glazed pot used by apothecaries for ointments and medicines.
2. Keats wrote "honeysickles."

To Fanny Brawne
8 JULY 1819

July 8th

My sweet Girl,

Your Letter gave me more delight than any thing in the world but yourself could do; indeed I am almost astonished that any absent one should
have that luxurious power over my senses which I feel. Even when I am not
thinking of you I receive your influence and a tenderer nature steeling upon
me. All my thoughts, my unhappiest days and nights have I find not at all
cured me of my love of Beauty, but made it so intense that I am miserable
that you are not with me; or rather breathe in that dull sort of patience that
cannot be called Life. I never knew before what such a love as you have
made me feel was. I did not believe in it. My Fancy was afraid of it, lest it
should burn me up. But if you will fully love me, though there may be

some fire, 'twill not be more than we can bear when moistened and be-dewed with Pleasures. You mention "horrid people" and ask me whether it depend upon them whether I see you again. Do understand me, my love, in this. I have so much of you in my heart that I must turn Mentor when I see a chance of harm befalling you. I would never see anything but Pleasure in your eyes, love on your lips, and Happiness in your steps. I would wish to see you among those amusements suitable to your inclinations and spir-its, so that our loves might be a delight in the midst of Pleasures agreeable enough, rather than a resource from vexations and cares. But I doubt much, in case of the worst, whether I shall be philosopher enough to follow my own Lessons. If I saw my resolution give you a pain I could not. Why may I not speak of your Beauty, since without that I could never have lov'd you? I cannot conceive any beginning of such love as I have for you but Beauty. There may be a sort of love for which, without the least sneer at it, I have the highest respect, and can admire it in others, but it has not the rich-ness, the bloom, the full form, the enchantment of love after my own heart. So let me speak of your Beauty, though to my own endangering if you could be so cruel to me as to try elsewhere its Power. You say you are afraid I shall think you do not love me. In saying this you make me ache the more to be near you. I am at the diligent use of my faculties here, I do not pass a day without sprawling some blank verse or tagging some rhymes; and here I must confess, that (since I am on that subject), I love you the more in that I believe you have liked me for my own sake and for nothing else. I have met with women whom I really think would like to be married to a Poem and to be given away by a Novel. I have seen your Comet, and only wish it was a sign that poor Rice would get well whose illness makes him rather a mel-ancholy companion; and the more so as so to conquer his feelings and hide them from me, with a forc'd Pun. I kiss'd your writing over in the hope you had indulg'd me by leaving a trace of honey. What was your dream? Tell it me and I will tell you the interpretation thereof.

Ever yours my love!
John Keats—

Do not accuse me of delay. We have not here an opportunity of sending
letters every day. Write speedily—

To J. H. Reynolds
II JULY 1819[1]

My dear Reynolds,

* * *

You will be glad to hear under my own hand (tho' Rice says we are like sauntering Jack and Idle Joe) how diligent I have been, and am being. I have finish'd the Act[2] and in the interval of beginning the 2nd have proceeded pretty well with Lamia, finishing the 1st part which consists of about 400 lines. I have great hopes of success, because I make use of my Judgment more deliberately than I yet have done; but in Case of failure with the world, I shall find my content. And here (as I know you have my good at heart as much as a Brother), I can only repeat to you what I have said to George; that however I should like to enjoy what the competences of life procure, I am in no wise dashed at a different prospect. I have spent too many thoughtful days and moralized thro' too many nights for that, and fruitless would they be indeed, if they did not by degrees make me look upon the affairs of the world with a healthy deliberation. I have of late been moulting—not for fresh feathers and wings—they are gone—and in their stead I hope to have a pair of patient sublunary legs. I have altered, not from a Chrysalis into a butterfly, but the Contrary, having two little loopholes, whence I may look out into the stage of the world; and that world on our coming here I almost forgot. The first time I sat down to write, I could scarcely believe in the necessity of so doing. It struck me as a great oddity, yet the very corn which is now so beautiful, as if it had only took to ripening yesterday, is for the market. So, why should I be delicate?

* * *

1. Asterisks indicate missing portions of the transcript.
2. Of *Otho the Great.*

To Fanny Brawne
15 (?) JULY 1819

Shanklin,
Thursday Evening

My love,

I have been in so irritable a state of health these two or three last days, that I did not think I should be able to write this week. Not that I was so ill, but so much so as only to be capable of an unhealthy teasing letter. To-night I am greatly recovered only to feel the languor I have felt after you touched with ardency. You say you perhaps might have made me better; you would then have made me worse. Now you could quite effect a cure; what fee my sweet Physician would I not give you to do so? Do not call it folly when I tell you I took your letter last night to bed with me. In the morning I found your name on the sealing wax obliterated. I was startled at the bad omen till I recollected that it must have happened in my dreams, and they you know fall out by contraries. You must have found out by this time I am a little given to bode ill like the raven. It is my misfortune not my fault; it has proceeded from the general tenor of the circumstances of my life, and rendered every event suspicious. However, I will no more trouble either you or myself with sad Prophecies, though so far I am pleased at it as it has given me opportunity to love your disinterestedness towards me. I can be a raven no more; you and pleasure take possession of me at the same moment. I am afraid you have been unwell. If through me illness have touched you (but it must be with a very gentle hand) I must be selfish enough to feel a little glad at it. Will you forgive me this? I have been reading lately an oriental tale of a very beautiful color. It is of a city of melancholy men, all made so by this circumstance. Through a series of adven-

tures each one of them by turns reach some gardens of Paradise where they
meet with a most enchanting Lady; and just as they are going to embrace
her, she bids them shut their eyes. They shut them, and on opening their
eyes again find themselves descending to the earth in a magic basket. The
remembrance of this Lady and their delights lost beyond all recovery render
them melancholy ever after.[1] How I applied this to you, my dear; how I pal-
pitated at it; how the certainty that you were in the same world with myself, and though as beautiful, not so talismanic as that Lady; how I could
not bear you should be so you must believe because I swear it by yourself. I
cannot say when I shall get a volume ready. I have three or four stories half
done, but as I cannot write for the mere sake of the press, I am obliged to
let them progress or lie still as my fancy chooses. By Christmas perhaps they
may appear, but I am not yet sure they ever will. 'Twill be no matter, for
Poems are as common as newspapers and I do not see why it is a greater
crime in me than in another to let the verses of an half-fledged brain tumble into the reading rooms and drawing room windows. Rice has been
better lately than usual: he is not suffering from any neglect of his parents
who have for some years been able to appreciate him better than they did in
his first youth, and are now devoted to his comfort. Tomorrow I shall, if my
health continues to improve during the night, take a look farther about the
country, and spy at the parties about here who come hunting after the picturesque like beagles. It is astonishing how they raven down scenery like
children do sweetmeats. The wondrous Chine here is a very great Lion. I
wish I had as many guineas as there have been spy-glasses in it. I have been,
I cannot tell why, in capital spirits this last hour. What reason? When I have
to take my candle and retire to a lonely room, without the thought as I fall
asleep, of seeing you tomorrow morning, or the next day, or the next? It
takes on the appearance of impossibility and eternity. I will say a month. I
will say I will see you in a month at most, though no one but yourself
should see me, if it be but for an hour. I should not like to be so near you as
London without being continually with you. After having once more kissed
you, Sweet, I would rather be here alone at my task than in the bustle and
hateful literary chitchat. Meantime you must write to me, as I will every

week, for your letters keep me alive. My sweet Girl I cannot speak my love for you. Good night! and

Ever yours
John Keats

1. In Henry Weber's *Tales of the East* (1812), II:666–674.

To Fanny Brawne
25 JULY 1819

Sunday Night

My sweet Girl,

I hope you did not blame me much for not obeying your request of a Letter on Saturday. We have had four in our small room playing at cards night and morning leaving me no undisturb'd opportunity to write. Now Rice and Martin are gone I am at liberty. Brown to my sorrow confirms the account you give of your ill health. You cannot conceive how I ache to be with you, how I would die for one hour, for what is in the world? I say you cannot conceive. It is impossible you should look with such eyes upon me as I have upon you; it cannot be. Forgive me if I wander a little this evening for I have been all day employ'd in a very abstract Poem and I am in deep love with you—two things which must excuse me. I have, believe me, not been an age in letting you take possession of me. The very first week I knew you I wrote myself your vassal, but burnt the Letter as the very next time I saw you I thought you manifested some dislike to me. If you should ever feel for Man at the first sight what I did for you, I am lost. Yet I should not quarrel with you, but hate myself if such a thing were to happen. Only I should burst if the thing were not as fine as a Man as you are as a Woman.

Perhaps I am too vehement; then fancy me on my knees, especially when I mention a part of your Letter which hurt me. You say, speaking of Mr. Severn, "but you must be satisfied in knowing that I admired you much more than your friend." My dear love, I cannot believe there ever was or ever could be anything to admire in me especially as far as sight goes. I cannot be admired; I am not a thing to be admired. You are. I love you. All I can bring you is a swooning admiration of your Beauty. I hold that place among Men which snub-nos'd brunettes with meeting eyebrows do among women; they are trash to me, unless I should find one among them with a fire in her heart like the one that burns in mine. You absorb me in spite of myself, you alone. For I look not forward with any pleasure to what is call'd being settled in the world. I tremble at domestic cares. Yet for you I would meet them, though if it would leave you the happier I would rather die than do so. I have two luxuries to brood over in my walks, your Loveliness and the hour of my death. O that I could have possession of them both in the same minute. I hate the world; it batters too much the wings of my self-will, and would I could take a sweet poison from your lips to send me out of it. From no others would I take it. I am indeed astonish'd to find myself so careless of all charms but yours, remembering as I do the time when even a bit of ribband was a matter of interest with me. What softer words can I find for you after this? What it is I will not read. Nor will I say more here, but in a Postscript answer anything else you may have mentioned in your Letter in so many words, for I am distracted with a thousand thoughts. I will imagine you Venus tonight and pray, pray, pray to your star like a Hethen.

Your's ever, fair Star,
John Keats

My seal is mark'd like a family tablecloth with my Mother's initial F for Fanny put between my Father's initials. You will soon hear from me again. My respectful Compliments to your Mother. Tell Margaret I'll send her a reef of best rocks and tell Sam I will give him my light bay hunter if he will tie the Bishop hand and foot and pack him in a

hamper and send him down for me to bathe him for his health with a
Necklace of good snubby stones about his Neck.[1]

1. This sentence remains unexplained.

To C. W. Dilke (With Charles Brown)
31 JULY 1819

Shanklin, Saturday Evening

My dear Dilke,

I will not make my diligence an excuse for not writing to you sooner—
because I consider idleness a much better plea. A Man in the hurry of business of any sort is expected and ought to be expected to look to everything.
His mind is in a whirl, and what matters it, what whirl? But to require a
Letter of a Man lost in idleness is the utmost cruelty; you cut the thread of
his existence, you beat, you pummel him, you sell his goods and chattels,
you put him in prison, you impale him, you crucify him. If I had not put
pen to paper since I saw you this would be to me a vi et armis[1] taking up
before the Judge, but having got over my darling lounging habits a little it
is with scarcely any pain I come to this dating from Shanklin and Dr.
Dilke, the Isle of Wight is but so so, etc. Rice and I passed rather a dull
time of it. I hope he will not repent coming with me. He was unwell and I
was not in very good health and I am afraid we made each other worse by
acting upon each other's spirits. We would grow as melancholy as need be. I
confess I cannot bear a sick person in a House especially alone. It weighs
upon me day and night, and more so when perhaps the Case is irretriev-
able. Indeed, I think Rice is in a dangerous state. I have had a Letter from
him which speaks favourably of his health at present. Brown and I are
pretty well harnessed again to our dog-cart. I mean the Tragedy which goes

on sinkingly. We are thinking of introducing an Elephant but have not historical reference within reach to determine us as to Otho's Menagerie.
When Brown first mention'd this I took it for a Joke; however he brings
such plausible reasons, and discourses so eloquently on the dramatic effect
that I am giving it a serious consideration. The Art of Poetry is not sufficient for us, and if we get on in that as well as we do in painting we shall
by next winter crush the Reviews and the royal Academy. Indeed if Brown
would take a little of my advice he could not fail to be first pallet of his day.
But odd as it may appear, he says plainly that he cannot see any force in my
plea for putting Skies in the background and leaving indian ink out of an
ash tree. The other day he was sketching Shanklin Church and as I saw how
the business was going on, I challenged him to a trial of Skill. He lent me
Pencil and Paper. We keep the Sketches to contend for the Prize at the Gallery. I will not say whose I think best, but really I do not think Brown's
done to the top of the Art. A word or two on the Isle of Wight. I have been
no further than Steephill. If I may guess I should say that there is no finer
part in the Island than from this Place to Steephill. I do not hesitate to say
it is fine. Bonchurch is the best. But I have seen so many finer walks, with a
background of lake and mountain instead of the sea, that I am not much
touch'd with it, though I credit it for all the Surprise I should have felt if it
had taken my cockney maidenhead. But I may call myself an old Stager in
the picturesque, and unless it be something very large and overpowering I
cannot receive any extraordinary relish. I am sorry to hear that Charles is so
much oppress'd at Westminster, though I am sure it will be the finest
touchstone for his Metal in the world. His troubles will grow day by day
less, as his age and strength increase. The very first Battle he wins will lift
him from the Tribe of Manassah.[2] I do not know how I should feel were I a
Father, but I hope I should strive with all my Power not to let the present
trouble me. When your Boy shall be twenty, ask him about his childish
troubles and he will have no more memory of them than you have of yours.
Brown tells me Mrs. Dilke sets off today for Chichester. I am glad. I was
going to say she had a fine day, but there has been a great Thunder cloud
muttering over Hampshire all day. I hope she is now at supper with a good
Appetite. So Reynolds's Piece succeeded.[3] That is all well. Papers have with

thanks been duly received. We leave this Place on the 13th and will let you know where we may be a few days after. Brown says he will write when the fit comes on him. If you will stand law expenses I'll beat him into one before his time. When I come to town I shall have a little talk with you about Brown and one Jenny Jacobs. Open daylight! He don't care. I am afraid there will be some more feet for little stockings[4]—*of Keats' making (I mean the feet)*. Brown here tried at a piece of Wit but it failed him, as you see though long a-brewing. *This is a 2d lie.*[5] Men should never despair. You see he has tried again and succeeded to a miracle. He wants to try again, but as I have a right to an inside place in my own Letter, I take possession.

Your sincere friend
John Keats—

1. By force of arms.
2. Judges vi.15, I Chronicles v.18.
3. A farce, *One, Two, Three, Four, Five: By Advertisement,* first performed 17 July 1819.
4. Slang for illegitimate children.
5. The two italicized remarks were written by Brown.

To Fanny Brawne
5, 6 AUGUST 1819

Shanklin, Thursday Night—

My dear Girl,

You say you must not have any more such Letters as the last. I'll try that you shall not by running obstinate the other way; Indeed, I have not fair play. I am not idle enough for proper downright love-letters. I leave this minute a scene in our Tragedy and see you (think it not blasphemy) through the mist of Plots, speeches, counterplots and counter speeches. The Lover is madder than I am. I am nothing to him. He has a figure like

the Statue of Maleager[1] and double-distilled fire in his heart. Thank God
for my diligence! Were it not for that I should be miserable. I encourage it,
and strive not to think of you. But when I have succeeded in doing so all
day and as far as midnight, you return as soon as this artificial excitement
goes off more severely from the fever I am left in. Upon my soul I cannot
say what you could like me for. I do not think myself a fright any more
than I do Mr. A, Mr. B and Mr. C, yet if I were a woman I should not like
A, B, C. But enough of this. So you intend to hold me to my promise of
seeing you in a short time. I shall keep it with as much sorrow as gladness,
for I am not one of the Paladins of old who liv'd upon water grass and
smiles for years together. What though would I not give tonight for the
gratification of my eyes alone? This day week we shall move to Winchester,
for I feel the want of a Library. Brown will leave me there to pay a visit to
Mr. Snook at Bedhampton. In his absence I will flit to you and back. I will
stay very little while, for as I am in a train of writing now I fear to disturb
it. Let it have its course bad or good. In it I shall try my own strength and
the public pulse. At Winchester I shall get your Letters more readily, and it
being a cathedral City I shall have a pleasure—always a great one to me
when near a Cathedral—of reading them during the service up and down
the Aisle.

Friday Morning. Just as I had written thus far last night, Brown came
down in his morning coat and nightcap, saying he had been refresh'd by a
good sleep and was very hungry. I left him eating and went to bed being
too tired to enter into any discussions. You would delight very greatly in
the walks about here, the Cliffs, woods, hills, sands, rocks, etc. about here.
They are however not so fine but I shall give them a hearty good bye to
exchange them for my Cathedral. Yet again I am not so tired of Scenery
as to hate Switzerland. We might spend a pleasant Year at Berne or Zurich,
if it should please Venus to hear my "Beseech thee to hear us, O Goddess."[2] And if she should hear, god forbid we should what people call, *settle,*
turn into a pond, a stagnant Lethe, a vile crescent, row of buildings. Better
be imprudent moveables than prudent fixtures—Open my Mouth at the
Street door like the Lion's head at Venice to receive hateful cards, Letters,
messages. Go out and wither at tea parties, freeze at dinners, bake at
dances, simmer at routs. No my love, trust yourself to me and I will find

you nobler amusements, fortune favouring. I fear you will not receive this till Sunday or Monday. As the irishman would write, do not in the meanwhile hate me. I long to be off for Winchester for I begin to dislike the very door posts here, the names, the pebbles. You ask after my health, not telling me whether you are better. I am quite well. You going out is no proof that you are. How is it? Late hours will do you great harm. What fairing is it? I was alone for a couple of days while Brown went gadding over the country with his ancient knapsack. Now I like his society as well as any Man's, yet regretted his return. It broke in upon me like a Thunderbolt. I had got in a dream among my Books, really luxuriating in a solitude and silence you alone should have disturb'd.

Your ever affectionate
John Keats—

1. Keats probably had in mind an engraving of the admirable statue of Meleager in the Museo Pio-Clementino division of the Vatican Museum.
2. A profanation of the Anglican litany.

To Benjamin Bailey
14 AUGUST 1819[1]

* * *

We removed to Winchester for the convenience of a Library and find it an exceeding pleasant Town, enriched with a beautiful Cathedral and surrounded by a fresh-looking country. We are in tolerably good and cheap Lodgings. Within these two Months I have written 1500 Lines, most of which besides many more of prior composition you will probably see by next Winter. I have written two Tales, one from Boccaccio call'd the Pot of Basil, and another call'd St Agnes' Eve on a popular superstition; and a third call'd Lamia (half finished; I have also been writing parts of my Hyperion[2] and completed 4 Acts of a Tragedy). It was the opinion of most of my friends that I should never be able to write a scene. I will endeavour to wipe away the prejudice. I sincerely hope you will be pleased when my Labours since we last saw each other shall reach you. One of my Ambitions is to make as great a revolution in modern dramatic writing as Kean has done in acting; another to upset the drawling of the bluestocking literary world. If in the course of a few years I do these two things I ought to die content and my friends should drink a dozen of Claret on my Tomb. I am convinced more and more every day that (excepting the human friend Philosopher) a fine writer is the most genuine Being in the World. Shakespeare and the paradise Lost every day become greater wonders to me. I look upon fine Phrases like a Lover. I was glad to see, by a Passage in one of Brown's Letters some time ago from the north, that you were in such good Spirits. Since that you have been married and in congratulating you I wish you every continuance of them. Present my Respects to Mrs. Bailey. This sounds oddly to me, and I dare say I do it awkwardly enough, but I suppose by this time it is nothing new to you. Brown's remembrances to you. As far as I know we shall remain at Winchester for a goodish while.

Ever your sincere friend
John Keats

1. A fragment.
2. That is, "The Fall of Hyperion."

To Fanny Brawne
16 AUGUST 1819

Winchester, August 17th
My dear Girl,
What shall I say for myself? I have been here four days and not yet written you. 'Tis true I have had many teasing letters of business to dismiss, and I have been in the Claws, like a Serpent in an Eagle's, of the last act of our

Tragedy. This is no excuse. I know it. I do not presume to offer it. I have no right either to ask a speedy answer to let me know how lenient you are. I must remain some days in a Mist. I see you through a Mist, as I dare say you do me by this time. Believe in the first Letters I wrote you. I assure you I felt as I wrote. I could not write so now. The thousand images I have had pass through my brain—my uneasy spirits, my unguess'd fate—all spread as a veil between me and you. Remember I have had no idle leisure to brood over you. 'Tis well perhaps I have not. I could not have endured the throng of Jealousies that used to haunt me before I had plunged so deeply into imaginary interests. I would feign, as my sails are set, sail on without an interruption for a Brace of Months longer. I am in complete cue—in the fever—and shall in these four Months do an immense deal. This Page as my eye skims over it I see is excessively unloverlike and ungallant. I cannot help it. I am no officer in yawning quarters, no Parson-romeo. My Mind is heap'd to the full, stuff'd like a cricket ball. If I strive to fill it more it would burst. I know the generality of women would hate me for this; that I should have so unsoften'd, so hard a Mind as to forget them, forget the brightest realities for the dull imaginations of my own Brain. But I conjure you to give it a fair thinking, and ask yourself whether 'tis not better to explain my feelings to you than write artificial Passion. Besides, you would see through it. It would be vain to strive to deceive you. 'Tis harsh, harsh, I know it; my heart seems now made of iron. I could not write a proper answer to an invitation to Idalia. You are my Judge. My forehead is on the ground. You seem offended at a little simple innocent childish playfulness in my last. I did not seriously mean to say that you were endeavouring to make me keep my promise. I beg your pardon for it. 'Tis but *just* your Pride should take the alarm. *Seriously*, you say I may do as I please. I do not think with any conscience I can; my cash-recourses are for the present stopp'd, I fear for some time. I spend no money but it increases my debts. I have all my life thought very little of these matters; they seem not to belong to me. It may be a proud sentence, but by heaven I am as entirely above all matters of interest as the Sun is above the Earth, and though of my own money I should be careless, of my Friends I must be spare. You see how I go on, like so many strokes of a Hammer. I cannot help it. I am impell'd, driven to it. I am not happy enough for silken Phrases and silver sentences. I can no more use soothing words to you than if I were at this moment engaged in a charge of Cavalry. Then you will say I should not write at all. Should I not?

This Winchester is a fine place, a beautiful Cathedral and many other ancient buildings in the Environs. The little coffin of a room at Shanklin is changed for a large room where I can promenade at my pleasure. Looks out onto a beautiful—blank side of a house. It is strange I should like it better than the view of the sea from our window at Shanklin. I began to hate the very posts there. The voice of the old Lady over the way was getting a great Plague. The Fisherman's face never altered any more than our black tea-pot. The nob however was knock'd off to my little relief. I am getting a great dislike of the picturesque, and can only relish it over again by seeing you enjoy it. One of the pleasantest things I have seen lately was at Cowes. The Regent in his Yatch[1] (I think they spell it) was anchored opposite—a beautiful vessel—and all the Yatchs and boats on the coast were passing and repassing it, and curcuiting and tacking about it in every direction. I never beheld anything so silent, light, and graceful. As we pass'd over to Southampton, there was nearly an accident. There came by a Boat wellmann'd with two naval officers at the stern. Our Bow-lines took the top of their little mast and snapped it off close by the bord. Had the mast been a little stouter they would have been upset. In so trifling an event I could not help admiring our seamen. Neither Officer nor man in the whole Boat moved a Muscle; they scarcely notic'd it even with words.

Forgive me for this flint-worded Letter and believe and see that I cannot think of you without some sort of energy, though mal a propos. Even as I leave off, it seems to me that a few more moments thought of you would uncrystallize and dissolve me. I must not give way to it, but turn to my writing again. If I fail I shall die hard. O my love, your lips are growing sweet again to my fancy. I must forget them. Ever your affectionate

Keats—

---

1. A contemporary spelling of "yacht."

To John Taylor

23 AUGUST 1819

Winchester, Monday morn.

24 August

My dear Taylor,

You will perceive that I do not write you till I am forced by necessity; that I am sorry for. You must forgive me for entering abruptly on the subject, merely prefixing an entreaty that you will not consider my business manner of wording and proceeding any distrust of, or stirrup standing against you, but put it to the account of a desire of order and regularity. I have been rather unfortunate lately in money concerns from a threatened chancery suit. I was deprived at once of all recourse to my Guardian. I relied a little on some of my debts being paid, which are of a tolerable amount, but I have not had one pound refunded. For these three Months Brown has advanced me money. He is not at all flush and I am anxious to get some elsewhere. We have together been engaged (this I should wish to remain secret) in a Tragedy which I have just finish'd and from which we hope to share moderate Profits. Being thus far connected, Brown proposed to me to stand with me responsible for any money you may advance to me to drive through the summer. I must observe again that it is not from want of reliance on your readiness to assist me that I offer a Bill, but as a relief to myself from a too lax sensation of Life, which ought to be responsible, which requires chains for its own sake, duties to fulfil with the more earnestness the less strictly they are imposed. Were I completely without hope it might be different, but am I not right to rejoice in the idea of not being Burthensome to my friends? I feel every confidence that if I choose I may be a popular writer; that I will never be, but for all that I will get a livelihood. I equally dislike the favour of the public with the love of a woman. They are both a cloying treacle to the wings of independence. I shall ever consider them (People) as debtors to me for verses, not myself to them for admiration, which I can do without. I have of late been indulging my spleen by composing a preface *at* them, after all resolving never to write a preface at all. "There are so many verses," would I have said to them, "give me so much means to buy pleasure with as a relief to my hours of labour." You will observe at the end of this if you put down the Letter, "How a solitary life engenders pride and egotism!" True. I know it does, but this Pride and egotism will enable me to write finer things than anything else could. So I will indulge it. Just so much as I am humbled by the genius above my grasp, am I exalted and look with hate and contempt upon the literary world. A Drummer boy who holds out his hand familiarly to a field marshal, that Drummer boy with me is the good word and favour of the public. Who would wish to be among the commonplace crowd of the little-famous, who are each individually lost in a throng made up of themselves? Is this worth louting[1] or playing the hypocrite for? To beg suffrages for a seat on the benches of a myriad aristocracy in Letters? This is not wise. I am not a wise man. 'Tis Pride. I will give you a definition of a proud Man: He is a Man who has neither vanity nor wisdom. One fill'd with hatreds cannot be vain, neither can he be wise. Pardon me for hammering instead of writing. Remember me to Woodhouse, Hessey and all in Percey street.

Ever yours sincerely
John Keats

P.S. I have read what Brown has said on the other side. He agrees with me that this manner of proceeding might appear too harsh, distant and indelicate with you. This however will place all in a clear light. Had I to borrow money of Brown and were in your house, I should request the use of your name in the same manner—

---

1. Bowing, cringing.

To J. H. Reynolds
24 AUGUST 1819

Winchester, August 25th—

My dear Reynolds,

By this Post I write to Rice who will tell you why we have left Shanklin and how we like this Place. I have indeed scarcely anything else to say, leading so monotonous a life, except I was to give you a history of sensations and day nightmares. You would not find me at all unhappy in it, as all my thoughts and feelings which are of the selfish nature, home speculations everyday continue to make me more Iron. I am convinced more and more day by day that fine writing is next to fine doing the top thing in the world; the Paradise Lost becomes a greater wonder. The more I know what my diligence may in time probably effect, the more does my heart distend with Pride and Obstinacy. I feel it in my power to become a popular writer. I feel it in my strength to refuse the poisonous suffrage of a public. My own being which I know to be becomes of more consequence to me than the crowds of Shadows in the Shape of Man and women that inhabit a kingdom. The Soul is a world of itself and has enough to do in its own home. Those whom I know already and who have grown as it were a part of myself I could not do without, but for the rest of Mankind, they are as much a dream to me as Milton's Hierarchies. I think if I had a free and healthy and lasting organisation of heart and Lungs, as strong as an ox's so as to be able to bear unhurt the shock of extreme thought and sensation without weariness, I could pass my Life very nearly alone though it should last eighty years. But I feel my Body too weak to support me to the height. I am obliged continually to check myself and strive to be nothing. It would be vain for me to endeavour after a more reasonable manner of writing to you. I have nothing to speak of but myself, and what can I say but what I feel? If you should have any reason to regret this state of excitement in me, I will turn the tide of your feelings in the right channel by mentioning that it is the only state for the best sort of Poetry. That is all I care for, all I live for. Forgive me for not filling up the whole sheet. Letters become so irksome to me that the next time I leave London I shall petition them all to be spar'd me. To give me credit for constancy and at the same time wave letter writing will be the highest indulgence I can think of.

Ever your affectionate friend
John Keats

❦

To Fanny Keats

28 AUGUST 1819

Winchester, August 28th

My dear Fanny,

You must forgive me for suffering so long a space to elapse between the dates of my letters. It is more than a fortnight since I left Shanklin, chiefly for the purpose of being near a tolerable Library, which after all is not to be found in this place. However, we like it very much. It is the pleasantest Town I ever was in, and has the most recommendations of any. There is a fine Cathedral which to me is always a source of amusement, part of it built 1400 years ago, and the more modern by a magnificent Man you may have read of in our History called William of Wickham.[1] The whole town is beautifully wooded. From the Hill at the eastern extremity you see a prospect of Streets and old Buildings mixed up with Trees—Then There are the most beautiful streams about I ever saw—full of Trout. There is the Foundation of St. Croix about half a mile in the fields, a charity greatly abused. We have a Collegiate School, a roman catholic School, a chapel ditto and a Nunnery! And what improves it all is the fashionable inhabitants are all gone to Southampton. We are quiet, except a fiddle that now and then goes like a gimlet through my Ears—Our Landlady's Son not being quite a Proficient. I have still been hard at work, having completed a Tragedy I think I spoke of to you. But there I fear all my labour will be thrown away for the present, as I hear Mr. Kean is going to America. For all I can guess I shall remain here till the middle of October, when Mr. Brown will return to his house at Hampstead whither I shall return with him. I some time since sent the Letter I told you I had received from George to Haslam with a request to let you and Mrs. Wylie see it. He sent it back to me for very insufficient reasons, without doing so, and I was so irritated by it that I would not send it travelling about by the post any more. Besides, the postage is very expensive. I know Mrs. Wylie will think this a great neglect. I am sorry to say my temper gets the better of me. I will not send it again. Some correspondence I have had with Mr. Abbey about George's affairs, and I must confess he has behaved very kindly to me as far as the wording of his Letter went. Have you heard any further mention of his retiring from Business? I am anxious to hear wether Hodgkinson, whose name I cannot bear to write, will in any likelihood be thrown upon himself. The delightful Weather we have had for two Months is the highest gratification I could receive. No chill'd red noses, no shivering, but fair Atmosphere to think in, a clean towel mark'd with the mangle, and a basin of clear Water to drench one's face with ten times a day. No need of much exercise, a Mile a day being quite sufficient. My greatest regret is that I have not been well enough to bathe, though I have been two Months by the seaside and live now close to delicious bathing. Still, I enjoy the Weather. I adore fine Weather as the greatest blessing I can have. Give me Books, fruit, french wine and fine weather and a little music out of doors, played by somebody I do not know—not pay the price of one's time for a gig—but a little chance music, and I can pass a summer very quietly without caring much about Fat Louis, fat Regent or the Duke of Wellington.

Why have you not written to me? Because you were in expectation of George's Letter and so waited? Mr. Brown is copying out our Tragedy of Otho the great in a superb style, better than it deserves. There as I said is labour in vain for the present. I had hoped to give Kean another opportunity to shine. What can we do now? There is not another actor of Tragedy in all

London or Europe. The Covent Garden Company is execrable. Young[2] is the best among them and he is a ranting, coxcombical, tasteless Actor, A Disgust, A Nausea, and yet the very best after Kean. What a set of barren asses are actors! I should like now to promenade round your Gardens—apple-tasting, pear-tasting, plum-judging, apricot-nibbling, peach-scrunching, Nectarine-sucking and Melon-carving. I have also a great feeling for antiquated cherries full of sugar cracks and a white currant tree kept for company. I admire lolling on a lawn by a water-lillied pond to eat white currants and see gold fish, and go to the Fair in the Evening if I'm good. There is not hope for that. One is sure to get into some mess before evening. Have these hot days I brag of so much been well or ill for your health? Let me hear soon.

Your affectionate Brother
John—

1. William of Wykeham (1324–1404), bishop of Winchester.
2. Charles Mayne Young (1777–1856). Kean had planned to leave for America in September 1819, but his contract with Drury Lane prevented his departure for over a year.

To John Taylor
31 AUGUST 1819

Winchester, Sept. 1st

My dear Taylor,

Brown and I have been employed for these three weeks past from time to time in writing to our different friends. A dead silence is our ownly answer. We wait morning after morning and nothing. Tuesday is the day for the Examiner to arrive. This is the second tuesday which has been barren even of a newspaper. Men should be in imitation of Spirits, "responsive to each other's note."[1] Instead of that I pipe and no one hath danced. We have been

cursing this morning like Mandeville and Lisle.[2] With this I shall send by
the same Post a third Letter to a friend of mine, who though it is of consequence has neither answered right or left. We have been much in want of
news from the Theatres, having heard that Kean is going to America, but
no, not a word. Why I should come on you with all these complaints, I
cannot explain to myself, especially as I suspect you must be in the Country. Do answer me soon for I really must know something. I must steer myself by the rudder of information, and I am in want of a Month's cash. Now
believe me I do not apply to you as if I thought you had a gold Mine. No. I
understand these matters well enough now having become well acquainted
with the disbursements every Man is tempted to make beyond his means.
From this time I have resolved myself to refuse all such requests. Tell me
you are not flush and I shall thank you heartily. That is a duty you owe
to yourself as well as to *me*. I have mulcted Brown too much; let it be my
last sin of the kind. I will try what use it will be to insist on my debts being paid.

> Ever yours sincerely
> *John Keats—*

1. *Paradise Lost,* IV.683.
2. Characters in William Godwin's novel *Mandeville.*

To J. A. Hessey
5 SEPTEMBER 1819

> Winchester, Sunday, Sep. 5th

My dear Hessey,

I received this morning yours of yesterday enclosing a 30£ bank post bill.
I have been in fear of the Winchester Jail for some time. Neither Brown nor
myself could get an answer from anyone. This morning I hear that some

unknown part of a Sum due to me and for which I had been waiting three weeks has been sent to Chichester by mistake. Brown has borrow'd money of a friend of his in Hampshire. A few days ago we had but a few shillings left, and now between us we have 60£ besides what is waiting in the Chichester post office. To be a complete Midas I suppose someone will send me a pair of asses ears by the wagon. There has been such an embargo laid on our correspondence that I can scarcely believe your Letter was only dated yesterday. It seems miraculous.

Ever yours sincerely
John Keats

I am sorry to hear such a bad account of himself from Taylor.

❧

To John Taylor
5 SEPTEMBER 1819

Winchester, Sept. 5th

My dear Taylor,

This morning I received yours of the 2nd and with it a Letter from Hessey enclosing a Bank post Bill of £30, an ample sum I assure you; more I had no thought of. You should not have delay'd so long in fleet Street. Leading an inactive life as you did was breathing poison. You will find the country air do more for you than you expect. But it must be proper country air; you must choose a spot. What sort of a place is Retford? You should live in a dry, gravelly, barren, elevated country open to the currents of air, and such a place is generally furnnish'd with the finest springs. The neighbourhood of a rich enclosed fulsome manured arable Land, especially in a valley and almost as bad on a flat, would be almost as bad as the smoke of fleetstreet. Such a place as this was shanklin, only open to the southeast and surrounded by hills in every other direction. From this southeast came the damps from the sea which having no egress the air would for days together

TO JOHN TAYLOR ♣ 5 SEPTEMBER 1819   335

take on an unhealthy idiosyncrasy altogether enervating and weakening as a city Smoke. I felt it very much. Since I have been at Winchester I have been improving in health. It is not so confined and there is on one side of the city a dry chalky down where the air is worth six pence a pint. So if you do not get better at Retford do not impute it to your own weakness before you have well considered the nature of the air and soil, especially as Autumn is encroaching, for the autumn fogs over a rich land is like the steam from cabbage water. What makes the great difference between valemen, flatland men, and Mountaineers? The cultivation of the earth in a great measure. Our health, temperament and dispositions are taken more (notwithstanding the contradiction of the history of cain and abel) from the air we breathe than is generally imagined. See the difference between a Peasant and a Butcher. I am convinced a great cause of it is the difference of the air they breathe. The one takes his mingled with the fume of slaughter, the other with the damp exhalement from the glebe. The teeming damp that comes from the plough furrow is of great effect in taming the fierceness of a strong Man more than his labour. Let him be mowing furze upon a Mountain and at the day's end his thoughts will run upon a withe[1] axe if he ever had handled one; let him leave the Plough and he will think quietly of his supper. Agriculture is the tamer of men. The steam from the earth is like drinking their mother's milk; it enervates their natures. This appears a great cause of the imbecility of the Chinese. And if this sort of atmosphere is a mitigation to the energies of a strong man, how much more must it injure a weak one—unoccupied—unexercised. For what is the cause of so many men maintaining a good state in Cities but occupation. An idle man, a man who is not sensitively alive to self interest in a city cannot continue long in good Health. This is easily explained. If you were to walk leisurely through an unwholesome path in the fens, with a little horror of them you would be sure to have your ague. But let macbeth cross the same path, with the dagger in the air leading him on, and he would never have an ague or anything like it. You should give these things a serious consideration. Notts I believe is a flat County. You should be on the slope of one of the dry barren hills in somersetshire. I am convinced there is as harmful Air to be breath'd in the country as in Town.

I am greatly obliged to you for your Letter. Perhaps if you had had strength and spirits enough you would have felt offended by my offering a note of hand; or rather express'd it. However, I am sure you will give me credit for not in any wise mistrusting you, or imagining you would take advantage of any power I might give you over me. No, it proceeded from my serious resolve not to be a gratuitous borrower, from a great desire to be correct in money matters, to have in my desk the Chronicles of them to refer to, and know my worldly non-estate. Besides, in case of my death such documents would be but just, if merely as memorials of the friendly turns I had had done to me. Had I known of your illness I should not of written in such fiery phrase in my first Letter. I hope that shortly you will be able to bear six times as much. Brown likes the Tragedy very much, but he is not a fit judge, as I have only acted as Midwife to his plot, and of course he will be fond of his child. I do not think I can make you any extracts without spoiling the effect of the whole when you come to read it. I hope you will then not think my labour mispent. Since I finish'd it I have finish'd Lamia and am now occupied in revising St Agnes' Eve and studying Italian. Ariosto I find as diffuse, in parts, as Spenser. I understand completely the difference between them. I will cross the letter with some lines from Lamia. Brown's kindest remembrances to you; and I am ever your most sincere friend

John Keats—

A haunting music, sole perhaps and lone
Supportress of the faery roof, made moan
Throughout, as fearful the whole charm might fade.
Fresh-carved cedar, mimicking a glade
Of Palm and Plantain, met, from either side,
High in the midst in honour of the bride.
Two palms, and then two plantains, and so on,
From either side, their stems branch'd one to one
All down the aisled place; and beneath all,
There ran a stream of lamps straight on from wall to wall.
So canopied lay an untasted feast

Teeming a perfume. Lamia regal drest
Silverly pac'd about, and as she went
In pale contented sort of discontent
Mission'd her viewless Servants to enrich
The splendid cornicing of nook and niche.
Between the Tree stems, wainscoated at first
Came jasper panels; then, anon, there burst
Forth creeping imagery of slighter trees
And with the larger wove in small intricacies.
Approving all, she faded at self will,
And shut the chamber up close-hush'd and still,
Complete, and ready for the revels rude,
When dreadful guests would come to spoil her solitude.
    The day came soon and all the gossip rout.
O senseless Lycius! Dolt! Fool! Madman! Lout!
Why would you murder happiness like yours,
And show to common eyes these secret bowers?
    The Herd came; and each guest, with buzzy brain,
Arriving at the Portal, gaz'd amain,
And enter'd won'dring; for they knew the Street,
Remember'd it from childhood all complete,
Without a gap, but ne'er before had seen
That royal Porch, that high built fair demesne;
So in went one and all maz'd, curious and keen.
Save one, who look'd thereon with eye severe,
And, with calm-planted steps, walk'd in austere;
'Twas Apollonius. Something to he laught,
As though some knotty problem, that had daft
His patient thought, had now begun to thaw,
And solve, and melt; 'twas just as he foresaw!
    Soft went the music, and the tables all
Sparkled beneath the viewless banneral
Of Magic; and dispos'd in double row
Seem'd edged Parterres of white-bedded snow,

Adorn'd along the sides with living flowers
Conversing, laughing after sunny showers.
And, as the pleasant appetite entic'd,
Gush came the wine, and sheer the meats were slic'd.
Soft went the Music; the flat salver sang
Kiss'd by the emptied goblet, and again it rang.
Swift bustled by the servants: here's a health
Cries one—another—then, as if by stealth,
A Glutton drains a cup of Helicon,
Too fast down, down his throat the brief delight is gone.
"Where is that Music?" cries a Lady fair.
"Aye, where is it my dear? Up in the air"?
Another whispers "Poo!" saith Glutton "Mum!"
Then makes his shiny mouth a napkin for his thumb, etc., etc.

This is a good sample of the Story.[2] Brown is going to Chister and Bed-hampton a-visiting. I shall be alone here for three weeks—expecting accounts of your health.

1. A primitive axe with a flexible handle.
2. But largely altered and cut in the final, printed version.

To Fanny Brawne
13 SEPTEMBER 1819

Fleet Street,[1] Monday Morn.

My dear Girl,
    I have been hurried to Town by a Letter from my brother George; it is not of the brightest intelligence.[2] Am I mad or not? I came by the Friday night coach and have not yet been to Hampstead. Upon my soul it is not

my fault; I cannot resolve to mix any pleasure with my days. They go one like another undistinguishable. If I were to see you today it would destroy the half comfortable sullenness I enjoy at present into downright perplexities. I love you too much to venture to Hampstead. I feel it is not paying a visit, but venturing into a fire. Que ferai-je?[3] as the french novel writers say in fun, and I in earnest. Really, what can I do? Knowing well that my life must be passed in fatigue and trouble, I have been endeavouring to wean myself from you, for to myself alone what can be much of a misery? As far as they regard myself I can despise all events, but I cannot cease to love you. This morning I scarcely know what I am doing. I am going to Walthamstow. I shall return to Winchester tomorrow, whence you shall hear from me in a few days. I am a Coward. I cannot bear the pain of being happy. 'Tis out of the question. I must admit no thought of it.

Yours ever affectionately
John Keats

1. Written from Taylor and Hessey's office, 93 Fleet Street.
2. It announced that he was in financial difficulties in America.
3. "What will I do?"

Richard Woodhouse to John Taylor
19, 20 SEPTEMBER 1819

Weymouth, Monday 20 Sept. 1819

My dear John,

I begin to find out that there is no getting pen to paper anywhere but in London. For tho' I do literally nothing here it is as exclusionary an employment as I ever met with. Godwin (whose life of Chaucer I am skimming over) says there is no doing anything in the writing way, out of one's own study. What with the dearths of pens, Ink, paper, knives, wax, etc., it is quite an attempt to begin a letter, and quite an achievement to have finished one. I left Town on Sunday Evening (12th) and arrived here on the Monday about 1. I found the place as it always was, and ever will be, very dull. To me this is a recommendation rather than otherwise, for I get bustle and bother enough in Town, and gladly hail *quietude* in the Country. I walk or run till breakfast time, after which I amuse myself with books for about 2 hours, and I am then at my Sister's disposal for the rest of the day, till 9 o'Clock, when the family go to roost. But I generally keep my vigils till near twelve, thanks to those habits of *industry* you and I imbibed from Lord Sommers. I was very much out of order when I came down here, but I am getting to rights gradually. I have not bathed yet; the smell of the sea and the air bath that blows from it have been sufficient for me. Freeman is I suppose in Town by this time, and occupied in discussing with the Squire[1] the terms and times of his receiving that portion of his "existence" which is in your hands. I take it for granted he will have left England in regret for his departure before I return to Town.

Keats was in Town the day before I left. He came into 93[2] unexpectedly, while I was in the midst of a recapitulation to Hessey of the strong points of the matter between yourselves and the Capt. for his government in case Parsons should set himself to wonder and be astonished, etc. at anything that has happened. In such Cases, a strong point, well put, and coming out pat, often does wonders. K. came about his Chancery Suit that is to be, or rather that is not to be, if he succeeds in the object of his Journey to London, which is to dissuade some old aunt[3] from going into that Court. He took his breakfast with me on the Sunday, and remained with me till I stepped into the Coach for this place at 3 o'Clock. I was much gratified with his Company. He wanted I believe to publish the Eve of St. Agnes and Lamia *immediately,* but Hessey told him it could not answer to do so now. I wondered why he said nothing of Isabella and assured him it would please more than the Eve of St. Agnes. He said he could not bear the former now. It appeared to him mawkish. This certainly cannot be so. The feeling is very likely to come across an author on review of a former work of his own, particularly where the objects of his present meditations are of a more sobered and unpassionate Character. The feeling of mawkishness seems to me to be that which comes upon us where anything of great tenderness and ex-cessive simplicity is met with when we are not in a sufficiently tender and simple frame of mind to bear it, when we experience a sort of revulsion or resiliency (if there be such a word) from the sentiment or expression. Now I believe there is nothing in any of the most passionate parts of Isabella to ex-cite this feeling. It may, as may Lear, leave the reader far behind, but there is none of that sugar and butter sentiment that cloys and disgusts. He had the Eve of St. A. copied fair. He has made trifling alterations, inserted an addi-tional stanza early in the poem to make the *legend* more intelligible and cor-respondent with what afterwards takes place, particularly with respect to the supper and the playing on the Lute. He retains the name of Porphyro, has altered the last 3 lines to leave on the reader a sense of pettish disgust by bringing Old Angela in (only) dead, stiff and ugly. He says he likes that the poem should leave off with this Change of Sentiment. It was what he aimed at and was glad to find from my objections to it that he had suc-ceeded. I apprehend he had a fancy for trying his hand at an attempt to play with his reader and fling him off at last. I should have thought he af-fected the "Don Juan" style of mingling up sentiment and sneering, but that he had before asked Hessey if he could procure him a sight of that work, as he had not met with it, and if the E. of St. A. had not in all proba-bility been altered before his Lordship had thus flown in the face of the public.

There was another alteration, which I abused for "a full hour by the *Temple* clock."[4] You know if a thing has a decent side, I generally look no further. As the Poem was originally written, *we* innocent ones (ladies and myself) might very well have supposed that Porphyro, when acquainted with Madeline's love for him, and when "he arose, Ethereal, flush'd, etc., etc" (turn to it) set himself at once to persuade her to go off with him, and succeeded and went over the "Dartmoor black" (now changed for some other place) to be married, in right honest chaste and sober-wise. But, as it is now altered, as soon as M. has confessed her love, P. winds by degrees his arm round her, presses breast to breast, and acts all the acts of a bonâfide husband, while she fancies she is only playing the part of a Wife in a dream. This alteration is of about 3 stanzas and tho' there are no improper expressions but all is left to inference, and tho' profanely speaking, the Interest on the reader's imagination is greatly heightened, yet I do apprehend it will render the poem unfit for ladies, and indeed scarcely to be mentioned to them among the "things that are." He says he does not want ladies to read his poetry, that he writes for men and that if in the former poem there was an opening for doubt what took place, it was his fault for not writing clearly and comprehensibly; that he should despise a man who would be such an eunuch in sentiment as to leave a maid, with that Character about her, in such a situation, and should despise himself to write about it, etc., etc., and all this sort of Keats-like rhodomontade. But you will see the work I dare say.

He then read to me Lamia, which he has half fair Copied; the rest is rough. I was much pleased with it. I can use no other terms, for you know how badly he reads his own poetry and you know how slow I am in Catching even the sense of poetry read by the best reader for the 1st time. And his poetry really must be studied to be properly appreciated. The Story is to this effect: Hermes is hunting for a Nymph, when from a wood he hears his name and a song relating to his loss. Mercury finds out that it comes from a serpent, who promises to show him his Nymph if he will turn the serpent into a Woman. This he agrees to, upon which the serpent breathes on his eyes when he sees his Nymph who had been beside them listening invisibly. The serpent had seen a young Man of Corinth with whom she had fallen desperately in Love. She is metamorphosed into a beautiful Woman, the Change is quite Ovidian, but better. She then finds the Youth and they live together in a palace in the Middle of Corinth (described, or rather pictured out in very good costume), the entrance of which no one can see (like the Cavern Prince Ahmed found in the Arabian Nights, when searching for his lost arrow). Here they live and love, "the world forgetting; of the world forgot."[5] He wishes to marry her and introduce her to his friends as his Wife, But this would be a forfeiture of her immortality and she refuses, but at length (for, says K, "Women love to be forced to do a thing, by a fine fellow—*such as this*—I forget his name— *was*") she consents. The Palace door becomes visible—to the "astonishment of the Natives"—the friends are invited to the wedding feast and K. wipes the Cits and the low-lived ones, of some of whom he says "who make their mouth a napkin to their thumb" in the midst of this Imperial splendour. The lover had seen his tutor Apollonius that morning while in a car with his Lamia; he had a scowl on his brow, which makes the hearts of the lovers sink, and she asks him, who that frowning old fellow was, as soon as A. passed. He appears at the feast, damps the joy of the two by his presence, sits over against the woman. He is a Magician. He looks earnestly at the woman, so intently and to such effect, that she reads in his eyes that she is discovered and vanishes away, shrieking. The lover is told she was a "Lamia" and goes mad for the loss of her and dies.

You may suppose all these Events have given K. scope for some beautiful poetry, which even in this Cursory hearing of it, came every now and then upon me, and made me "start, as tho' a Sea Nymph quired."[6] The metre is Drydenian heroic with many triplets and many alexandrines. But this K. observed, and I agreed, was required, or rather quite in character with the language and sentiment in those particular parts. K. has a fine feeling when and where he may use poetical licenses with effect. He very kindly reproach'd me with never writing to him. You may suppose I promised amendment and stipulated (as Paddy says) "that all the reciprocity should not be on one side." The last thing, as he shook me by the hand, he promised to drop me a line to Bath: "and if (said he) it *should be in verse,* I dare say you will forgive me." He parted with me at the Coach door. I had the inside all to myself and I amused myself with diving into a deep reverie and recalling all that had passed during the 6 hours we were tête-à-tête.

I make no apology for stuffing my letter with these Keatsiana. I am sure nothing else I could say would have half the Interest, and I deem myself in luck to have such a subject to write about. I shall leave this place for Bath on Wednesday and be there to dinner. I shall remain in Bath till the end of the month, perhaps later. As soon as I get there I shall write to Reynolds. Let me have a line from you to "R.W. Jr, 8 Duke St., Bath." This letter tho' dated on Monday was written thus far on Sunday night to the Music of someone snoring. This morning I have been taking a six or seven mile walk round an Inland lake; it was a journey of discovery, but I found contrary to Expectation all the passages practicable. I am just going to break my fast.

Our post leaves us at that unseasonable hour 10 o' Clock. So Adieu and re-member me kindly wherever remembrances will be acceptable. I suppose you are ere this returned to Retford. I have tried for a frank but there is no Member here into whose hand I can put a cover. I am, Dear John, yours, as ever, most truly

Richard Woodhouse

P.S. Do not lose Keats's letter to Reynolds.

1. Hessey.
2. That is, 93 Fleet Street, Taylor and Hessey's bookshop.
3. Mrs. Midgley Jennings.
4. Compare *1 Henry IV,* V.iv.150f., "fought a long hour by Shrewsbury clock."
5. Pope, *Eloisa to Abelard,* line 208.
6. Misquoted from Keats's sonnet "On the Sea," line 14.

To J. H. Reynolds

21 SEPTEMBER 1819

Winchester, Tuesday

My dear Reynolds,

I was very glad to hear from Woodhouse that you would meet in the Country. I hope you will pass some pleasant time together, which I wish to make pleasanter by a brace of letters, very highly to be estimated, as really I have had very bad luck with this sort of game this season. I "kepen in solitarinesse,"[1] for Brown has gone a-visiting. I am surprized myself at the pleasure I live alone in. I can give you no news of the place here, or any other idea of it but what I have to this effect written to George. Yesterday I say to him was a grand day for Winchester. They elected a Mayor. It was in-deed high time the place should receive some sort of excitement. There was nothing going on—all asleep—not an old maid's sedan returning from a

card party, and if any old woman got tipsy at Christenings they did not expose it in the streets. The first night tho' of our arrival here, there was a
slight uproar took place at about 10 o' the Clock. We heard distinctly a
noise patting down the high Street as of a walking cane of the good old
Dowager breed; and a little minute after we heard a less voice observe,
"What a noise the ferril made; it must be loose." Brown wanted to call the
Constables, but I observed 'twas only a little breeze, and would soon pass
over. The side streets here are excessively maiden ladylike, the door steps always fresh from the flannel. The knockers have a staid serious, nay almost
awful quietness about them. I never saw so quiet a collection of Lions' and
Rams' heads, the doors most part black, with a little brass handle just above
the keyhole, so that in Winchester a man may very quietly shut himself out
of his own house. How beautiful the season is now, how fine the air, a temperate sharpness about it. Really, without joking, chaste weather, Dian
skies. I never lik'd stubble fields so much as now—Aye, better than the
chilly green of the spring. Somehow a stubble plain looks warm—in the
same way that some pictures look warm—this struck me so much in my
sunday's walk that I composed upon it.[2]

I hope you are better employed than in gaping after weather. I have been
at different times so happy as not to know what weather it was. No, I will
not copy a parcel of verses. I always somehow associate Chatterton with autumn. He is the purest writer in the English Language. He has no French
idiom, or particles like Chaucer; 'tis genuine English Idiom in English
words. I have given up Hyperion.[3] There were too many Miltonic inversions in it. Miltonic verse cannot be written but in an artful or rather artist's
humour. I wish to give myself up to other sensations. English ought to be
kept up. It may be interesting to you to pick out some lines from Hyperion
and put a mark X to the false beauty proceeding from art, and one | | to the
true voice of feeling. Upon my soul 'twas imagination—I cannot make the
distinction. Every now and then there is a Miltonic intonation, but I cannot make the division properly. The fact is I must take a walk, for I am
writing so long a letter to George, and have been employed at it all the
morning. You will ask, have I heard from George? I am sorry to say not the
best news; I hope for better. This is the reason among others that if I write

to you it must be in such a scrap-like way. I have no meridian to date Interests from, or measure circumstances. Tonight I am all in a mist. I scarcely know what's what, but you knowing my unsteady and vagarish[4] disposition, will guess that all this turmoil will be settled by tomorrow morning. It strikes me tonight that I have led a very odd sort of life for the two or three last years—Here and there—No anchor—I am glad of it. If you can get a peep at Babbicomb before you leave the country, do. I think it the finest place I have seen, or is to be seen in the South. There is a Cottage there I took warm water at, that made up for the tea. I have lately skirk'd some friends of ours, and I advise you to do the same, I mean the blue-devils. I am never at home to them. You need not fear them while you remain in Devonshire. There will be some of the family waiting for you at the Coach office, but go by another Coach. I shall beg leave to have a third opinion in the first discussion you have with Woodhouse—just half way—between both. You know I will not give up my argument. In my walk today I stoop'd under a railway that lay across my path and ask'd myself, "Why I did not get over." Because, answered I, "no one wanted to force you under." I would give a guinea to be a reasonable man, good sound sense; a says-what-he-thinks, and does-what-he-says man, and did not take snuff. They say men near death however mad they may have been, come to their senses. I hope I shall here in this letter. There is a decent space to be very sensible in; many a good proverb has been in less. Nay, I have heard of the statutes at large being chang'd into the Statutes at Small and printed for a watch paper. Your sisters by this time must have got the Devonshire ees—short ees—you know 'em; they are the prettiest ees in the Language. O, how I admire the middle-siz'd delicate Devonshire girls of about 15. There was one at an Inn door holding a quartern of brandy. The very thought of her kept me warm a whole stage—and a 16-miler too. "You'll pardon me for being jocular."[5]

Ever your affectionate friend
John Keats—

1. Keats's "The Eve of St. Mark," line 106.
2. See "To Autumn."

3. "The Fall of Hyperion."
4. "Disposed to wander, whimsical, erratic." *(OED)*
5. Master Vellum three times makes this remark in Addison's *Drummer*.

To Richard Woodhouse

21, 22 SEPTEMBER 1819

Tuesday—

Dear Woodhouse,

If you see what I have said to Reynolds before you come to your own dose you will put it between the bars unread, provided they have begun fires in Bath. I should like a bit of fire tonight. One likes a bit of fire. How glorious the Blacksmiths' shops look now. I stood tonight before one till I was very near listing for one. Yes I should like a bit of fire, at a distance about 4 feet "not quite hob nob,"[1] as wordsworth says. The fact was I left Town on Wednesday determined to be in a hurry. You don't eat travelling. You're wrong—beef—beef. I like the look of a sign. The Coachman's face says eat, eat, eat. I never feel more contemptible than when I am sitting by a good-looking coachman. One is nothing. Perhaps I eat to persuade myself I am somebody. You must be when slice after slice—but it won't do. The Coachman nibbles a bit of bread; he's favour'd, he's had a Call, a Hercules Methodist. Does he live by bread alone? O, that I were a Stage Manager! Perhaps that's as old as "doubling the Cape." "How are ye old 'un? Hey! why dont'e speak?" O, that I had so sweet a Breast to sing as the Coachman hath![2] I'd give a penny for his Whistle and bow to the Girls on the road. Bow, nonsense, 'tis a nameless graceful slang action. Its effect on the women suited to it must be delightful. It touches 'em in the ribs—en passant—very off hand—very fine—Sed thongum formosa vale vale inquit Heigh ho la![3] You like Poetry better, so you shall have some I was going to give Reynolds.

Season of Mists and mellow fruitfulness,
   Close bosom friend of the maturing sun;
Conspiring with him how to load and bless
   The vines with fruit that round the thatch eves run;
To bend with apples the moss'd cottage trees,
   And fill all fruit with ripeness to the core;
     To swell the gourd, and plump the hazle-shells
With a white kernel; to set budding more,
   And still more, later flowers for the bees
   Until they think warm days will never cease
     For summer has o'er-brimm'd their clammy Cells.

Who hath not seen thee oft amid thy stores?
   Sometimes, whoever seeks abroad may find
Thee sitting careless on a granary floor,
   Thy hair soft-lifted by the winnowing[4] wind;
Or on a half-reap'd furrow sound asleep,
   Dased with the fume of poppies, while thy hook
     Spares the next swath and all its twined flowers;
And sometimes like a gleaner thou dost keep
   Steady thy laden head across a brook;
   Or by a Cyder press, with patient look,
     Thou watchest the last oozings hours by hours—

Where are the songs of spring? Aye, Where are they?
   Think not of them, thou hast thy music too.
While barred clouds bloom the soft-dying day
   And touch the stubble plains with rosy hue:
Then in a wailful choir[5] the small gnats mourn
   Among the river sallows, borne aloft
     Or sinking as the light wind lives and dies;
And full grown Lambs loud bleat from hilly bourne:
   Hedge crickets sing, and now with treble soft
   The Red breast whistles from a garden Croft
And gather'd Swallows twitter in the Skies—

I will give you a few lines from Hyperion[6] on account of a word in the last line of a fine sound.

> Mortal! that thou may'st understand aright
> I humanize my sayings to thine ear,
> Making comparisons of earthly things;
> Or thou might'st better listen to the wind
> Though it blows *legend-laden* through the trees.

I think you will like the following description of the Temple of Saturn:

> I look'd around upon the carved sides
> Of an old sanctuary, with roof august
> Builded so high, it seem'd that filmed clouds
> Might sail beneath, as o'er the stars of heaven.
> So old the place was I remember none
> The like upon the earth; what I had seen
> Of grey Cathedrals, buttress'd walls, rent towers
> The superannuations of sunk realms,
> Or nature's rocks hard-toil'd in winds and waves,
> Seem'd but the failing of decrepit things
> To that eternal-domed monument.
> Upon the marble, at my feet, there lay
> Store of strange vessels and large draperies
> Which needs had been of dyed asbestus wove,
> Or in that place the moth could not corrupt,
> So white the linen, so, in some, distinct
> Ran imageries from a sombre loom.
> All in a mingled heap confused there lay
> Robes, golden tongs, censer and chafing dish
> Girdles, and chains and holy jewelries.
> Turning from these, with awe once more I rais'd
> My eyes to fathom the space every way;
> The embossed roof, the silent massive range
> Of Columns north and south, ending in Mist

Of nothing; then to the eastward where black gates
Were shut against the Sunrise evermore.

I see I have completely lost my direction, so I e'n make you pay double postage. I had begun a sonnet in french of Ronsard. On my word 'tis very capable of poetry. I was stop'd by a circumstance not worth mentioning. I intended to call it La Platonique Chevalresque. I like the second line:

Non ne suis si audace a languire
    De m'empresser au coeur vos tendres mains, etc.[7]

Here is what I had written for a sort of induction[8]:

Fanatics have their dreams wherewith they weave
A Paradise for a Sect; the savage too
From forth the loftiest fashion of his sleep
Guesses at Heaven: pity these have not
Trac'd upon vellum, or wild indian leaf
The shadows of melodious utterance:
But bare of laurel they live, dream, and die,
For Poesy alone can tell her dreams,
With the fine spell of words alone can save
Imagination from the sable charm
And dumb enchantment.

My Poetry will never be fit for anything; it doesn't cover its ground well. You see he she is off her guard and doesn't move a peg though Prose is coming up in an awkward style enough. Now a blow in the spondee will finish her, but let it get over this line of circumvallation[9] if it can. These are unpleasant Phrases.

    Now for all this you two must write me a letter apiece, for as I know you will interread one another. I am still writing to Reynolds as well as yourself. As I say to George, I am writing *to* you but *at* your Wife. And don't forget to tell Reynolds of the fairy tale Undine.[10] Ask him if he has read any of the American Brown's novels that Hazlitt speaks so much of. I have read one call'd Wieland.[11] Very powerful. Something like Godwin, between Schiller and Godwin. A Domestic prototype of Schiller's Armenian.[12] More clever in plot and incident than Godwin; a strange american scion of the German trunk. Powerful genius, accomplish'd horrors. I shall proceed tomorrow.

Wednesday.[13] I am all in a Mess here embowell'd in Winchester. I wrote two Letters to Brown, one from said Place and one from London, and neither of them has reach'd him. I have written him a long one this morning and am so perplex'd as to be an object of Curiosity to you quiet People. I hire myself a show wagon and trumpetour. Here's the wonderful Man whose Letters won't go! All the infernal imaginary thunderstorms from the Post office are beating upon me, so that "unpoeted I write." Some curious body has detained my Letters, I am sure of it. They know not what to make of me, not an acquaintance in the Place. What can I be about? So they open my Letters—Being in a lodging house, and not so self-will'd, but I am a little cowardly, I dare not spout my rage against the Ceiling. Besides, I should be run through the Body by the major in the next room. I don't think his wife would attempt such a thing.

Now I am going to be serious. After revolving certain circumstances in my Mind, chiefly connected with a late american letter, I have determined to take up my abode in a cheap Lodging in Town and get employment in some of our elegant Periodical Works. I will no longer live upon hopes. I shall carry my plan into execution speedily. I shall live in Westminster, from which a walk to the British Museum will be noisy and muddy but otherwise pleasant enough. I shall enquire of Hazlitt how the figures of the market stand. O, that I could write something agrest rural,[14] pleasant, fountainvoic'd, not plague you with unconnected nonsense. But things won't leave me *alone*. I shall be in Town as soon as either of you. I only wait for an answer from Brown, if he receives mine, which is now a very moot point. I will give you a few reasons why I shall persist in not publishing The Pot of Basil. It is too smokeable. I can get it smoak'd at the Carpenter's shaving chimney much more cheaply. There is too much inexperience of life and simplicity of knowledge in it, which might do very well after one's death but not while one is alive. There are very few would look to the reality. I intend to use more finesse with the Public. It is possible to write fine things which cannot be laugh'd at in anyway. Isabella is what I should call were I a reviewer "a weak-sided Poem" with an amusing sober-sadness about it. Not that I do not think Reynolds and you are quite right about it; it is enough for me. But this will not do to be public. If I may so say, in my dramatic capacity I enter fully into the feeling, but in Propria Persona I should be apt to quiz it myself. There is no objection of this kind to Lamia, a good deal to St. Agnes Eve, only not so glaring. Would, as I say, I could write you something sylvestran. But I have no time to think. I am an otiosus-peroccupatus Man.[15] I think upon crutches, like the folks in your Pump room. Have you seen old Bramble yet? They say he's on his last legs. The gout did not treat the old Man well so the Physician superseded it, and put the dropsy in office, who gets very fat upon his new employment, and behaves worse than the other to the old Man. But he'll have his house about his ears soon. We shall have another fall of Siege-arms. I suppose Mrs. Humphrey persists in a big-belley; poor thing, she little thinks how she is spoiling the corners of her mouth and making her nose quite a piminy.[16] Mr. Humphrey I hear was giving a Lecture in the gaming-room when someone call'd out Spousey! I hear too he has received a challenge from a gentleman who lost that evening. The fact is Mr. H. is a mere nothing out of his Rod-room. Old Tabitha died in being bolstered up for a whist-party. They had to cut again. Chowder died long ago. Mrs. H. laments that the last time they *put him* (i.e. to breed) he didn't take. They say he was a direct descendent of Cupid and Veney in the Spectator. This may be easily known by the Parish Books. If you do not write in the course of a day or two, direct to me at Rice's. Let me know how you pass your times and how you are.

Your sincere friend
John Keats—

Haven't heard from Taylor—

1. "The Idiot Boy," line 289.
2. *Twelfth Night*, II.iii.19–21.
3. A punning adaptation and parody of Virgil's *Eclogues*, III.79. Virgil's line reads "et longum 'formose, vale, vale,' inquit, 'Iolla'" ("and for a long time she said, 'Farewell, farewell, handsome Iollas'"). Keats's line offers a choice of translations, though the likeliest is "but, beautiful woman, the thong said 'Farewell, farewell, heigh ho

la!'" *Thongum* (English *thong*) means leather strip or whip. The line could also be translated, "Whip, the beautiful woman says 'Farewell, farewell, heigh ho la!'" *Thongum* is also slang for penis, adding yet another level of witty vulgarity to the line.

4. Keats wrote "winmowing."
5. Keats wrote "quire."
6. "The Fall of Hyperion," II.1–4, 6.
7. "Nor am I so bold / As to long to press your tender hands to my heart."
8. "The Fall of Hyperion," I.1–11.
9. This paragraph, written at right angles to the verse, is curved to fit in with the varying length of the lines of verse.
10. George Soane's *Undine: Or, The Spirit of the Waters, A Melo Dramatic Romance, in Two Acts,* translated from the German of Baron de la Motte Fouqué.
11. Published in 1798 by Charles Brockden Brown (1771–1810).
12. He refers to William Render's translation, *The Arminian; Or, The Ghost Seer* (1800).
13. That is, 22 September.
14. Keats meant "something rustic and rural," same as "sylvestran" below.
15. Presumably he meant "a leisurely-terribly-busy man."
16. Adapted from the game-expression "miminy piminy," one meaning of which is "mincing, affected."

To Charles Brown

22 SEPTEMBER 1819[1]

* * *

Now I am going to enter on the subject of self. It is quite time I should set myself doing something, and live no longer upon hopes. I have never yet exerted myself. I am getting into an idle-minded, vicious way of life, almost content to live upon others. In no period of my life have I acted with any self-will, but in throwing up the apothecary profession. That I do not repent of. Look at x x x x x x.[2] If he was not in the law, he would be acquiring, by his abilities, something towards his support. My occupation is entirely literary; I will do so too. I will write, on the liberal side of the question, for whoever will pay me. I have not known yet what it is to be diligent. I purpose living in town in a cheap lodging, and endeavouring, for a beginning, to get the theatricals of some paper. When I can afford to compose deliberate poems I will. I shall be in expectation of an answer to this. Look on my side of the question. I am convinced I am right. Suppose the Tragedy should succeed; there will be no harm done. And here I will take an opportunity of making a remark or two on our friendship, and all your good offices to me. I have a natural timidity of mind in these matters, liking better to take the feeling between us for granted, than to speak of it. But, good God! What a short while you have known me! I feel it a sort of duty thus to recapitulate, however unpleasant it may be to you. You have been living for others more than any man I know. This is a vexation to me because it has been depriving you, in the very prime of your life, of pleasures which it was your duty to procure. As I am speaking in general terms this may appear nonsense; you perhaps will not understand it, but if you can go over, day by day, any month of the last year, you will know what I mean. On the whole, however, this is a subject that I cannot express myself upon. I speculate upon it frequently; and, believe me, the end of my speculations is always an anxiety for your happiness. This anxiety will not be one of the least incitements to the plan I purpose pursuing. I had got into a habit of mind of looking towards you as a help in all difficulties. This very habit would be the parent of idleness and difficulties. You will see it is a duty I owe myself to break the neck of it. I do nothing for my subsistence, make no exertion. At the end of another year, you shall applaud me, not for verses, but for conduct. If you live at Hampstead next winter ———.[3] I like x x x x x x x x x[4] and I cannot help it. On that account I had better not live there. While I have some immediate cash, I had better settle myself quietly, and fag on as others do. I shall apply to Hazlitt, who knows the market as well as anyone, for something to bring me in a few pounds as soon as possible. I shall not suffer my pride to hinder me. The whisper may go round; I shall not hear it. If I can get an article in the "Edinburg," I will. One must not be delicate. Nor let this disturb you longer than a moment. I look forward, with a good hope, that we shall one day be passing free, untrammelled, unanxious time together. That can never be if I continue a dead lump. x x x x x x x x x x x x x x I shall be expecting anxiously an answer from you. If it does not arrive in a few days, this will have miscarried, and I shall come straight to x x x x[5] before I go to town, which you, I am sure, will agree had better be done while I still have some ready cash. By the middle of October I shall expect you in London. We will then set at the Theatres. If you have anything to gainsay, I shall be even as the deaf adder which stoppeth her ears.[6]

* * *

1. A fragmentary letter, taken from Brown's *Life of John Keats.*
2. Reynolds.
3. Text missing.
4. Fanny Brawne?
5. Bedhampton or Chichester?
6. Psalm lviii.4.

To C. W. Dilke
22 SEPTEMBER 1819[1]

Winchester, Wednesday Eve—

My dear Dilke,

Whatever I take to for the time I cannot leave off in a hurry; letter writing is the go now. I have consumed a Quire at least. You must give me credit now for a free Letter when it is in reality an interested one on two points, the one requestive, the other verging to the pros and cons. As I expect they will lead me to seeing and conferring with you in a short time, I shall not enter at all upon a letter I have lately received from george of not the most comfortable intelligence, but proceed to these two points, which if you can theme out in sections and subsections,[2] for my edification, you will oblige me. The first I shall begin upon, the other will follow like a tail to a Comet. I have written to Brown on the subject, and can but go over the same Ground with you in a very short time, it not being more in length than the ordinary paces between the Wickets.[3] It concerns a resolution I have taken to endeavour to acquire something by temporary writing in periodical works. You must agree with me how unwise it is to keep feeding upon hopes, which depending so much on the state of temper and imagination, appear gloomy or bright, near or afar off just as it happens. Now an act has three parts: to act, to do, and to perform.[4] I mean I should *do* something for my immediate welfare. Even if I am swept away like a Spider from a drawing room I am determined to spin, home spun anything for sale. Yea, I will traffic. Anything but Mortgage my Brain to Blackwood. I am determined not to lie like a dead lump. If Reynolds had not taken to the law, would he not be earning something? Why cannot I? You may say I want tact; that is easily acquired. You may be up to the slang of a cockpit in three battles. It is fortunate I have not before this been tempted to venture on the common. I should a year or two ago have spoken my mind on every subject with the utmost simplicity. I hope I have learnt a little better and am confident I shall be able to cheat as well as any literary Jew of the Market and shine up an article on anything without much knowledge of the subject, aye like an orange. I would willingly have recourse to other means. I cannot; I am fit for nothing but literature. Wait for the issue of this Tragedy? No. There cannot be greater uncertainties east, west, north, and south[5] than concerning dramatic composition. How many months must I wait! Had I not better begin to look about me now? If better events supersede this necessity what harm will be done? I have no trust whatever on Poetry. I don't wonder at it. The marvel is to me how people read so much of it. I think you will see the reasonableness of my plan. To forward it I purpose living in cheap Lodging in Town, that I may be in the reach of books and information, of which there is here a plentiful lack.[6] If I can find any place tolerably comfitable I will settle myself and fag till I can afford to buy Pleasure, which if I never can afford I must go Without. Talking of Pleasure, this moment I was writing with one hand and with the other holding to my Mouth a Nectarine. Good god, how fine. It went down soft pulpy, slushy, oozy; all its delicious embonpoint melted down my throat like a large beatified Strawberry. I shall certainly breed.

Now I come to my request. Should you like me for a neighbour again? Come, plump it out, I won't blush. I should also be in the neighbourhood of Mrs. Wylie, which I should be glad of, though that of course does not influence me. Therefore will you look about Marsham, or rodney street for a couple of rooms for me? Rooms like the gallant's legs in massinger's time, "as good as the times allow, Sir."[7] I have written today to Reynolds, and to Woodhouse. Do you know him? He is a Friend of Taylor's at whom Brown has taken one of his funny odd dislikes. I'm sure he's wrong, because Woodhouse likes my Poetry—conclusive. I ask your opinion and yet I must say to you as to him, Brown, that if you have anything to say against it I shall be as obstinate and heady as a Radical. By the Examiner coming in your handwriting you must be in Town. They have put into spirits; notwithstanding[8] my aristocratic temper, I cannot help being very much pleas'd with the present public proceedings.[9] I hope sincerely I shall be able to put a Mite of help to the Liberal side of the Question before I die. If you should have left Town again (for your Holidays cannot be up yet) let me know when this is forwarded to you. A most extraordinary mischance has befallen two Letters I wrote Brown: one from London whither I was obliged to go on business for George, the other from this place since my return. I can't make it out. I am excessively sorry for it. I shall hear from Brown and from you almost together for I have sent him a Letter today. You must positively agree with me or by the delicate toenails of the virgin I will not open your Letters. If they are, as David says, "suspicious looking letters," I won't open them. If St. John had been half as cunning he might have seen the revelations comfortably in his own room, without giving Angels the trouble of breaking open Seals.[10] Remember me to Mrs. D. and the Westmonisteranian, and believe me

Ever your sincere friend
John Keats—

1. This letter was not mailed to Dilke, but was replaced by another of 1 October 1819 not included here.
2. A reference to Burton's *Anatomy of Melancholy.* Keats spelled the words "sexions" and "subsexions."
3. A reference to the game of cricket.
4. *Hamlet,* V.i.11–13.
5. *Love's Labor's Lost,* V.ii.566.
6. *Hamlet,* II.ii.202.
7. *A Very Woman,* III.i.

8. Keats wrote "notwithstand."
9. He had been reading in the *Examiner* about public meetings, Henry Hunt, and the Reformers.
10. Revelation v, vi.

To Charles Brown

23 SEPTEMBER 1819[1]

* * *

Do not suffer me to disturb you unpleasantly. I do not mean that you should not suffer me to occupy your thoughts, but to occupy them pleasantly, for, I assure you, I am as far from being unhappy as possible. Imaginary grievances have always been more my torment than real ones. You know this well. Real ones will never have any other effect upon me than to stimulate me to get out of or avoid them. This is easily accounted for. Our imaginary woes are conjured up by our passions, and are fostered by passionate feeling; our real ones come of themselves, and are opposed by an abstract exertion of mind. Real grievances are displacers of passion. The imaginary nail a man down for a sufferer, as on a cross; the real spur him up into an agent. I wish, at one view, you could see my heart towards you. 'Tis only from a high tone of feeling that I can put that word upon paper—out of poetry. I ought to have waited for your answer to my last before I wrote this. I felt, however, compelled to make a rejoinder to your's. I had written to x x x x x^2 on the subject of my last. I scarcely know whether I shall send my letter now. I think he would approve of my plan; it is so evident. Nay, I am convinced, out and out, that by prosing for awhile in periodical works I may maintain myself decently.

* * *

1. A fragmentary letter, taken from Brown's *Life of John Keats*.
2. Dilke.

To George and Georgiana Keats
17, 18, 20, 21, 24, 25, 27 SEPTEMBER 1819

Winchester, Sept. Friday—

My dear George,

I was closely employed in reading and composition in this place, whither I had come from Shanklin for the convenience of a library, when I received your last, dated July 24th. You will have seen by the short Letter I wrote from Shanklin how matters stand between us and Mrs. Jennings. They had not at all mov'd and I knew no way of overcoming the inveterate obstinacy of our affairs. On receiving your last I immediately took a place in the same night's coach for London. Mr. Abbey behaved extremely well to me, appointed Monday evening at 7 to meet me and observed that he should drink tea at that hour. I gave him the enclosed note and showed him the last leaf of yours to me. He really appeared anxious about it; promised he would forward your money as quickly as possible. I think I mention'd that Walton was dead. He will apply to Mr. Gliddon the partner, endeavour to get rid of Mrs. Jennings's claim and be expeditious. He has received an answer from my Letter to Fry.[1] That is something. We are certainly in a very low estate. I say we, for I am in such a situation that were it not for the assistance of Brown and Taylor, I must be as badly off as a Man can be. I could not raise any sum by the promise of any Poem, no, not by the mortgage of my intellect. We must wait a little while. I really have hopes of success. I have finish'd a Tragedy[2] which if it succeeds will enable me to sell what I may have in manuscript to a good advantage. I have pass'd my time in reading, writing and fretting. The last I intend to give up and stick to the other two. They are the only chances of benefit to us. Your wants will be a fresh spur to me. I assure you, you shall more than share what I can get, whilst I am still young. The time may come when age will make me more selfish. I have not been well-treated by the world, and yet I have capitally well. I do not know a Person to whom so many purse strings would fly open as to me—if I could possibly take advantage of them—which I cannot do for none of the owners of these purses are rich. Your present situation I will not suffer myself to dwell upon. When misfortunes are so real we are glad enough to escape them, and the thought of them. I cannot help thinking Mr. Audubon a dishonest man. Why did he make you believe that he was a Man of Property?[3] How is it his circumstances have altered so suddenly? In truth, I do not believe you fit to deal with the world, or at least the american world. But good God, who can avoid these chances? You have done your best. Take matters as coolly as you can and confidently expecting help from England, act as if no help was nigh. Mine I am sure is a tolerable tragedy. It would have been a bank to me, if just as I had finish'd it I had not heard of Kean's resolution to go to America. That was the worst news I could have had. There is no actor can do the principal character besides Kean. At Covent Garden there is a great chance of its being damn'd. Were it to succeed even there it would lift me out of the mire. I mean the mire of a bad reputation which is continually rising against me. My name with the literary fashionables is vulgar. I am a weaver boy to them. A Tragedy would lift me out of this mess. And mess it is as far as it regards our Pockets. But be not cast down any more than I am. I feel I can bear real ills better than imaginary ones. Whenever I find myself growing vapourish, I rouse myself, wash and put on a clean shirt, brush my hair and clothes, tie my shoestrings neatly and in fact adonize as I were going out. Then all clean and comfortable I sit down to write. This I find the greatest relief. Besides, I am becoming accustom'd to the privations of the pleasures of sense. In the midst of the world I live like a Hermit. I have forgot how to lay plans for enjoyment of any Pleasure. I feel I can bear anything, any misery, even imprisonment, so long as I have neither wife nor child. Perhaps you will say yours are your only comfort; they must be.

I return'd to Winchester the day before yesterday and am now here alone, for Brown some days before I left went to Bedhampton and there he will be for the next fortnight. The term of his house will be up in the middle of next month when we shall return to Hampstead. On Sunday I dined with your Mother and Henry and Charles in Henrietta Street. Mrs. and Miss Millar were in the Country. Charles had been but a few days returned from Paris. I dare say you will have letters expressing the motives of his Journey. Mrs. Wylie and Miss Waldegrave seem as quiet as two Mice there alone. I did not show your last; I thought it better not. For better times will certainly come and why should they be unhappy in the main time? On Monday Morning I went to Walthamstow. Fanny look'd better than I had seen her for some time. She complains of not hearing from you, appealing to me as if it was half my fault. I had been so long in retirement that London appeared a very odd place. I could not make out I had so many acquaintance, and it was a whole day before I could feel among Men. I had another strange sensation. There was not one house I felt any pleasure to call at. Reynolds was in the Country and saving himself. I am prejudiced against all that family. Dilke and his wife and child were in the Country. Taylor was at Nottingham. I was out and everybody was out. I walk'd about the Streets as in a strange land. Rice was the only one at home. I pass'd some time with him. I know him better since we have liv'd a month together in the isle of Wight. He is the most sensible, and even wise Man I know. He has a few John Bull prejudices, but they improve him. His illness is at times alarming. We are great friends, and there is no one I like to pass a day with better. Martin call'd in to bid him good bye before he set out for Dublin. If you would like to hear one of his jokes, here is one which at the time we laugh'd at a good deal. A Miss ———— with three young Ladies, one of them Martin's sister, had come a gadding in the Isle of wight and took for a few days a Cottage opposite ours. We dined with them one day, and as I was saying they had fish. Miss ———— said she thought *they tasted of the boat*. No, says Martin very seriously, they haven't been kept long enough.

I saw Haslam. He is very much occupied with love and business, being one of Mr. Saunders' executors and Lover to a young woman. He show'd me her Picture by Severn. I think she is, though not very cunning, too cunning for him. Nothing strikes me so forcibly with a sense of the rediculous as love. A Man in love I do think cuts the sorryest figure in the world. Even when I know a poor fool to be really in pain about it, I could burst out laughing in his face. His pathetic visage becomes irresistible. Not that I take Haslam as a pattern for Lovers. He is a very worthy man and a good friend.

His love is very amusing. Somewhere in the Spectator is related an account
of a Man inviting a party of stutterers and squinters to his table. 'Twould
please me more to scrape together a party of Lovers, not to dinner, no to
tea. There would be no fighting as among Knights of old:

> Pensive they sit, and roll their languid eyes
> Nibble their toasts, and cool their tea with sighs,
> Or else forget the purpose of the night
> Forget their tea, forget their appetite.
> See with cross'd arms they sit; ah, hapless crew,
> The fire is going out, and no one rings
> For coals, and therefore no coals Betty brings.
> A Fly is in the milk pot; must he die
> Circled by a humane society?
> No, no, there Mr. Werter takes his spoon,
> Inverts it, dips the handle and lo, soon
> The little struggler sav'd from perils dark
> Across the teaboard draws a long wet mark.
> Romeo! Arise! Take Snuffers by the handle,
> There's a large Cauliflower in each candle.
> A winding-sheet. Ah me! I must away
> To no. 7 just beyond the Circus gay.
> "Alas," my friend! Your Coat sits very well:
> Where may your Taylor live?" "I may not tell.
> "O pardon me, I'm absent now and then."
> Where *might* my Taylor live? I say again
> I cannot tell. Let me no more be teas'd,
> He lives in wapping, *might* live where he pleas'd.

You see I cannot get on without writing as boys do at school a few nonsense
verses. I begin them and before I have written six the whim has pass'd, if
there is anything deserving so respectable a name in them. I shall put in a
bit of information anywhere just as it strikes me. Mr. Abbey is to write to
me as soon as he can bring matters to bear, and then I am to go to Town to
tell him the means of forwarding to you through Capper and Hazlewood. I

wonder I did not put this before. I shall go on tomorrow. It is so fine now I must take a bit of a walk.

Saturday[4]

With my inconstant disposition it is no wonder that this morning, amid all our bad times and misfortunes, I should feel so alert and well-spirited. At this moment you are perhaps in a very different state of Mind. It is because my hopes are very paramount to my despair. I have been reading over a part of a short poem I have composed lately call'd "Lamia," and I am certain there is that sort of fire in it which must take hold of people in some way, give them either pleasant or unpleasant sensation. What they want is a sensation of some sort. I wish I could pitch the key of your spirits as high as mine is, but your organ loft is beyond the reach of my voice. I admire the exact admeasurement of my niece in your Mother's letter. O, the little span long elf.[5] I am not in the least judge of the proper weight and size of an infant. Never trouble yourselves about that; she is sure to be a fine woman. Let her have only delicate nails both on hands and feet and teeth as small as a May-fly's who will live you his life on a square inch of oak-leaf. And nails she must have quite different from the market women here who plough into the butter and make a quatter pound taste of it. I intend to write a letter to your Wifie and there I may say more on this little plump subject; I hope she's plump—"Still harping on my daughter."[6]

This Winchester is a place tolerably well-suited to me. There is a fine Cathedral, a College, a Roman-Catholic Chapel, a Methodist do, an independent do, and there is not one loom or anything like manufacturing beyond bread and butter in the whole City. There are a number of rich Catholics in the place. It is a respectable, ancient, aristocratical place, and moreover it contains a nunnery. Our set are by no means so hail fellow, well met on literary subjects as we were wont to be. Reynolds has turn'd to the law. Bye the bye, he brought out a little piece at the Lyceum call'd *one, two, three, four by advertisement*. It met with complete success. The meaning of this odd title is explained when I tell you the principal actor is a mimic who takes off four of our best performers in the course of the farce. Our stage is loaded with mimics. I did not see the Piece being out of Town the whole time it was in progress. Dilke is entirely swallowed up in his boy. 'Tis really lamentable to what a pitch he carries a sort of parental mania. I had a Letter from him at Shanklin. He went on a word or two about the isle of Wight which is a bit of hobbyhorse of his, but he soon deviated to his boy. "I am sitting," says he, "at the window expecting my Boy from School." I suppose I told you somewhere that he lives in Westminster and his boy goes to the School there where he gets beaten, and every bruise he has and I dare say deserves is very bitter to Dilke. The Place I am speaking of puts me in mind of a circumstance occured lately at Dilke's. I think it very rich and dramatic and quite illustrative of the little quiet fun that he will enjoy sometimes. First I must tell you their house is at the corner of Great Smith Street, so that some of the windows look into one Street, and the back windows into another round the corner. Dilke had some old people to dinner, I know not who, but there were two old ladies among them. Brown was there. They had known him from a Child. Brown is very pleasant with old women, and on that day, it seems, behaved himself so winningly that they became hand and glove together and a little complimentary. Brown was obliged to depart early. He bid them good bye and pass'd into the passage. No sooner was his back turn'd than the old women began lauding him. When Brown had reach'd the Street door and was just going, Dilke threw up the Window and call'd "Brown! Brown! They say you look younger than ever you did!" Brown went on and had just turn'd the corner into the other street when Dilke appeared at the back window crying "Brown! Brown! By God, they say you're handsome!" You see what a many words it requires to give any identity to a thing I could have told you in half a minute.

I have been reading lately Burton's Anatomy of Melancholy, and I think you will be very much amused with a page I here copy for you.[7] I call it a Feu de joie round the batteries of Fort St. Hyphen-de-Phrase on the birth-day of the Digamma. The whole alphabet was drawn up in a Phalanx on the cover of an old Dictionary. Band playing "Amo, Amas, etc.": "Every Lover admires his Mistress, though she be very deformed of herself, ill-favored, wrinkled, pimpled, pale, red, yellow, tann'd, tallow-fac'd, have a swoln jugler's platter face, or a thin, lean, chitty face, have clouds in her face, be crooked, dry, bald, goggle-eyed, blear-eyed or with staring eyes, she looks like a squis'd cat, hold her head still awry, heavy, dull, hollow-eyed, black or yellow about the eyes, or squint-eyed, sparrow-mouth'd, Persian-hook-nosed, have a sharp fox nose, a red nose, China flat, great nose, nare simo patuloque,[8] a nose like a promontory, gubber-tush'd, rotten teeth, black, uneven, brown teeth, beetle-brow'd, a witch's beard, her breath stink all over the room, her nose drop winter and summer, with a Bavarian poke under her chin, a sharp chin, lave-eared, with a long crane's neck, which stands awry too, pendulis mammis her dugs like two double jugs, or else no dugs in the other extream, bloody-fallen fingers, she have filthy, long, unpaired, nails, scabbed hands or wrists, a tann'd skin, a rotton carcass, crooked back, she stoops, is lame, splay-footed, as slender in the middle as a cow in the wast, gouty legs, her ankles hang over her shoes, her feet stink, she breed lice, a mere changeling, a very monster, an aufe imperfect, her whole complexion savors, an harsh voice, incondite gesture, vile gate, a vast virago, or an ugly tit, a slug, a fat fustilugs, a trusse, a long lean rawbone, a Skeleton, a Sneaker, (si qua patent meliora puta)[9] and to thy Judgement looks like a mard in a Lanthorn, whom thou couldst not fancy for a world, but hatest, loathest, and wouldst have spit in her face, or blow thy nose in her bosom, remedium amoris[10] to another man, a dowdy, a Slut, a scold, a nasty rank, rammy, filthy, beastly quean, dishonest peradventure, obscene, base, beggarly, rude, foolish, untaught, peevish, Irus' daughter, Thersite's sister, Grobian's Scholler; if he love her once, he admires her for all this, he takes no notice of any such errors or imperfections of body or mind." There's a dose for you—fine!! I would give my favourite leg to have written this as a speech in a Play. With what effect could Mathews[11] pop-gun it at the pit! This I think will amuse you more than so much Poetry. Of that I do not like to copy any as I am afraid it is too mal apropo for you at present; and yet I will send you some, for by the time you receive it things in England may have taken a different turn. When I left Mr. Abbey on monday evening, I walk'd up Cheapside but returned to put some letters in the Post and met him again in Bucklersbury. We walk'd together through the Poultry as far as the hatter's shop he has some concern in. He spoke of it in such a way to me, I thought he wanted me to make an offer to assist him in it. I do believe if I could be a hatter I might be one. He seems anxious about me. He began blowing up Lord Byron while I was sitting with him; however, Says he, the fellow says true things now and then, at which he took up a Magasine and read me some extracts from Don Juan (Lord Byron's last flash poem) and particularly one against literary ambition.[12] I do think I must be well spoken of among sets, for Hodgkinson is more than polite, and the coffee-german[13] endeavour'd to be very close to me the other night at covent garden where I went at half-price before I tumbled into bed. Everyone however distant an acquaintance behaves in the most conciliating manner to me. You will see I speak of this as a matter of interest. On the next Sheet I will give you a little politics. In every age there has been in England for some two or three centuries subjects of great popular interest on the carpet, so that however great the uproar one can scarcely prophesy any material change in the government; for as loud disturbances have agitated this country many times. All civiled countries become gradually more enlighten'd and there should be a continual change for the better. Look at this Country at present and remember it when it was even thought impious to doubt the justice of a trial by Combat. From that time there has been a gradual change. Three great changes have been in progress; First for the better, next for the worse, and a third time for the better once more. The first was the gradual annihilation of the tyranny of the nobles when kings found it their interest to conciliate the common people, elevate them and be just to them. Just when baronial Power ceased and before standing armies were so dangerous, Taxes were few. Kings were lifted by the people over the heads of their nobles, and those people held a rod over kings. The change for the worse in Europe was again this. The obligation of kings to the Multitude began to be forgotten. Custom had made noblemen the humble servants of kings. Then kings turned to the Nobles as the adorners of their power, the slaves of it, and from the people as creatures continually endeavouring to check them. Then in every kingdom there was a long struggle of kings to destroy all popular privileges. The english were the only people in europe who made a grand kick at this. They were slaves to Henry 8th but were freemen under william 3rd. At the time the french were abject slaves under Lewis 14th. The example of England and the liberal writers of france and england sowed the seed of opposition to this Tyranny—and it

was swelling in the ground till it burst out in the french revolution—That
has had an unlucky termination. It put a stop to the rapid progress of free
sentiments in England; and gave our Court hopes of turning back to the
despotism of the 16th century. They have made a handle of this event in every way to undermine our freedom. They spread a horrid superstition
against all innovation and improvement. The present struggle in England
of the people is to destroy this superstition. What has rous'd them to do it is
their distresses. Perhaps on this account the present distresses of this nation
are a fortunate thing—tho' so horrid in their experience. You will see I
mean that the french Revolution put a temporary stop to this third change,
the change for the better. Now it is in progress again and I think in an effectual one. This is no contest between whig and tory, but between right and
wrong. There is scarcely a grain of party spirit now in England. Right and
Wrong considered by each man abstractedly is the fashion. I know very little of these things. I am convinced however that apparently small causes
make great alterations. There are little signs whereby we may know how
matters are going on. This makes the business about Carlisle the Bookseller
of great moment in my mind. He has been selling deistical pamphlets, republished Tom Paine and many other works held in superstitious horror.
He even has been selling for some time immense numbers of a work called
"The Deist" which comes out in weekly numbers. For this Conduct he, I
think, has had above a dozen inditements issued against him, for which he
has found Bail to the amount of many thousand Pounds. After all, they are
afraid to prosecute; they are afraid of his defence. It would be published in
all the papers all over the Empire. They shudder at this. The Trials would
light a flame they could not extinguish. Do you not think this of great im-
port? You will hear by the papers of the proceedings at Manchester and
Hunt's triumphal entry into London.[14] It would take me a whole day and a
quire of paper to give you anything like detail. I will merely mention that it
is calculated that 30,000 people were in the streets waiting for him. The
whole distance from the Angel Islington to the Crown and anchor[15] was
lined with Multitudes. As I pass'd Colnaghi's window I saw a profile Portrait of Sands the destroyer of Kotzebue. His very look must interest everyone in his favour. I suppose they have represented him in his college dress.

He seems to me like a young Abelard: A fine Mouth, cheek bones (and this is no joke) full of sentiment, a fine unvulgar nose and plump temples. On looking over some Letters I found the one I wrote intended for you from the foot of Helvellyn to Liverpool, but you had sail'd and therefore it was returned to me. It contained among other nonsense an Acrostic of my Sister's name, and a pretty long name it is. I wrote it in a great hurry which you will see. Indeed I would not copy it if I thought it would ever be seen by any but yourselves.[16]

I ought to make a large Q[17] here, but I had better take the opportunity of telling you I have got rid of my haunting sore throat and conduct myself in a manner not to catch another. You speak of Lord Byron and me. There is this great difference between us: he describes what he sees, I describe what I imagine. Mine is the hardest task. You see the immense difference. The Edinburgh review are afraid to touch upon my Poem. They do not know what to make of it. They do not like to condemn it and they will not praise it for fear. They are as shy of it as I should be of wearing a Quaker's hat. The fact is they have no real taste. They dare not compromise their Judgements on so puzzling a Question. If on my next Publication they should praise me and so lug in Endymion, I will address them in a manner they will not at all relish. The Cowardliness of the Edinburgh is worse than the abuse of the Quarterly.

Monday. This day is a grand day for winchester; they elect the Mayor. It was indeed high time the place should have some excitement. There was nothing going on—all asleep—Not an old Maid's Sedan returning from a card party, and if any old women have got tipsy at christenings they have not exposed themselves in the Street. The first night tho' of our arrival here there was a slight uproar took place at about ten of the clock. We heard distinctly a noise patting down the high street as of a walking Cane of the good old dowager breed; and a little minute after we heard a less voice observe, "what a noise the ferril made; it must be loose." Brown wanted to call the Constables, but I observed 'twas only a little breeze and would soon pass over. The side-streets here are excessively maiden lady-like, the door steps always fresh from the flannel. The knockers have a very staid serious, nay almost awful quietness about them. I never saw so quiet a collection of Lions, and rams heads—The doors most part black with a little brass handle just above the key hole—so that you may easily shut yourself out of your own house—he! he! There is none of your Lady Bellaston[18] rapping and ringing here. No thundering-Jupiter footmen, no opera-trebble-tattoos, but a modest lifting up of the knocker by a set of little wee old fingers that peep through the grey mittens, and a dying fall thereof. The great beauty of Poetry is that it makes everything every place interesting; The palatine venice and the abbotine Winchester are equally interesting. Some time since I began a Poem call'd "The Eve of St. Mark" quite in the spirit of Town quietude. I think it will give you the sensation of walking about an old county Town in a coolish evening. I know not yet whether I shall ever finish it. I will give it far as I have gone. *Ut tibi placent!*[19]

> Upon a Sabbath day it fell;
> Thrice holy was the sabbath bell
> That call'd the folk to evening prayer.
> The City Streets were clean and fair
> From wholesome drench of April rains,
> And on the western window pains
> The chilly sunset faintly told
> Of immatur'd, green vallies cold,
> Of the green, thorny, bloomless hedge,
> Of Rivers new with spring tide sedge,
> Of Primroses by shelter'd rills,
> And Dasies on the aguish hills.
> Thrice holy was the sabbath bell:
> The silent streets were crowded well
> With staid and pious companies
> Warm from their fireside oratries,
> And moving with demurest air
> To evensong and vesper prayer.
> Each arched porch and entry low

Was fill'd with patient crowd and slow,
With whispers hush, and shuffling feet
While play'd the organs loud and sweet.

    The Bells had ceas'd, the Prayers begun,
And Bertha had not yet half done
A curious volume, patch'd and torn,
That all day long, from earliest morn,
Had taken captive her fair eyes
Among its golden broideries:
Perplex'd her with a thousand things
The Stars of heaven, and Angels wings;
Martyrs in a fiery blaze;
Azure Saints 'mid silver rays;
Aron's breastplate, and the seven
Candlesticks John saw in heaven;
The winged Lion of St. Mark,
And the Covenental Arck
With its many Misteries
Cherubim and golden Mice.

    Bertha was a Maiden fair,
Dwelling in the old Minster square
From her fireside she could see
Sidelong its rich antiquity,
Far as the Bishop's garden wall,
Where sycamores and elm trees tall
Full-leav'd the forest had outstript,
By no sharp north wind ever nipt,
So sheltered by the mighty pile.

    Bertha arose, and read awhile
With forehead 'gainst the window pane,
Again she tried, and then again,

Until the dusk eve left her dark
Upon the Legend of St. Mark:

   From pleated lawn-frill fine and thin
She lifted up her soft warm chin
With aching neck and swimming eyes
All daz'd with saintly imageries.

   All was gloom, and silent all,
Save now and then the still footfall
Of one returning homewards late
Past the echoing minster gate.
The clamourous daws that all the day
Above tree tops and towers play,
Pair by Pair had gone to rest,
Each in their ancient belfry nest
Where asleep they fall betimes
To music of the drowsy chimes.

   All was silent, all was gloom
Abroad and in the homely room;
Down she sat, poor cheated soul,
And struck a swart Lamp from the coal,
Leaned forward with bright drooping hair
And slant book full against the glare.
Her shadow, in uneasy guise,
Hover'd about, a giant size,
On ceiling, beam, and old oak chair,
The Parrot's cage and pannel square,
And the warm-angled winter screne,
On which were many monsters seen,
Call'd Doves of Siam, Lima Mice,
And legless birds of Paradise,
Macaw, and tender Av'davat,
And silken-furr'd Angora Cat.

Untir'd she read; her shadow still
Glower'd about as it would fill
The room with gastly forms and shades,
As though some ghostly Queen of Spades
Had come to mock behind her back,
And dance, and ruffle her garments black.

Untir'd she read the Legend page
Of holy Mark from youth to age,
On Land, on sea, in pagan-chains,
Rejoicing for his many pains.
Sometimes the learned Eremite
With golden star, or dagger bright,
Refer'd to pious poesies
Written in smallest crow quill size
Beneath the text and thus the rhyme
Was parcell'd out from time to time.

What follows is an imitation of the Authors in Chaucer's time. 'Tis more ancient than Chaucer himself and perhaps between him and Gower:

——Als writeth he of swevenis
Men han beforne they waken in blis,
When that hir friendes thinke hem bounde
In crimpide shroude farre under grounde:
And how a litling childe mote be
A scainte er its natavitie,
Gif that the modre (Gode her blesse)
Kepen in Solitarinesse,
And kissen devoute the holy croce.
Of Goddis love and Sathan's force
He writithe; and things many moe,
Of swiche thinges I may not show,
Bot I must tellen verilie
Somedele of Saintè Cicilie,

And chieflie what he auctoreth
Of Saintè Markis life and dethe.

I hope you will like this for all its Carelessness. I must take an opportunity here to observe that though I am writing *to* you, I am all the while writing *at* your Wife. This explanation will account for my speaking sometimes *hoity-toityishly.* Whereas if you were alone I should sport a little more sober sadness. I am like a squinting gentleman who saying soft things to one Lady ogles another, or what is as bad, in arguing with a person on his left hand appeals with his eyes to one on the right. His Vision is elastic, he bends it to a certain object but having a patent spring it flies off. Writing has this disadvantage of speaking: one cannot write a wink, or a nod, or a grin, or a purse of the Lips, or a *smile—O law!* One cannot put one's finger to one's nose, or yerk ye in the ribs,[20] or lay hold of your button in writing, but in all the most lively and titterly parts of my Letter you must not fail to imagine me as the epic poets say, now here, now there, now with one foot pointed at the ceiling, now with another, now with my pen on my ear, now with my elbow in my mouth. O, my friends, you lose the action, and attitude is everything, as Fusili[21] said when he took up his leg like a Musket to shoot a Swallow just darting behind his shoulder. And yet does not the word "mum!" go for one's finger beside the nose? I hope it does. I have to make use of the word "Mum!" before I tell you that Severn has got a little Baby, all his own let us hope. He told Brown he had given up painting and had turn'd modeler. I hope sincerely 'tis not a party concern, that no Mr. ⸺ or **** is the real *Pinxit* and Severn the poor *Sculpsit* to this work of art. You know he has long studied in the Life-Academy.[22]

Haydon. Yes, your wife will say, "here is a sum total account of Haydon again, I wonder your Brother don't put a monthly bulleteen in the Philadelphia Papers about him. I won't hear—no—skip down to the bottom—aye, and there are some more of his verses, skip (lullaby-by) them too." "No, let's go regularly through." "I won't hear a word about Haydon. Bless the child, how rioty she is! There go on there." Now pray go on here for I have a few words to say about Haydon. Before this Chancery threat had cut off every legitimate supply of Cash from me I had a little at my disposal.

Haydon being very much in want, I lent him £30 of it. Now in this see-saw game of Life I got nearest to the ground and this chancery business riveted me there so that I was sitting in that uneasy position where the seat slants so abominably. I applied to him for payment—he could not—that was no wonder. But goodman Delver,[23] where was the wonder then, why marry, in this? He did not seem to care much about it and let me go without my money with almost nonchalance when he aught to have sold his drawings to supply me. I shall perhaps still be acquainted with him, but for friendship that is at an end. Brown has been my friend in this; he got him to sign a Bond payable at three Months. Haslam has assisted me with the return of part of the money you lent him. Hunt—"there," says your wife, "there's another of those dull folks—not a syllable about my friends—well, Hunt—what about Hunt, pray? You little thing, see how she bites my finger? My! Is not this a tooth?" Well, when you have done with the tooth, read on—Not a syllable about your friends. Here are some syllables. As far as I could smoke[24] things, on the Sunday before last thus matters stood in Henrietta street. Henry was a greater blade than ever I remember to have seen him. He had on a very nice coat, a becoming waistcoat and buff trowsers. I think his face has lost a little of the spanish-brown, but no flesh. He carv'd some beef exactly to suit my appetite, as if I had been measured for it. As I stood looking out of the window with Charles after dinner, quizzing the Passengers, at which, I am sorry to say he is too apt, I observed that his young son-of-a-gun's whiskers had begun to curl and curl, little twists and twists all down the sides of his face getting properly thickish on the angles of the visage. He certainly will have a notable pair of Whiskers. "How shiny your gown is in front," says Charles, "Why, don't you see 'tis an apron," says Henry, Whereat I scrutiniz'd and behold your mother had a purple stuff gown on, and over it an apron of the same colour, being the same cloth that was used for the lining, and furthermore to account for the shining it was the first day of wearing. I guess'd as much of the Gown, but that is entrenous.[25] Charles likes england better than france. They've got a fat, smiling, fair Cook as ever you saw. She is a little lame, but that improves her; it makes her go more swimmingly. When I ask'd, "Is Mrs. Wylie within?" she gave such a large, five-and-thirty-year-old smile, it made me look round

upon the forth stair—it might have been the fifth—but that's a puzzle. I
shall never be able if I were to set myself a recollecting for a year, to recollect
that. I think I remember two or three specks in her teeth but I really can't
say exactly. Your mother said something about Miss Keasle; what that was is
quite a riddle to me now. Whether she had got fatter or thinner, or broader
or longer, straiter, or had taken to the zigzags; Whether she had taken to, or
left off, asses Milk. That, by the by, she ought never to touch. How much
better it would be to put her out to nurse with the Wise woman of
Brentford.[26] I can say no more on so spare a subject. Miss Millar now is a
different morsel if one knew how to divide and subdivide, theme her out
into sections and subsections—Say a little on every part of her body as it is
divided in common with all her fellow creatures, in Moor's Almanac. But
Alas! I have not heard a word about her, no cue to begin upon. There was
indeed a buzz about her and her mother's being at old Mrs. So and So's *who
was like to die,* as the jews say, but I dare say, keeping up their dialect, *she
was not like to die.* I must tell you a good thing Reynolds *did:* 'twas the best
thing he ever *said.* You know at taking leave of a party at a doorway, sometimes a Man dallies and foolishes and gets awkward, and does not know
how to make off to advantage. Good bye, well, good-bye—and yet he does
not go—good bye and so on—well—good bless you—You know what I
mean. Now Reynolds was in this predicament and got out of it in a very
witty way. He was leaving us at Hampstead. He delay'd, and we were joking
at him and even said, "be off," at which he put the tails of his coat between
his legs, and sneak'd off as nigh like a spanial as could be. He went with flying colours; this is very clever. I must, being upon the subject, tell you another good thing of him; He began, for the service it might be of to him in
the law, to learn french. He had Lessons at the cheap rate of 2.6 per fag[27]
and observed to Brown, "Gad," says he, "the man sells his Lessons so cheap
he must have stolen 'em." You have heard of Hook the farce writer.[28] Horace Smith said to one who ask'd him if he knew Hook, "Oh yes, Hook and
I are very intimate." There's a page of Wit for you to put John Bunyan's
emblems[29] out of countenance.

   Tuesday.[30] You see I keep adding a sheet daily till I send the packet off,
which I shall not do for a few days as I am inclined to write a good deal, for

there can be nothing so remembrancing and enchaining as a good long letter be it composed of what it may. From the time you left me, our friends
say I have altered completely, am not the same person. Perhaps in this letter
I am, for in a letter one takes up one's existence from the time we last met. I
dare say you have altered also; every man does. Our bodies every seven
years are completely fresh-material'd; seven years ago it was not this hand
that clench'd itself against Hammond.[31] We are like the relic garments of a
Saint—the same and not the same—for the careful Monks patch it and
patch it till there's not a thread of the original garment left, and still they
show it for St. Anthony's shirt. This is the reason why men who had been
bosom friends, on being separated for any number of years, afterwards
meet coldly, neither of them knowing why. The fact is they are both altered. Men who live together have a silent moulding and influencing power
over each other. They interassimulate. 'Tis an uneasy thought that in seven
years the same hands cannot greet each other again. All this may be obvi-
ated by a willful and dramatic exercise of our Minds towards each other.
Some think I have lost that poetic ardour and fire 'tis said I once had. The
fact is perhaps I have, but instead of that I hope I shall substitute a more
thoughtful and quiet power. I am more frequently, now, contented to read
and think, but now and then haunted with ambitious thoughts. Quieter in
my pulse, improved in my digestion, exerting myself against vexing speculations, scarcely content to write the best verses for the fever they leave behind. I want to compose without this fever. I hope I one day shall. You
would scarcely imagine I could live alone so comfortably, "Kepen in solitarinesse." I told Anne, the servent here, the other day to say I was not at
home if anyone should call. I am not certain how I should endure loneliness and bad weather together. Now the time is beautiful. I take a walk every day for an hour before dinner and this is generally my walk. I go out at
the back gate across one street, into the Cathedral yard, which is always interesting; then I pass under the trees along a paved path, pass the beautiful
front of the Cathedral, turn to the left under a stone doorway, then I am on
the other side of the building, which leaving behind me I pass on through
two college-like squares seemingly built for the dwelling place of Deans and
Prebendaries, garnished with grass and shaded with trees. Then I pass

through one of the old city gates and then you are in one College Street through which I pass and at the end thereof crossing some meadows and at last a country alley of gardens, I arrive, that is, my worship arrives at the foundation of Saint Cross, which is a very interesting old place, both for its gothic tower and alms-square and for the appropriation of its rich rents to a relation of the Bishop of Winchester. Then I pass across St. Cross meadows till you come to the most beautifully clear river. Now this is only one mile of my walk. I will spare you the other two till after supper when they would do you more good. You must avoid going the first mile just after dinner. I could almost advise you to put by all this nonsense until you are lifted out of your difficulties, but when you come to this part feel with confidence what I now feel, that though there can be no stop put to troubles we are in-heritors of, there can be and must be an end to immediate difficulties. Rest in the confidence that I will not omit any exertion to benefit you by some means or other. If I cannot remit you hundreds, I will tens, and if not that ones. Let the next year be managed by you as well as possible, the next month I mean, for I trust you will soon receive Abbey's remittance. What he can send you will not be a sufficient capital to ensure you any command in America. What he has of mine I nearly have anticipated by debts. So I would advise you not to sink it, but to live upon it in hopes of my being able to increase it. To this end I will devote whatever I may gain for a few years to come, at which period I must begin to think of a security of my own comforts when quiet will become more pleasant to me than the World. Still I would have you doubt my success. 'Tis at present the cast of a die with me. You say, "these things will be a great torment to me." I shall not suffer them to be so. I shall only exert myself the more, while the seri-ousness of their nature will prevent me from missing imaginary griefs. I have not had the blue devils once since I received your last. I am advised not to publish till it is seen whether the Tragedy will or not succeed. Should it, a few months may see me in the way of acquiring property. Should it not, it will be a drawback and I shall have to perform a longer literary Pil-grimage. You will perceive that it is quite out of my interest to come to America. What could I do there? How could I employ myself? Out of the reach of Libraries.

You do not mention the name of the gentleman who assists you.[32] 'Tis an extraordinary thing. How could you do without that assistance? I will not trust myself with brooding over this. The following is an extract from a Letter of Reynolds to me: "I am glad to hear you are getting on so well with your writings. I hope you are not neglecting the revision of your Poems for the press: from which I expect more than you do." The first thought that struck me on reading your last, was to mortgage a Poem to Murray, but on more consideration I made up my mind not to do so. My reputation is very low; he would perhaps not have negociated my bill of intellect or given me a very small sum. I should have bound myself down for some time. 'Tis best to meet present misfortunes, not for a momentary good to sacrifice great benefits which one's own untramell'd and free industry may bring one in the end. In all this do never think of me as in anyway unhappy. I shall not be so. I have a great pleasure in thinking of my responsibility to you and shall do myself the greatest luxury if I can succeed in any way so as to be of assistance to you. We shall look back upon these times—even before our eyes are at all dim—I am convinced of it. But be careful of those Americans. I could almost advise you to come whenever you have the sum of £500 to England. Those Americans will, I am afraid, still fleece you. If ever you should think of such a thing you must bear in mind the very different state of society here—The immense difficulties of the times—The great sum required per annum to maintain yourself in any decency. In fact the whole is with Providence. I know not how to advise you but by advising you to advise with yourself. In your next tell me at large your thoughts about america, what chance there is of succeeding there, for it appears to me you have as yet been somehow deceived. I cannot help thinking Mr. Audubon has deceived you. I shall not like the sight of him. I shall endeavour to avoid seeing him. You see how puzzled I am. I have no meridian to fix you to, being the Slave of what is to happen. I think I may bid you finally remain in good hopes and not tease yourself with my changes and variations of Mind. If I say nothing decisive in any one particular part of my Letter you may glean the truth from the whole pretty correctly. You may wonder why I had not put your affairs with Abbey in train on receiving your Letter before last, to which there will reach you a short answer[33] dated from shanklin. I did write and speak to Abbey but to no purpose. Your last, with the enclosed note has appealed home to him. He will not see the necessity of a thing till he is hit in the mouth. 'Twill be effectual.

I am sorry to mix up foolish and serious things together, but in writing so much I am obliged to do so, and I hope sincerely the tenor of your mind will maintain itself better. In the course of a few months I shall be as good an Italian Scholar as I am a french one. I am reading Ariosto at present, not managing more than six or eight stanzas at a time. When I have done this language so as to be able to read it tolerably well, I shall set myself to get complete in latin and there my learning must stop. I do not think of venturing upon Greek. I would not go even so far if I were not persuaded of the power the knowlege of any language gives one. The fact is I like to be acquainted with foreign languages. It is besides a nice way of filling up intervals, etc. Also the reading of Dante is well worth the while. And in latin there is a fund of curious literature of the middle ages, the Works of many great Men—Aretine and Sanazarius and Machievel. I shall never become attach'd to a foreign idiom so as to put it into my writings. The Paradise lost though so fine in itself is a curruption of our Language. It should be kept as it is, unique, a curiosity, a beautiful and grand Curiosity, the most remarkable Production of the world, a northern dialect accommodating itself to greek and latin inversions and intonations. The purest english I think, or what ought to be the purest, is Chatterton's. The Language had existed long enough to be entirely uncorrupted of Chaucer's gallicisms and still the old words are used. Chatterton's language is entirely northern. I prefer the native music of it to Milton's cut by feet. I have but lately stood on my guard against Milton. Life to him would be death to me. Miltonic verse cannot be written but in the vein of art; I wish to devote myself to another sensation.

I have been obliged to intermiten[34] your Letter for two days (this being Friday morn)[35] from having had to attend to other correspondence. Brown who was at Bedhampton, went thence to Chichester, and I still directing my letters Bedhampton. There arose a misunderstand about them. I began to suspect my Letters had been stopped from curiosity. However, yesterday Brown had four Letters from me all in a Lump and the matter is clear'd up.

Brown complained very much in his Letter to me of yesterday of the great alteration the Disposition of Dilke has undergone; He thinks of nothing but "Political Justice"[36] and his Boy. Now the first political duty a Man ought to have a Mind to is the happiness of his friends. I wrote Brown a comment on the subject, wherein I explained what I thought of Dilke's Character, which resolved itself into this conclusion. That Dilke was a Man who cannot feel he has a personal identity unless he has made up his Mind about everything. The only means of strengthening one's intellect is to make up one's mind about nothing, to let the mind be a thoroughfare for all thoughts. Not a select party. The genus is not scarce in population. All the stubborn arguers you meet with are of the same brood—They never begin upon a subject they have not pre-resolved on. They want to hammer their nail into you and if you turn the point, still they think you wrong. Dilke will never come at a truth as long as he lives because he is always trying at it. He is a Godwin-methodist. I must not forget to mention that your mother show'd me the lock of hair. 'Tis of a very dark colour for so young a creature. When it is two feet in length I shall not stand a barley corn higher. That's not fair; one ought to go on growing as well as others. At the end of this sheet I shall stop for the present and send it off. You may expect another Letter immediately after it. As I never know the day of the month but by chance, I put here that this is *the 24th September.* I would wish you here to stop your ears, for I have a word or two to say to your Wife. My dear sister, In the first place I must quarrel with you for sending me such a shabby sheet of paper, though that is in some degree made up for by the beautiful impression of the seal. You should like to know what I was doing—The first of May—let me see—I cannot recollect. I have all the Examiners ready to send; They will be a great treat to you when they reach you. I shall pack them up when my Business with Abbey has come to a good conclusion and the remittance is on the road to you. I have dealt round your best wishes to our friends like a pack of cards, but being always given to cheat myself, I have turned up ace. You see I am making game of you. I see you are not all happy in that America. England however would not be over happy for us if you were here. Perhaps 'twould be better to be teased here than there. I must preach patience to you both. No step hasty or injurious to you must be taken. Your observation on the moschetos[37] gives me great pleasure. 'Tis excessively poetical and humane. You say let one large sheet be all to me: You will find more than that in different parts of this packet for you. Certainly I have been caught in rains. A Catch in the rain occasioned my last sore throat, but As for red-hair'd girls, upon my word I do not recollect ever having seen one. Are you quizzing me or Miss Waldegrave when you talk of promenading? As for Pun-making, I wish it was as good a trade as pin-making. There is very little business of that sort going on now. We struck for wages like the manchester weavers, but to no purpose, so we are all out of employ. I am more lucky than some you see by having an opportunity of exporting a few, getting into a little foreign trade, which is a comfortable thing. I wish one could get change for a pun in silver currency. I would give three and a half any night to get into Drury-pit, but they won't ring at all. No more will notes you will say, but notes are differing things, though they make together a Pun mote,[38] as the term goes. If I were your Son I shouldn't mind you, though you rapt me with the Scissars. But lord! I should be out of favor sin the little un be comm'd. You have made an Uncle of me, you have, and I don't know what to make of myself. I suppose next there'll be a Nevey. You say—in may last—write directly. I have not received your Letter above 10 days. The thought of you[r] little girl puts me in mind of a thing I heard a Mr. Lamb say. A child in arms was passing by his chair toward the mother in the nurse's arms. Lamb took hold of the long clothes saying, "Where, god bless me, Where does it leave off?"

Saturday. If you would prefer a joke or two to anything else I have two for you fresh hatch'd, just ris as the Baker's wives say by the rolls. The first I play'd off at Brown; the second I play'd *on* on myself. Brown when he left me, "Keats!" says he, "my good fellow (staggering upon his left heel, and fetching an irregular pirouette with his right) "Keats," says he (depressing his left eyebrow and elevating his right one ((tho' by the way, at the moment, I did not know which was the right one)) "Keats," says he (still in the same posture but forthermore both his hands in his waistcoat pockets and jutting out his stomach) "Keats—my—go-o-ood fell o-o-o-ooh!" says he (interlarding his exclamation with certain ventriloquial parentheses)—no, this is all a lie—He was as sober as a Judge when a judge happens to be sober; and said "Keats, if any Letters come for me—Do not forward them, but open them and give me the marrow of them in few words." At the time when I wrote my first to him no Letters had arrived. I thought I would invent one, and as I had not time to manufacture a long one I dabbed off a short one, and that was the reason of the joke succeeding beyond my expectations. Brown let his house to a Mr. Benjamin, a Jew. Now the water which furnishes the house is in a tank sided with a composition of lime and the lime impregnates the water unpleasantly. Taking advantage of this circumstance I pretended that Mr. Benjamin had written the following short note: "Sir. By drinking your damn'd tank water I have got the gravel. What reparation can you make to me and my family? Nathan Benjamin." By a fortunate hit, I hit upon his right hethen name, his right Pronomen. Brown, in consequence it appears, wrote to the surprised Mr. Benjamin the following: "Sir, I cannot offer you any remuneration until your gravel shall have formed itself into a Stone when I will cut you with Pleasure. C. Brown." This of Brown's Mr. Benjamin has answered insisting on an explanation of this singular circumstance. B. says "when I read your Letter and his following I roared, and in came Mr. Snook who on reading them seem'd likely to burst the hoops of his fat sides"—so the Joke has told well. Now for the one I played on myself. I must first give you the scene and the dramatis Personae. There are an old Major and his youngish wife live in the next apartments to me. His bedroom door opens at an angle with my sitting room door. Yesterday I was reading as demurely as a Parish Clerk when I heard a rap at the door. I got up and opened it. No one was to be seen. I listened and heard some one in the Major's room. Not content with this I went upstairs and down, look'd in the cupboards and watch'd. At last I set myself to read again not quite so demurely when there came a louder rap. I arose determined to find out who it was. I look out, the Stair cases were all silent: "This must be the Major's wife," said I, "at all events I will see the truth." So I rapt me at the Major's door and went in to the utter surprise and confusion of the Lady who was in reality there. After a little explanation, which I can no more describe than fly, I made my retreat from her convinced of my mistake. She is to all appearance a silly body and is really surprised about it. She must have been, for I have discovered that a little girl in the house was the Rappee. I assure you she has nearly make me sneeze.[39] If the Lady tells tits I shall put a very grave and moral face on the matter with the old Gentleman, and make his little Boy a present of a humming top.

My Dear George—This Monday morning the 27th I have received your last dated July 12th. You say you have not heard from England these three months. Then my Letter from Shanklin written I think at the end of July cannot have reach'd you. You shall not have cause to think I neglect you. I have kept this back a little time in expectation of hearing from Mr. Abbey. You will say I might have remained in Town to be Abbey's messenger in these affairs. That I offer'd him, but he in his answer convinced me he was anxious to bring the Business to an issue. He observed that by being himself the agent in the whole, people might be more expeditious. You say you have not heard for three months and yet your letters have the tone of knowing how our affairs are situated, by which I conjecture I acquainted you with them in a Letter previous to the Shanklin one. That I may not have done. To be certain I will here state that it is in consequence of Mrs. Jennings threatening a Chancery suit that you have been kept from the receipt of monies and myself deprived of any help from Abbey. I am glad you say you keep up your Spirits. I hope you make a true statement on that score. Still keep them up, for we are all young. I can only repeat here that you shall hear from me again immediately. Notwithstanding their bad intelligence, I have experienced some pleasure in receiving so correctly two Letters from you, as it gives me, if I may so say, a distant Idea of Proximity. This last improves upon my little niece. Kiss her for me. Do not fret yourself about the delay of money on account of any immediate opportunity being lost, for in a new country whoever has money must have opportunity of employing it in many ways. The report runs now more in favor of Kean stopping in England. If he should I have confident hopes of our Tragedy. If he smokes the hot-blooded character of Ludolph—and he is the only actor that can do it—he will add to his own fame, and improve my fortune. I will give you a half dozen lines of it before I part as a specimen:

> "Not as a Swordsman would I pardon crave,
> But as a Son: the bronz'd Centurion
> Long-toil'd in foreign wars, *and whose high deeds*

Are shaded in a forest of tall spears,
Known only to his troop, hath greater plea
Of favour with my Sire than I can have."[40]

Believe me my dear brother and Sister—

Your affectionate and anxious Brother
John Keats

1. Probably the other trustee for the Keats property, appointed by Abbey after the death in 1816 of John Nowland Sandell.
2. *Otho the Great.*
3. George had dealings with the famous naturalist John James Audubon (1785–1851), who suggested that George invest his inheritance money in a riverboat that subsequently sank.
4. That is, 18 September.
5. Ben Jonson, *The Sad Shepherd,* II.viii.53.
6. *Hamlet,* II.ii.188f.
7. The passage is from III.2.iv.1 of Burton's *Anatomy of Melancholy* (1806 edition).
8. "A flat and open nose."
9. Consider whether any better things "lie open" (or whether there are better images of openness).
10. A remedy for love. Ovid wrote a book in elegiac verse on this subject *(Remedia Amoris)* to follow his three books titled *The Art of Love (Ars Amatoria).*
11. Charles Mathews (1776–1835), comedian, friend of Coleridge, the Lambs, James and Horace Smith.
12. *Don Juan,* Canto I, stanza 218.
13. This may be another term for Hodgkinson, from whom Keats had borrowed money previously, or a relative of Abbey in the coffee business.
14. Henry Hunt (1773–1835), political orator, presided at the reform meeting in St. Peter's Fields, Manchester, 16 August 1819, that was broken up by government troops (the "Peterloo Massacre"). He was greeted by an estimated 200,000 people in London after being released on bail.
15. Edward Ottey's tavern in the Strand.
16. Keats copies here the acrostic in addition to a large section of his "Scotch letter" of 23, 26 July to Tom, both with slight variations and additions, omitted here.
17. "Query"?
18. In Fielding's *Tom Jones.*
19. "May it be pleasing to you."
20. *Othello,* I.ii.5.
21. Keats is punning on the name of Henry Fuseli (1741–1825), painter and author, and "fusil," a musket.
22. "Academy" is slang for brothel.

23. *Hamlet*, V.i.14.
24. That is, understand.
25. "Between you and me."
26. *The Merry Wives of Windsor*, IV.v.27.
27. Lesson.
28. Theodore Edward Hook (1788–1841), humorist and novelist.
29. *A Book for Boys and Girls: Or, Country Rhimes for Children* (1686), in later editions called *Divine Emblems*.
30. That is, 21 September.
31. Thomas Hammond, surgeon, of 7 Church Street, Edmonton, with whom Keats quarrelled during his apprenticeship.
32. He was William Bakewell, Audubon's brother-in-law.
33. Now unknown.
34. That is, discontinue.
35. That is, 24 September.
36. By William Godwin (1793).
37. An obsolete form of "mosquitoes."
38. The word is a pun on *bon mot* as well as on "pound note."
39. A pun on "rappee," a kind of snuff.
40. *Otho the Great*, I.iii.24–29.

To C. W. Dilke

I OCTOBER 1819

Winchester, Friday Oct. 1st

My dear Dilke,

For sundry reasons, which I will explain to you when I come to Town, I have to request you will do me a great favor, as I must call it, knowing how great a Bore it is. That your imagination may not have time to take too great an alarm, I state immediately that I want you to hire me a *couple of rooms in Westminster. Quietness and cheapness are the essentials. But as I shall with Brown be returned by next Friday, you cannot in that space have sufficient time to make any choice selection, and need not be very particu-

*A Sitting Room and bed room for myself alone.

lar, as I can when on the spot suit myself at leisure. Brown bids me remind you not to send the Examiners after the third. Tell Mrs. D. I am obliged to her for the late ones which I see are directed in her hand. Excuse this mere business letter, for I assure you I have not a syllable at hand on any subject in the world.

Your sincere friend
John Keats—

To B. R. Haydon (With Charles Brown)
3 OCTOBER 1819

Winchester, Sunday Morn.

My dear Haydon,

Certainly I might,[1] but a few Months pass away before we are aware. I have a great aversion to letter writing which grows more and more upon me; and a greater to summon up circumstances before me of an unpleasant nature. I was not willing to trouble you with them. Could I have dated from my Palace in Milan you would have heard from me. Not even now will I mention a word of my affairs, only that "I Rab am here,"[2] but shall not be here more than a Week more, as I purpose to settle in Town and work my way with the rest. I hope I shall never be so silly as to injure my health and industry for the future by speaking, writing or fretting about my non-estate. I have no quarrel, I assure you, of so weighty a nature with the world on my own account as I have on yours. I have done nothing, except for the amusement of a few people who refine upon their feelings till anything in the ununderstandable way will go down with them, people predisposed for sentiment. I have no cause to complain because I am certain anything really fine will in these days be felt. I have no doubt that if I had written Othello I should have been cheered by as good a Mob as Hunt.[3] So would you be now if the operation of painting was as universal as that of writing. It is not, and therefore it did behoove men I could mention, among whom I must place Sir G. Beaumont, to have lifted you up above sordid cares. That this has not been done is a disgrace to the country. I know very little of Painting, yet your pictures follow me into the Country. When I am tired with reading I often think them over and as often condemn the spirit of modern Connoisseurs. Upon the whole indeed you have no complaint to make, being able to say what so few Men can—"I have succeeded." On sitting down to write a few lines to you these are the uppermost in my mind, and however I may be beating about under the arctic while your spirit has passed the line, you may lay to a minute and consider I am earnest as far as I can see. Though at this present "I have great dispositions to *write,*"[4] I feel every day more and more content to read. Books are becoming more interesting and valuable to me. I may say I could not live without them. If in the course of a fortnight you can procure me a ticket to the british museum I will make a better use of it than I did in the first instance. I shall go on with patience in the confidence that if I ever do anything worth remembering the Reviewers will no more be able to stumbleblock me than the Academy could you. They have the same quarrel with you that the scotch nobles had with Wallace. The fame they have lost through you is no joke to them. Had it not been for you, Fuseli would have been not as he is major but maximus domo. What the Reviewers can put a hindrance to must be a nothing, or mediocre, which is worse. I am sorry to say that since I saw you I have been guilty of a practical Joke upon Brown which has had all the success of an innocent Wild fire among people. Some day in the next week you shall hear it from me by word of Mouth. I have not seen the portentous Book which was scimmer'd[5] at you just as I left town. It may be light enough to serve you as a Cork Jacket and save you for awhile the trouble of swimming. I heard the Man went raking and rummaging about like any Richardson. That and the Memoirs of Menage[6] are the first I shall be at. From Sir G. B.'s, Lord M.'s,[7] and particularly Sir John Leicester's, good lord deliver us. I shall expect to see your Picture plumped out like a ripe Peach. You would not be very willing to give me a slice of it. I came to this place in the hopes of meeting with a Library but was disappointed. The High Street is as quiet as a Lamb; the knockers are dieted to three raps per diem. The walks about are interesting, from the many old Buildings and archways. The view of the high street through the Gate of the City in the beautiful September evening light has amused me frequently. The bad singing of the Cathedral I do not care to smoke. Being by myself I am not very coy in my taste. At St. Cross there is an interesting Picture of Albert Durer's, who living in such warlike times perhaps was forced to paint in his Gauntlets—so we must make all allowances.

I am my dear Haydon

yours ever

John Keats

Brown has a few words to say to you and will cross this.

My dear Sir, I heard yesterday you had written to me at Hampstead. I have not received your letter. You must, I think, accuse me of neglect, but indeed I do not merit it. This many-worded Keats has left me no room to say more. I shall be in Town in a few days.

Your's truly

Chas. Brown.

1. Evidently, "I might have written to you."
2. Burns, "Second Epistle to J. Lapraik," line 60, "I, Rob," etc.
3. Henry Hunt (1773–1835), politician and reformer, who was greeted by immense throngs of people in London after being released from jail.
4. *The Merry Wives of Windsor*, III.i.22, "I have a great dispositions to cry."
5. Perhaps the word means "scumbered, voided (ordure) at."
6. Gilles Ménage, *Menagiana ou les bons mots et remarques critiques, historiques, morales and d'érudition, de Monsieur Menage*, 3d ed., 4 vols. (Paris, 1715).
7. Sir George Beaumont (1753–1827) and Sir Henry Phipps, first earl of Mulgrave (1755–1831), long-suffering patrons of Haydon.

To Fanny Brawne
11 OCTOBER 1819

College Street

My sweet Girl,

I am living today in yesterday. I was in a complete fascination all day. I feel myself at your mercy. Write me ever so few lines and tell me you will never forever be less kind to me than yesterday. You dazzled me. There is nothing in the world so bright and delicate. When Brown came out with that seemingly true story against me last night, I felt it would be death to me if you had ever believed it, though against anyone else I could muster up my obstinacy. Before I knew Brown could disprove it I was for the moment miserable. When shall we pass a day alone? I have had a thousand kisses, for which with my whole soul I thank love, but if you should deny me the thousand and first 'twould put me to the proof how great a misery I could live through. If you should ever carry your threat yesterday into execution, believe me 'tis not my pride, my vanity or any petty passion would torment me; really, 'twould hurt my heart. I could not bear it. I have seen Mrs. Dilke this morning; she says she will come with me any fine day.

Ever yours
John Keats

Ah hertè mine![1]

---

1. This expression occurs often in Chaucer's *Troilus and Criseyde*.

To Fanny Brawne
13 OCTOBER 1819

25 College Street

My dearest Girl,

This moment I have set myself to copy some verses out fair. I cannot proceed with any degree of content. I must write you a line or two and see if that will assist in dismissing you from my Mind for ever so short a time. Upon my Soul I can think of nothing else. The time is passed when I had power to advise and warn you against the unpromising morning of my Life. My love has made me selfish. I cannot exist without you. I am forgetful of everything but seeing you again. My Life seems to stop there; I see no further. You have absorb'd me. I have a sensation at the present moment as though I was dissolving. I should be exquisitely miserable without the hope of soon seeing you. I should be afraid to separate myself far from you. My sweet Fanny, will your heart never change? My love, will it? I have no limit now to my love. Your note came in just here. I cannot be happier away from you; 'tis richer than an Argosy of Pearles. Do not threat me even in jest. I have been astonished that Men could die Martyrs for religion. I have shudder'd at it. I shudder no more. I could be martyr'd for my Religion. Love is my religion. I could die for that; I could die for you. My Creed is Love and you are its only tenet. You have ravish'd me away by a Power I cannot resist, and yet I could resist till I saw you, and even since I have seen you I have endeavoured often "to reason against the reasons of my Love."[1] I can do that no more. The pain would be too great. My Love is selfish. I cannot breathe without you.

Yours forever
John Keats

1. John Ford, *'Tis Pity She's a Whore*, I.iii.78.

To Fanny Brawne
19 OCTOBER 1819

Great Smith Street[1]
Tuesday Morn

My sweet Fanny,

On awakening from my three days dream ("I cry to dream again"),[2] I find one and another astonish'd at my idleness and thoughtlessness. I was miserable last night. The morning is always restorative. I must be busy, or try to be so. I have several things to speak to you of tomorrow morning. Mrs. Dilke I should think will tell you that I purpose living at Hampstead. I must impose chains upon myself. I shall be able to do nothing. I should like to cast the die for Love or death. I have no Patience with anything else. If you ever intend to be cruel to me, as you say in jest now but perhaps may sometime be in earnest, be so now—and I will. My mind is in a tremble, I cannot tell what I am writing.

Ever my love yours
John Keats

1. Dilke's house.
2. *The Tempest*, III.ii.155.

To Fanny Keats
26 (?) OCTOBER 1819

Wentworth Place

My dear Fanny,

My Conscience is always reproaching me for neglecting you for so long a time. I have been returned from Winchester this fortnight and as yet I have not seen you. I have no excuse to offer. I should have no excuse. I shall expect to see you the next time I call on Mr. A about George's affairs which perplex me a great deal. I should have today gone to see if you were in Town, but as I am in an industrious humour (which is so necessary to my livelihood for the future) I am loath to break through it though it be merely for one day, for when I am inclined I can do a great deal in a day. I am more fond of pleasure than study (many men have prefer'd the latter) but I have become resolved to do something which you will credit when I tell you I have left off animal food that my brains may never henceforth be in a greater mist than is theirs by nature. I took Lodgings in Westminster for the purpose of being in the reach of Books, but am now returned to Hampstead, being induced to it by the habit I have acquired of this room I am now in and also from the pleasure of being free from paying any petty attentions to a diminutive housekeeping. Mr. Brown has been my great friend for some time. Without him I should have been in, perhaps, personal distress. As I know you love me though I do not deserve it, I am sure you will take pleasure in being a friend to Mr. Brown even before you know him. My Lodgings for two or three days were close in the neighbourhood of Mrs. Dilke who never sees me but she enquires after you. I have had letters from George lately which do not contain, as I think I told you in my last, the best news. I have hopes for the best. I trust in a good termination to his affairs which you, please god, will soon hear of. It is better you should not be teased with the particulars. The whole amount of the ill news is that his mercantile speculations have not had success in consequence of the general depression of trade in the whole province of Kentucky and indeed all america. I have a couple of shells for you you will call pretty.

Your affectionate Brother
John—

To William Haslam
2 NOVEMBER 1819[1]

Wentworth Place[2]

My dear Haslam,

My disposition is of so careless a nature that it is continually tormenting me for my neglect of matters of consequence. My debt to Sawrey has been of very long standing, and my Character with him must be so low that I really should not like to meet him. I call'd on you a day or two since for the purpose of talking with you on the subject. I need say no more and only have to hope you can almost immediately command £30 to present him with. If you can do this you will ease me of a disease which at intervals comes upon me like a fever fit. I shall have some Cash from Abbey in a short time, and if you should be obliged to borrow the sum I will engage in a short time to set you square with the lender. I shall see you in a few days, I hope a little recover'd from your fatigues, when I will explain why I did no[t] keep my "demi" appointment with you.

Your sincere friend
John Keats

---

1. This letter is printed in full for the first time here. Its whereabouts were unknown at the time of Rollins's edition and he was able to print only two sentences from different sales catalogs. The second sentence is inaccurate in his edition. Happily,

the letter is now in the possession of the Denison Library, Scripps College Campus, Claremont, California.

2. The address on the envelope reads, "Mr. Wm. Haslam, Frampton & Co., Leadenhall Street."

To Joseph Severn
15 NOVEMBER 1819

Wentworth Place
Monday Morn—

My dear Severn,

I am very sorry that on Tuesday I have an appointment in the City of an undeferable nature and Brown on the same day has some business at Guildhall. I have not been able to figure your manner of executing the Cave of despair, therefore it will be at any rate a novelty and surprise to me, I trust on the right side. I shall call upon you some morning shortly early enough to catch you before you can get out, when we will proceed to the Academy. I think you must be suited with a good painting light in your Bay window. I wish you to return the Compliment by going with me to see a Poem I have hung up for the Prize in the Lecture Room of the surry Institution. I have many Rivals: the most threatning are An Ode to Lord Castlereagh, and a new series of Hymns for the New, new Jerusalem Chapel. You had best put me into your Cave of despair.

Ever yours sincerely
John Keats

To John Taylor
17 NOVEMBER 1819

Wentworth Place
Wednesday

My dear Taylor,

I have come to a determination not to publish anything I have now ready written, but for all that to publish a Poem before long and that I hope to make a fine one. As the marvelous is the most enticing and the surest guarantee of harmonious numbers, I have been endeavouring to persuade myself to untether Fancy and let her manage for herself. I and myself cannot agree about this at all. Wonders are no wonders to me. I am more at home amongst Men and women. I would rather read Chaucer than Ariosto. The little dramatic skill I may as yet have, however badly it might show in a Drama, would I think be sufficient for a Poem. I wish to diffuse the colouring of St. Agnes' eve throughout a Poem in which Character and Sentiment would be the figures to such drapery. Two or three such Poems, if God should spare me, written in the course of the next six years, would be a famous gradus ad Parnassum altissimum;[1] I mean they would nerve me up to the writing of a few fine Plays, my greatest ambition when I do feel ambitious. I am sorry to say that is very seldom. The subject we have once or twice talked of appears a promising one, The Earl of Leicester's history. I am this morning reading Holingshed's Elisabeth.[2] You had some Books awhile ago you promised to lend me, illustrative of my Subject. If you can lay hold of them or any others which may be serviceable to me I know you will encourage my low-spirited Muse by sending them or rather by letting me know when our Errand cart Man shall call with my little Box. I will endeavour to set my self selfishly at work on this Poem that is to be—

Your sincere friend
John Keats—

1. "A step toward Parnassus most high." Mount Parnassus is the home of the Muses.
2. Raphael Holinshed, *Chronicles of England, Scotland, and Ireland* (1577).

To James Rice

DECEMBER 1819

Wentworth Place

My dear Rice,

As I want the coat on my back mended, I would be obliged if you will send me the one Brown left at your house, by the Bearer. During your late contest I heard regular reports of you; how that your time was entirely taken up, and your health improving. I shall call in the course of a few days and see whether your promotion has made any difference in your Behaviour to us. I suppose Reynolds has given you an account of Brown and Elliston. As he has not rejected our Tragedy I shall not venture to call him directly a fool, but as he wishes to put it off till next season I can't help thinking him little better than a Knave. That it will not be acted this Season is yet uncertain; perhaps we may give it another furbish and try it at covent Garden. 'Twould do one's heart good to see Macready[1] in Ludolph. If you do not see me soon it will be from the humour of writing, which I have had for three days continuing. I must say to the Muses what the maid says to the Man, "take me while the fit is on me."[2] Would you like a true Story? "There was a Man and his Wife who being to go a long journey on foot, in the course of their travels came to a River which rolled knee deep over the pebbles. In these cases the Man generally pulls off his shoes and stockings and carries the woman over on his Back. This Man did so; and his Wife being pregnant and troubled, as in such cases is very common, with strange longings, took the strangest that ever was heard of. Seeing her Husband's foot, a hansome one enough, look very clean and tempting in the clear water, on their arrival at the other bank she earnestly demanded a bit of it; he being an affectionate fellow and fearing for the comeliness of his child gave her a bit which he cut off with his Clasp knife. Not satisfied, she asked another morsel; supposing there might be twins, he gave her a slice more. Not yet contented, she craved another Piece. 'You Wretch,' cries the Man, 'would you wish me to kill myself? Take that!' Upon which he stabb'd her with the knife, cut her open and found three Children in her Belly, two of them very comfortable with their mouth's shut, the third with its eyes and mouth stark staring open. 'Who would have thought it,' cried the Widower, and pursued his journey." Brown has a little rumbling in his Stomach this morning—

Ever yours sincerely
John Keats—

1. William Charles Macready (1793–1873), actor and manager.
2. Beaumont and Fletcher, *Wit without Money,* V.iv.55.

❦

To Fanny Keats
20 DECEMBER 1819

Wentworth Place
Monday Morn—

My dear Fanny,

When I saw you last, you ask'd me whether you should see me again before Christmas. You would have seen me if I had been quite well. I have not, though not unwell enough to have prevented me—not indeed at all—but fearful lest the weather should affect my throat which on exertion or cold continually threatens me. By the advice of my Doctor I have had a warm great Coat made and have ordered some thick shoes. So furnish'd I shall be with you if it holds a little fine before Christmas day. I have been very busy since I saw you, especially the last Week, and shall be for some time in preparing some Poems to come out in the Spring and also in hightening the interest of our Tragedy. Of the Tragedy I can give you but news semi-good. It is accepted at Drury Lane with a promise of coming out next season. As that will be too long a delay we have determined to get Elliston to bring it out this Season or to transfer it to Covent Garden. This Elliston will not like, as we have every motive to believe that Kean has perceived how suitable the principal Character will be for him. My hopes of success in the literary world are now better than ever. Mr. Abbey, on my calling on him lately, appeared anxious that I should apply myself to something else. He mentioned Tea Brokerage. I supposed he might perhaps mean to give me the Brokerage of his concern, which might be executed with little trouble and a good profit; and therefore said I should have no objection to it especially as at the same time it occured to me that I might make over the business to George. I questioned him about it a few days after. His mind takes odd turns. When I became a Suitor he became coy. He did not seem so much inclined to serve me. He described what I should have to do in the progress of business. It will not suit me. I have given it up. I have not heard again from George which rather disappoints me, as I wish to hear before I make any fresh remittance of his property. I received a note from Mrs. Dilke a few days ago inviting me to dine with her on Xmas day, which I shall do. Mr. Brown and I go on in our old dog trot of Breakfast, dinner (not tea for we have left that off), supper, Sleep, Confab, stirring the fire and reading. Whilst I was in the Country last summer Mrs. Bentley tells me a woman in mourning call'd on me and talk'd something of an aunt of ours. I am so careless a fellow I did not enquire, but will particularly. On Tuesday I am going to hear some Schoolboys Speechify on breaking up day. I'll lay you a pocket piece we shall have "My name is norval."[1] I have not yet look'd for the Letter you mention'd as it is mix'd up in a box full of papers. You must tell me, if you can recollect, the subject of it. This moment Bentley brought a Letter from George for me to deliver to Mrs. Wylie. I shall see her and it before I see you. The direction was in his best hand, written with a good Pen and sealed with a Tassi's Shakespeare such as I gave you. We judge of people's hearts by their Countenances; may we not judge of Letters in the same way? If so, the Letter does not contain unpleasant news. Good or bad spirits have an effect on the handwriting. This direction is at least unnervous and healthy. Our Sister is also well, or George would have made strange work with K's and W's. The little Baby is well or he would have formed precious vowels and Consonants. He sent off the Letter in a hurry, or the mail bag was rather a warm birth, or he has worn out his Seal, for the Shakespeare's head is flattened a little. This is close muggy weather as they say at the Ale houses.

I am, ever, my dear Sister

Yours affectionately

John Keats—

1. The opening line of *Douglas,* the once famous tragedy by John Home (1722–1808).

1820

To Georgiana Wylie Keats
13, 15, 17, 28 JANUARY 1820

Thursday, Jan. 13th 1820—

My dear Sister,

By the time you receive this your troubles will be over. I wish you knew they were half over, I mean that George is safe in England and in good health. To write to you by him is almost like following one's own Letter in the Mail. That it may not be quite so I will leave common intelligence out of the question and write wide of him as I can. I fear I must be dull having had no good-natured flip from fortune's finger since I saw you, and no side way comfort in the success of my friends. I could almost promise that if I had the means I would accompany George back to america and pay you a Visit of a few Months. I should not think much of the time or my absence from my Books, or I have no right to think, for I am very idle. But then I ought to be diligent and at least keep myself within the reach of materials for diligence. Diligence! That I do not mean to say; I should say dreaming over my Books, or rather other people's Books. George has promised to bring you to England when the five years have elapsed. I regret very much that I shall not be able to see you before that time; and even then I must hope that your affairs will be in so prosperous a way as to induce you to stop longer. Yours is a hardish fate to be so divided from your friends and settled among a people you hate. You will find it improve. You have a heart that will take hold of your Children. Even George's absence will make things better. His return will banish what must be your greatest sorrow and at the same time minor ones with it. Robinson Crusoe when he saw himself in danger of perishing on the Waters look'd back to his island as to the haven of his Happiness and on gaining it once more was more content with his Solitude.

We smoke George about his little Girl. He runs the common beaten road of every father, as I dare say you do of every Mother. There is no Child like his Child; so original! Original forsooth. However, I take you at your words. I have a lively faith that yours is the very gem of all Children—Ain't I its Unkle? On Henry's Marriage there was a piece of Bride cake sent me. It miss'd its way. I suppose the Carrier or Coachman was a Conjurer and wanted it for his own private use. Last Sunday George and I dined at Millar's. There were your Mother and Charles with Fool Lacon, Esq. who sent the sly disinterested Shawl to Miss Millar with his own heathen name engraved in the Middle. Charles had a silk Handkerchief belonging to a Miss Grover with whom he pretended to be smitten and for her sake kept exhibiting and adoring the Handkerchief all the evening. Fool Lacon, Esq. treated it with a little venturesome trembling Contumely, whereon Charles set him quietly down on the floor, from where he as quietly got up. This process was repeated at supper time, when your Mother said, "if I were you Mr. Lacon, I would not let him do so." Fool Lacon, Esq. did not offer any remark. He will undoubtedly die in his bed. Your Mother did not look quite so well on Sunday. Mrs. Henry Wylie is excessively quiet before people; I hope she is always so.

Yesterday we dined at Taylor's in Fleet Street. George left early after dinner to go to Deptford. He will make all square there for me. I could not go with him. I did not like the amusement. Haslam is a very good fellow indeed; he has been excessively anxious and kind to us. But is this fair? He has an inamorata at Deptford and he has been wanting me for some time past to see her. This is a thing which it is impossible not to shirk. A Man is like a Magnet, he must have a repelling end. So how am I to see Haslam's lady and family if I even went, for by the time I got to greenwich I should have repell'd them to Blackheath and by the time I got to Deptford, they would be on Shooters hill. When I came to shooters Hill, they would alight at Chatham, and so on till I drove them into the Sea, which I think might be inditeable.

The Evening before yesterday we had a piano forte hop at Dilkes. There was very little amusement in the room but a Scotchman to hate. Some people you must have observed have a most unpleasant effect upon you when you see them speaking in profile. This Scotchman is the most accomplish'd fellow in this way I ever met with. The effect was complete. It went down like a dose of bitters and I hope will improve my digestion. At Taylor's too there was a Scotchman, not quite so bad for he was as clean as he could get himself. Not having succeeded at Drury Lane with our Tragedy, we have been making some alterations and are about to try Covent Garden. Brown has just done patching up the Copy, as it is altered. The only reliance I had on it was in Kean's acting. I am *not* afraid it will be damn'd in the Garden. You said in one of your Letters that there was nothing but Haydon and Co. in mine. There can be nothing of him in this for I never see him or Co. George has introduc'd to us an American of the Name of Hart. I like him in a Modrate way. He was at Mrs. Dilke's party, and sitting by me, we begun talking about english and american ladies. The Miss Reynolds' and some of their friends made not a very inticing row opposite us. I bade him mark them and form his Judgement of them. I told him I hated Englishmen because they were the only Men I knew. He does not understand this. Who would be Braggadocio to Johnny Bull? Johnny's house is his Castle, and a precious dull Castle it is. What a many Bull Castles there are in So-and-So Crescent.

I never wish myself an unvers'd visitor and newsmonger but when I write to you. I should like for a day or two to have somebody's knowledge, Mr. Lacon's for instance, of all the different folks of a wide acquaintance to tell you about. Only let me have his knowledge of family minutiae and I would set them in a proper light, but bless me I never go anywhere. My pen is no more garrulous than my tongue. Any third person would think I was addressing myself to a Lover of Scandal. But we know we do not love scandal but fun, and if Scandal happens to be fun that is no fault of ours. There were very pretty pickings for me in George's Letters about the Prairie Settlement, if I had had any taste to turn them to account in England. I knew a friend of Miss Andrews yet I never mention'd her to him, for after I had read the letter I really did not recollect her Story. Now I have been sitting here a half hour with my invention at work to say something about your

Mother or Charles or Henry but it is in vain. I know not what to say. Three nights since George went with your Mother to the play. I hope she will soon see mine acted. I do not remember ever to have thank'd you for your tassels to my Shakespeare; there he hangs so ably supported opposite me. I thank you now. It is a continual memento of you. If you should have a Boy do not christen him John,[1] and persuade George not to let his partiality for me come across. 'Tis a bad name and goes against a Man. If my name had been Edmund[2] I should have been more fortunate. I was surprised to hear of the State of Society[3] at Louisville; it seems you are just as rediculous there as we are here—threepenny parties, half penny Dances. The best thing I have heard of is your Shooting, for it seems you follow the Gun. Give my Compliments to Mrs. Audubon and tell her I cannot think her either good-looking or honest. Tell Mr. Audubon he's a fool and Briggs that 'tis well I was not Mr. A.

Saturday, Jan. 15. It is strange that George having to stop so short a time in England I should not have seen him for nearly two days. He has been to Haslam's and does not encourage me to follow his example. He had given promise to dine with the same party tomorrow, but has sent an excuse which I am glad of as we shall have a pleasant party with us tomorrow. We expect Charles here today. This is a beautiful day; I hope you will not quarrel with it if I call it an american one. The Sun comes upon the snow and makes a prettier candy than we have on twelfth cakes. George is busy this morning in making copies of my verses. He is making now one of an Ode to the nightingale, which is like reading an account of the black hole at Calcutta on an ice bergh. You will say this is a matter of course, I am glad it is, I mean that I should like your Brothers more, the more I know them. I should spend much more time with them if our lives were more run in parallel, but we can talk but on one subject—that is you. The more I know of Men the more I know how to value entire liberality in any of them. Thank God there are a great many who will sacrifice their worldly interest for a friend. I wish there were more who would sacrifice their passions. The worst of Men are those whose self interests are their passion; the next those whose passions are their self-interest. Upon the whole I dislike Mankind.

Whatever people on the other side of the question may advance they cannot deny that they are always surprised at hearing of a good action and
never of a bad one. I am glad you have something to like in America,
Doves. Gertrude of Wyoming[4] and Birkbeck's book[5] should be bound up
together like a Brace of Decoy Ducks; one is almost as poetical as the other.
Precious miserable people at the Prairie. I have been sitting in the Sun
whilst I wrote this till it became quite oppressive; this is very odd for January. The vulcan fire is the true natural heat for Winter. The Sun has nothing to do in winter but to give a "little grooming light much like a Shade."[6]
Our irish servant has piqued me this morning by saying that her Father in
Ireland was very much like my Shakespeare[7] only he had more color than
the Engraving. You will find on George's return that I have not been neglecting your affairs. The delay was unfortunate, not faulty; perhaps by this
time you have received my three last letters, not one of which had reach'd
you before George sail'd. I would give two pence to have been over the
world as much as he has. I wish I had money enough to do nothing but
travel about for years. Were you now in England I dare say you would be
able (setting aside the pleasure you would have in seeing your mother) to
suck out more amusemement for Society than I am able to do. To me it is
all as dull here as Louisville could be. I am tired of the Theatres. Almost all
the parties I may chance to fall into I know by heart. I know the different
Styles of talk in different places, what subjects will be started, how it will
proceed like an acted play from the first to the last Act. If I go to Hunt's I
run my head into manytimes heard puns and music; to Haydon's worn out
discourses of poetry and painting. The Miss Reynolds I am afraid to speak
to for fear of some sickly reiteration of Phrase or Sentiment. When they were
at the dance the other night I tried manfully to sit near and talk to them,
but to no purpose, and if I had 'twould have been to no purpose still. My
question or observation must have been an old one, and the rejoinder very
antique indeed. At Dilke's I fall foul of Politics. 'Tis best to remain aloof
from people and like their good parts without being eternally troubled with
the dull processes of their everyday Lives. When once a person has smok'd
the vapidness of the routine of Society he must have either self-interest or

the love of some sort of distinction to keep him in good humour with it. All I can say is that standing at Charing cross and looking east, west, north and south I can see nothing but dullness. I hope while I am young to live retired in the Country. When I grow in years and have a right to be idle I shall enjoy cities more. If the American Ladies are worse than the English they must be very bad. You say you should like your Emily brought up here. You had better bring her up yourself. You know a good number of english Ladies; what encomium could you give of half a dozen of them? The greater part seem to me downright American. I have known more than one Mrs. Audubon. Their affection of fashion and politeness cannot transcend ours. Look at our Cheapside Tradesmans' sons and daughters—only fit to be taken off by a plague. I hope now soon to come to the time when I shall never be forc'd to walk through the City and hate as I walk.

Monday, Jan. 17 George had a quick rejoinder to his Letter of excuse to Haslam so we had not his company yesterday which I was sorry for, as there was our old set. I know three witty people all distinct in their excellence: Rice, Reynolds and Richards. Rice is the wisest, Reynolds the playfullest, Richards the out o' the wayest. The first makes you laugh and think, the second makes you laugh and not think, the third puzzles your head. I admire the first, I enjoy the second, I stare at the third. The first is Claret, the second Ginger beer, the third Crême de Bzrapqmdrag. The first is inspired by Minerva, the second by Mercury, the third by Harlequin Epigram, Esq. The first is neat in his dress, the second slovenly, the third uncomfortable. The first speaks adagio, the second alegretto, the third both together. The first is swiftean, the second Tom cribean,[8] the third Shandean, and yet these three Eans are not three Eans but one Ean. Charles came on Saturday, but went early. He seems to have schemes and plans and wants to get off. He is quite right, I am glad to see him employed at his years. You remember I wrote you a Story about a woman named Alice being made young again or some such stuff. In your next Letter tell me whether I gave it as my own or whether I gave it as a matter Brown was employed upon at the time. He read it over to George the other day, and George said he had heard it all before. So Brown suspects I have been giving You his Story as my own. I should like to set him right in it by your Evidence. George has not return'd from Town. When he does I shall tax his memory. We had a young, long, raw, lean Scotchman with us yesterday, called Thornton. Rice for fun or for mistake would persist in calling him Stevenson. I know three people of no wit at all, each distinct in his excellence: A, B and C. A is the foolishest, B the sulkiest, C is a negative. A makes you yawn, B makes you hate, as for C you never see him though he is six feet high. I bear the first; I forbear the second; I am not certain that the third is. The first is gruel, the Second Ditch water, the third is spilt. He ought to be wip'd up. A is inspired by Jack o' the Clock; B has been dull'd by a russian Sargeant; C they say is not his Mother's true Child but that she bought him of the Man who cries "young Lambs to sell."

   T wang dillo dee.[9] This you must know is the Amen to nonsense. I know many places where Amen should be scratched out, rubb'd over with pounce made of Momus's[10] little finger bones, and in its place "T wang-dillo-dee" written. This is the word I shall henceforth be tempted to write at the end of most modern Poems. Every American Book ought to have it. It would be a good distinction in Society. My Lords Wellington, Castlereagh and Canning and many more would do well to wear T wang-dillo-dee written on their Backs instead of wearing ribbands in their Buttonholes. How many people would go sideways along walls and quickset hedges to keep their T wang dillo dee out of sight, or wear large pigtails to hide it? However there would be so many that the T wang dillo dees would keep one another in Countenance, which Brown cannot do for me. I have fallen away lately. Thieves and Murderers would gain rank in the world, for would any one of them have the poorness of Spirit to condescend to be a T wang dillo dee? "I have robb'd in many a dwelling house, I have kill'd many a fowl, many a goose and many a Man," (would such a gentleman say) "but thank heaven I was never yet a T wang dillo dee." Some philosophers in the Moon who spy at our Globe as we do at theirs say that T wang dillo dee is written in large Letters on our Globe of Earth. They say the beginning of the T is just on the spot where London stands, London being built within the Flourish; *wan* reaches downward and slant as far as Tumbutoo in africa;

the tail of the G. goes slap across the Atlantic into the Rio della Plata; the remainder of the Letters wrap round new holland, and the last e terminates on land we have not yet discovered. However I must be silent. These are dangerous times to libel a man in, much more a world.

Friday 27th[11] I wish you would call me names. I deserve them so much. I have only written two sheets for you to carry by George, and those I forgot to bring to town and have therefore to forward them to Liverpool. George went this morning at 6 o'Clock by the Liverpool Coach. His being on his journey to you, prevents me regretting his short stay. I have no news of any sort to tell you. Henry is wife-bound in Camden Town; there is no getting him out. I am sorry he has not a prettier wife; indeed 'tis a shame. She is not half a wife. I think I could find some of her relations in Buffon, or Capt. Cook's voyages, or the hie*rogue*glyphics in Moor's almanack, or upon a chinese Clock door, the Shepherdesses on her own mantlepiece, or in a *cruel* sampler in which she may find herself worsted, or in a dutch toyshop window, or one of the Daughters in the Ark, or in any picture shop window. As I intend to retire into the Country where there will be no sort of news, I shall not be able to write you very long Letters. Besides I am afraid the Postage comes to too much, which till now I have not been aware of. We had a fine Packing up at {. . .} other things I saw {. . .}.[12] People in military Bands are generally seriously occupied. None may or can laugh at their work but the Kettle Drums, Long drum, D° Triangle, and Cymbals. Thinking you might want a Rat-catcher, I put your mother's old quaker-colour'd Cat into the top of your bonnet. She's wi' kitten, so you may expect to find a whole family. I hope the family will not grow too large for its Lodging. I shall send you a close-written Sheet on the first of next Month, but for fear of missing the Liverpool Post I must finish here. God bless you and your little Girl.

Your affectionate Brother
John Keats—

1. Advice that Georgiana did not follow.
2. The name of Fanny Brawne Lindon's first child.

3. Spelled "Saciety" throughout the letter.
4. A poem dealing with Pennsylvania by Thomas Campbell (1777–1844).
5. Morris Birkbeck, *Notes on a Journey in America from the Coast of Virginia to the Territory of Illinois* (1818).
6. *The Faerie Queen*, I.i.14.
7. The tasseled picture mentioned above and in earlier letters.
8. Thomas Moore, *Tom Crib's Memorial to Congress.*
9. Nonsense refrain to a number of popular songs of the day.
10. The spirit of satire.
11. Friday was the 28th.
12. About twenty words are missing in these two places.

To Fanny Brawne
4 (?) FEBRUARY 1820

Dearest Fanny,

I shall send this the moment you return. They say I must remain confined to this room for some time. The consciousness that you love me will make a pleasant prison of the house next to yours. You must come and see me frequently—this evening, without fail—when you must not mind about my speaking in a low tone for I am ordered to do so, though I *can* speak out.

Yours ever
sweetest love
J Keats

turn over

Perhaps your Mother is not at home and so you must watch till she
comes. You must see me tonight and let me hear you promise to come
tomorrow. Brown told me you were all out. I have been looking for the
Stage the whole afternoon. Had I known this, I could not have
remain'd so silent all day.

To Fanny Keats

6 FEBRUARY 1820

Wentworth Place
Sunday Morning

My dear Sister,

I should not have sent those Letters[1] without some notice if Mr. Brown had not persuaded me against it on account of an illness with which I was attacked on Thursday.[2] After that I was resolved not to write till I should be on the mending hand. Thank God, I am now so. From imprudently leaving off my great coat in the thaw I caught cold which flew to my Lungs. Every remedy that has been applied has taken the desired effect, and I have nothing now to do but stay within doors for some time. If I should be confined long I shall write to Mr. Abbey to ask permission for you to visit me. George has been running great chance of a similar attack, but I hope the sea air will be his Physician in case of illness. The air out at sea is always more temperate than on land. George mentioned in his Letters to us something of Mr. Abbey's regret concerning the silence kept up in his house. It is entirely the fault of his Manner.

You must be careful always to wear warm cloathing not only in frost but in a Thaw. I have no news to tell you. The half-built houses opposite us stand just as they were and seem dying of old age before they are brought up. The grass looks very dingy, the Celery is all gone, and there is nothing to enliven one but a few Cabbage Stalks that seem fix'd on the superannuated List. Mr. Dilke has been ill but is better. Several of my friends have been to see me. Mrs. Reynolds was here this morning and the two Mr. Wylies. Brown has been very alert about me, though a little wheezy himself this weather. Everybody is ill. Yesterday evening Mr. Davenport, a gentleman of hampstead, sent me an invitation to supper instead of his coming to see us, having so bad a cold he could not stir out. So you see 'tis the weather and I am among a thousand. Whenever you have an inflammatory fever never mind about eating. The day on which I was getting ill I felt this fever to a great height, and therefore almost entirely abstained from food the whole day. I have no doubt experienc'd a benefit from so doing. The Papers I see are full of anecdotes of the late king;[3] how he nodded to a Coal-heaver and laugh'd with a Quaker and lik'd boil'd Leg of Mutton. Old Peter Pindar is just dead. What will the old king and he say to each other? Perhaps the king may confess that Peter was in the right, and Peter maintain himself to have been wrong. You shall hear from me again on tuesday.

Your affectionate Brother
John

1. Probably from George Keats.
2. That is, 3 February, the date of the hemorrhage, which, according to Brown's *Life of John Keats,* made Keats exclaim: "I know the colour of that blood; it is arterial blood; I cannot be deceived in that colour; that drop of blood is my death-warrant; I must die."
3. George III died on 29 January.

To Fanny Keats
8 FEBRUARY 1820

Wentworth Place
Tuesday morn.

My dear Fanny,

I had a slight return of fever last night, which terminated favourably, and I am now tolerably well, though weak from small quantity of food to which I am obliged to confine myself. I am sure a mouse would starve upon it. Mrs. Wylie came yesterday. I have a very pleasant room for a sick person. A Sopha bed is made up for me in the front Parlour which looks on to the grass plot as you remember Mrs. Dilke's does. How much more comfortable than a dull room upstairs, where one gets tired of the pattern of the bed curtains. Besides, I see all that passes. For instance, now, this morning, if I had been in my own room I should not have seen the coals brought in. On sunday between the hours of twelve and one I descried a Pot boy. I conjectured it might be the one o' Clock beer. Old women with bobbins and red cloaks and unpresuming bonnets I see creeping about the heath; Gipseys after hare skins and silver spoons. Then goes by a fellow with a wooden clock under his arm that strikes a hundred and more. Then comes the old french emigrant (who has been very well-to-do in france) with his hands joined behind on his hips, and his face full of political schemes. Then passes Mr. David Lewis, a very good-natured, good-looking old gentleman who has been very kind to Tom and George and me. As for those fellows the Brick-makers they are always passing to and fro. I musn't forget the two old maiden Ladies in well walk who have a Lap dog between them that they are very anxious about. It is a corpulent Little Beast whom it is necessary to coax along with an ivory-tipp'd cane. Carlo, our Neighbour Mrs. Brawne's dog, and it meet sometimes. Lappy thinks Carlo a devil of a fellow and so do his Mistresses. Well they may. He would sweep 'em all down at a run; all for the Joke of it. I shall desire him to peruse the fable of the Boys and the frogs, though be prefers the tongues and the Bones.[1] You shall hear from me again the day after tomorrow.

Your affectionate Brother

John Keats

1. *A Midsummer Night's Dream,* IV.i.32, "the tongs and the bones."

※
————

To Fanny Brawne
10 (?) FEBRUARY 1820

My dearest Girl,

If illness makes such an agreeable variety in the manner of your eyes I should wish you sometimes to be ill. I wish I had read your note before you went last night that I might have assured you how far I was from suspecting any coldness. You had a just right to be a little silent to one who speaks so plainly to you. You must believe, you shall, you will, that I can do nothing, say nothing, think nothing of you but what has its spring in the Love which has so long been my pleasure and torment. On the night I was taken ill when so violent a rush of blood came to my Lungs that I felt nearly suffocated, I assure you I felt it possible I might not survive and at that moment thought of nothing but you. When I said to Brown, "this is unfortunate," I thought of you. 'Tis true that since the first two or three days other subjects have entered my head. I shall be looking forward to Health and the Spring and a regular routine of our old Walks. Your affectionate,

JK—

To Fanny Brawne
FEBRUARY (?) 1820

My sweet love,

I shall wait patiently till tomorrow before I see you and in the meantime, if there is any need of such a thing, assure you by your Beauty, that whenever I have at any time written on a certain unpleasant subject, it has been with your welfare impress'd upon my mind. How hurt I should have been had you ever acceded to what is, notwithstanding, very reasonable! How much the more do I love you from the general result![1] In my present state of Health I feel too much separated from you and could almost speak to you in the words of Lorenzo's Ghost to Isabella:

> Your Beauty grows upon me and I feel
> A greater love through all my essence steal.[2]

My greatest torment since I have known you has been the fear of you being a little inclined to the Cressid, but that suspicion I dismiss utterly and remain happy in the surety of your Love, which I assure you is as much a wonder to me as a delight. Send me the words "Good night" to put under my pillow.

Dearest Fanny,
Your affectionate
J. K.

1. Keats is referring to his earlier suggestion that they break their engagement.
2. "Isabella," xl.7f.

To Fanny Keats

14 FEBRUARY 1820

Wentworth Place
Monday Morn—

My dear Fanny,

I am improving but very gradually and suspect it will be a long while before I shall be able to walk six miles. The Sun appears half inclined to shine; if he obliges us I shall take a turn in the garden this morning. No one from Town has visited me since my last. I have had so many presents of jam and jellies that they would reach side by side the length of the sideboard. I hope I shall be well before it is all consumed. I am vex'd that Mr. Abbey will not allow you pocket money sufficient. He has not behaved well. By detaining money from me and George when we most wanted it he has increased our expences. In consequence of such delay George was obliged to take his voyage to england which will be £150 out of his Pocket. I enclose you a Note. You shall hear from me again the day after tomorrow.

Your affectionate Brother
John

To Fanny Brawne
FEBRUARY (?) 1820

My dearest Girl,

According to all appearances I am to be separated from you as much as possible. How I shall be able to bear it, or whether it will not be worse than your presence now and then, I cannot tell. I must be patient, and in the meantime you must think of it as little as possible. Let me not longer detain you from going to Town. There may be no end to this emprisoning of you. Perhaps you had better not come before tomorrow evening. Send me however without fail a good night. You know our situation. What hope is there if I should be recover'd ever so soon? My very health will not suffer me to make any great exertion. I am recommended not even to read poetry, much less write it. I wish I had even a little hope. I cannot say forget me, but I would mention that there are impossibilities in the world. No more of this. I am not strong enough to be weaned. Take no notice of it in your good night. Happen what may I shall ever be my dearest Love,

Your affectionate
J—K—

To Fanny Brawne
FEBRUARY (?) 1820

My dearest Girl,

How could it ever have been my wish to forget you? How could I have said such a thing? The utmost stretch my mind has been capable of was to endeavour to forget you for your own sake seeing what a chance there was of my remaining in a precarious state of health. I would have borne it as I would bear death if fate was in that humour, but I should as soon think of choosing to die as to part from you. Believe too, my Love, that our friends think and speak for the best, and if their best is not our best it is not their fault.[1] When I am better I will speak with you at large on these subjects, if there is any occasion. I think there is none. I am rather nervous today perhaps from being a little recovered and suffering my mind to take little excursions beyond the doors and windows. I take it for a good sign, but as it must not be encouraged you had better delay seeing me till tomorrow. Do not take the trouble of writing much; merely send me my goodnight. Remember me to your Mother and Margaret. Your affectionate

J—K—

1. He refers very temperately to friends who disapproved of their engagement.

To Fanny Brawne
FEBRUARY (?) 1820

My dearest Fanny,

Then[1] all we have to do is to be patient. Whatever violence I may sometimes do myself by hinting at what would appear to anyone but ourselves a matter of necessity, I do not think I could bear any approach of a thought of losing you. I slept well last night, but cannot say that I improve very fast. I shall expect you tomorrow, for it is certainly better that I should see you seldom. Let me have your good night. Your affectionate

J—K—

1. That is, evidently, if she does not wish to break their engagement.

To James Rice

14, 16 FEBRUARY 1820

Wentworth Place
Monday Morn.

My dear Rice,

　I have not been well enough to make any tolerable rejoinder to your kind Letter. I will as you advise be very chary of my health and spirits. I am sorry to hear of your relapse and hypochondriac symptoms attending it. Let us hope for the best as you say. I shall follow your example in looking to the future good rather than brooding upon present ill. I have not been so worn with lengthen'd illnesses as you have, therefore cannot answer you on your own ground with respect to those haunting and deformed thoughts and feelings you speak of. When I have been or supposed myself in health I have had my share of them, especially within this last year. I may say that for 6 Months before I was taken ill I had not passed a tranquil day, either that gloom overspread me or I was suffering under some passionate feeling, or if I turn'd to versify that acerbated the poison of either sensation. The Beauties of Nature had lost their power over me. How astonishingly (here I must premise that illness as far as I can judge in so short a time has relieved my Mind of a load of deceptive thoughts and images and makes me perceive things in a truer light), how astonishingly does the chance of leaving the world impress a sense of its natural beauties on us. Like poor Falstaff, though I do not babble, I think of green fields.[1] I muse with the greatest affection on every flower I have known from my infancy. Their shapes and colours are as new to me as if I had just created them with a superhuman fancy. It is because they are connected with the most thoughtless and happiest moments of our Lives. I have seen foreign flowers in hothouses of the most beautiful nature, but I do not care a straw for them. The simple flowers of our spring are what I want to see again.

Brown has left the inventive and taken to the imitative art. He is doing his forte which is copying Hogarth's heads. He has just made a purchase of the methodist meeting Picture, which gave me a horrid dream a few nights ago. I hope I shall sit under the trees with you again in some such place as the isle of Wight. I do not mind a game at cards in a saw pit or wagon, but if ever you catch me on a stage coach in the winter full against the wind bring me down with a brace of bullets and I promise not to "peach."[2] Remember me to Reynolds and say how much I should like to hear from him, that Brown returned immediately after he went on Sunday, and that I was vex'd at forgetting to ask him to lunch, for as he went towards the gate I saw he was fatigued and hungry.

I am

my dear Rice

ever most sincerely yours

John Keats

I have broken this open to let you know I was surprised at seeing it on the table this morning, thinking it had gone long ago.

1. *Henry V,* II.iii.17f.
2. *1 Henry IV,* II.ii.47, "I'll peach for this"; "to peach": to inform against an accomplice; to turn informer.

⚜

To Fanny Brawne

FEBRUARY (?) 1820

My dearest Fanny,

I read your note in bed last night, and that might be the reason of my sleeping so much better. I think Mr. Brown is right in supposing you may stop too long with me, so very nervous as I am. Send me every evening a written Good night. If you come for a few minutes about six it may be the best time. Should you ever fancy me too low-spirited I must warn you to ascribe it to the medicine I am at present taking which is of a nerve-shaking nature. I shall impute any depression I may experience to this cause. I have been writing with a vile old pen the whole week, which is excessively ungallant. The fault is in the Quill. I have mended it and still it is very much inclin'd to make blind e's. However these last lines are in a much better style of penmanship though a little disfigured by the smear of black currant jelly, which has made a little mark on one of the Pages of Brown's Ben Jonson, the very best book he has. I have lick'd it but it remains very purple. I did not know whether to say purple or blue, so in the mixture of the thought wrote purplue which may be an excellent name for a colour made up of those two, and would suit well to start next spring. Be very careful of open doors and windows and going without your duffle grey. God bless you, Love!

J. Keats—

P.S. I am sitting in the back room. Remember me to your Mother.

To Fanny Brawne
FEBRUARY (?) 1820

My dear Fanny,

Do not let your mother suppose that you hurt me by writing at night. For some reason or other your last night's note was not so treasureable as former ones. I would fain that you call me *Love* still. To see you happy and in high spirits is a great consolation to me. Still let me believe that you are not half so happy as my restoration would make you. I am nervous, I own, and may think myself worse than I really am. If so you must indulge me, and pamper with that sort of tenderness you have manifested towards me in different Letters. My sweet creature, when I look back upon the pains and torments I have suffer'd for you from the day I left you to go to the Isle of Wight, the ecstasies in which I have pass'd some days and the miseries in their turn, I wonder the more at the Beauty which has kept up the spell so fervently. When I send this round I shall be in the front parlour watching to see you show yourself for a minute in the garden. How illness stands as a barrier betwixt me and you! Even if I was well, I must make myself as good a Philosopher as possible. Now I have had opportunities of passing nights anxious and awake I have found other thoughts intrude upon me. "If I should die," said I to myself, "I have left no immortal work behind me, nothing to make my friends proud of my memory, but I have lov'd the principle of beauty in all things, and if I had had time I would have made myself remember'd." Thoughts like these came very feebly whilst I was in health and every pulse beat for you. Now you divide with this (may *I* say it?) "last infirmity of noble minds"[1] all my reflection.

God bless you, Love,
J. Keats

1. A misquotation of Milton's "Lycidas," line 71.

To Fanny Brawne
FEBRUARY (?) 1820

My dearest Girl,

You spoke of having been unwell in your last note. Have you recover'd? That Note has been a great delight to me. I am stronger than I was. The Doctors say there is very little the matter with me, but I cannot believe them till the weight and tightness of my Chest is mitigated. I will not indulge or pain myself by complaining of my long separation from you. God alone knows whether I am destined to taste of happiness with you. At all events I myself know thus much, that I consider it no mean Happiness to have lov'd you thus far. If it is to be no further I shall not be unthankful. If I am to recover, the day of my recovery shall see me by your side from which nothing shall separate me. If well you are the only medicine that can keep me so. Perhaps, aye, surely I am writing in too depress'd a state of mind. Ask your Mother to come and see me; she will bring you a better account than mine.

Ever your affectionate
John Keats—

To Fanny Brawne
24 (?) FEBRUARY 1820

My dearest Girl,

Indeed I will not deceive you with respect to my Health. This is the fact as far as I know. I have been confined three weeks and am not yet well. This proves that there is something wrong about me which my constitution will either conquer or give way to. Let us hope for the best. Do you hear the Thrush singing over the field? I think it is a sign of mild weather—so much the better for me. Like all Sinners now I am ill, I philosophise, aye, out of my attachment to everything, Trees, flowers, Thrushes, Spring, Summer, Claret, etc., etc.—aye, everything but you. My Sister would be glad of my company a little longer. That Thrush is a fine fellow. I hope he was fortunate in his choice this year. Do not send any more of my Books home. I have a great pleasure in the thought of you looking on them.

Ever yours
my sweet Fanny
J—K—

To Fanny Brawne
27 (?) FEBRUARY 1820

My dearest Fanny,

I had a better night last night than I have had since my attack, and this morning I am the same as when you saw me. I have been turning over two volumes of Letters written between Rousseau and two Ladies in the perplexed strain of mingled finesse and sentiment in which the Ladies and gentlemen of those days were so clever, and which is still prevalent among Ladies of this Country who live in a state of reasoning romance. The Likeness however only extends to the mannerism not to the dexterity. What would Rousseau have said at seeing our little correspondence! What would his Ladies have said! I don't care much. I would sooner have Shakespeare's opinion about the matter. The common gossiping of washerwomen must be less disgusting than the continual and eternal fence and attack of Rousseau and these sublime Petticoats. One calls herself Clara and her friend Julia, two of Rousseau's Heroines. They all the same time christen poor Jean Jacques, "St. Preux," who is the pure cavalier of his famous novel.[1] Thank God I am born in England with our own great Men before my eyes. Thank god that you are fair and can love me without being Letter-written and sentimentaliz'd into it. Mr. Barry Cornwall[2] has sent me another Book, his first, with a polite note. I must do what I can to make him sensible of the esteem I have for his kindness. If this northeast would take a turn it would be so much the better for me. Good bye, my love, my dear love, my beauty—

love me forever—

J—K—

1. *La nouvelle Héloïse.*
2. Pseudonym of Bryan Waller Procter (1787–1874).

To J. H. Reynolds
28 FEBRUARY 1820

My dear Reynolds,

I have been improving since you saw me. My nights are better which I think is a very encouraging thing. You mention your cold in rather too slighting a manner. If you travel outside have some flannel against the wind, which I hope will not keep on at this rate when you are in the Packet boat. Should it rain, do not stop upon deck though the Passengers should vomit themselves inside out. Keep under Hatches from all sort of wet. I am pretty well provided with Books at present; when you return I may give you a commission or two. Mr. B.C.[1] has sent me not only his Sicilian Story but yesterday his Dramatic Scenes. This is very polite and I shall do what I can to make him sensible I think so. I confess they tease me. They are composed of Amiability, the Seasons, the Leaves, the Moon, etc., upon which he rings (according to Hunt's expression) triple bob majors.[2] However, that is nothing. I think he likes poetry for its own sake, not his. I hope I shall soon be well enough to proceed with my fairies[3] and set you about the notes on sundays and Stray-days. If I had been well enough I should have liked to cross the water with you. Brown wishes you a pleasant voyage. Have fish for dinner at the sea ports, and don't forget a bottle of Claret. You will not meet with so much to hate at Brussels as at Paris. Remember me to all my friends. If I were well enough I would paraphrase an ode of Horace's for you, on your embarking in the seventy years ago style. The Packet will bear a comparison with a roman galley at any rate.

Ever yours affectionately
J. Keats

1. "Barry Cornwall," or Bryan Waller Procter (1787–1874). His *Dramatic Scenes* was published in 1819, *A Sicilian Story* in 1820.

2. Peals rung on eight bells.
3. The "fairies" means "The Cap and Bells, Or, The Jealousies," which never was finished.

To Fanny Brawne
28 (?) FEBRUARY 1820

My dearest Girl,

I continue much the same as usual, I think a little better. My Spirits are better also, and consequently I am more resign'd to my confinement. I dare not think of you much or write much to you. Remember me to all.

Ever your affectionate
John Keats—

To Fanny Brawne
29 (?) FEBRUARY 1820

My dear Fanny,

I think you had better not make any long stay with me when Mr. Brown is at home. Whenever he goes out you may bring your work. You will have a pleasant walk today. I shall see you pass. I shall follow you with my eyes over the Heath. Will you come towards evening instead of before dinner? When you are gone, 'tis past. If you do not come till the evening I have something to look forward to all day. Come round to my window for a moment when you have read this. Thank your Mother for the preserves for me. The raspberry will be too sweet not having any acid, therefore as you are so good a girl I shall make you a present of it. Good bye

my sweet Love!

J. Keats

🐚

───────

To Fanny Brawne

1 MARCH (?) 1820

My dearest Fanny,

The power of your benediction is of not so weak a nature as to pass from the ring[1] in four-and-twenty hours; it is like a sacred Chalice once consecrated and ever consecrate. I shall kiss your name and mine where your Lips have been. Lips! Why should a poor prisoner as I am talk about such things? Thank God, though I hold them the dearest pleasures in the universe, I have a consolation independent of them in the certainty of your affection. I could write a song in the style of Tom Moore's Pathetic about Memory if that would be any relief to me. No, it would not. I will be as obstinate as a Robin. I will not sing in a cage. Health is my expected heaven and you are the Houri. This word I believe is both singular and plural. If only plural, never mind—you are a thousand of them.

Ever yours affectionately

my dearest—

J. K.

You had better not come today—

1. A seal ring of agate or carnelian with their joint names engraved on it.

To C. W. Dilke
4 MARCH 1820

My dear Dilke,

Since I saw you I have been gradually, too gradually perhaps, improving; and though under an interdict with respect to animal food living upon pseudo victuals, Brown says I have pick'd up a little flesh lately. If I can keep off inflammation for the next six weeks I trust I shall do very well. You certainly should have been at Martin's dinner, for making an index is surely as dull work as engraving. Have you heard that the Bookseller is going to tie himself to the manger eat or not as he pleases? He says Rice shall have his foot on the fender notwithstanding. Reynolds is going to sail on the salt seas. Brown has been mightily progressing with his Hogarth. A damn'd melancholy picture it is, and during the first week of my illness it gave me a psalm-singing nightmare that made me almost faint away in my sleep. I know I am better, for I can bear the Picture. I have experienced a specimen of great politeness from Mr. Barry Cornwall. He has sent me his books. Some time ago he had given his first publish'd book to Hunt for me. Hunt forgot to give it and Barry Cornwall thinking I had received it must have thought me a very neglectful fellow. Notwithstanding, he sent me his second book and on my explaining that I had not received his first he sent me that also. I am sorry to see by Mrs. D's note that she has been so unwell with the spasms. Does she continue the Medicines that benefited her so much? I am afraid not. Remember me to her and say I shall not expect her at Hampstead next week unless the Weather changes for the warmer. It is better to run no chance of a supernumerary cold in March. As for you, you must come. You must improve in your penmanship; your writing is like the speaking of a child of three years old, very understandable to its father but to no one else. The worst is it looks well—no, that is not the worst—the worst is, it is worse than Bailey's. Bailey's looks illegible and may perchance be read. Your's looks very legible and may perchance not be read. I would endeavour to give you a facsimile of your word Thistlewood if I were not minded on the instant that Lord chesterfield has done some such thing to his Son. Now I would not bathe in the same River with lord C. though I had the upper hand of the stream. I am grieved that in writing and speaking it is necessary to make use of the same particles as he did. Cobbet is expected to come in.[1] O, that I had two double plumpers[2] for him. The ministry are not so inimical to him but it would like to put him out of Coventry. Casting my eye on the other side I see a long word written in a most vile manner, unbecoming a Critic. You must recollect I have served no apprenticeship to old plays. If the only copies of the greek and Latin Authors had been made by you, Bailey and Haydon they Were as good as lost. It has been said that the Character of a Man may be known by his handwriting. If the Character of the age may be known by the average goodness of said, what a slovenly age we live in. Look at Queen Elizabeth's Latin exercises and blush. Look at Milton's hand. I can't say a word for shakespeare.

Your sincere friend
John Keats

1. William Cobbett returned from America to England in November 1819, and shortly afterwards became a candidate for Parliament from Coventry. He lost by only 352 votes.
2. A vote given solely to one candidate at an election when one has the right to vote for two or more.

To Fanny Brawne
MARCH (?) 1820

My dearest Love,

You must not stop so long in the cold. I have been suspecting that window to be open. Your Note half-cured me. When I want some more oranges I will tell you; these are just a propos. I am kept from food so feel rather weak, otherwise very well. Pray do not stop so long upstairs—it makes me uneasy. Come every now and then and stop a half minute. Remember me to your Mother.

Your ever affectionate

J—Keats—

To Fanny Brawne
MARCH (?) 1820

Sweetest Fanny,

You fear, sometimes, I do not love you so much as you wish? My dear Girl, I love you ever and ever and without reserve. The more I have known you the more have I lov'd—in every way—even my jealousies have been agonies of Love. In the hottest fit I ever had I would have died for you. I have vex'd you too much. But for Love! Can I help it? You are always new. The last of your kisses was ever the sweetest; the last smile the brightest; the last movement the gracefullest. When you pass'd my window home yesterday, I was fill'd with as much admiration as if I had then seen you for the first time. You uttered a half complaint once that I only lov'd your Beauty. Have I nothing else then to love in you but that? Do not I see a heart naturally furnish'd with wings imprison itself with me? No ill prospect has been able to turn your thoughts a moment from me. This perhaps should be as much a subject of sorrow as joy, but I will not talk of that. Even if you did not love me I could not help an entire devotion to you. How much more deeply then must I feel for you knowing you love me? My Mind has been the most discontented and restless one that ever was put into a body too small for it. I never felt my Mind repose upon anything with complete and undistracted enjoyment, upon no person but you. When you are in the room my thoughts never fly out of window; you always concentrate my whole senses. The anxiety shown about our Loves in your last note is an immense pleasure to me; however, you must not suffer such speculations to molest you any more. Nor will I any more believe you can have the least pique against me. Brown is gone out but here is Mrs. Wylie. When she is gone I shall be awake for you. Remembrances to your Mother.

Your affectionate

J. Keats

To Fanny Brawne

MARCH (?) 1820

My dearest Fanny,

Whenever you know me to be alone, come, no matter what day. Why will you go out this weather? I shall not fatigue myself with writing too much, I promise you. Brown says I am getting stouter. I rest well and from last night do not remember anything horrid in my dream, which is a capital symptom, for any organic derangement always occasions a Phantasmagoria. It will be a nice idle amusement to hunt after a motto for my Book, which I will have if lucky enough to hit upon a fit one—not intending to write a preface. I fear I am too late with my note. You are gone out. You will be as cold as a topsail in a north latitude. I advise you to furl yourself and come in a doors.

Good bye Love,

J. K.

To Fanny Brawne
MARCH (?) 1820

My dearest Fanny,

I slept well last night and am no worse this morning for it. Day by day if I am not deceived I get a more unrestrain'd use of my Chest. The nearer a racer gets to the Goal the more his anxiety becomes, so I lingering upon the borders of health feel my impatience increase. Perhaps on your account I have imagined my illness more serious than it is. How horrid was the chance of slipping into the ground instead of into your arms. The difference is amazing, Love. Death must come at last; Man must die, as Shallow says,[1] but before that is my fate I feign would try what more pleasures than you have given so sweet a creature as you can give. Let me have another opportunity of years before me and I will not die without being remember'd. Take care of yourself, dear, that we may both be well in the Summer. I do not at all fatigue myself with writing, having merely to put a line or two here and there, a Task which would worry a stout state of the body and mind, but which just suits me as I can do no more.

Your affectionate
J. K—

1. *2 Henry IV,* III.ii.41f.

To Fanny Brawne
MARCH (?) 1820

My dearest Fanny,

Though I shall see you in so short a time I cannot forbear sending you a few lines. You say I did not give you yesterday a minute account of my health. Today I have left off the Medicine which I took to keep the pulse down and I find I can do very well without it, which is a very favourable sign, as it shows there is no inflammation remaining. You think I may be wearied at night, you say. It is my best time. I am at my best about eight o' Clock. I received a Note from Mr. Proctor[1] today. He says he cannot pay me a visit [in] this weather as he is fearful of an inflammation in the Chest. What a horrid climate this is, or what careless inhabitants it has. You are one of them. My dear girl, do not make a joke of it; do not expose yourself to the cold. There's the Thrush again. I can't afford it. He'll run me up a pretty Bill for Music. Besides, he ought to know I deal at Clementi's.[2] How can you bear so long an imprisonment at Hampstead? I shall always remember it with all the gusto that a monopolizing carle[3] should. I could build an Altar to you for it.

Your affectionate
J. K.

1. B. W. Proctor, alias Barry Cornwall, the poet.
2. Music publishers and makers of musical instruments.
3. Spenserian for "fellow."

To Fanny Brawne
MARCH (?) 1820

Dear Girl,

Yesterday you must have thought me worse than I really was. I assure you there was nothing but regret at being obliged to forego an embrace which has so many times been the highest gust of my Life. I would not care for health without it. Sam would not come in. I wanted merely to ask him how you were this morning. When one is not quite well we turn for relief to those we love. This is no weakness of spirit in me. You know when in health I thought of nothing but you. When I shall again be so it will be the same. Brown has been mentioning to me that some hint from Sam, last night, occasions him some uneasiness. He whispered something to you concerning Brown and old Mr. Dilke which had the complexion of being something derogatory to the former. It was connected with an anxiety about Mr. D. Sr's death and an anxiety to set out for Chichester. These sort of hints point out their own solution. One cannot pretend to a delicate ignorance on the subject. You understand the whole matter. If anyone, my sweet Love, has misrepresented, to you, to your Mother or Sam, any circumstances which are at all likely, at a tenth remove, to create suspicions among people who from their own interested notions slander others, pray tell me, for I feel the least attaint on the disinterested character of Brown very deeply. Perhaps Reynolds or some other of my friends may come towards evening, therefore you may choose whether you will come to see me early today before or after dinner as you may think fit. Remember me to your Mother and tell her to drag you to me if you show the least reluctance.[1]

* * *

1. The signature to this letter is missing.

To Fanny Keats
20 MARCH 1820

My dear Fanny,

According to your desire I write today. It must be but a few lines for I have been attack'd several times with a palpitation at the heart and the Doctor says I must not make the slightest exertion. I am much the same today as I have been for a week past. They say 'tis nothing but debility and will entirely cease on my recovery of my strength, which is the object of my present diet. As the Doctor will not suffer me to write I shall ask Mr. Brown to let you hear news of me for the future if I should not get stronger soon. I hope I shall be well enough to come and see your flowers in bloom.

Ever your most
affectionate Brother
John—

To Fanny Brawne
MARCH (?) 1820

My dearest Girl,

As from the last part of my note you must see how gratified I have been by your remaining at home, you might perhaps conceive that I was equally bias'd the other way by your going to Town. I cannot be easy tonight without telling you you would be wrong to suppose so. Though I am pleased with the one, I am not displeased with the other. How do I dare to write in this manner about my pleasures and displeasures? I will tho' whilst I am an invalid, in spite of you. Good night, Love!

J. K.

To Fanny Brawne
MARCH (?) 1820

My dearest Girl,

In consequence of our company I suppose I shall not see you before to-morrow. I am much better today; indeed, all I have to complain of is want of strength and a little tightness in the Chest. I envied Sam's walk with you today, which I will not do again as I may get very tired of envying. I imagine you now sitting in your new black dress which I like so much and if I were a little less selfish and more enthusiastic[1] I should run round and surprise you with a knock at the door. I fear I am too prudent for a dying kind of Lover. Yet, there is a great difference between going off in warm blood like Romeo, and making one's exit like a frog in a frost. I had nothing particular to say today, but not intending that there shall be any interruption to our correspondence (which at some future time I propose offering to Murray),[2] I write something! God bless you, my sweet Love! Illness is a long lane, but I see you at the end of it, and shall mend my pace as well as possible.

J—K

1. Spelled "enthousiastic."
2. The publisher.

To Mrs. James Wylie
24 (?) MARCH 1820

Wentworth Place
Friday Morn.

My dear Mrs. Wylie,

I have been very negligent in not letting you hear from me for so long a time considering the anxiety I know you feel for me. Charles has been here this morning and will tell you that I am better. Just as he came in I was sitting down to write to you, and I shall not let his visit supersede these few lines. Charles enquired whether I had heard from George. It is impossible to guess whether he has landed yet, and if he has, it will take at least a month for any communication to reach us. I hope you keep your spirits a great height above the freezing point, and live in expectation of good news next summer. Louisville is not such a Monstrous distance; if Georgiana liv'd at york it would be just as far off. You see George will make nothing of the journey here and back. His absence will have been perhaps a fortunate event for Georgiana, for the pleasure of his return will be so great that it will wipe away the consciousness of many troubles felt before very deeply. She will see him return'd from us and be convinced that the separation is not so very formidable although the Atlantic is between. If George succeeds it will be better certainly that they should stop in America. If not, why not return? It is better in ill luck to have at least the comfort of one's friends than to be shipwreck'd among American's. But I have good hopes as far as I can judge from what I have heard from George. He should by this time be taught Alertness and Carefulness. If they should stop in America for five or six years let us hope they may have about three Children. Then the eldest will be getting old enough to be society. The very crying will keep their ears employed and their spirits from being melancholy. Mrs. Millar I hear continues confined to her Chamber. If she would take my advice I should recommend her to keep it till the middle of april and then go to some Sea-town in Devonshire which is sheltered from the east wind, which blows down the channel very briskly even in april. Give my Compliments to Miss Millar and Miss Waldegrave.[1]

* * *

1. The letter is missing a signature.

To Fanny Keats

I APRIL 1820

Wentworth Place
April 1st

My dear Fanny,

I am getting better every day and should think myself quite well were I not reminded every now and then by faintness and a tightness in the Chest. Send your Spaniel over to Hampstead for I think I know where to find a Master or Mistress for him. You may depend upon it if you were even to turn it loose in the common road it would soon find an owner. If I keep improving as I have done I shall be able to come over to you in the course of a few weeks. I should take the advantage of your being in Town but I cannot bear the City though I have already ventured as far as the west end for the purpose of seeing Mr. Haydon's Picture which is just finished and has made its appearance.[1] I have not heard from George yet since he left liverpool. Mr. Brown wrote to him as from me the other day. Mr. B. wrote two Letters to Mr. Abbey concerning me. Mr. A. took no notice and of course Mr. B. must give up such a correspondence when, as the man said, all the Letters are on one side. I write with greater ease than I had thought, therefore you shall soon hear from me again.

Your affectionate Brother
John—

1. *Christ's Entry into Jerusalem* was privately exhibited in Egyptian Hall, Piccadilly, on Saturday, 25 March. It is now at Mount Saint Mary's Seminary, Norwood, Ohio.

To Fanny Keats
12 APRIL 1820

Wentworth Place

My dear Fanny,

Excuse these shabby scraps of paper I send you and also from endeavouring to give you any consolation just at present, for though my health is tolerably well I am too nervous to enter into any discussion in which my heart is concerned. Wait patiently and take care of your health being especially careful to keep yourself from low spirits which are great enemies to health. You are young and have only need of a little patience. I am not yet able to bear the fatigue of coming to Walthamstow, though I have been to Town once or twice. I have thought of taking a change of air. You shall hear from me immediately on my moving anywhere. I will ask Mrs. Dilke to pay you a visit if the weather holds fine the first time I see her. The Dog is being attended to like a Prince.

Your affectionate Brother
John

To Fanny Keats
21 APRIL 1820

My dear Fanny,

I have been slowly improving since I wrote last. The Doctor assures me that there is nothing the matter with me except nervous irritability and a general weakness of the whole system which has proceeded from my anxiety of mind of late years and the too great excitement of poetry. Mr. Brown is going to Scotland by the Smack, and I am advised for change of exercise and air to accompany him and give myself the chance of benefit from a Voyage. Mr. H. Wylie call'd on me yesterday with a letter from George to his mother. George is safe on the other side of the water, perhaps by this time arrived at his home. I wish you were coming to town that I might see you. If you should be coming write to me, as it is quite a trouble to get by the coaches to Walthamstow. Should you not come to Town I must see you before I sail at Walthamstow. They tell me I must study lines and tangents and squares and circles to put a little Ballast into my mind. We shall be going in a fortnight and therefore you will see me within that space. I expected sooner, but I have not been able to venture to walk across the Country. Now the fine Weather is come you will not find your time so irksome. You must be sensible how much I regret not being able to alleviate the unpleasantness of your situation, but trust my dear Fanny that better times are in wait for you.

Your affectionate Brother
John—

To Fanny Keats

4 MAY 1820

Wentworth Place
Thursday—

My dear Fanny,

I went for the first time into the City the day before yesterday, for before I was very disinclined to encounter the Scuffle, more from nervousness than real illness, which notwithstanding I should not have suffered to conquer me if I had not made up my mind not to go to Scotland but to remove to Kentish Town till Mr. Brown returns. Kentish Town is a Mile nearer to you than Hampstead. I have been getting gradually better but am not so well as to trust myself to the casualties of rain and sleeping out which I am liable to in visiting you. Mr. Brown goes on Saturday and by that time I shall have settled in my new Lodging when I will certainly venture to you. You will forgive me, I hope, when I confess that I endeavour to think of you as little as possible and to let George dwell upon my mind but slightly. The reason being that I am afraid to ruminate on anything which has the shade of difficulty or melancholy in it, as that sort of cogitation is so pernicious to health, and it is only by health that I can be enabled to alleviate your situation in future. For some time you must do what you can of yourself for relief, and bear your mind up with the consciousness that your situation cannot last forever, and that for the present you may console yourself against the reproaches of Mrs. Abbey. Whatever obligations you may have had to her (or her Husband) you have none now as she has reproach'd you. I do not know what property you have, but I will enquire into it. Be sure however that beyond the obligations that a Lodger may have to a Landlord you have none to Mr. Abbey. Let the surety of this make you laugh at Mrs. A's foolish tattle. Mrs. Dilke's Brother has got your Dog. She is not very well, still liable to Illness. I will get her to come and see you if I can make up my mind on the propriety of introducing a Stranger into Abbey's House. Be careful to let no fretting injure your health as I have suffered it. Health is the greatest of blessings. With *health* and *hope* we should be content to live, and so you will find as you grow older. I am

my dear Fanny
your affectionate Brother
John—

To Fanny Brawne
MAY (?) 1820

Tuesday Morn—

My dearest Girl,

I wrote a Letter for you yesterday expecting to have seen your mother. I shall be selfish enough to send it though I know it may give you a little pain, because I wish you to see how unhappy I am for love of you, and endeavour as much as I can to entice you to give up your whole heart to me whose whole existence hangs upon you. You could not step or move an eyelid but it would shoot to my heart. I am greedy of you. Do not think of anything but me. Do not live as if I was not existing. Do not forget me. But have I any right to say you forget me? Perhaps you think of me all day. Have I any right to wish you to be unhappy for me? You would forgive me for wishing it, if you knew the extreme passion I have that you should love me. And for you to love me as I do you, you must think of no one but me, much less write that sentence.

Yesterday and this morning I have been haunted with a sweet vision. I have seen you the whole time in your shepherdess dress. How my senses have ached at it! How my heart has been devoted to it! How my eyes have been full of Tears at it! Indeed, I think a real Love is enough to occupy the widest heart. Your going to town alone, when I heard of it, was a shock to me. Yet I expected it. *Promise me you will not for some time, till I get better.* Promise me this and fill the paper full of the most endearing names. If you cannot do so with good will, do my Love tell me—say what you think—confess if your heart is too much fasten'd on the world. Perhaps then I may see you at a greater distance, I may not be able to appropriate you so closely to myself. Were you to lose a favorite bird from the cage, how would your eyes ache after it as long as it was in sight; when out of sight you would recover a little. Perhaps if you would, if so it is, confess to me how many things are necessary to you besides me, I might be happier, by being less tantaliz'd. Well may you exclaim, how selfish, how cruel, not to let me enjoy my youth! To wish me to be unhappy! You must be so if you love me. Upon my Soul I can be contented with nothing else. If you could really what is call'd enjoy yourself at a Party; if you can smile in peoples' faces, and wish them to admire you *now,* you never have nor ever will love me. I see *life* in nothing but the certainty of your Love; convince me of it my sweetest. If I am not somehow convinc'd I shall die of agony. If we love we must not live as other men and women do. I cannot brook the wolfsbane of fashion and foppery and tattle. You must be mine to die upon the rack if I want you. I do not pretend to say I have more feeling than my fellows, but I wish you seriously to look over my letters kind and unkind and consider whether the Person who wrote them can be able to endure much longer the agonies and uncertainties which you are so peculiarly made to create. My recovery of bodily health will be of no benefit to me if you are not all mine when I am well. For god's sake save me, or tell me my passion is of too awful a nature for you. Again God bless you,

J. K.

No—my sweet Fanny—I am wrong. I do not want you to be unhappy—
    and yet I do, I must while there is so sweet a Beauty—my loveliest, my
    darling! Good bye! I kiss you—O, the torments!

To Fanny Brawne
JUNE (?) 1820

My dearest Fanny,

My head is puzzled this morning, and I scarce know what I shall say though I am full of a hundred things. 'Tis certain I would rather be writing to you this morning, notwithstanding the alloy of grief in such an occupation, than enjoy any other pleasure, with health to boot, unconnected with you. Upon my soul I have loved you to the extreme. I wish you could know the Tenderness with which I continually brood over your different aspects of countenance, action and dress. I see you come down in the morning; I see you meet me at the Window. I see everything over again eternally that I ever have seen. If I get on the pleasant clue I live in a sort of happy misery, if on the unpleasant 'tis miserable misery. You complain of my ill treating you in word, thought and deed. I am sorry. At times I feel bitterly sorry that I ever made you unhappy. My excuse is that those words have been wrung from me by the sharpness of my feelings. At all events and in any case I have been wrong; could I believe that I did it without any cause, I should be the most sincere of Penitents. I could give way to my repentant feelings now; I could recant all my suspicions; I could mingle with you heart and Soul, though absent, were it not for some parts of your Letters. Do you suppose it possible I could ever leave you? You know what I think of myself and what of you. You know that I should feel how much it was my loss and how little yours. My friends laugh at you! I know some of them; when I know them all I shall never think of them again as friends or even acquaintance. My friends have behaved well to me in every instance but one, and there they have become tattlers and inquisitors into my conduct, spying upon a secret I would rather die than share it with anybody's confidence. For this I cannot wish them well. I care not to see any of them again. If I am the Theme, I will not be the Friend of idle Gossips. Good gods what a shame it is our Loves should be so put into the microscope of a Coterie. Their laughs should not affect you (I may perhaps give you reasons some day for these laughs, for I suspect a few people to hate me well enough, *for reasons I know of,* who have pretended a great friendship for me) when in competition with one, who if he never should see you again would make you the saint of his memory. These Laughers, who do not like you, who envy you for your Beauty, who would have God-bless'd-me from you forever, who were plying me with disencouragements with respect to you eternally. People are revengeful. Do not mind them. Do nothing but love me. If I knew that for certain life and health will in such event be a heaven, and death itself will be less painful. I long to believe in immortality. I shall never be able to bid you an entire farewell. If I am destined to be happy with you here, how short is the longest Life. I wish to believe in immortality. I wish to live with you forever. Do not let my name ever pass between you and those laughers. If I have no other merit than the great Love for you, that were sufficient to keep me sacred and unmentioned in such society. If I have been cruel and injust I swear my love has ever been greater than my cruelty which lasts but a minute, whereas my Love, come what will, shall last forever. If concessions to me has hurt your Pride, god knows I have had little pride in my heart when thinking of you. Your name never passes my Lips; do not let mine pass yours. Those People do not like me. After reading my Letter you even then wish to see me, I am strong enough to walk over. But I dare not. I shall feel so much pain in parting with you again. My dearest love, I am afraid to see you. I am strong but not strong enough to see you. Will my arm be ever round you again? And if so shall I be obliged to leave you again? My sweet Love! I am happy whilst I believe your first Letter. Let me be but certain that you are mine heart and soul, and I could die more happily than I could otherwise live. If you think me cruel, if you think I have slighted you, do muse it over again and see into my heart. My Love to you is "true as truth's simplicity and simpler than the infancy of truth,"[1] as I think I once said before. How could I slight you? How threaten to leave you? Not in the spirit of a Threat to you—no—but in the spirit of Wretchedness in myself. My fairest, my delicious, my angel Fanny! Do not believe me such a vulgar fellow. I will be as patient in illness and as believing in Love as I am able.

Yours forever my dearest
John Keats—

1. *Troilus and Cressida,* III.ii.176f.

To John Taylor
11 (?) JUNE 1820

My dear Taylor,

In reading over the proof of St Agnes' Eve since I left Fleet street I was struck with what appears to me an alteration in the 7th Stanza very much for the worse. The passage I mean stands thus:

> "her maiden eyes incline
> Still on the floor, while many a sweeping train
> Pass by—"

Twas originally written

> "her maiden eyes divine
> Fix'd on the floor saw many a sweeping train
> Pass by—"

My meaning is quite destroyed in the alteration. I do not use *train* for *concourse of passers by* but for *Skirts* sweeping along the floor. In the first Stanza my copy reads, 2nd line

> "bitter *chill* it was"

to avoid the echo cold in the next line.

ever yours sincerely
John Keats

To Charles Brown
ABOUT 21 JUNE 1820[1]

My dear Brown,

I have only been to x x x's[2] once since you left, when x x x x[3] could not find your letters. Now this is bad of me. I should, in this instance, conquer the great aversion to breaking up my regular habits, which grows upon me more and more. True, I have an excuse in the weather, which drives one from shelter to shelter in any little excursion. I have not heard from George. My book[4] is coming out with very low hopes, though not spirits on my part. This shall be my last trial; not succeeding, I shall try what I can do in the Apothecary line. When you hear from or see x x x x x x[5] it is probable you will hear some complaints against me, which this notice is not intended to forestall. The fact is I did behave badly, but it is to be attributed to my health, spirits, and the disadvantageous ground I stand on in society. I would go and accommodate matters, if I were not too weary of the world. I know that they are more happy and comfortable than I am; therefore why should I trouble myself about it? I foresee I shall know very few people in the course of a year or two. Men get such different habits that they become as oil and vinegar to one another. Thus far I have a consciousness of having been pretty dull and heavy, both in subject and phrase; I might add, enigmatical. I am in the wrong, and the world is in the right, I have no doubt. Fact is, I have had so many kindnesses done me by so many people, that I am cheveaux-defrised[6] with benefits, which I must jump over or break down. I met x x x[7] in town a few days ago, who invited me to supper to meet Wordsworth, Southey, Lamb, Haydon, and some more. I was too careful of my health to risk being out at night. Talking of that, I continue to improve slowly, but I think surely. All the talk at present x x x x x x x x. There is a famous exhibition in Pall Mall[8] of the old english portraits by Van Dyck and Holbein, Sir Peter Lely and the great Sir Godfrey. Pleasant countenances predominate, so I will mention two or three unpleasant ones.

There is James the first, whose appearance would disgrace a "Society for the suppression of women," so very squalid, and subdued to nothing he looks. Then, there is old Lord Burleigh, the high priest of economy, the political save-all, who has the appearance of a Pharisee just rebuffed by a gospel bon-mot. Then, there is George the second, very like an unintellectual Voltaire, troubled with the gout and a bad temper. Then, there is young Devereux, the favourite, with every appearance of as slang a boxer as any in the court; his face is cast in the mould of blackguardism with jockey-plaster. x x x x x I shall soon begin upon *Lucy Vaughan Lloyd*.[9] I do not begin composition yet, being willing, in case of a relapse, to have nothing to reproach myself with. I hope the weather will give you the slip; let it show itself, and steal out of your company. x x x x x When I have sent off this, I shall write another to some place about fifty miles in advance of you.

Good morning to you.
Your's ever sincerely,
John Keats

1. Printed from Brown's *Life of John Keats.*
2. Dilke's.
3. Probably Dilke.
4. *Lamia, Isabella, The Eve of St. Agnes, and Other Poems.*
5. Bailey.
6. A cryptic idiom. Literally, "taken the curls out of my hair." More generally, "overwhelmed."
7. Monkhouse.
8. The British Institution, 52 Pall Mall, opened on 15 June.
9. "The Cap and Bells."

To Fanny Keats
23 JUNE 1820

Friday Morn—

My dear Fanny,

I had intended to delay seeing you till a Book which I am now publishing was out, expecting that to be the end of this Week when I would have brought it to Walthamstow. On receiving your Letter of course I set myself to come to town, but was not able for just as I was setting out yesterday morning a slight spitting of blood came on which returned rather more copiously at night. I have slept well and they tell me there is nothing material to fear. I will send my Book soon with a Letter which I have had from George, who is with his family quite well.

Your affectionate Brother
John—

To Fanny Brawne
4 JULY (?) 1820

Tuesday Aft.

My dearest Fanny,

For this Week past I have been employed in marking the most beautiful passages in Spenser, intending it for you, and comforting myself in being somehow occupied to give you however small a pleasure. It has lightened my time very much. I am much better.

God bless you.

Your affectionate
J. Keats

To Fanny Brawne
5 JULY (?) 1820

Wednesday Morn.

My dearest Girl,

I have been a walk this morning with a book in my hand, but as usual I have been occupied with nothing but you, I wish I could say in an agreeable manner. I am tormented day and night. They talk of my going to Italy. 'Tis certain I shall never recover if I am to be so long separate from you; yet with all this devotion to you I cannot persuade myself into any confidence of you. Past experience connected with the fact of my long separation from you gives me agonies which are scarcely to be talked of. When your mother comes I shall be very sudden and expert in asking her whether you have been to Mrs. Dilke's, for she might say no to make me easy. I am literally worn to death, which seems my only recourse. I cannot forget what has pass'd. What? Nothing with a man of the world, but to me deathful. I will get rid of this as much as possible. When you were in the habit of flirting with Brown you would have left off, could your own heart have felt one half of one pang mine did. Brown is a good sort of Man; he did not know he was doing me to death by inches. I feel the effect of every one of those hours in my side now; and for that cause, though he has done me many services, though I know his love and friendship for me, though at this moment I should be without pence were it not for his assistance, I will never see or speak to him until we are both old men, if we are to be. I *will* resent my heart having been made a football. You will call this madness. I have heard you say that it was not unpleasant to wait a few years. You have amusements; your mind is away. You have not brooded over one idea as I have, and how should you? You are to me an object intensely desireable; the air I breathe in a room empty of you is unhealthy. I am not the same to you. No, you can wait. You have a thousand activities. You can be happy without me. Any party, anything to fill up the day has been enough. How have you pass'd this month? Who have you smil'd with? All this may seem savage in me. You do not feel as I do. You do not know what it is to love. One day you may; your time is not come. Ask yourself how many unhappy hours Keats has caused you in Loneliness. For myself I have been a Martyr the whole time, and for this reason I speak. The confession is forc'd from me by the torture. I appeal to you by the blood of that Christ you believe in: Do not write to me if you have done anything this month which it would have pained me to have seen. You may have altered. If you have not, if you still behave in dancing rooms and other societies as I have seen you, I do not want to live. If you have done so, I wish this coming night may be my last. I cannot live without you, and not only you but *chaste you; virtuous you*. The Sun rises and sets, the day passes, and you follow the bent of your inclination to a certain extent. You have no conception of the quantity of miserable feeling that passes through me in a day. Be serious! Love is not a plaything. And again do not write unless you can do it with a crystal conscience. I would sooner die for want of you than—

Yours forever

J. Keats

To Fanny Keats
5 JULY 1820

Mortimer Terrace
Wednesday

My dear Fanny,

I have had no return of the spitting of blood and for two or three days have been getting a little stronger. I have no hopes of an entire reestablishment of my health under some months of patience. My Physician[1] tells me I must contrive to pass the Winter in Italy. This is all very unfortunate for us. We have no recourse but patience, which I am now practicing better than ever I thought it possible for me. I have this moment received a Letter from Mr. Brown, dated Dunvegan Castle, Island of Skye. He is very well in health and Spirits. My new publication[2] has been out for some days and I have directed a Copy to be bound for you, which you will receive shortly. No one can regret Mr. Hodgkinson's ill fortune. I must own illness has not made such a Saint of me as to prevent my rejoicing at his reverse. Keep yourself in as good hopes as possible. In case my illness should continue an unreasonable time many of my friends would I trust for my Sake do all in their power to console and amuse you, at the least word from me. You may depend upon it that in case my strength returns I will do all in my power to extricate you from the Abbies. Be above all things careful of your health, which is the cornerstone of all pleasure.

Your affectionate Brother
John—

1. Dr. George Darling, physician to Taylor, Hessey, Hazlitt, Haydon, John Scott, and many other important men.
2. *Lamia, Isabella, The Eve of St. Agnes, and Other Poems.*

Joseph Severn to William Haslam
12 (?) JULY 1820

6 Goswell St. Road

Wednesday M

My dear Haslam,

I have been away from home until Monday on a face-making expedition, so that your letter has been to Hampton Court, Teddington and Richmond before I received it. It shall be done as you say, next week.

Poor Keats has been still nearer the next world. A Fortnight back he ruptured a blood-vessel in the Chest. I have seen him many times, particularly previous to this accident—once since—and it will give you pleasure to say I think he will still recover. His appearance is shocking and now reminds me of poor Tom, and I have been inclined to think him in the same way. For himself he makes sure of it, and seems prepossessed that he cannot recover. Now I seem more than ever *not* to think so and I know you will agree with me when you see him. Are you aware another volume of Poems was published last week in which is "Lovely Isabel—poor simple Isabel"? I have been delighted with this volume and think it will even please the Million. Keats has been for some time at Leigh Hunt's on account of the attention he requires. Most certain his body cannot be in better hands. But for his soul . . . Altho' I can see in Keats such a deep thinking, determined, silent spirit that I am doing him the greatest injustice to suppose for a moment that such a man as L——H—— can ever taint him with his principles *now*, or even school him with his learning. I think the house is 13 Mortimer Terrace, Kentish Town. It is only a few doors from Keats's lodging (2 Weslyan Place). I shall continue to visit Keats very much at every opportunity, perhaps twice a week.

Now about your "dearer self." I am quite ashamed that I have not succeeded; the white satin gown looks most vile after all my trouble. Now if I may be favored with a sitting, I will succeed. To this purpose I think I can manage. Some day next week I shall be going to Deptford Dock Yard, say Thursday. Now, I can call on Mrs. H and regain my lost favor.[1] Present my respects and say that from any silk dress I can paint white satin. It is merely the light and shade and the form I want. I met your Servant on monday but I could not return from the East India Dock Yard in time to call. Try to see me. Sincerely yours,

Josh. Severn

No, I'll give you another half sheet and fill this bit with self. I have been very much occupied with my Miniatures, am at home finishing 5 now. I cannot tell how they will turn out for they are all new faces to me. I am glad to be going this way altho' it takes me entirely from my other Painting. But soon I begin and continue until the end of the year. My reputation is increasing most largely and nobly and I hope soon to reap much profit. Tell Kent that the [a sketch of a flag appears here] are being gilt. I expect them soon to be complete.

1. Severn was attempting to paint a portrait of Mrs. Haslam.

To Fanny Keats
22 JULY 1820

My dear Fanny,

I have been gaining Strength for some days. It would be well if I could at the same time say I am gaining hopes of a speedy recovery. My constitution has suffered very much for two or three years past, so as to be scarcely able to make head against illness, which the natural activity and impatience of my Mind renders more dangerous. It will at all events be a very tedious affair, and you must expect to hear very little alteration of any sort in me for some time. You ought to have received a copy of my Book ten days ago. I shall send another message to the Booksellers. One of the Mr. Wylies will be here today or tomorrow when I will ask him to send you George's Letter. Writing the smallest note is so annoying to me that I have waited till I shall see him. Mr. Hunt does everything in his power to make the time pass as agreeably with me as possible. I read the greatest part of the day, and generally take two half hour walks a day up and down the terrace, which is very much pester'd with cries, ballad singers, and street music. We have been so unfortunate for so long a time, every event has been of so depressing a nature that I must persuade myself to think some change will take place in the aspect of our affairs. I shall be upon the look out for a trump card.

Your affectionate Brother,
John—

From Percy Bysshe Shelley
27 JULY 1820

Pisa—July 27, 1820

My dear Keats,

I hear with great pain the dangerous accident that you have undergone, and Mr. Gisborne, who gives me the account of it, adds that you continue to wear a consumptive appearance. This consumption is a disease particularly fond of people who write such good verses as you have done, and with the assistance of an English winter it can often indulge its selection. I do not think that young and amiable poets are at all bound to gratify its taste; they have entered into no bond with the Muses to that effect . . . But seriously (for I am joking on what I am very anxious about) I think you would do well to pass the winter after so tremendous an accident in Italy, and (if you think it as necessary as I do) so long as you could find Pisa or its neighbourhood agreeable to you, Mrs. Shelley unites with myself in urging the request that you would take up your residence with us. You might come by sea to Leghorn (France is not worth seeing and the sea air is particularly good for weak lungs) which is within a few miles of us. You ought at all events to see Italy, and your health, which I suggest as a motive, might be an excuse to you. I spare declamation about the statues and the paintings and the ruins, and what is a greater piece of forbearance, about the mountains, the Streams and the fields, the colours of the sky, and the sky itself.

I have lately read your Endymion again and ever with a new sense of the treasures of poetry it contains, though treasures poured forth with indistinct profusion. This, people in general will not endure, and that is the cause of the comparatively few copies which have been sold. I feel persuaded that you are capable of the greatest things, so you but will. I always tell Ollier to send you Copies of my books. "Prometheus Unbound" I imagine you will receive nearly at the same time with this letter. "The Cenci" I hope you have already received. It was studiously composed in a different style "below the *good* how far! But far above the *great*."[1] In poetry *I* have sought to avoid system and mannerism. I wish those who excel me in genius would pursue the same plan.

Whether you remain in England or journey to Italy, believe that you carry with you my anxious wishes for your health, happiness and success, wherever you are or whatever you undertake, and that I am

Yours sincerely, *P. B. Shelley*

1. The last line of Thomas Gray's "Progress of Poetry."

To Fanny Brawne

AUGUST (?) 1820

I do not write this till the last, that no eye
may catch it.[1]

My dearest Girl,

I wish you could invent some means to make me at all happy without
you. Every hour I am more and more concentrated in you. Everything else
tastes like chaff in my Mouth. I feel it almost impossible to go to Italy. The
fact is I cannot leave you, and shall never taste one minute's content until it
pleases chance to let me live with you for good. But I will not go on at this
rate. A person in health as you are can have no conception of the horrors
that nerves and a temper like mine go through. What Island do your
friends propose retiring to? I should be happy to go with you there alone,
but in company I should object to it. The back-bitings and jealousies of
new colonists who have nothing else to amuse themselves is unbearable.
Mr. Dilke came to see me yesterday, and gave me a very great deal more
pain than pleasure. I shall never be able any more to endure the society of
any of those who used to meet at Elm Cottage and Wentworth Place. The
last two years taste like brass upon my Palate. If I cannot live with you I will
live alone. I do not think my health will improve much while I am separated from you. For all this I am averse to seeing you. I cannot bear flashes
of light and return into my glooms again. I am not so unhappy now as I
should be if I had seen you yesterday. To be happy with you seems such an
impossibility! It requires a luckier Star than mine! It will never be.

I enclose a passage from one of your Letters which I want you to alter a
little. I want (if you will have it so) the matter express'd less coldly to me. If
my health would bear it, I could write a Poem which I have in my head,
which would be a consolation for people in such a situation as mine. I
would show someone in Love as I am, with a person living in such Liberty

as you do. Shakespeare always sums up matters in the most sovereign manner. Hamlet's heart was full of such Misery as mine is when he said to Ophelia: "Go to a Nunnery, go, go!"[2] Indeed I should like to give up the matter at once. I should like to die. I am sickened at the brute world which you are smiling with. I hate men and women more. I see nothing but thorns for the future. Wherever I may be next winter, in Italy or nowhere, Brown will be living near you with his indecencies.[3] I see no prospect of any rest. Suppose me in Rome. Well, I should there see you as in a magic glass going to and from town at all hours. I wish you could infuse a little confidence in human nature into my heart. I cannot muster any. The world is too brutal for me. I am glad there is such a thing as the grave. I am sure I shall never have any rest till I get there. At any rate I will indulge myself by never seeing any more Dilke or Brown or any of their Friends. I wish I was either in your arms full of faith or that a Thunderbolt would strike me.

God bless you, *J. K—*

1. Keats probably wrote the letter and then added this sentence and the words "My dearest girl." The letter was written in Hunt's crowded house, where privacy was impossible. It is perhaps the last letter that Keats ever wrote to Fanny Brawne.
2. *Hamlet,* III.i.121, 131f.
3. A reference to Brown's liaison with Abigail O'Donaghue, their Irish servant.

To Fanny Keats
13 AUGUST 1820

Wentworth Place

My dear Fanny,

'Tis a long time since I received your last. An accident of an unpleasant nature occurred at Mr. Hunt's and prevented me from answering you, that is to say made me nervous. That you may not suppose it worse I will mention that some one of Mr. Hunt's household opened a Letter of mine, upon which I immediately left Mortimer Terrace with the intention of taking to Mrs. Bentley's again. Fortunately I am not in so lone a situation, but am staying a short time with Mrs. Brawne who lives in the House which was Mrs. Dilke's. I am excessively nervous; a person I am not quite used to entering the room half chokes me. 'Tis not yet Consumption I believe, but it would be were I to remain in this climate all the Winter, so I am thinking of either voyaging or travelling to Italy. Yesterday I received an invitation from Mr. Shelley, a Gentleman residing at Pisa, to spend the Winter with him. If I go I must be away in a Month or even less. I am glad you like the Poems. You must hope with me that time and health will produce you some more. This is the first morning I have been able to sit to the paper and have many Letters to write if I can manage them. God bless you my dear Sister.

Your affectionate Brother
John—

To John Taylor
13 AUGUST 1820

Wentworth Place
Sat. Morn.

My dear Taylor,

My Chest is in so nervous a State, that any thing extra such as speaking to an unaccustomed Person or writing a Note half suffocates me. This Journey to Italy wakes me at daylight every morning and haunts me horribly. I shall endeavour to go though it be with the sensation of marching up against a Battery. The first step towards it is to know the expense of a Journey and a year's residence, which if you will ascertain for me and let me know early, you will greatly serve me. I have more to say but must desist, for every line I write increases the tightness of the Chest, and I have many more to do. I am convinced that this sort of thing does not continue for nothing. If you can come with any of our friends do.

Your sincere friend
John Keats—

To Leigh Hunt
13 (?) AUGUST 1820

(An Amyntas)[1]

Wentworth Place

My dear Hunt,

You will be glad to hear I am going to delay a little time at Mrs. Brawne's. I hope to see you whenever you can get time, for I feel really attach'd to you for your many sympathies with me, and patience at my lunes. Will you send by the Bearess Lucy Vaughn Lloyd?[2] My best rems. to Mrs. Hunt.

Your affectionate friend
John Keats

1. A reference to Hunt's *Amyntas, A Tale of the Woods; from the Italian of Torquato Tasso* (1820), which is dedicated to Keats.
2. The manuscript of "The Cap and Bells."

To John Taylor
14 AUGUST 1820

Wentworth Place

My dear Taylor,

I do not think I mentioned anything of a Passage to Leghorn by Sea. Will you join that to your enquiries, and, if you can, give a peep at the Birth[1] if the Vessel is in our river?

Your sincere friend
John Keats

over

P.S. Somehow a Copy of Chapman's Homer, lent to me by Haydon, has disappeared from my Lodgings. It has quite flown I am afraid, and Haydon urges the return of it so that I must get one at Longman's and send it to Lisson grove, or you must, or as I have given you a job on the River, ask Mistessey.[2] I had written a Note to this effect to Hessey some time since but crumpled it up in hopes that the Book might come to Light. This morning Haydon has sent another messenger. The Copy was in good condition, with the head.[3] Damn all thieves! Tell Woodhouse I have not lost his Blackwood.

[Endorsement by Taylor:] Inclosed in this Letter I received a Testamentary Paper in John Keats's Handwriting without Date on which I have indorsed a Memorandum to this Effect for the purpose of identifying it, and for better Security it is here unto annexed.

John Taylor

22 Sep 1820

[The Testament]

In case of my death this scrap of Paper may be serviceable in your possession.

All my estate real and personal consists in the hopes of the sale of books publish'd or unpublish'd. Now I wish *Brown* and you to be the first paid Creditors. The rest is in nubibus.[4] But in case it should shower pay my Taylor the few pounds I owe him.

My Chest of Books divide among my friends—

[Endorsed by Taylor:] NB on the 14th August or the 15th, 1820 I received this paper which is in John Keats's Handwriting enclosed in the annexed Letter which came by the 3 day Post, 22 Sept. 1820.

John Taylor

 1. Keats's own misspelling of "berth."
 2. Mr. Hessey.
 3. The head of Chapman, engraved on the verso of the title page.
 4. In the clouds.

To Charles Brown
14 AUGUST 1820[1]

My dear Brown,

   You may not have heard from x x x x or x x x x, or in any way that an attack of spitting of blood, and all its weakening consequences, has prevented me from writing for so long a time. I have matter now for a very long letter, but not news; so I must cut everything short. I shall make some confession, which you will be the only person, for many reasons, I shall trust with. A winter in England would, I have not a doubt, kill me; so I have resolved to go to Italy, either by sea or land. Not that I have any great hopes of that, for I think there is a core of disease in me not easy to pull out.

   *(Note) x x x x x x x x x x x x x x x x If I should die x x x x x I shall be obliged to set off in less than a month. Do not, my dear Brown, tease your-

---

*(Note) The omitted passage contained the secret.[2] He went to Italy in pursuance of his physician's urgent advice.

self about me. You must fill up your time as well as you can, and as happily. You must think of my faults †(Note) as lightly as you can. When I have health I will bring up the long arrears of letters I owe you. x x x x x x My book has had good success among literary people, and, I believe, has a moderate sale. I have seen very few people we know. x x x has visited me more than any one. I would go to x x x x x and make some inquiries after you, if I could with any bearable sensation, but a person I am not quite used to causes an oppression on my chest. Last week I received a letter from Shelley, at Pisa, of a very kind nature, asking me to pass the winter with him. Hunt has behaved very kindly to me. You shall hear from me again shortly.

Your affectionate friend,
John Keats

1. Printed from Brown's *Life of John Keats.*
2. No doubt of his engagement to Fanny Brawne.

To Percy Bysshe Shelley
16 AUGUST 1820

Hampstead, August 16th

My dear Shelley,

I am very much gratified that you, in a foreign country, and with a mind almost over occupied, should write to me in the strain of the Letter beside me. If I do not take advantage of your invitation it will be prevented by a circumstance I have very much at heart to prophesy. There is no doubt that an english winter would put an end to me, and do so in a lingering hateful

---

†(Note) Sixteen years have not changed my opinion. I thought then, and I think now, he had no fault. On the faulty side he was scarcely human.

manner, therefore I must either voyage or journey to Italy as a soldier marches up to a battery. My nerves at present are the worst part of me, yet they feel soothed when I think that come what extreme may, I shall not be destined to remain in one spot long enough to take a hatred of any four particular bed-posts. I am glad you take any pleasure in my poor Poem which I would willingly take the trouble to unwrite, if possible, did I care so much as I have done about Reputation. I received a copy of the Cenci, as from yourself from Hunt. There is only one part of it I am judge of—the Poetry and dramatic effect—which by many spirits nowadays is considered the mammon. A modern work it is said must have a purpose, which may be the God. *An artist* must serve Mammon;[1] he must have "self-concentration," selfishness perhaps. You, I am sure, will forgive me for sincerely remarking that you might curb your magnanimity and be more of an artist, and "load every rift" of your subject with ore.[2] The thought of such discipline must fall like cold chains upon you, who perhaps never sat with your wings furl'd for six Months together. And is not this extraordinary talk for the writer of Endymion whose mind was like a pack of scattered cards? I am pick'd up and sorted to a pip. My Imagination is a Monastry and I am its Monk. You must explain my metaphysics to yourself. I am in expectation of Prometheus every day. Could I have my own wish for its interest effected you would have it still in manuscript, or be but now putting an end to the second act. I remember you advising me not to publish my first-blights, on Hampstead heath. I am returning advice upon your hands. Most of the Poems in the volume I send you[3] have been written above two years, and would never have been publish'd but from a hope of gain; so you see I am inclined enough to take your advice now. I must express once more my deep sense of your kindness, adding my sincere thanks and respects for Mrs. Shelley. In the hope of soon seeing you I remain

most sincerely yours,
John Keats—

1. Matthew vi.24; Luke xvi.13.
2. *The Faerie Queene*, II.vii.28, line 5.

3. In his *Autobiography*, Leigh Hunt wrote of Shelley's corpse that Keats's last volume of poems was found open in the jacket pocket: "He had probably been reading it, when surprised by the storm. It was my copy . . . It was burnt with his remains" (III:15). Shelley drowned in the Bay of Spezia in the summer of 1822.

To Charles Brown
AUGUST (?) 1820

My dear Brown,

x x x x x x x¹ I ought to be off at the end of this week, as the cold winds begin to blow towards evening, but I will wait till I have your answer to this. I am to be introduced, before I set out, to a Dr. Clarke, a physician settled at Rome, who promises to befriend me in every way at Rome. The sale of my book is very slow, though it has been very highly rated. One of the causes, I understand from different quarters, of the unpopularity of this new book, and the others also, is the offence the ladies take at me. On thinking that matter over, I am certain that I have said nothing in a spirit to displease any woman I would care to please, but still there is a tendency to class women in my books with roses and sweetmeats. They never see themselves dominant.² If ever I come to publish "Lucy Vaughan Lloyd" there will be some delicate picking for squeamish stomachs. I will say no more, but waiting in anxiety for your answer, doff my hat, and make a purse as long as I can.

Your affectionate friend,
John Keats

1. Brown said that the words he omitted here were "a continuation of the secret in his former letter, ending with a request that I would accompany him to Italy."
2. Here Brown adds an asterisk and at the foot of the page the following commentary: "On what grounds can this opinion rest? Is not 'Isabella' dominant to an extreme, in affection and in heroism? Are not his other poetic women mentally dominant, only in a minor degree? As for what he says respecting his poem by the supposed

'Lucy Vaughan Lloyd,' there is nothing in the fragment he has left, nothing in the intended construction of the story (for I knew all, and was to assist him in the machinery of one part), but to the honour of women. Lord Byron, really popular among women, reduced them, to the offence of some men, to 'roses and sweetmeats.'"

To Fanny Keats

23 AUGUST 1820

Wentworth Place
Wednesday Morning

My dear Fanny,

It will give me great Pleasure to see you here, if you can contrive it, though I confess I should have written instead of calling upon you before I set out on my journey, from the wish of avoiding unpleasant partings. Meantime I will just notice some parts of your Letter. The Seal-breaking business is overblown—I think no more of it. A few days ago I wrote to Mr. Brown, asking him to befriend me with his company to Rome. His answer is not yet come, and I do not know when it will, not being certain how far he may be from the Post Office to which my communication is addressed. Let us hope he will go with me. George certainly ought to have written to you. His troubles, anxieties and fatigues are not quite a sufficient excuse. In the course of time you will be sure to find that this neglect is not forgetfulness. I am sorry to hear you have been so ill and in such low spirits. Now you are better, keep so. Do not suffer Your Mind to dwell on unpleasant reflections. That sort of thing has been the destruction of my health. Nothing is so bad as want of health. It makes one envy Scavengers and Cinder-sifters. There are enough real distresses and evils in wait for everyone to try the most vigorous health. Not that I would say yours are not real, but they are such as to tempt you to employ your imagination on them, rather than endeavour to dismiss them entirely. Do not diet your mind with grief, it destroys the constitution, but let your chief care be of your health, and with that you will meet with your share of Pleasure in the world. Do not doubt it. If I return well from Italy I will turn over a new leaf for you. I have been improving lately, and have very good hopes of "turning a Neuk"[1] and cheating the Consumption. I am not well enough to write to George myself. Mr. Haslam will do it for me, to whom I shall write today, desiring him to mention as gently as possible your complaint. I am, my dear Fanny,

your affectionate Brother
John

1. Burns, "To Miss Ferrier," line 15.

To Fanny Keats
II SEPTEMBER 1820

Monday Morn.

My dear Fanny,

In the hope of entirely re-establishing my health I shall leave England for Italy this week and of course I shall not be able to see you before my departure. It is not illness that prevents me from writing, but as I am recommended to avoid every sort of fatigue I have accepted the assistance of a friend,[1] who I have desired to write to you when I am gone and to communicate any intelligence she may hear of me. I am as well as I can expect and feel very impatient to get on board, as the sea air is expected to be of great benefit to me. My present intention is to stay some time at Naples and then to proceed to Rome where I shall find several friends or at least several acquaintances. At any rate it will be a relief to quit this cold, wet, uncertain climate. I am not very fond of living in cities but there will be too much to amuse me—as soon as I am well enough to go out—to make me feel dull. I have received your parcel and intend to take it with me. You shall hear from me as often as possible. If I feel too tired to write myself I shall have some friend to do it for me. I have not yet heard from George nor can I expect to receive any letters from him before I leave.

Your affectionate brother
John—

1. Fanny Brawne, who wrote and signed the letter. She carried on a correspondence with Fanny Keats beginning the day after Keats embarked for Italy.

❦

Joseph Severn to William Haslam
19 SEPTEMBER 1820

Tuesday Morn.
½ past 8

My dear Haslam,

We are going on well, capitally well so far. Keats is seeming and looking better. Yesterday he was not so well, but I think today he looks promising. I have the best possible hopes.

We are going on most delightfully. The second Lady[1] has joined us, and it is a most singular coincidence that she is laboring under the very same complaint as Keats, the same symptoms, and the same manner of cure. One very good hope is we find sick people insisting and quarreling about being worse than each other. Nothing could make my poor Mother angry but for a sick person to insist on being worse than herself in any denomination of sickness. Now here we are better off, for the Lady who is a very sweet girl about 18 but quite a martyr to the complaint, she insists on being better than Keats, and Keats feels she is certainly worse than himself. Here I must stop for I begin to break down. We are now 13 miles from Margate. I

Joseph Severn, by John Partridge (1825).
National Portrait Gallery, London.

am pumping away. All the circumbendibusses of my craw are in motion. My breakfast is a matter just come to light; from the Severn it has gone to some salmon. Keats I think looks very happy. For myself I would not change with anyone. The Ladies are the quintessence of good nature and prettiness. I don't know which I like best. This is written on the side of the Ship.[2]

* * *

1. Miss Cotterell (the first lady passenger being Mrs. Pidgeon), who died in Naples before 1825.
2. It is unclear whether the letter is complete.

Joseph Severn to William Haslam
21 SEPTEMBER 1820

Dungee Ness—near the Down's
on Deck—Thursday Morn.
20th Sept[1]
1820

My dear Haslam,

It will be best to make a kind of journal in my letters to you, making a Quartet, for we are "hail fellow well met." The Ladies seem to wish communication to be made in London and by including theirs in this that object will be gained. Respecting Mrs. Pidgeon. You will call on Mr. Taylor, the half moon, Gracechurch St., and for Miss Cotterell, apply to her father, No. 9 Richmond Terrace, Walworth.

Sunday, 17 Sept. 1820

Keats thought I had neglected you: "Severn, you should see your friends[2] to the Ship-side." I had seen my brother off in the Morning and it was not a little painful to me, at the same time painful to no purpose. We were soon reconciled to everything about from the Captain down to his Cat. Is it not most delightful that the less we have the less we want? This little Cabin with 6 beds and at first sight every inconvenience in one hour was more endeared to us and to our every purpose than the most stately Palace. Keats seem'd happy, seem'd to have got at the thing he wanted. He cracked his jokes at tea and was quite the "special fellew" of olden time. The kind Mrs. Pidgeon, our Lady passenger, did the honors of the tea table with the most unaffected good nature, and we repaid her most gallantly by falling into a sound sleep and serenading her with a snoring duet, for I have the vanity to think that Keats and myself would continue our harmony even in sleep. I awoke several times with the oddest notions: the first time in a Shoemaker's shop, the next down in a wine cellar pretty well half seas over, but we came to the last snore of our duet, rubbed our eyes and said, "we'll go to bed." We slept most soundly. Mrs. P. has a side scene to retire to.

18 Sept. Monday
I arose soon and looked at Keats. He felt faint in his voice but in other respects well. Our fair passenger came about 8, quite well. We took breakfast and I can assure you enjoy'd it. Our Captain is a good fellow; if he makes us happy his object is gain'd. Keats took his breakfast well. I had proposed to go ashore to Gravesend. He thought this a good opportunity to have some things from the Chymist's,[3] which I got him, with 1/2 hundred Apples and 2 Dozen Biscuits, etc., etc. The Captain was trying to buy a Goat for him, but was not successful. We all returned in a real full boat to dinner. Keats was full of his waggery, looked well, ate well, and was well. At six came down my passport. We were not surprised, for we made sure of it since our oak friend Haslam had the getting of it. The other Lady passenger arrived soon after, a Miss Cotterell—very lady like—but a sad martyr to her illness, which is to a jot the same as Keats. (I told a fib just before, nothing new with me). The passport coming had unloosed all my prattle, and in a short time Keats backing me with his golden jokes in support of my tinsel, began to sail. We recovered Miss Cotterell to laugh and be herself. My wit would have dropt in a minute but for Keats plying me, but I was done up for all

that leaving him sole Master. But I struck up again in my own language or Keats would have born the Lady off in triumph. I began drawing my picture for my dear Sister Maria. Having received great supply in my cheek from the Captain's beefs and tongues, this is it done to the life.[4] Fancy me with two things not knowing which to prefer, my eyes devouring both. After this I drew a Moonlight scene from the Sea which took until 12 (middle watch) after "the house had gone to rest." Keats was in a sound sleep.

19th Sept. Tuesday, off Dover Castle, etc. I arose at daybreak to see the glorious eastern gate. Keats slept till 7. Miss C was rather ill this Morning. I prevailed on her to walk the deck with me at 1/2 past 6. She recovered much. Keats was still better this Morning and Mrs. Pidgeon looked and was the picture of health, but poor me! I began to feel a waltzing on my stomach at breakfast when I wrote the note to you. I was going it most soundly; Miss Cotterell followed me, then Keats, who did it in the most gentlemanly manner, and then the saucy Mrs. Pidgeon who had been laughing at us. Four faces bequeathing to the mighty deep their breakfasts. Here I must change to a Minor Key. Miss C fainted. We soon recovered her. I was very ill; nothing but laying down would do for me. Keats ascended his bed, from which he dictated surgically like Esculapius of old in baso-relievo. Through him Miss C was recovered. We had a cup of tea each and no more. Went to bed and slept until it was time to go to bed. We could not get up again and slept in our cloths all night, Keats the King not even looking pale.

19 Sept. Wednesday,[5] off Brighton Beautiful Morning. We all breakfasted on deck and recovered as we were could enjoy it. About 10 Keats said a storm was hatching. He was right. The rain came on and we retired to our Cabin. It abated and once more we came on deck. At 2 the Storm came on furiously; we retired to our beds. The rolling of the ship was death to us. Towards 4 it increased and our situation was alarming. The trunks rolled across the Cabin, the water poured in from the skylight and we were tumbled from one side to the other of our beds. My curiosity was raised to see the storm and my anxiety to see Keats, for I could only speak to him when in bed. I got up and fell down on the floor from my weakness and the rolling of the ship. Keats was very calm.

The ladies were much frightened and could scarce speak. When I got up to the deck I was astounded. The waves were in Mountains and washed the ship. The watery horizon was like a Mountainous Country, but the ship's motion was beautifully to the sea, falling from one wave to the other in a very lovely manner, the sea each time crossing the deck and one side of the ship being level with the water. This when I understood gave me perfect ease. I communicated below and it did the same, but when the dusk came the sea began to rush in from the side of our Cabin from an opening in the planks. This made us rather long-faced, for it came by pails-full. Again I got out and said to Keats, "here's pretty music for you." With the greatest calmness he answered me, only "Water parted from the sea."[6] I staggered up again and the storm was awful. The Captain and Mate soon came down, for our things were squashing about in the dark. They struck a light and I succeeded in getting my desk off the ground, with clothes, books, etc. The Captain finding it could not be stopped, tacked about from our voyage and the sea ceased to dash against the Cabin for we were sailing against wind and tide, but the horrible agitation continued in the ship lengthways. Here were the pumps working, the sails squalling, the confused voices of the sailors, the things rattling about in every direction, and us poor devils pinn'd up in our beds like ghosts by daylight. Except Keats, he was himself all the time. The ladies suffered the most, but I was out of bed a dozen times to wait on them and tell them there *was* no danger. My sickness made me get into bed very soon each time, but Keats this Morning brags of my sailorship; he says could I have kept on my legs in the water cabin I should have been a standing Miracle.

20th Sept.

I caught a sight of the moon about 3 o' clock this Morning[7] and ran down to tell the glad tidings, but the surly rolling of the sea was worse than the storm. The ship trembled to it and the sea was scarcely calmed by daylight so that we were kept from 2 o' clock yesterday until 6 this Morning without anything. Well, it has done us good. We are like a Quartet of Fighting Cocks this Morning. The Morning is serene. We [have] now [gone] back again some 20 Miles, waiting for a wind, but full of spirits. Keats is without even complaining and Miss Cotterell has a colour in her face. The sea has done his worst upon us. I am better than I have been for years. Farewell my dear fellow,

Josh. Severn

Show this to my family with my love to them. When you read this you
will excuse the manner. I am quite beside myself and have written the
whole this Morning, Thursday, on the deck after a sleepless night and
with a head full of care. You shall have a better the next time.

1. Thursday was 21 September.
2. Taylor, Haslam, Woodhouse.
3. Including the laudanum for which Keats vainly begged on his deathbed.
4. The piece of paper on which Severn drew the portrait has been torn off.
5. Wednesday was 20 September.
6. A popular song from T. A. Arne's opera *Artaxerxes* (1762).
7. Really 21 September.

To Charles Brown
30 SEPTEMBER 1820

Saturday, Sept. 28[1]
Maria Crowther,
off Yarmouth, isle
of wight

My dear Brown,

The time has not yet come for a pleasant Letter from me. I have delayed
writing to you from time to time because I felt how impossible it was to enliven you with one heartening hope of my recovery. This morning in bed
the matter struck me in a different manner. I thought I would write "while
I was in some liking"[2] or I might become too ill to write at all and then if
the desire to have written should become strong it would be a great affliction to me. I have many more Letters to write and I bless my stars that
I have begun, for time seems to press; this may be my best opportunity.

We are in a calm and I am easy enough this morning. If my spirits seem too low you may in some degree impute it to our having been at sea a fortnight without making any way. I was very disappointed at not meeting you at bedhampton, and am very provoked at the thought of you being at Chichester today. I should have delighted in setting off for London for the sensation merely, for what should I do there? I could not leave my lungs or stomach or other worse things behind me. I wish to write on subjects that will not agitate me much. There is one I must mention and have done with it. Even if my body would recover of itself, this would prevent it. The very thing which I want to live most for will be a great occasion of my death. I cannot help it. Who can help it? Were I in health it would make me ill, and how can I bear it in my state? I dare say you will be able to guess on what subject I am harping. You know what was my greatest pain during the first part of my illness at your house. I wish for death every day and night to deliver me from these pains, and then I wish death away, for death would destroy even those pains which are better than nothing. Land and Sea, weakness and decline are great separators, but death is the great divorcer forever. When the pang of this thought has passed through my mind, I may say the bitterness of death is passed. I often wish for you that you might flatter me with the best. I think without my mentioning it for my sake you would be a friend to Miss Brawne when I am dead. You think she has many faults, but for my sake, think she has not one. If there is anything you can do for her by word or deed, I know you will do it. I am in a state at present in which woman merely as woman can have no more power over me than stocks and stones, and yet the difference of my sensations with respect to Miss Brawne and my Sister is amazing. The one seems to absorb the other to a degree incredible. I seldom think of my Brother and Sister in america. The thought of leaving Miss Brawne is beyond everything horrible—the sense of darkness coming over me. I eternally see her figure eternally vanishing. Some of the phrases she was in the habit of using during my last nursing at Wentworth Place ring in my ears. Is there another Life? Shall I awake and find all this a dream? There must be; we cannot be created for this sort of suffering. The receiving of this letter is to be one of yours. I will say nothing about our friendship or rather yours to me more than that as you deserve to escape you will never be so unhappy as I am. I should think of you in my last moments. I shall endeavour to write to Miss Brawne if possible today. A sudden stop to my life in the middle of one of these Letters would be no bad thing for it keeps one in a sort of fever awhile. Though fatigued with a Letter longer than any I have written for a long while it would be better to go on forever than awake to a sense of contrary winds. We expect to put into Portland roads tonight. The Captain, the Crew and the Passengers are all ill-temper'd and weary. I shall write to dilke. I feel as if I was closing my last letter to you, my dear Brown.

Your affectionate friend
John Keats

1. Saturday was 30 September.
2. *1 Henry IV,* III.iii.5.

Joseph Severn to William Haslam
22 OCTOBER 1820

Naples, Oct. 22, 1820

My dear Haslam,

Here we are, thank God, but in quarantine,[1] *therefore accordingly.* Close upon when I wrote you Keats began to droop and the many privations coming in the want of fair winds, nice provisions, airing of beds, and {. . .}[2] made him impatient. This brings on fever and at times he has been very bad, but mind you I think from these things, for our passage has been most horribly rough. Keats has lived through it, but it is a wonder; no way could be worse for him. I had determined on returning with him to London from the conviction that he would die on the passage—and should—but from the English Channel (in which we were groaning for a fortnight) the difficulties seem'd to decrease. We skipp'd the rest in 3 Weeks, though quick yet not well. In the Straits of Gibralter I perceived great changes in Keats for the better. He seem'd recovering, at least looked like it, but in two days

the blood came from his stomach with fever at night and violent perspira-
tion. All this had its cause in—but here is our courier. This is only an opportunity—

farewell Sincerely
Joseph Severn

Keats now is in a doubtful state—I cannot guess what this climate will
  do—

   1. The *Maria Crowther* entered the Bay of Naples on 21 October, only to be quaran-
     tined for ten days.
   2. Missing word.

To Mrs. Samuel Brawne
24 (?) OCTOBER 1820

Oct. 24, Naples Harbour—
care Giovanni[1]

My dear Mrs. Brawne,
   A few words will tell you what sort of a Passage we had and what situation we are in, and few they must be on account of the Quarantine, our
Letters being liable to be opened for the purpose of fumigation at the
Health Office. We have to remain in the vessel ten days and are at present
shut in a tier of ships. The sea air has been beneficial to me about to as great
an extent as squally weather and bad accommodations and provisions has
done harm. So I am about as I was. Give my Love to Fanny and tell her, if I
were well there is enough in this Port of Naples to fill a quire of Paper, but
it looks like a dream. Every man who can row his boat and walk and talk
seems a different being from myself. I do not feel in the world. It has been
unfortunate for me that one of the Passengers is a young Lady in a Consumption; her imprudence has vexed me very much. The knowledge of her
complaint, the flushings in her face, all her bad symptoms have preyed

Fanny Brawne, an ambrotype (ca. 1850).
*Keats House, Hampstead. By permission of
the London Metropolitan Archives.*

upon me. They would have done so had I been in good health. Severn now is a very good fellow but his nerves are too strong to be hurt by other people's illnesses. I remember poor Rice wore me in the same way in the isle of wight. I shall feel a load off me when the Lady vanishes out of my sight. It is impossible to describe exactly in what state of health I am. At this moment I am suffering from indigestion very much, which makes such stuff of this Letter. I would always wish you to think me a little worse than I really am; not being of a sanguine disposition I am likely to succeed. If I do not recover your regret will be softened; if I do your pleasure will be doubled. I dare not fix my Mind upon Fanny. I have not dared to think of her. The only comfort I have had that way has been in thinking for hours together of having the knife she gave me put in a silver-case, the hair in a Locket and the Pocket Book in a gold net. Show her this. I dare say no more, yet you must not believe I am so ill as this Letter may look, for if ever there was a person born without the faculty of hoping I am he. Severn is writing to Haslam, and I have just asked him to request Haslam to send you his account of my health. O, what an account I could give you of the Bay of Naples if I could once more feel myself a Citizen of this world. I feel a Spirit in my Brain would lay it forth pleasantly. O, what a misery it is to have an intellect in splints! My Love again to Fanny. Tell Tootts[2] I wish I could pitch her a basket of grapes, and tell Sam[3] the fellows catch here with a line a little fish much like an anchovy, pull them up fast. Remember me to Mrs. and Mr. Dilke. Mention to Brown that I wrote him a letter at Portmouth which I did not send and am in doubt if he ever will see it.

My dear Mrs. Brawne,
yours sincerely and affectionately
John Keats—

Good bye Fanny! god bless you.

1. Possibly the courier mentioned by Severn in the previous letter.
2. Presumably her daughter Margaret.
3. Her son.

To Charles Brown
I, 2 NOVEMBER 1820[1]

Naples, Wednesday, first in November
My dear Brown,
    Yesterday we were let out of Quarantine, during which my health suffered more from bad air and a stifled cabin than it had done the whole voyage. The fresh air revived me a little, and I hope I am well enough this

morning to write to you a short calm letter, if that can be called one in which I am afraid to speak of what I would the fainest dwell upon. As I have gone thus far into it, I must go on a little. Perhaps it may relieve the load of WRETCHEDNESS which presses upon me. The persuasion that I shall see her no more will kill me. I cannot q———.[2] My dear Brown, I should have had her when I was in health, and I should have remained well. I can bear to die. I cannot bear to leave her. Oh, God! God! God! Everything I have in my trunks that reminds me of her goes through me like a spear. The silk lining she put in my travelling cap scalds my head. My imagination is horribly vivid about her. I see her. I hear her. There is nothing in the world of sufficient interest to divert me from her a moment. This was the case when I was in England. I cannot recollect, without shuddering, the time that I was prisoner at Hunt's, and used to keep my eyes fixed on Hampstead all day. Then there was a good hope of seeing her again. Now! O, that I could be buried near where she lives! I am afraid to write to her, to receive a letter from her. To see her handwriting would break my heart; even to hear of her anyhow, to see her name written would be more than I can bear. My dear Brown, what am I to do? Where can I look for consolation or ease? If I had any chance of recovery, this passion would kill me. Indeed through the whole of my illness, both at your house and at Kentish Town, this fever has never ceased wearing me out. When you write to me, which you will do immediately, write to Rome (poste restante). If she is well and happy, put a mark thus +, — if — Remember me to all. I will endeavour to bear my miseries patiently. A person in my state of health should not have such miseries to bear. Write a short note to my sister, saying you have heard from me. Severn is very well. If I were in better health I should urge your coming to Rome. I fear there is no one can give me any comfort. Is there any news of George? O, that something fortunate had ever happened to me or my brothers! Then I might hope, but despair is forced upon me as a habit. My dear Brown, for my sake, be her advocate forever. I cannot say a word about Naples. I do not feel at all concerned in the thousand novelties around me. I am afraid to write to her. I should like her to know that I do not forget her. Oh, Brown, I have coals of fire in my breast. It surprised me that the human heart is capable of containing and bearing so much misery. Was I born for this end? God bless her, and her mother, and my sister, and George, and his wife, and you, and all!

Your ever affectionate friend,
John Keats

Thursday. I was a day too early for the courier. He sets out now. I have
been more calm today, though in a half dread of not continuing so. I
said nothing of my health. I know nothing of it. You will hear Severn's
account from X X X X X X.[3] I must leave off. You bring my thoughts
too near to ————[4]

God bless you!

1. Printed from Brown's *Life of John Keats*.
2. Here Brown added an asterisk and the note: "He could not go on with this sentence, nor even write the word 'quit,' as I suppose. The word WRETCHEDNESS above he himself wrote in large characters."
3. Haslam.
4. Fanny Brawne.

Joseph Severn to William Haslam
1, 2 NOVEMBER 1820

Naples—Nov. 1—1820

My dear Haslam,

We are just released from the loathsome misery of Quarantine.[1] Foul
weather and foul air for the whole 10 days kept us to the small Cabin surrounded by about 2000 ships in a wretched Mole[2] not sufficient for half the
number. Yet Keats is still living. May I not have hopes of him? He has
passed what I must have thought would kill myself. Now that we are on

shore and feel the fresh air I am horror struck at his sufferings on this voyage. All that could be fatal to him in air and diet, with the want of medicine and conveniences he has weather'd, if I may call his poor shattered frame and broken heart weathering it. For myself I have stood it firmly until this Morning when in a moment my spirits dropt at the sight of his suffering. A plentiful shower of tears (which he did not see) has relieved me somewhat, but what he has passed still unnerves me. But now we are breathing in a large room with Vesuvius in our view. Keats has become calm and thinks favorably of this place, for we are meeting with much kind treatment on every side, more particularly from an English Gentleman[3] here (brother to Miss Cotterell, one of our Lady passengers), who has shown unusually humane treatment to Keats—unasked. These, with very good accommodations at our Inn (Villa da Londra), have kept him up through dinner, but on the other hand, Dr. Milne is at Rome (wither Keats is proposing to go). The weather is now cold, wet and foggy, and we find ourselves on the wrong side for his hope for recovery. (For the present I will talk to him; he is disposed to it. I will talk him to sleep for he has suffered much fatigue).

Nov. 2nd

Keats went to bed much recover'd. I took every means to remove from him a heavy grief that may tend more than anything to be fatal. He told me much, very much, and I don't know whether it was more painful for me or himself, but it had the effect of much relieving him. He went very calm to bed. Poor fellow! He is still sleeping at 1/2 past nine. If I can but cure his mind I will bring him back to England—*well*—but I fear it never can be done in this world. The grand scenery here effects him a little, but he is too infirm to enjoy it. His gloom deadens his sight to everything and but for intervals of something like ease he must soon end it. You will like to know how I have managed in respect to self. I have had a most severe task, full of contrarieties. What I did one way was undone another. The lady passenger, though in the same state as Keats yet differing in constitution, required almost everything the opposite to him; for instance, if the cabin windows were not open she would faint and remain entirely insensible 5 or 6 hours together. If the windows were open, poor Keats would be taken with a cough (a violent one, caught from this cause) and sometimes spitting of blood. Now I had this to manage continually for our other passenger is a most consummate brute. She would see Miss Cotterell stiffened like a corpse—I have sometimes thought her dead—nor ever lend the least aid. Full a dozen times I have recovered this Lady and put her to bed. Sometimes she would faint 4 times in a day, yet at intervals would seem quite well and was full of spirits. She is both young and lively and but for her we should have had more heaviness, though much less trouble. She has benefited by Keats' advice. I used to act under him and reduced the fainting each time. She has recovered very much and gratefully ascribes it to us, her brother the same. The Captain has behaved with great kindness to us all, but more particularly Keats. Everything that could be got or done was at his service without asking. He is a good-natured man to his own injury, strange for a Captain. I won't say so much for his ship. It's a black hole—5 sleeping in one Cabin—the one you saw, the only one. During the voyage I have been frequently sea-sick, sometimes severely 2 days together. We have had only one real fright on the seas, not to mention continued squalls and a storm. "All's well that ends well," and these ended well. Our fright was from two Portuegese Ships of War. They brought us to with a shot which passed close under our stern. This was not pleasant for us you will allow, nor was it decreased when they came up, for a more infernal set I never could imagine. After some trifling questions they allowed us to go on to our no small delight. Our captain was afraid they would plunder the ship. This was in the Bay of Biscay over which we were carried by a good wind. Keats has written to Brown and in quarantine another to Mrs. Brawn. He requests you will tell Mrs. Brawn what I think of him for he is too bad to judge of himself. This Morning he is still very much better. We are in good spirits and I may say hopeful fellows, at least I may say as much for Keats. He made an Italian Pun today. The rain is coming down in torrents. When you write, direct Post office, Rome.

1. They landed on 31 October, Keats's twenty-fifth birthday.
2. "Hole"?
3. Charles Cotterell, Miss Cotterell's brother.

Dr. James Clark to ?

27 NOVEMBER 1820[1]

* * *

Keats arrived here about a week ago[2] and I have got him into comfortable lodgings. I can hardly yet give you a decided opinion of his case but will in my next. The chief part of his disease, as far as I can yet see, seems seated in his Stomach. I have some suspicion of disease of the heart and it may be of the lungs, but of this say nothing to his friends as in my next I shall be able to give you something more satisfactory. His mental exertions and application have I think been the sources of his complaints. If I can put his mind at ease, I think he'll do well. Get Mr. Taylor or some of his friends to write him. I'm afraid the Idea of his expenses operates on his mind and some plan must be adopted to remove this if possible. The truth is, having come abroad for the purpose of restoring his health, everything must be done to favor the change of climate. I mean that he shall buy or hire by the month a horse to ride out whenever the weather permits and so forth. After all, his expenses will be very little, and he's too noble an animal to be allowed to sink without some sacrifice being made to save him. I wish I were rich enough his living here should cost him nothing. He has a friend with him who seems very attentive to him but between you and I is not the best suited for his companion, but I suppose poor fellow he had no choice. I fear much there is something operating on his mind—at least so it appears to me. He either feels that he is now living at the expense of someone else or something of that kind. If my opinion be correct, we may throw medicine to the dogs. Let everything be done to relieve his mind from any Idea of that kind as far as possible. I feel very much interested in him and believe me will do everything in my power to be of service to him. I am glad to find the Edinburgh Reviewers have been just towards him.[3] He seems much pleased with Rome and prefers it greatly to Naples. I was writing to some friends at Naples about him at the moment he unexpectedly made his appearance here.

* * *

1. A transcript made by Hessey of part of a letter to an unknown person, possibly Samuel F. Gray, a medical writer, or an agent of Taylor and Hessey's.
2. He reached Rome at least as early as 15 November.
3. A reference to Jeffrey's August review.

To Charles Brown
30 NOVEMBER 1820[1]

Rome, 30 November 1820

My dear Brown,

'Tis the most difficult thing in the world to me to write a letter. My stomach continues so bad, that I feel it worse on opening any book, yet I am much better than I was in Quarantine. Then I am afraid to encounter the proing and conning of anything interesting to me in England. I have an habitual feeling of my real life having past, and that I am leading a posthumous existence. God knows how it would have been, but it appears to me. However, I will not speak of that subject. I must have been at Bedhampton nearly at the time you were writing to me from Chichester. How unfortunate, and to pass on the river too! There was my star predominant! I cannot answer anything in your letter, which followed me from Naples to Rome, because I am afraid to look it over again. I am so weak (in mind) that I cannot bear the sight of any handwriting of a friend I love so much as I do you. Yet I ride the little horse, and at my worst, even in Quarantine, summoned up more puns, in a sort of desperation, in one week than in any year of my life. There is one thought enough to kill me. I have been well, healthy, alert etc., walking with her, and now the knowledge of contrast, feeling for light and shade, all that information (primitive sense) necessary for a poem are great enemies to the recovery of the stomach. There, you rogue, I put you to the torture, but you must bring your philosophy to bear as I do mine, really, or how should I be able to live? Dr. Clarke is very attentive to me; he says there is very little the matter with my lungs, but my stomach, he says, is very bad. I am well disappointed in hearing good news from George, for it runs in my head we shall all die young. I have not written to x x x x x yet, which he must think very neglectful. Being anxious to send him a good account of my health, I have delayed it from week to week. If I recover, I will do all in my power to correct the mistakes made during sickness, and if I should not, all my faults will be forgiven. I shall write to x x x tomorrow, or next day. I will write to x x x x x in the middle of next week. Severn is very well, though he leads so dull a life with me. Remember me to all friends, and tell x x x x^2 I should not have left London without taking leave of him, but from being so low in body and mind. Write to George as soon as you receive this, and tell him how I am, as far as you can guess, and also a note to my sister, who walks about my imagination like a ghost; she is so like Tom. I can scarcely bid you good bye even in a letter. I always made an awkward bow.

God bless you!
John Keats

1. Printed from Brown's *Life of John Keats.*
2. The deleted names may refer to Haslam, Dilke, Woodhouse, and Reynolds.

Joseph Severn to Charles Brown
14, 17 DECEMBER 1820

Rome, Dec. 14, 1820

My dear Brown,

I fear our poor Keats is at his worst. A most unlooked-for relapse has confined him to his bed with every chance against him. It has been so sudden upon what I almost thought convalescence and without any seeming cause that I cannot calculate on the next change. I dread it, for his suffering is so great, so continued, and his fortitude so completely gone, that any further change must make him delirious. This is the fifth day and I see him get worse, but stop. I will tell you the manner of this relapse from the first.

Dec. 17, 4 Morning

Not a moment can I be from him. I sit by his bed and read all day and at night I humour him in all his wanderings. He has just fallen asleep, the first for 8 nights, and now from mere exhaustion. I hope he will not wake until I have written this, for I am anxious beyond measure to have you know this worse and worse state. Yet I dare not let him see I think it dangerous. I had seen him wake on the morning of this attack, and to all appearance he was going on merrily and had unusual good spirits, when in an instant a Cough seized him and he vomited near two Cupfuls of blood. In a moment I got Dr. Clark, who saw the manner of it, and immediately took away about 8 ounces of blood from the Arm; it was black and thick in the extreme. Keats was much alarmed and dejected. O, what an awful day I had with him! He rush'd out of bed and said "this day shall be my last," and but for me most certainly it would. At the risk of losing his confidence I took every destroying means from his reach, nor let him be from my sight one minute. The blood broke forth again in like quantity the next morning, and the doctor thought it expedient to take away the like quantity of blood; this was in the same dismal state, and must have been from the horrible state of despair he was in. But I was so fortunate as to talk him into a little calmness, and with some English newspapers he became quite patient under the necessary arrangements.

This is the 9th day, and no change for the better. Five times the blood has come up in coughing, in large quantities generally in the morning, and nearly the whole time his saliva has been mixed with it. But this is the lesser evil when compared with his Stomach. Not a single thing will digest. The torture he suffers all and every night and best part of the day is dreadful in the extreme. The distended stomach keeps him in perpetual hunger or craving, and this is augmented by the little nourishment he takes to keep down the blood. Then his mind is worse than all—despair in every shape. His imagination and memory present every image in horror, so strong that morning and night I tremble for his Intellect. The recollection of England, of his "good friend Brown," and his happy few weeks in Mrs. Brawne's Care, his Sister and brother—O, he will mourn over every circumstance to me whilst I cool his burning forehead until I tremble through every vein in concealing my tears from his staring glassy eyes. How he can be Keats again from all this I have little hope, but I may see it too gloomy since each coming night I sit up adds its dismal contents to my mind.

Dr. Clark will not say so much, although there is no bounds to his attention, yet with little success "can he administer to a mind diseased."[1] Yet all that can be done most kindly he does whilst his Lady, like himself in refined feeling, prepares and cooks all that poor Keats takes. For in this wilderness of a place (for an Invalid) there was no alternative. Yesterday Dr. Clark went all over Rome for a certain kind of fish, and got it, but just as I received it from Mrs. C delicately prepared, Keats was taken by the spitting of blood and is now gone back all the 9 days. This was occasioned by disobeying the Doctor's commands. Keats is required to be kept as low as possible to check the blood, so that he is weak and gloomy. Every day he raves that he will die from hunger, and I was obliged to give him more than allowed. You cannot think how dreadful this is for me. The Doctor on the one hand tells me I shall kill him to give him more than he allows, and

Keats raves for more till I am in complete tremble for him. But I have talked him over now. We have the best opinion of Dr. C's skill. He seems to understand the case, and comes over 4 and 5 times a day. He left word at 12 this morning to call any time in case of danger.

I heard Keats say how he should like Mrs. Brawne and Mrs. Dilke to visit his sister at Walthamstow. Will you say this for me, and to Mr. Taylor that Keats was about to write favorably on the very time of his relapse? For myself I am keeping up beyond my most sanguine expectations; 8 Nights I have been up, and in the days never a moment away from my patient but to run over to the Doctor. But I will confess my spirits have been sometimes quite pulled down, for these wretched Romans have no Idea of comfort. Here I am obliged to wash up, cook, and read to Keats all day. Added to this I have had no letters yet from my family. This is a damp to me for I never knew how dear they were to me. I think of my Mother and I think of Keats for they are something the same in this tormenting Indigestion. But if Keats recovers, and then letters bring good news, why I shall take upon myself to be myself again. I wrote last to my good friend Haslam. It will tell you all the events up to the relapse of Keats. I had put the letters in post on the same morning. It was my custom to walk until Keats awoke. We did breakfast about 9 o' Clock. My head begins to sally round so much that I cannot recollect. I will write to Mr. Taylor on the next change in my friend, and to the Kind Mrs. Brawne when I have any good news. Will you re-member me to this lady? Little did I dream on THIS when I saw her last in London. Will you, my dear Brown, write to me, for a letter to Keats now would almost kill him. Give Haslam this sad news. I am quite exhausted. Farewell. I wish you were here my dear Brown.

Sincerely,   *Joseph Severn* (Signed)

I have just looked at him. This will be a good night.

---

1. *Macbeth,* V.iii.40.

Joseph Severn to John Taylor
24 DECEMBER 1820[1]

Rome, Dec. 24, 1820
1/2 past 4 morn.

My dear Sir,

Keats has changed somewhat for the worse, at least his mind has much, very, very much, and this leaves his state much the same, and quite as hopeless. Yet the blood has ceased to come, his digestion is better and but for a cough he must be improving, that is as far as respects his body. But the fatal prospect of Consumption hangs before his "mind's eye"[2] and turns everything to despair and wretchedness. He will not bear the idea of living, much less strive to live. I seem to lose his confidence by trying to give him this hope. He will not hear that his future prospects are favorable. He says that the continued stretch of his imagination has killed him and were he to recover he could not write another line. Then his good friends in England. He only cherishes the idea of what they have done and this he turns to a load of care for the future. The high hopes of him, his certain success, his experience, he shakes his head at it and bids it farewell. The remembrance of his brother's death I cannot keep from him; all his own symptoms he recollects in him and this with every cough and pain. The many troubles, persecutions, and I may say cruelties he has borne now weigh heavy on him. If he dies I am witness that he dies of a broken heart and spirit. Would that his enemies could see this martyrdom of the most noble feeling and brightest genius to be found in existence. I only wish this for their punishment. He is now only a wreck of his former self. The gnawing weight upon his mind with the entire loss of bodily strength and appearance push him to malevolence, suspicion and impatience, yet everyone is struck with him and interested about him. I am astonished and delighted at the respect paid him, but even this—I mean the general utmost endeavour he receives—his dreadful state of mind turns to persecution and sometimes even murder. He is now under the {. . .}[3] was administered to him by an individual in London. All that fortitude and as it were bravery of mind against bodily suffering are away from him, and the want of some kind hope to feed his voracious imagination leaves him to the wreck of ideas without purpose, imagination without philosophy. Yet this night he said to me: "I think a malignant being must have power over us, over whom the Almighty has little or no influence. Yet you know Severn, I cannot believe in your book, the Bible, but I feel the horrible want of some faith, some hope, something to rest on now. There must be such a book and I know that is it, but I can't believe it. I am destined to every torment in this world, even to this little comfort on my deathbed {. . .}."

O, my dear Sir, you cannot imagine what I sometimes feel. I have read to him incessantly until no more books could be had, for they must be new to him, and above all the book he has set his mind upon all through this last week is not to be had, the works of Jeremy Taylor. His desire to have these read to him is very great, and yet not to be had. Is not this hard? The other books he wished me write down are not in Rome. They were Madam Dacier's Plato[4] and the Pilgrim's Progress. I have read to him Don Quixote at his request and some of Miss Edgeworth's novels, but there are no Books in Rome. We sometimes get some English papers.

Now observe, my dear Sir, I don't for a moment push my little but honest Religious faith upon poor Keats, except as far as my feelings go, but these I try to keep from him. I fall into his views sometimes to quiet him and tincture them with a somewhat of mine, but his many changes both body and mind render my charge most affecting and even dangerous, for I cannot leave him without someone with him that he likes.[5] This is the third week and I have not left him more than two hours. He has not been out of bed the whole time; he says this alone is enough to kill him was he in health, and then seeing no face but mine {. . .} him he {. . .} say it makes him worse to think how I should be occupied and how I am. Sometimes I succeed in persuading him that he will recover and go back with me to England. I do lament a thousand times that he ever left England, not from the want of medical aid or even friends, for nothing can be superior to the kindness of Dr. Clark, etc., but the journey of 2000 Miles was too much for his state, even when he left England, and now he has most surely broken down under it. I have thought he would die before he reached this place. Journeys to and about Jatatu [?] are not for an Invalid.

Dr. Clark gives very little hope of him. He says he may recover from this by some change in his mind, but he will most certainly die (at some not distant period) of Consumption. No disorganisation exists at present, but a total derangement of the digestive powers. They have nearly lost their functions and it is this cause that produces the blood from the heads of {. . .} on the chest. It does not come at present.

For myself, my dear Sir, I still keep up nearly as well as I did, altho' I have not got any person to relieve me. Keats makes me careful of myself. He is my doctor. A change of scene might make me better, but I can do without it. It is 6 o' clock in the Morning. I have been writing all night. This is my 5th Letter. Keats has just awoken. I must leave off and boil my kettle; he hears me writing and inquires, "Tell Taylor I shall soon be in a second Edition—in sheets—and cold dress." He desired me tell you some time since that he would have written you but felt he could not say anything; it gave him pain. We have received 5 Letters, 3 to Keats. He read one from Mr. Hessey and another from Mr. Brown, but the third he could not read and was effected most bitterly. He says no more letters for him. Even good news will not lift him up. He is too far gone. But he does not know I think this, nor does he know Dr. C's opinion, but his own knowledge of Anatomy is unfortunate. Farewell, my dear Sir,

Josh. Severn

Tell my friend Haslam I will write him by next post, and the first good
    news shall be for the kind Mrs. Brawn. I still hope to have Keats better.
    He has waked very calm. I have got leave to have him up today. He will
    not take any food. I have been afraid that he would refuse to take food,
    and the like of medicine. The Doctor seem'd to think this yesterday. He
    is much changed this Morning in appearance for the worse, but he
    remains (9 o' clock) very calm and good-natured (4 o' clock) dozing

between wiles. He has eaten a small pudding and taken his milk. He is
still composed, but low. I am rather alarmed about money. At Naples I
expended nearly all my stock. Here I can get more by my Miniature
Painting, perhaps quite as much as we could want should Keats fail, but
now I am kept from it. No one to relieve me with Keats. I dare say I
shall manage well, for here are above a dozen to sit to me. I am quite
concerned at the expences here for an invalid. Italy is only for persons
in health, for had I fallen into Keats's views and these cursed Italians'
imposition all his money must have been gone, but the kindness of
Dr. C has saved much expence. Horses and Coaches have been the
greatest charge. Proper lodging is dear, and as for proper food, it cannot
be got for money; that is, it cannot be got. Dr. Clark went all over
Rome for a fish proper for Keats. If I get a proper thing one day I can't
get it the next. They cannot make 2 pudding three [?]. The price of a
Horse per month in English Money: £6; lodging: £4.16; and a dinner 4
sh. The money remaining at the Bankers: 260 Scudi, about £52, with
here £70.

    4 o' clock. This moment the doctor sends me word that my
Landlady has reported to the Police that Keats is dying of a
Consumption. Now this has made me vent some curses against her.
The words "dying" and "Consumption" have rather dampt my spirits.
The laws are very severe. I do not know the extent of them. Should
poor Keats die, everything in his room is condemned to be burned even
to paper on the walls. The Italians are so alarmed at Consumption. The
expences are enormous after a death for examinations and precautions
to contagion. Fools. I can hardly contain myself. O! I will be revenged
on this old Cat for putting the notion in my head of my friend's dying,
and of Consumption; but stop, I know the Doctor half thinks so, but
will not say it. He has brought an Italian Physician here who thinks
Keats has a malformed chest. Should he die the law will demand him to
be opened. I have got some books, Scots Monastery and some travels.
He seems inclined to hear me read all this evening. Keats has just said it
is his last request that no mention be made of him in any manner

publicly—in Reviews, Magazines or Newspapers—that no Engraving be taken from any Picture of him. Once more, farewell.

1. This letter was first printed in Hyder Rollins, ed., *The Keats Circle,* 2 vols. (Cambridge, Mass.: Harvard University Press, 1948).
2. *Hamlet,* I.ii.185.
3. Four or five words missing or illegible, though editors have added, "impression that poison." Subsequent brackets indicate one to two words missing.
4. Anne Lefèvre Dacier, *The Works of Plato Abridg'd* (1749).
5. Here Severn added an asterisk and at the bottom of the sheet wrote: "He does not like anyone. He says a strange face makes him miserable."

1821

Dr. James Clark to ?

3 JANUARY 1821[1]

* * *

In my last I said a few words about poor Keats. Since that date he has had another attack of bleeding from the lungs which has weakened him greatly, and he is now in a most deplorable state. His stomach is ruined and the state of his mind is the worst possible for one in his condition, and will undoubtedly hurry on an event that I fear is not far distant and even in the best frame of mind would not probably be long protracted. His digestive organs are sadly deranged and his lungs are also diseased. Either of these would be a great evil, but to have both under the state of mind which he unfortunately is in must soon kill him. I fear he has long been governed by his imagination and feelings and now has little power and less inclination to endeavour to keep them under. I feel much interested in the poor fellow indeed. It is most distressing to see a mind like his (what it might have been) in the deplorable state in which it is. His friend Mr. Severn is most attentive to him. Were Christianity of no use but to give tranquillity to the sickbed, it were the greatest blessing on earth. I am sorry indeed, and much disappointed in having to communicate such sad accounts of poor K. When I first saw him I thought something might be done, but now I fear the prospect is a hopeless one.

* * *

1. A transcript by Hessey of part of a letter possibly addressed to Samuel F. Gray.

Joseph Severn to Mrs. Samuel Brawne
11 JANUARY 1821[1]

Rome, Jan. 11, 1821
1 o' clock morning

My dear Madam,

I said that "the first good news I had should be for the kind Mrs. Brawn." I am thankful and delighted to make good my promise, to be at all able to do it, for among all the horrors hovering over poor Keats this was the most dreadful: that I could see no possible way and but a fallacious hope for his recovery. But now, thank God, I have a real one. I most certainly think I shall bring him back to England, at least my anxiety for his recovery and comfort make me think this, for half the cause of his danger has arisen from the loss of England, from the dread of never seeing it more. O, this hung upon him like a torture; never may I behold the like again even in my direst enemy. Little did I think what a task of affliction and danger I had undertaken, for I only thought of the beautiful mind of Keats, my attachment to him, and his convalescence.

But I will tell you dear Madam the singular reason I have for hoping his recovery. In the first fortnight of this attack his memory presented to him everything that was dear and delightful, even to the minutiae, and with it all the persecution and I may say villainy practised upon him, his exquisite sensibility for everyone save his poor self, all his own means and comfort expended upon others, almost in vain. These he would contrast with his present suffering and say that all was brought on by them. And he was right. Now he has changed to calmness and quietude, as singular as productive of good, for his mind was certainly killing him. He has now given up all thoughts, hopes, or even wish for recovery. His mind is in a state of peace from the final leave he has taken of this world and all its future hopes.

This has been an immense weight for him to rise from. He remains quiet and submissive under his heavy fate.

Now if anything will recover him it is this absence of himself. I have perceived for the last 3 days symptoms of recovery. Dr. Clark even thinks so. Nature again revives in him, I mean where art was used before. Yesterday he permitted me to carry him from his bedroom to our sitting room, to put him clean things on, and to talk about my Painting to him. This is my good news. Don't think it otherwise, my dear Madam, for I have been in such a state of anxiety and discomfiture in this barbarous place that the least hope of my friend's recovery is a heaven to me.

For Three weeks I have never left him. I have sat up at night. I have read to him nearly all day and even in the night. I light the fire, make his breakfast and sometimes am obliged to cook, make his bed and even sweep the room. I can have these things done, but never at the time when they ought and must be done, so that you will see my alternative. What enrages me most is making a fire. I blow, blow, for an hour. The smoke comes fuming out. My kettle falls over on the burning sticks—no stove—Keats calling me to be with him, the fire catching my hands and the door bell ringing. All these to one quite unused and not all capable, with the want of every proper material, come not a little galling.

But to my great surprise I am not ill, or even restless, nor have I been all the time. There is nothing but what I will do for him. There is no alternative but what I think and provide myself against, except his death. Not the loss of him, I am not prepared to bear that. But the inhumanity, the barbarism of these Italians. So far I have kept everything from poor Keats, but if he did know but part of what I suffer for them and their cursed laws it would kill him. Just to instance one thing among many: news was brought me the other day that our gentle landlady had reported to the Police that my friend was dying of consumption. Now their law is that every individual thing in each room the patient has been in shall without reserve even to the paper on the walls be destroyed by fire. This startled me not a little, for in our sitting room where I wanted to bring him there is property worth about £150 besides all our own books, etc. invaluable. Now my difficulty was to shift him to this room and let no one know it. This was a heavy task from the unfortunate manner of the place. Our landlady's apartments are on the same floor with ours. Her servant waits on me when it pleases her and enters from an adjoining room. I was determined on removing Keats, let what would be the consequence. The change was most essential to his health and spirits, and the following morning I set about accomplishing it. In the first place I blocked up the door so that they could not enter, then made up a bed on the Sofa and removed my friend to it. The greatest difficulty was in keeping all from him. I succeeded in this too by making his bed and sweeping the room where it is, and going dinnerless with all the pretensions of dining, persuading him that the Servant had made his bed and I had been dining. He half-suspected this but as he could not tell the why and the wherefore there it ended. I got him back in the afternoon and no one save Dr. Clark knew of it.

Dr. C still attends him with his usual kindness and shows his good heart in everything he does; the like of his lady. I cannot tell which shows us the most kindness. I am even a mark of their care; mince pies and numberless nice things come over to keep me alive, and but for their kindness I am afraid we should go on very gloomily. Now my dear Madam I must leave off. My eyes are beginning to be unruly, and I must write a most important letter to our President, Sir Thomas Lawrence, before I suffer myself to sleep.

Will you be so kind as to write Mr. Taylor that it was at Messrs. Torlonia's Advice Mr. Keats drew a Bill for the whole Sum £120? This was to save the trouble and expense of many small bills. He now draws in small sums. I have the whole of affairs under charge and am trying the nearest possible way. Mr. Taylor will hear from Dr C. about the bill; it will be well arranged. Present my respectful Compliments to Miss B who I hope and trust is quite well. Now that I think of her my mind is carried to your happy Wentworth Place. O, I would my unfortunate friend had never left it for the hopeless disadvantage of this comfortless Italy. He has many many times talked over the few happy days at your House, the only time when his mind was at ease. I hope still to see him with you again. Farewell, my dear

Madam. One more thing I must say. Poor Keats cannot see any letters, at least he will not. They affect him so much and increase his danger. The two last I repented giving. He made me put them into his box unread. More of these when I write again; meanwhile, any matter of moment had better come to me. I will be very happy to receive advice and remembrance from you. Once more farewell,

(signed) *Josh. Severn*

I have just looked at him. He is in a beautiful sleep. In look he is very
   much more himself. I have the greatest hopes of him.

1. This letter was first printed in Hyder Rollins, ed., *The Keats Circle,* 2 vols. (Cambridge, Mass.: Harvard University Press, 1948).

Joseph Severn to William Haslam
15 JANUARY 1821

Rome—Jan. 15th 1821
Sunday Night, 1/2 past 11—

My dear Haslam,

   Poor Keats has just fallen asleep. I have watched him and read to him to his very last wink. He has been saying to me, "Severn, I can see under your quiet look immense twisting and contending. You don't know what you are reading. You are enduring for me more than I'd have you. O! that my last hour was come. What is it puzzles you now? What is it happens?" I tell him that "nothing happens, nothing worries me beyond his seeing, that it has been the dull day." Getting from myself to his recovery, and then my painting, and then England, and then—but they are all lies; my heart almost leaps to deny them, for I have the veriest load of care that ever came upon these shoulders of mine. For Keats is sinking daily. He is dying of a consumption, of a confirmed consumption. Perhaps another three weeks may lose me him forever. This alone would break down the most gallant spirit. I had made sure of his recovery when I set out. I was selfish and thought of his value to me and made a point of my future success depending on his candor to me. This is not all. I have prepared myself to bear this now, now that I must and should have seen it before, but Torlonia's the bankers have refused any more money. The bill is returned unaccepted, "no effects," and I tomorrow must—aye, *must*—pay the last solitary Crowns for this cursed lodging place. Yet more. Should our unfortunate friend die, all the furniture will be burnt; beds, sheets, curtains and even the walls must be scraped. And these devils will come upon me for £100 or £150, the making good.

But above all, this noble fellow lying on the bed is dying in horror: no kind hope smoothing down his suffering, no philosophy, no religion to support him, yet with all the most gnawing desire for it, yet without the possibility of receiving it. It is not from any religious principles I feel this, but from the individual sufferings of his mind in this point. I would not care from what source, so he could understand his misfortunes and glide into his lot. O! My dear Haslam, this is my greatest care, a care that I pray to God may soon end, for he says in words that tear my very heartstrings: "Miserable wretch I am. This last cheap comfort which every rogue and fool have is denied me in my last moments. Why is this? O! I have serv'd everyone with my utmost good, yet why is this? I cannot understand this." And then his chattering teeth. If I do break down it will be under this. But I pray that some kind of comfort may come to his lot, that some angel of goodness will lead him through this dark wilderness.

Now Haslam, what do you think of my situation? For I know not what may come with tomorrow. I am hedg'd in every way that you can look at me. If I could leave Keats for a while everyday I could soon raise money by my face painting, but he will not let me out of his sight. He cannot bear the face of a stranger. He has made me go out twice and leave him solus. I'd rather cut my tongue out than tell him that money I must get; that would kill him at a word. I will not do anything that may add to his misery, for I have tried on every point to leave for a few hours in the day, but he won't unless he is left alone. This won't do, nor shall, not for another minute whilst he is John Keats.

Yet will I not bend down under these. I will not give myself a jot of credit unless I stand firm, and will too. You'd be rejoiced to see how I am kept up. Not a flinch yet. I read, cook, make the beds and do all the menial offices, for no soul comes near Keats except the Doctor and myself. Yet I do all this with a cheerful heart, for I thank God my little but honest religion stays me up all through these trials. I'll pray to God tonight that he may look down with mercy on my poor friend and myself. I feel no dread of what more I am to bear but look to it with confidence.

You see my hopes of being kept by the Royal Academy will be cut off unless I send a picture by the Spring. I have written Sir T. Lawrence some bold things that I have been feasting my mind on in this confinement; no less than a project by which to copy (same size) Raphael's grand pictures in the Vatican—the Sanctum Sanctorum of Painting—8 in number. I think this will save me at all events.

I have got a volume of Jeremy Taylor's Works which Keats has heard me read tonight. This is a treasure and came when I thought it hopeless. Why may not other good things come, and even money? I will still keep myself up with the best hope. Dr. Clark is still the same altho' he has received notice about this bill. I have said to him that if Keats is wanting in any possible thing now that would give him ease but would be out of his agreement, or at least fears the payment for, I will be answerable in any way he may think fit. But no, he does his everything. I lament a thousand times that Mr. Taylor did not tell me about this money, that it was to be drawn in small bills. I could have stopped this. As it is I don't know what to do, unless money is coming through your means, altho' I know you cannot. But farewell. Pray, my dear fellow, don't ask me for journals. Every day's would have been more or less like this. Not a word at my Father's.

Sincerely, ever
Joseph Severn

This letter is for thine own eye and own heart, or as you see fit. I wrote by last post to Mrs. Brawne. I think she should know these, but it will be a severe blow. See Brown too, though I do you injustice to tell you. On Wednesday I write to Mr. *Hunt.*

The proofs of Keats's present state are expectoration continually of a fawn colour, sometimes streaked with blood. He's still wasting away, altho' he takes as much food as myself, a dry cough, night sweats, with great uneasiness in his chest. Dr. C is afraid the next change will be to diarrhea. Keats sees all this. His knowledge of anatomy makes it tenfold worse at every change. Every way he is unfortunate. I cannot see him any way without something to "dash the cup from his lip,"[1] yet everyone offers me aid on his account. But he cannot bear it. I must not leave him night or day. I am quite well, thank God. Once more, good bye. Only one letter from you yet. I am in doubt whether you shall have harrowing things like this. Poor Keats cannot read any letters. He has made me put 2 by unopened. They tear him to pieces. He dare not look upon the outside of any more—make this known—and should any communication be required to make let it come to me. I will frame it to his ear. He places the greatest confidence in me.

1. He was thinking of Matthew xxvi.39, 42, and so on.

Joseph Severn to John Taylor
25, 26 JANUARY 1821

Rome, Jan. 25th, 1821—

My dear Sir,

Another week and less and less hope. I have still greater cause to fear that poor Keats is now upon his deathbed. He has shown still worse symptoms every day: clay-like expectoration in large quantities, night sweats, a ghastly wasting-away of his body and extremities with the approaches to a diarrhea by laxity and griping of the bowels, his food passing through him very quick and but little digested. Yet from all this he might get up if he could bear over that intense feeling and those unfortunate combinations and passions of mind from which no medicine in the world can relieve him, nor any other means, for they are a part of his nature. It now quite astonishes me that he has lived so long without the almost essence of human-life. I mean that sometimes calm of mind to keep the machinery of the body going. This I am certain poor Keats never possessed or even felt. He has described to me many parts of his life, of various changes, but all moving to this restless ferment. No doubt all the emotions of his mind even to his happiest sensations have brought him to this dreary point from which I pray God speedily to lift him up. His suffering now is beyond description and it increases with increasing acuteness of his memory and imagination. His nerves will not bear the only dreary comfort from things that "smell of mortality,"[1] and to any other source he has still greater horror. He cannot bear any books; the fact is he cannot bear anything. His state is so irritable, is so every way unfortunate that I begin to sink under the very seeing him. Without the labor, without the want of rest and occupation, I shall be ill from this cause alone. The hardest point between us is that cursed bottle of Opium. He had determined on taking this the instant his recovery should stop, he says to save him the extended misery of a long illness. In his own mind he saw this fatal prospect: the dismal nights, the impossibility of receiving any sort of comfort, and above all the wasting of his body and helplessness. These he had determined on escaping, and but for me, he would have swallowed this draught 3 Months since in the ship. He says 3 wretched months I have kept him alive, and for it, no name, no treatment, no privations can be too bad for me. I cannot reason him out of this even on his own ground, but now I fall into his views on every point. Before I made every sacrifice for his personal comfort in his own way, trying every manner to satisfy him; now I must do the same mentally. I even say he should have this bottle, but I have given it to Dr. Clark. The fact is I dare not trust myself with it—so anxious I was to satisfy him in everything.

Poor fellow! He could not read your letter when it came, altho' he opened it. I did not regret it for not a syllable had I let him know about the Bill. It would have killed him. I trembled when he looked at your name, but he wept most bitterly, and gave the Letter to me. Dr. Clark has received yours respecting the Bill. It is now quite right. You will have received my explanations about it, and I am once more at rest about it.

I have been taken ill in this last week. In 6 weeks I have not had 6 hours fresh air and sometimes sitting up 3 nights together. Now I cannot sleep, although I may, and the consequence is a heaviness of mind, no power of thinking. But at my altered appearance today Keats is much alarmed. He has talked it over and proposed having a nurse, for no one has come near him but the Doctor and myself. I hope this will soon bring me round, but my anxiety would alone make me ill without the bodily fatigue I am under. Everyone is astonished that I have kept up so long.

The Doctor has most certainly done all that could be done, but he says Keats should never have left England. The disorder had made too great a progress to receive benefit from this Climate. He says nothing in the world could cure him, even when he left England. By this journey his life has been shortened and rendered more painful. Yet it will be a satisfaction to you as it is to me that for delicate climate nothing could exceed this in mildness; the fruit trees have been long in blossom. Perhaps everything that could be done for Keats has been. You will have seen my friend Haslam. I have been in great trouble about a most painful letter I wrote him. Say to him that I was in a dreadful state of mind but could not wait sending. The post goes once a week. Yours very truly,

Joseph Severn

If I can get a nurse I shall not leave Keats for more than an hour in the day, merely to keep up my health.

26th

The nurse has just been, but I am afraid she won't do. There are so many little things that no one can do but myself that I think I will not leave poor Keats at all. I feel something better this Morning and have determined to keep on without any more going out. Keats is wanting to say something or have something done every minute in the day. No one to do these, he may become irritated, for I can assure you his mind is bordering on the insane.

II o' clock. The doctor has just been. Nature cannot hold out another fortnight, he says. The mucus is collecting in such quantities the body and the extremity receive no nourishment, and above all poor Keats's mind is determined on being worse and worse nearer and nearer his death that he cannot possibly last but a short time. Keats is desiring his death with dreadful earnestness. The idea of death seems his only comfort, the only prospect of ease. He talks of it with delight; it sooths his present torture. The strangeness of his mind everyday surprises us, no one feeling or one notion like any other being.

1. *King Lear,* IV.vi.136.

Joseph Severn to William Haslam
22 FEBRUARY 1821

Rome, Feb. 22, 1821

My dear Haslam,

O! how anxious I am to hear from you. None of yours has come but in answer to mine from Naples. I have nothing to break this dreadful solitude but Letters. Day after day, night after night here I am by our poor dying friend. My spirits, my intellects and my health are breaking down. I can get no one to change me. No one will relieve me. They all run away. And even if they did not, poor Keats could not do without me. I prepare everything he eats.

Last night I thought he was going. I could hear the Phlegm in his throat. He bade me lift him up in the bed, or he would die with pain. I watched him all night. At every cough I expected he would suffocate. Death is very fast approaching, for this Morning by the pale daylight the change in him frightened me. He has sunk in the last three days to a most ghastly look. I have these three nights set up with him from the apprehension of his dying. Dr. Clark has prepared me for it, but I shall be but little able to bear it. Even this my horrible situation I cannot bear to cease by the loss of him. As regards Money, my dear Haslam, you will have known that the kindness of Mr. Taylor sets me quite easy.

I have at times written a favorable letter to my sister. You will see this is best, for I hope that staying by my poor friend to close his eyes in death will not add to my other unlucky hits, for I am still quite prevented from painting and what the consequence may be. Poor Keats keeps me by him and shadows out the form of one solitary friend. He opens his eyes in great horror and doubt, but when they fall upon me they close gently, and open and close until he falls into another sleep. The very thought of this keeps me by him until he dies. And why did I say I was losing my time? The advantages I have gained by knowing John Keats would to gain any other way have doubled and trebled the time. They could not have gain'd. I won't try to write any more; the want of sleep has almost taken away the power. The Post is going so I would try. Think of me, my dear Haslam, as doing well and happy, as far as will allow.

> Farewell—God bless you
> Sincerely,
> J. Severn

I will write by next post to Brown—a 2nd letter has just come from
  him—

Deathbed portrait of Keats, by Joseph Severn (1821).
Keats House, Hampstead. By permission of the London Metropolitan Archives.

Joseph Severn to John Taylor
6 MARCH 1821

Rome, March 6, 1821

My dear Sir,

I have tried many times to write you, but no, I could not. It has been too much for me to think on it. I have been ill from the fatigue and pain I have suffered. The recollection of poor Keats hangs dreadfully upon me. I see him at every glance. I cannot be alone now, my nerves are so shattered. These brutal Italians have nearly finished their monstrous business. They have burned all the furniture and are now scraping the walls, making new windows, new doors, and even a new floor. You will see all the miseries attendant on these laws. I verily think I have suffered more from their cursed cruelties than from all I did for Keats. These wretches have taken the moments when I was suffering in mind and body; they have enraged me day after day until I trembled at the sound of every voice. I will try now once more to write you on our poor Keats. You will have but little for I can hardly dare to think on it, but I will write at intervals and pray you to take it as my utmost endeavour. When I am stronger I will send you every word. The remembrance of this scene of horror will be fresh upon my mind to the end of my days.

Four days previous to his death, the change in him was so great that I passed each moment in dread, not knowing what the next would have. He was calm and firm at its approaches to a most astonishing degree. He told me not to tremble for he did not think that he should be convulsed. He said, "did you ever see anyone die?" No. "Well then I pity you, poor Severn, what trouble and danger you have got into for me. Now you must be firm for it will not last long. I shall soon be laid in the quiet grave. Thank God for the quiet grave. O! I can feel the cold earth upon me, the daisies growing over me. O, for this quiet. It will be my first." When the morning light came and still found him alive, O how bitterly he grieved. I cannot bear his cries.

Each day he would look up in the doctor's face to discover how long he should live. He would say, "how long will this posthumous life of mine last?" That look was more than we could ever bear. The extreme brightness of his eyes, with his poor pallid face, were not earthly.

These four nights I watch him, each night expecting his death. On the fifth day the doctor prepared me for it—23rd, at 4 o' clock afternoon—The poor fellow bade me lift him up in bed. He breathed with great difficulty and seem'd to lose the power of coughing up the phlegm. An immense sweat came over him so that my breath felt cold to him: "Don't breath on me, it comes like Ice." He clasped my hand very fast as I held him in my arms. The mucus was boiling within him; it gurgled in his throat. This increased but yet he seem'd without pain. His eyes look'd upon me with extreme sensibility but without pain. At 11 he died in my arms. The English Nurse had been with me all this day. This was something to me, but I was very bad, no sleep that night. The next day the doctor had me over to his house. I was still the same. These kind people[1] did everything to comfort me. I must have sunk under it all but for them. On the following day a cast was taken[2] and his death made known to the brutes here, yet we kept a strong hand over them. We put them off until the poor fellow was laid in his grave. On Sunday, the second day, Dr. Clark and Dr. Luby with an Italian Surgeon opened the body. They thought it the worst possible Consumption. The lungs were entirely destroyed. The cells were quite gone, but Doctor Clark will write you on this head. This was another night without sleep to me. I felt worse and worse. On the third day, Monday 26th, the funeral beasts came. Many English requested to follow him. Those who did so were Dr. Clark and Dr. Luby, Messrs. Ewing, Westmacott, Henderson, Pointer and the Revd. Mr. Wolf, who read the funeral service.[3] He was buried very near to the monument of Caius Cestius, a few yards from Dr. Bell and an infant of Mr. Shelley's.[4] The good-hearted Doctor made the men put turfs of daisies upon the grave. He said, "this would be poor Keats's

ould he know it." I will write again by next post, but I am still but in
    state. Farewell,

Josh. Severn

The expense I fear will be great, perhaps £50. I owe [?] still on the Doctor.
    I have not received the £50 you mention, at least Torlonia's have had no
    notice of it. The Doctor pays everything for me and would let me have
    any money I need.

1. Dr. Clark and his wife.
2. Keats's death mask.
3. William Ewing was a painter and ivory carver; Richard Westmacott, Jr. (1799–
   1872), a sculptor; Ambrose Poynter (1796–1886) a well-known architect; and Wolff
   the English chaplain at Rome.
4. John Bell (1763–1820) died at Rome on 15 April. Shelley's son William was buried
   there on 8 June 1819.

Charles Brown to William Haslam
18 MARCH 1821

Hampstead,
Sunday, 18 March

Dear Haslam,

It is all over. I had a letter from Severn last night, telling me poor Keats
died on 23rd Feb. The letter is forwarded to Taylor. I was about to write to
Mr. Abbey, to inform him of this sad news, but request you will without
delay call on him for that purpose. I say *without delay*, lest Miss Keats
should hear of it by the papers or through some other means. Taylor will
show you the letter. I can't write more.

Your's most truly
Charles Brown

Joseph Severn to William Haslam
5 MAY 1821[1]

Rome, May 5th 1821

Pardon me, my dear Haslam, that for a moment I should think you had forgotten me. I was worn down with nightwatchings, deprivation from my pursuits, and above all the prospect of poor Keats's death—the prospect of a scene which I trembled to think on. The Letters at this time were a great comfort to me, yet none came from my good friend Haslam. This was hard upon me when I felt to want your advice, but no more on this. I have said this much in excuse for myself. Your 2 letters of the 22nd March and 2nd April gave me very great pain. I knew how deeply you would feel these awful things, and I knew that the distance we were from you would increase these feelings. But now, thank God, it is all quit and over. Poor Keats has his wish, a humble wish indeed. He is at peace in the quiet grave. I walk'd there a few days ago and found the daisies had grown all over it. It is in one of the most lovely retired spots in Rome. The Pyramid of Caius Cestius and the Roman Walls are in the same place. The grave of Surgeon Bell is next to our poor friend and many other English are lying in the same romantic spot. You cannot have any such place in England. I visit the place with a most delicious melancholy which on many occasions has relieved my low spirits. When I recollect that Keats in his life had never one day without ferment or torture of mind and body and that now he lies at rest in a grave with the flowers he so much desired upon him, and in a place such as he must have form'd to his mind's eye with no other sound than a few simple sheep and goats with their tinkling bells, this is what I feel grateful for. It was what I pray'd might be. I did pray most earnestly that his sufferings might end; there was not one grain more of comfort for him in this world.

I will not as I intended say to you more on Keats's death now. It must still be at a future time. I am now ill and low in spirits and these very recollections will break me down, yet I have had one month in capital health and spirits and it is only in the changes of weather or the difficulties of my Painting that my spirits are low. Then comes Keats, Keats, to my mind. I can see his poor face and his poor still hands and I am no longer master of myself. It has been fortunate for me that my Painting required such a revolution in my ideas or I might have been laid up with a fever. But why am I writing all this low-spirited state to you? I should not be so, for I am certainly most fortunate. I have received the most polite attention here although we came strangers. You are right in your conjecture in my having friends, but you cannot imagine to what extent. I have received so many presents and so many introductions that I am astonished when I reflect on them. One good fellow[2] sent me a splendid paint box with everything; another lends me the finest Study in Rome;[3] a third brings a party of English Noblemen to see me. But more than all, and what I know will gladden my dear friend Haslam, is that I have above half finished an Historical Picture of 8 figures.[4] This is for the Council of the R. A., for my pension. So far it is much liked. I think I have gained very much by coming here. This place is a heaven for an Artist. Raphael's pictures I had so long wished to see and I knew them all so well from the prints in London that they have given me a most expanded notion of art.

There are here a number of English Artists but none of highest ability except the Sculptors. We have here Mr. Westmacott, a son of the celebrated Sculptor in London.[5] They are all kind and good fellows. So far I am astonished at their generosity; you will be thankful and say Providence is over me, upon me when I tell you that the Gentleman who has shown me the greatest respect and who gave me the paint box is in almost every point like poor Keats. His noble mind, his learning, his taste and his good heart remind me of Keats. Everyone here seems to love him and have something good to say of him. His name is Kirkup. He has a small fortune and is studying Historical painting. He is a fine Musician. This good little fellow (for he is just the same size as Keats) has done me most essential service. Fearing that I may lose the pension from the R. A., he has explained my case to all the higher classes of English here. He has shown to them that I must paint my Miniatures for support should I fail. I have already got 40

John Keats at Wentworth Place, by Joseph Severn (1821–23).
National Portrait Gallery, London.

Guineas and through him could have had a 150 Guineas in a short time, but my picture must be done so he has prepared my way for the next season. He talks to me and advises me with great honesty. I see him every day. This I can assure you is my greatest consolation for the loss of Keats. I should tell he has even purchased a Piano Forte for my playing on. He accompanies me on the Violin or Guittern.

Last night I had the honor to receive an Invitation with Lord Colchester and Riven and the Ladies Westmorland and Riven[6] with many others of the English gentry here. Ah, and I am quite at home with them. They look up to me as an English Painting. This invitation came from a Mr. Crawford, a most splendid man here. This Gentleman has invited me to dine with him every day for a long time past which I do not receive. Upon the whole this place is everything for me. I look forward with great hope and delight. I have the most glowing prospect before me: a noble profession, a prospect of capital health, in the finest situation in the World. I have youth and above all I have a very contented mind; anything satisfies me. I can live on very little. So my dear fellow, it will be a long time before you see me back. Thanks, thanks to the end of my days for making me come to Rome. Farewell. Remember me to your lovely partner and to all my friends. Tell them I am happy and successful. Farewell.

Ever yours
Joseph Severn

1. This letter was first printed in Hyder Rollins, ed., *The Keats Circle,* 2 vols. (Cambridge, Mass.: Harvard University Press, 1948).
2. Seymour Kirkup (1788–1880), artist, and friend of Haydon, Landor, the Brownings, and Trelawny.
3. Thomas Campbell (1790–1858), the sculptor, installed him in the study of Sir Charles Eastlake (1793–1865), artist.
4. *The Death of Alcibiades.*
5. The son of Sir Richard Westmacott (1775–1856).
6. Charles Abbot (1757–1829), first Baron Colchester; James Ruthven (1777–1853), seventh Baron Ruthven of Freeland, who married Mary Hamilton Campbell (d. 1885); Jane Huck-Saunders (d. 1857), second wife of John Fane (1759–1841), sixteenth earl of Westmorland.

INDEX